HOUSE *of* BUSH
HOUSE *of* SAUD

HOUSE *of* BUSH
HOUSE *of* SAUD

THE HIDDEN RELATIONSHIP BETWEEN THE WORLD'S
TWO MOST POWERFUL DYNASTIES

Craig Unger

GIBSON SQUARE BOOKS

London

—To my mother —

This edition published for the first time in 2004 in the UK by

Gibson Square Books Ltd
15 Gibson Square, London N1 0RD
Tel: +44 (0)20 7689 4790; Fax: +44 (0)20 7689 7395
info@gibsonsquare.com
www.gibsonsquare.com

© 2004 by Craig Unger

ISBN 1-903933-58-7

Sales by Signature
Castlegate 20, York YO1 9RP
Tel 01904 633 633; Fax 01904 675 445
sales@signaturebooks.co.uk
www.signaturebooks.co.uk

UK distribution by Central Books Ltd
99 Wallis Road, UK London E9 5LN
Tel +44 (0)845 458 9911; Fax +44 (0)845 458 9912
info@centralbooks.com
www.centralbooks.com

CONTENTS

HOUSE *of* BUSH
HOUSE *of* SAUD

CHAPTER ONE

The Great Escape

IT WAS THE SECOND Wednesday in September 2001, and for Brian Cortez, a desperately ill twenty-one-year-old man in Seattle, Washington State, the day he had long waited for. Two years earlier, Cortez had been diagnosed with congestive heart failure,[1] and since then his prognosis had become even worse: he suffered from dilated cardiomyopathy, a severe swelling of the heart for which the only permanent solution is a transplant.

Cortez had been on the official heart transplant waiting list for months. Now, thanks to an accident in Anchorage, Alaska, an organ was finally available. The transplant team from the University of Washington Medical Center chartered a plane to Alaska to retrieve it as quickly as possible. The human heart can last about eight hours outside the body before it loses its value as a transplanted organ. That was the length of time the medical team had to remove it from the victim's body, take it to the Anchorage airport, fly approximately fifteen hundred miles from Anchorage to Seattle, get it to the University of Washington Medical Center, and complete the surgery.

Sometime around midnight, the medical team boarded a chartered jet and flew back with its precious cargo. They passed over the Gulf of Alaska and the Queen Charlotte Islands, and finally, Vancouver, Canada. Before they crossed the forty-ninth parallel and reentered U.S. airspace, however, something unexpected happened.

Suddenly, two Royal Canadian Air Force fighters were at the chartered plane's side. The Canadian military planes then handed it off to two U.S. Air Force F/A-18 fighter jets, which forced it to land.[2] Less than twenty-four hours earlier, terrorists had hijacked four airliners in the worst atrocity in American history, crashing two of them into New York's World Trade Center and one into the Pentagon. Nearly three thousand people were dead. America was grounded. Brian Cortez's new heart was eighty miles short of its destination, and time was running out.[3]

Cortez's medical team was not alone in confronting a crisis caused by the shutdown of America's airspace. The terrorist attacks had grounded all commercial and private aviation throughout the entire United States for the first time in history. Former vice president Al Gore was stranded in Austria because his flight to the United States was canceled. Former president Bill Clinton was stuck in Australia. Major league baseball games were postponed. American skies were nearly as empty as they had been when the Wright brothers first flew at Kitty Hawk. America was paralyzed by terror, and for forty-eight hours, virtually no one could fly.

No one, that is, except for the Saudis.

At the same time that Brian Cortez's medical team was grounded, Prince Bandar bin Sultan bin Abdul Aziz, the Saudi Arabian ambassador to the United States, was orchestrating the exodus of more than 140 Saudis scattered throughout the country. They included members of two families: One was the royal House of Saud, the family that ruled the kingdom of Saudi Arabia, and which, thanks to the country's vast oil reserves, was without question the richest family in the world. The other family was the Sauds' close friends and allies, the bin Ladens, who in addition to owning a multibillion-dollar construction conglomerate had spawned the notorious terrorist Osama bin Laden.

At fifty-two, Prince Bandar had long been the most recognizable figure from his country in America. Widely known as the Arab Gatsby, with his trimmed goatee and tailored double-breasted suits, Bandar was the very embodiment of the contradictions inherent in being a modern, jet-setting, Western-leaning member of the royal House of Saud.

Flamboyant and worldly, Bandar entertained lavishly at his spectacular estates all over the world. Whenever he was safely out of Saudi Arabia and beyond the reach of the puritanical form of Islam it espoused, he puckishly flouted Islamic tenets by sipping brandy and smoking Cohiba cigars. And when it came to embracing the culture of the West, Bandar outdid even the most ardent admirers of Western civilization—that was him patrolling the sidelines of Dallas Cowboys football games with his friend Jerry Jones, the team's owner. To militant Islamic fundamentalists who loathed pro-West multibillionaire Saudi royals, no one fit the bill better than Bandar.

And yet, his guise as Playboy of the Western World notwithstanding, deep in his bones, Prince Bandar was a key figure in the world of Islam. His father, Defense Minister Prince Sultan, was second in line to the Saudi crown. Bandar was the nephew of King Fahd, the aging Saudi monarch, and the grandson of the late king Abdul Aziz, the founder of modern Saudi Arabia, who initiated his country's historic oil-for-security relationship with the United States when he met Franklin D. Roosevelt on the USS *Quincy* in the Suez Canal on February 14, 1945.[4] The enormous royal family in which Bandar played such an important role oversaw two of the most sacred places of Islamic worship, the holy mosques in Medina and Mecca.

As a wily international diplomat, Bandar also knew full well just how precarious his family's position was. For decades, the House of Saud had somehow maintained control of Saudi Arabia and the world's richest oil reserves by performing a seemingly untenable balancing act with two parties who had vowed to destroy each other.

On the one hand, the House of Saud was an Islamic theocracy whose power grew out of the royal family's alliance with Wahhabi fundamentalism, a strident and puritanical Islamic sect that provided a fertile breeding ground for a global network of terrorists urging a violent jihad against the United States.

On the other hand, the House of Saud's most important ally was the Great Satan itself, the United States. Even a cursory examination of the relationship revealed astonishing contradictions: America, the beacon of democracy, was to arm and protect a brutal theocratic monarchy. The United States, sworn defender of Israel, was also the guarantor of security to the guardians of Wahhabi Islam, the fundamentalist religious sect that was one of Israel's and America's mortal enemies.

Astoundingly, this fragile relationship had not only endured but in many ways had been spectacularly successful. In the nearly three decades since the oil embargo of 1973, the United States had bought hundreds of billions of dollars of oil at reasonable prices. During that same period, the Saudis had purchased hundreds of billions of dollars of weapons from the United States. The Saudis had supported the United States on regional security matters in Iran and Iraq and refrained from playing an aggressive role against Israel. Members of the Saudi royal family, including Bandar, became billionaires many times over, in the process quietly turning into some of the most powerful players in the American market, investing hundreds of billions of dollars in equities in the United States.[5] And the price of oil, the eternal bellwether of economic, political, and cultural anxiety in America, had remained low enough that enormous gas-guzzling SUVs had become ubiquitous on U.S. highways. During the Reagan and Clinton eras the economy boomed.

The relationship was a coarse weave of money, power, and trust. It had lasted because two foes, militant Islamic fundamentalists and the United States, turned a blind eye to each other. The U.S. military might have called the policy "Don't ask, don't tell." The Koran had its own version: "Ask not about things which, if made plain to you, may cause you trouble."[6]

But now, in the immediate aftermath of 9/11, the ugly seams of the relationship had been laid bare. Because thousands of innocent people had been killed and most of the killers were said to be Saudi, it was up to Bandar, ever the master illusionist, to assure Americans that everything was just fine between the United States and Saudi Arabia. Bandar had always been a smooth operator, but now he and his unflappable demeanor would be tested as never before.

Bandar desperately hoped that early reports of the Saudi role had been exaggerated—after all, Al Qaeda terrorist operatives were known to use false passports. But at 10 p.m. on the evening of September 12, about thirty-six hours after the attack, a high-ranking CIA official—according to *Newsweek* magazine, it was probably CIA director George Tenet—phoned Bandar at his home and gave him the bad news:[7] Fifteen of the nineteen hijackers were Saudis. Afterward, Bandar said, "I felt as if the Twin Towers had just fallen on my head."

Public relations had never been more crucial for the Saudis. Bandar swiftly retained PR giant Burson-Marsteller to place newspaper ads all over the country condemning the attacks and dissociating Saudi Arabia from them.[8] He went on CNN, the BBC, and the major TV networks and hammered home the same points again and again: The alliance with the United States was still strong. Saudi Arabia would support America in its fight against terrorism.

Prince Bandar also protested media reports that referred to those involved in terrorism as "Saudis." Asserting that no terrorists could ever be described as Saudi citizens, he urged the media and politicians to refrain from casting arbitrary accusations against Arabs and Muslims. "We in the kingdom, the government and the people of Saudi Arabia, refuse to have any person affiliated with terrorism to be connected to our country," Bandar said.[9] That included Osama bin Laden, the perpetrator of the attacks, who had even been disowned by his family. He was not really a Saudi, Bandar asserted, for the government had taken away his passport because of his terrorist activities.

But Osama bin Laden *was* Saudi, of course, and he was not just any Saudi. The bin Ladens were one of a handful of extremely wealthy families that were so close to the House of Saud that they effectively acted as extensions of the royal family. Over five decades, they had built their multibillion-dollar construction empire thanks to their intimate relationship with the royal family. Bandar himself knew them well. "They're really lovely human beings," he told CNN. "[Osama] is the only one ... I met him only once. The rest of them are well-educated, successful businessmen, involved in a lot of charities. It is—it is tragic. I feel pain for them, because he's caused them a lot of pain."[10]

Like Bandar, the bin Laden family epitomized the marriage between the United States and Saudi Arabia. Their huge construction company, the Saudi Binladin Group (SBG),* banked with Citigroup and invested with Goldman Sachs and Merrill Lynch.[11] Over time, the bin Ladens did business with such icons of Western[12] culture as Disney, the Hard Rock Café, Snapple, and Porsche. In the mid-nineties, they joined various members of the House of Saud in becoming business associates

---

*Due to inconsistencies in transliteration, the family company and various family members use the spelling *Binladin* rather than *bin Laden*, the spelling most frequently used for Osama.

with former secretary of state James Baker and former president George H. W. Bush by investing in the Carlyle Group, a gigantic Washington, D.C.-based private equity firm. As Charles Freeman, the former U.S. ambassador to Saudi Arabia, told the *Wall Street Journal*, "If there were ever any company closely connected to the U.S. and its presence in Saudi Arabia, it's the Saudi Binladin Group."[13]

The bin Ladens and members of the House of Saud who spent time in the United States were mostly young professionals and students attending high school or college.[14] Many lived in the Boston area, thanks to its high concentration of colleges. Abdullah bin Laden, a younger brother of Osama's,* was a 1994 graduate of Harvard Law School and had offices in Cambridge, Massachusetts.[15] Several bin Ladens had attended Tufts University, near Boston.[16] Sana bin Laden had graduated from Wheelock College in Boston and organized a Saudi festival at the Children's Museum in Boston.[17] Two bin Ladens—Mohammed and Nawaf—owned units in the Flagship Wharf condominium complex in Charlestown Navy Yard on Boston Harbor.[18]

Some of the young, chic, sophisticated members of the family appeared even more westernized than Bandar. Wafah† Binladin, a twenty-six-year-old graduate of Columbia Law School, lived in a $6,000-a-month rented loft in New York's fashionable SoHo[19] and was considering pursuing a singing career. Partial to Manhattan nightspots such as Lotus, the Mercer Kitchen, and Pravda,[20] she was in Geneva, Switzerland, at the time of the attack and simply did not return. Kameron bin Laden, a cousin of Osama's in his thirties, also frequented Manhattan nightspots and spent as much as $30,000 in one day on designer clothes at Prada's Fifth Avenue boutique.[21] He elected to stay in the United States.

But half brother Khalil Binladin wanted to go back to Jeddah. Khalil, who had a Brazilian wife, had been appointed as Brazil's honorary consul in Jeddah[22] and owned a sprawling twenty-acre estate in Winter Garden, Florida, near Orlando.[23]

---

*At least four members of the extended bin Laden family are named Abdullah bin Laden—Osama's uncle, a cousin, his younger brother, and his son.

†Sometimes spelled Waffa.

As for the Saudi royal family, many of them were scattered all over the United States. Some had gone to Lexington, Kentucky, for the annual September yearling auctions. The sale of the finest racehorses in the world had been suspended after the terrorist attacks on September 11, but resumed the very next day. Saudi prince Ahmed bin Salman bought two horses for $1.2 million on September 12.

Others felt more personally threatened. Shortly after the attack, one of the bin Ladens, an unnamed brother of Osama's, frantically called the Saudi embassy in Washington seeking protection. He was given a room at the Watergate Hotel and told not to open the door.[24] King Fahd, the aging and infirm Saudi monarch, sent a message to his emissaries in Washington. "Take measures to protect the innocents," he said.[25]

Meanwhile, a Saudi prince sent a directive to the Tampa Police Department in Florida that young Saudis who were close to the royal family and went to school in the area were in potential danger.[26]

Bandar went to work immediately. If any foreign official had the clout to pull strings at the White House in the midst of a grave national security crisis, it was he. A senior member of the Washington diplomatic corps, Bandar had played racquetball with Secretary of State Colin Powell in the late seventies. He had run covert operations for the late CIA director Bill Casey that were so hush-hush they were kept secret even from President Ronald Reagan. He was the man who had stashed away thirty locked attaché cases that held some of the deepest secrets in the intelligence world.[27] And for two decades, Bandar had built an intimate personal relationship with the Bush family that went far beyond a mere political friendship.

First, Bandar set up a hotline at the Saudi embassy in Washington for all Saudi nationals in the United States. For the forty-eight hours after the attacks, he stayed in constant contact with Secretary of State Colin Powell and National Security Adviser Condoleezza Rice.[28]

Before the attacks, Bandar had been invited to come to the White House to meet with President George W. Bush on September 13 to discuss the Middle East peace process.[29] Even though the fifty-five-year-old president and he were, roughly speaking, contemporaries, Bandar had not yet developed the same rapport with the younger Bush that he had enjoyed for decades with his father. Bandar and the elder Bush had participated in the shared rituals of manhood—hunting trips, vacations together, and the like. Bandar and the younger Bush were well-known to each other, but not nearly as close.

On the thirteenth, the meeting went ahead as scheduled. But in the wake of the attacks two days earlier, the political landscape of the Middle East had drastically changed. A spokesman for the Saudi embassy later said he did not know whether repatriation was a topic of discussion.

But the job had been started nonetheless. Earlier that same day, a forty-nine-year-old former policeman turned private investigator named Dan Grossi got a call from the Tampa (Florida) Police Department. Grossi had worked with the Tampa force for twenty years before retiring, and it was not particularly unusual for the police to recommend former officers for special security jobs. But Grossi's new assignment was very much out of the ordinary.

"The police had been giving Saudi students protection since September eleventh," Grossi recalls. "They asked if I was interested in escorting these students from Tampa to Lexington, Kentucky, because the police department couldn't do it."

Grossi was told to go to the airport, where a small charter jet would be available to take him and the Saudis on their flight. He was not given a specific time of departure, and he was dubious about the prospects of accomplishing his task. "Quite frankly, I knew that everything was grounded," he says. "I never thought this was going to happen." Even so, Grossi, who'd been asked to bring a colleague, phoned Manuel Perez, a former FBI agent, to put him on alert. Perez was equally unconvinced. "I said, 'Forget about it,'" Perez recalls. "Nobody is flying today."

The two men had good reason to be skeptical. Within minutes of the terrorist attacks on 9/11, the Federal Aviation Administration had sent out a special notification called a NOTAM—a notice to airmen—to airports all across the country, ordering every airborne plane in the United States to land at the nearest airport as soon as possible, and prohibiting planes on the ground from taking off. Initially, there were no exceptions whatsoever. Later, when the situation stabilized, several airports accepted flights for emergency medical and military operations—but those were few and far between.

Nevertheless, at 1:30 or 2 p.m. on the thirteenth, Dan Grossi received his phone call. He was told the Saudis would be delivered to Raytheon Airport Services, a private hangar at Tampa International Airport. When he arrived, Manny Perez was there to meet him.

At the terminal a woman laughed at Grossi for even thinking he would be flying that day. Commercial flights had slowly begun to resume, but at 10:57 a.m., the FAA had issued another NOTAM, a reminder that private aviation was still prohibited. Three private planes violated the ban that day, in Maryland, West Virginia, and Texas, and in each case a pair of jet fighters quickly forced the aircraft down. As far as private planes were concerned, America was still grounded.

Then one of the pilots arrived. "Here's your plane," he told Grossi. "Whenever you're ready to go."

What happened next was first reported by Kathy Steele, Brenna Kelly, and Elizabeth Lee Brown in the *Tampa Tribune* in October 2001. Not a single other American paper seemed to think the subject was newsworthy.[30]

Grossi and Perez say they waited until three young Saudi men, all apparently in their early twenties, arrived. Then the pilot took Grossi, Perez, and the Saudis to a well-appointed ten-passenger Learjet. They departed for Lexington at about 4:30 p.m.[31]

"They got the approval somewhere," said Perez. "It must have come from the highest levels of government."[32]

"Flight restrictions had not been lifted yet," Grossi said. "I was told it would take White House approval. I thought [the flight] was not going to happen."[33]

Grossi said he did not get the names of the Saudi students he was escorting. "It happened so fast," Grossi says. "I just knew they were Saudis. They were well connected. One of them told me his father or his uncle was good friends with George Bush senior."[34]

How did the Saudis go about getting approval? According to the Federal Aviation Administration, they didn't and the Tampa flight never took place. "It's not in our logs," Chris White, a spokesman for the FAA, told the *Tampa Tribune*. "... It didn't occur."[35] The White House also said that the flights to evacuate the Saudis did not take place.

According to Grossi, about one hour and forty-five minutes after takeoff they landed at Blue Grass Airport in Lexington, a frequent destination for Saudi horse-racing enthusiasts such as Prince Ahmed bin Salman. When they arrived, the Saudis were greeted by an American who took custody of them and helped them with their baggage. On the tarmac was a 747 with Arabic writing on the fuselage, apparently ready to take them back to Saudi Arabia. "My understanding is that there were other Saudis in Kentucky buying racehorses at that time, and they were going to fly back together," said Grossi.

With just three Saudis on it, the Tampa flight was hardly the only mysterious trip under way. All over the country, members of the extended bin Laden family, the House of Saud, and their associates were assembling in various locations. At least seven other planes were available for their transportation. Officially, the FBI says it had nothing to do with the repatriation of the Saudis. "I can say unequivocally that the FBI had no role in facilitating these flights one way or another," says Special Agent John Iannarelli.[36]

Bandar, however, characterized the role of the FBI very differently. "With coordination with the FBI," he said on CNN, "we got them all out."

Meanwhile, the Saudis had at least two of the planes on call to repatriate the bin Ladens. One of them began picking up family members all across the country. Starting in Los Angeles on an undetermined date, it flew first to Orlando, Florida, where Khalil Binladin, a sibling of Osama bin Laden's, boarded.[37] From Orlando, the plane continued to Dulles International Airport outside Washington, before going on to Logan Airport in Boston on September 19, picking up members of the bin Laden family along the way.

As the planes prepared for takeoff at each location across the country, the FBI repeatedly got into disputes with Rihab Massoud, Bandar's chargé d'affaires at the Saudi embassy in Washington. "I recall getting into a big flap with Bandar's office about whether they would leave without us knowing who was on the plane," said one former agent who participated in the repatriation of the Saudis.[38] "Bandar wanted the plane to take off and we were stressing that that plane was not leaving until we knew exactly who was on it."

In the end, the FBI was only able to check papers and identify everyone on the flights. In the past, the FBI had been constrained from arbitrarily launching investigations without a "predicate"—i.e., a strong reason to believe that an individual had been engaged in criminal activities. Spokesmen for the FBI assert that the Saudis had every right to leave the country.

Meanwhile, President Bush was in Washington working full-time at the White House to mobilize a global antiterror coalition. On Friday, September 14, a dozen ambassadors from Arab nations—Syria, the Palestinian Authority, Algeria, Lebanon, Saudi Arabia, Egypt, Jordan, and the Persian Gulf states—met at Prince Bandar's home in McLean, Virginia, to discuss how they would respond to Bush's new policies.[39] Bandar himself had pledged his support for the war on terror and, perhaps most important, vowed that Saudi Arabia would help stabilize the world oil markets. In a breathtaking display of their command over the oil markets, the Saudis dispatched 9 million barrels of oil to the United States. As a consequence, the price instantly dropped from $28 to $22 per barrel.[40]

On Tuesday, September 18, at Logan Airport, a specially reconfigured Boeing 727 with about thirty first-class seats had been chartered by the bin Ladens and flew five passengers, all of them members of the bin Laden family, out of the country from Boston.

The next day, September 19, President Bush met with the president of Indonesia, the world's most populous Muslim country, and with the foreign ministers of Russia and Germany. His speechwriting team was also working on a stirring speech to be delivered the next day, officially declaring a global war on terror. "Our war on terror ... will not end until every terrorist group of global reach has been found, stopped, and defeated," he vowed.[41]

Meanwhile, the plane that had originated in Los Angeles and gone to Orlando and Washington, another Boeing 727, was due to touch down at Boston's Logan International Airport.[42]

At the time, Logan was in chaos. The two hijacked planes that had crashed into the World Trade Center's Twin Towers had departed from Logan. The airport was reeling from criticism that its security failures had allowed the hijackings to take place, and exceptional measures were now being taken. Several thousand cars were towed from the airport's parking garages. "We didn't know if they were booby-trapped or what," said Tom Kinton, director of aviation at Logan.[43]

Even though the Federal Aviation Administration had allowed commercial flights to resume on September 13, because of various security issues, Logan did not reopen until September 15, two days later.[44] Even then, air traffic resumed slowly.

Then, in the early afternoon of September 19, a call came into Logan's Emergency Operations Center saying that the private charter aircraft was going to pick up members of the bin Laden family.[45] Both Kinton and Virginia Buckingham, the head of the Massachusetts Port Authority, which oversees Logan, were incredulous. "We were in the midst of the worst terrorist act in history," Kinton said. "And here we were seeing an evacuation of the bin Ladens!"

Like Kinton, Virginia Buckingham was stunned that the bin Laden family was being spirited out of the country. "My staff was told that a private jet was arriving at Logan from Saudi Arabia to pick up fourteen members of Osama bin Laden's family living in the Boston area," she later wrote in the *Boston Globe*.[46] "'Does the FBI know?' staffers wondered. 'Does the State Department know? Why are they letting these people go? Have they questioned them?' This was ridiculous."*

Yet there was little that Logan officials could do. Federal law did not give them much leeway in terms of restricting an individual flight. "So bravado would have to do in the place of true authority," wrote Buckingham.[47]

"Again and again, Tom Kinton asked for official word from the FBI. 'Tell the tower that plane is not coming in here until somebody in Washington tells us it's okay,' he said."

As the bin Ladens were about to land, the top brass at Logan Airport did not know what was going on. The FBI's counterterrorism unit should have been a leading force in the domestic battle against terror, but here it was not even going to interview the Saudis.

"Each time," Buckingham wrote, "the answer was the same: 'Let them leave.' On September 19, under the cover of darkness, they did."

---

*There are conflicting accounts about the exact number of bin Ladens who boarded in Boston on September 19. In another article, the *Boston Globe* reported eleven.

* * *

Of course, the vast majority of the Saudis on those planes had nothing whatsoever to do with Osama bin Laden. The bin Laden family itself had expressed "the strongest denunciation and condemnation of this sad event, which resulted in the loss of many innocent men, women, and children, and which contradicts our Islamic faith."[48] And a persuasive case could be made that it was against the interests of the royal family and the bin Ladens to have aided the terrorists.

On the other hand, this was the biggest crime in American history. A global manhunt of unprecedented proportions was under way. Thousands of people had just been killed by Osama bin Laden. Didn't it make sense to at least interview his relatives and other Saudis who, inadvertently or not, may have aided him?

Moreover, Attorney General John Ashcroft had asserted that the government "had a responsibility to use every legal means at our disposal to prevent further terrorist activity by taking people into custody who have violated the law and who may pose a threat to America."[49] All over the country Arabs were being rounded up and interrogated. By the weekend after the attacks, Ashcroft, to the dismay of civil libertarians, had already put together a package of proposals broadening the FBI's power to detain foreigners, wiretap them, and trace money-laundering to terrorists. Some suspects would be held for as long as ten months at the American naval base in Guantánamo, Cuba.

In an ordinary murder investigation, it is commonplace to interview relatives of the prime suspect. When the FBI talks to subjects during an investigation, the questioning falls into one of two categories. Friendly subjects are "interviewed" and suspects or unfriendly subjects are "interrogated." How did the Saudis get a pass?

And did a simple disclaimer from the bin Laden family mean no one in the entire family had any contacts or useful information whatsoever? Did that mean the FBI should simply drop all further inquiries? At the very least, wouldn't family members be able to provide U.S. investigators with some information about Osama's finances, people who might know who him or might be aiding Al Qaeda?

Moreover, national security experts found it hard to believe that no one in the entire extended bin Laden family had any contact whatsoever with Osama. "There is no reason to think that every single member of his family has shut him down," said Paul Michael Wihbey, a fellow at the Institute for Advanced Strategic and Political Studies.[50]

Vincent Cannistraro, a former CIA counterterrorism chief, told the *New Yorker*, "I've been following the bin Ladens for years, and it's easy to say, 'We disown him.' Many in the family have. But blood is usually thicker than water."[51]

In fact, Osama was not the only bin Laden who had ties to militant Islamic fundamentalists. As early as 1979, Mahrous bin Laden, an older half brother of Osama's, had befriended members of the militant Muslim Brotherhood and had, perhaps unwittingly, played a key role in a violent armed uprising against the House of Saud in Mecca in 1979, which resulted in more than one hundred deaths.

One Saudi who had married into the extended bin Laden family was widely reported to be an important figure in Al Qaeda and was tied to the men behind the 1993 World Trade Center bombing, to the October 2000 bombing of the USS *Cole,* and was alleged to have funded a Philippine terrorist group.

Another Saudi, who boarded one of the earliest planes to leave the United States, had won the attention of foreign investigators for possible terrorist connections. According to an international press agency, the Saudi had business connections in a Latin American city thought to to be a center for training terrorists, including members of the Hezbollah movement.

How is it possible that Saudis were allowed to fly even when all of America, FBI agents included, was grounded? Had the White House approved the operation—and, if so, why?

When Bandar arrived at the White House on Thursday, September 13, 2001, he and President Bush retreated to the Truman Balcony, a casual outdoor spot behind the pillars of the South Portico that also provided a bit of privacy. Over the years, any history made on the Truman Balcony had transpired in informal conversation. In 1992, nine years earlier, President Bush's father, George H. W. Bush, had walked out on the balcony with Boris Yeltsin, the first democratically elected president of Russia, to celebrate the end of the Cold War. In 1993, after First Lady Hillary Rodham Clinton put an end to smoking in the White

House, Bill Clinton would sometimes retreat there to smoke a cigar in a celebratory moment, as he did after the United States rescued a soldier in Bosnia.

This occasion may have marked the beginning of a new era, but Bandar and President Bush had nothing to celebrate. Thousands of Americans were dead. They had been killed in a terrorist operation largely run by Saudis. Nonetheless, the two men each lit up a Cohiba and began to discuss how they would work together in the war on terror. Bush said that the United States would hand over any captured Al Qaeda operatives to the Saudis if they would not cooperate. The implication was clear: the Saudis could use any means necessary—including torture—to get the suspects to talk.[52]

But the larger points went unspoken. The two men were scions of the most powerful dynasties in the world. The Bush family and its close associates—the House of Bush, if you will—included two presidents of the United States; former secretary of state James Baker, who had been a powerful figure in four presidential administrations; key figures in the oil and defense industries, the Carlyle Group, and the Republican Party; and much, much more. As for Bandar, his family effectively *was* the government of Saudi Arabia, the most powerful country in the Arab world. They had hundreds of billions of dollars and the biggest oil reserves in the world. The relationship was unprecedented. Never before had a president of the United States— much less, two presidents from the same family—had such close personal and financial ties to the ruling family of another foreign power.

Yet few Americans realized that these two dynasties, the Bush family and the House of Saud, had a history dating back more than twenty years. Not just business partners and personal friends, the Bushes and the Saudis had pulled off elaborate covert operations and gone to war together. They had shared secrets that involved unimaginable personal wealth, spectacular military might, the richest energy resources in the world, and the most odious crimes imaginable.

They had been involved in the Iran-contra scandal, and in secret U.S. aid in the Afghanistan War that gave birth to Osama bin Laden. Along with then Vice President Bush, the Saudis had joined the United States in supporting the brutal Iraqi dictator Saddam Hussein for seven full years after knowing that he had used weapons of mass destruction. In the private sector, the Saudis had supported George W. Bush's struggling oil company, Harken Energy, and in the nineties they made common cause with his father by investing in the Carlyle Group. In the 1991 Gulf War, the Saudis and the elder Bush had fought side by side. And now there was the repatriation of the bin Ladens, which could not have taken place without approval at the highest levels of the executive branch of President George W. Bush's administration.

Only Bush and Bandar know what transpired that day on the Truman Balcony. But the ties between the two families were so strong that allowing the Saudis to leave America would not have been difficult for Bush. It would also have been in character with a relationship in which decisions were often made through elaborate and contrived deniability mechanisms that allowed the principals to turn a blind eye to unseemly realities and to be intentionally "out of the loop."

The ties between the two families were an open secret that in some ways was as obvious as the proverbial elephant in the living room. Yet at the same time it was somehow hard to discern even for the most seasoned journalists. Perhaps that was because the relationship had been forged all over the globe and arced across different eras—from the Reagan-Bush years to the Clinton administration to the presidency of George W. Bush. To understand its scope and its meaning, one would have to search through tens of thousands of forgotten newspaper stories, read scores of books by journalists and historians, and study myriad "Secret" classified documents and the records of barely remembered congressional probes of corporate intrigue and Byzantine government scandals. One would have to journey back in time to the birth of Al Qaeda at the terrorist training camps during the Afghanistan War. One would have to study the Iran-Iraq War of the eighties, the 1991 Gulf War, and the Iraq War of 2003. One would have to try to deduce what had happened within the corporate suites of oil barons in Dallas and Houston, in the executive offices of the Carlyle Group, in the Situation Room of the White House, and in the grand royal palaces of Saudi billionaires. One would have to interview scores of politicians, oil executives, counterterrorism analysts, CIA operatives, and businessmen from Washington and Saudi Arabia and Texas. One would have to decipher brilliantly hidden agendas and purposefully murky corporate relationships.

Finally, one would have to put all this information together to shape a continuum, a narrative in which the House of Bush and the House of Saud dominated the world stage together in one era after another. Having done so, one would come to a singular inescapable conclusion: namely, that, horrifying as it sounds, the secret relationship between these two great families helped to trigger the Age of Terror and give rise to the tragedy of 9/11.

CHAPTER TWO

The Houston-Jeddah Connection

ON A WARM AUGUST night in 2002, James R. Bath, a little-known Texas businessman, opens the door to the front of his ranch in Liberty, a town of eight thousand people on the Trinity River outside Houston. His house is framed by trees silhouetted against a moonlit Texas sky.

About six feet tall, trim and balding, Bath mingles a wry, folksy Texas charm with some of the machismo of a veteran jet fighter pilot. The combination has served him well in cultivating relationships with some of the great Texas power brokers of the last generation—from former governor John Connally to the Bush family.

There are many ways to tell the story of the events leading up to September 11 and the Iraq War of 2003, and Bath is hardly the most important person through whom to view them. However, his very obscurity carries its own significance. Bath happens to have served as the intentionally low-profile middleman in a passion play of sorts, the saga of how the House of Saud and its surrogates first courted the Bush family.

Bath is disarmingly hospitable as he whips up a late-night dinner and recounts the story of the birth of the Houston-Jeddah connection in the 1970s. A native of Natchitoches, Louisiana, he moved to Houston in 1965 at the age of twenty-nine to join the Texas Air National Guard. In the late sixties, after working for Atlantic Aviation, a Delaware-based company that sold business aircraft, he moved to Houston and went on to become an airplane broker on his own.

Sometime around 1974—he doesn't recall the exact date—Bath was trying to sell a F-27 turboprop, a sluggish medium-range plane that was not exactly a hot ticket in those days, when he received a phone call that changed his life.

The voice on the other end belonged to Salem bin Laden, heir to the great Saudi Binladin Group fortune. Then only about twenty-five, Salem was the eldest of fifty-four children of Mohammed Awad bin Laden, a brilliant engineer who had built the multibillion-dollar construction empire in Saudi Arabia.*

Bath not only had a buyer for a plane no one else seemed to want, he had also stumbled upon a source of wealth and power that was certain to pique the interest of even the brashest Texas oil baron. Bath flew the plane to Saudi Arabia himself—no easy task since the aircraft could only do about 240 knots an hour—and ended up spending three weeks in Jeddah, where he befriended two key figures in the new generation of young Saudi billionaires.[1] One of them was Salem bin Laden. In addition, Salem introduced Bath to his family and friends, including Khalid bin Mahfouz, also about twenty-five, who was the heir to the National Commercial Bank of Saudi Arabia, the biggest bank in the kingdom.

Salem was of medium height, outgoing, and thoroughly Western in his manner, says Bath. Bin Mahfouz was taller—about six feet—rail thin, relatively quiet and reserved. One associate says that if he had not known bin Mahfouz was a Saudi billionaire, he would have mistaken him for a biker straight out of a Harley-Davidson ad.

Bath immediately took to the two young men. "I like the Saudi mentality. They like guns, horses, aviation, the outdoors," he said. "We had a lot in common."

In many ways, bin Mahfouz† and bin Laden were Saudi versions of the well-heeled good old boys whom Bath knew so well. "In Texas,

---

*Because the Hegira calendar used in Saudi Arabia does not consistently conform to the Gregorian calendar used in the West, the ages of many Saudis in this book are approximate.

†Bin Mahfouz has widely been identified in the media as the brother-in-law of Osama bin Laden, thanks to congressional testimony by former CIA director James Woolsey. But a spokesman for bin Mahfouz denies the assertion, and the author has found no evidence to back up Woolsey's charge.

you'll find the rich carrying on about being just poor country boys," he says.[2] "Well, these guys were masters of playing the poor, simple bedouin kid."

Poor, they were not. Salem and Khalid were both poised to take over the companies started by their billionaire fathers. In fact, they had almost identical family histories. Their fathers, Mohammed Awad bin Laden and Salem bin Mahfouz respectively, had both originally come from the Hadramawt, an oasislike valley in rugged, mountainous eastern Yemen. Both men were uneducated and poor— bin Laden was a brilliant but illiterate bricklayer who never even learned to sign his name—and had traveled the same 750-mile trek by foot. In Jeddah, the commercial capital of Saudi Arabia, they made their fortunes off the hajj, the sacred pilgrimages to the great mosques in Mecca and Medina, bin Laden through construction and bin Mahfouz through currency exchange.

In 1931, Salem's father, Mohammed Awad bin Laden, had formed what eventually became the Saudi Binladin Group as a modest general-contracting firm that first became known for building roads, including a stunning highway with precipitous hairpin turns between Jeddah and the resort city of Taif. Ambitious and highly disciplined, the elder bin Laden advanced his cause by submitting below-cost bids on palace construction projects, including palaces for members of the royal family.[3] His shrewdest innovation was to build a ramp to the palace bedroom of the aging and partially paralyzed King Abdul Aziz.[4] Subsequently, the king made him the royal family's favorite contractor for palaces and major governmental infrastructure projects.

As a result of this growing friendship, in 1951, bin Laden won the contract to build one of the kingdom's first major roads, running from Jeddah to Medina. Eventually, he became known as the king's private contractor. "He was a nice man, very well liked by the royals," says an American oil executive who knew Mohammed Awad bin Laden. "He had the reputation of a doer, of getting things done."

The most prestigious and lucrative prize given by the royal family to the bin Ladens was for the kingdom's biggest roads[5] and exclusive rights to all religious construction, including $17 billion in contracts to rebuild the holy sites at Medina and Mecca,[6] which carried enormous iconic significance. In the center of the Grand Mosque of Mecca was the Kaaba, the holiest place to worship in all of Islam. Legend has it that the Kaaba was built after God instructed the prophet Abraham to build a house of worship, and the Archangel Gabriel gave Abraham a black stone, thought to be a meteorite, which was placed in the north-east corner of the Kaaba. "If there is one single image that signifies the Muslim world, it is that of the hajj being performed in the Kaaba," says Adil Najam, a professor at Boston University.[7] "[Rebuilding these sites] would be the Western equivalent of restoring the Statue of Liberty, Mount Rushmore, and the Lincoln Memorial—multiplied by a factor of ten."

During the same period that Mohammed Awad bin Laden was cementing his ties with the royal family, Salem bin Mahfouz was using similar methods to woo King Abdul Aziz. After leaving the Hadramawt in 1915, bin Mahfouz had worked in various capacities for the wealthy Kaaki family of Mecca for thirty-five years, finally winning a partnership in the Kaakis' lucrative currency exchange business.[8] Because charging interest was condemned by the Koran as usury, at the time Saudi Arabia merely had money changers instead of a domestic banking industry. But bin Mahfouz went to the royal family and argued that Saudi Arabia would never be self-sufficient until the kingdom had a bank. Subsequently, bin Mahfouz won a license that allowed him to establish the National Commercial Bank of Saudi Arabia, the first bank in the kingdom.

By the early sixties, the bin Mahfouzes and the bin Ladens had made extraordinarily successful transitions from the tribal, Wild West-like Hadramawt in Yemen to the far more commercially sophisticated world of Jeddah. Since they were outsiders—both families were Yemenites—the bin Ladens and the bin Mahfouzes did not have the tribal allegiances that other Saudis had,[9] and it was easy for the royal family to build them into billionaire allies who did not bring with them the political baggage other Saudis may have had. Consequently, the two great merchant families had virtual state monopolies in construction and banking.

In effect, the Saudi Binladin Group was on its way to becoming a Saudi equivalent of Bechtel, the huge California-based construction and engineering firm.[10] Likewise, bin Mahfouz had begun to build the

National Commercial Bank into the Saudi version of Citibank, paving the way for it to enter the era of globalization.

Knowing full well the value of being close to the royal family in Saudi Arabia, Salem bin Laden and Khalid bin Mahfouz sought to have similar relationships in the United States. With Bath tutoring them in the ways of the West, they started coming to Houston regularly in the mid-seventies. Salem came first, buying planes and construction equipment for his family's company.[11] He bought houses in Marble Falls on Lake Travis in central Texas's Hill Country and near Orlando, Florida.[12] He started an aircraft-services company in San Antonio, Bin-laden Aviation, largely as a vehicle for managing his small fleet of planes.[13] He converted a BAC-111, a British medium-size commercial liner, for his own personal use, and for fun he flew Learjets, ultralights, and other planes around central Texas.

There were days that began in Geneva, continued in England, and ended up in New York.[14] Salem flew girlfriends over the Nile to see the Pyramids. "He loved to fly, and spent more time trying to entertain himself than anyone I know," says Dee Howard,[15] a San Antonio engineer who converted several aircraft for bin Laden, including the $92-million modification of a Boeing 747-400 for King Fahd's personal use,[16] the biggest such conversion in the world. The spectacularly outfitted jumbo jet boasted its own private hospital and was said to make Air Force One look modest by comparison.

From Texas to England, most Westerners who knew the bin Ladens found them irresistible. "Salem was a crazy bastard—and a delightful guy," says Terry Bennett, a doctor who attended the family in Saudi Arabia.[17] "All the bin Ladens filled the room. It was like being in the room with Bill Clinton or someone—you were aware that they were there. They may have had the normal human foibles, but they were good for their word and generous to a fault."

Salem loved music, the nightlife, and entertaining guests at dinner parties by playing guitar and singing "Deep in the Heart of Texas."[18] But Khalid bin Mahfouz was more reserved. "Khalid was a banker first and always acted as a banker should," remembers Bath. "He was extremely intelligent and quick to assess things."

For the most part, bin Laden and bin Mahfouz eschewed the gaudy public extravagance of sheikhs such as Mohammed al-Fassi, who in 1979 painted his Beverly Hills mansion in a color that evoked rotting limes and redid the statuary so that the genitals appeared more life-like.[19] Still, this was Texas. Bigger was better, and bin Mahfouz and bin Laden observed the prevailing mores. As they became entrenched in Texas in the seventies, bin Mahfouz bought an enormous, rambling $3.5-million faux château,[20] later known as Houston's Versailles,[21] in the posh River Oaks section of Houston. He also purchased a four-thousand-acre ranch in Liberty County on the Trinity River near James Bath's ranch.

These men, billionaires from a fundamentalist theocratic monarchy, had arrived in a wide-open American city where strip clubs and churches were often side by side, and they fit right in. "They loved the ranch and they loved the country life," says Bath. "There was a real affinity between Texas and life in the kingdom. Khalid would come out to the ranch with the family and the kids, to ride horses, shoot guns, fireworks. They'd been going to England forever. But Texas—there was the novelty."

Bin Laden and bin Mahfouz were not the only Saudis who started making the Saudi Arabia-Texas commute. Saudi arms dealer Adnan Khashoggi operated a small fleet of Boeing 727s for his private use.[22]* In 1970, Prince Bandar, later the ambassador on the Truman Balcony with President Bush, trained at Perrin Air Force Base near Sherman, Texas, as a fighter pilot[23] and became a daring acrobatic pilot who delighted in entertaining VIPs with his audacious aerial stunts. Joining them were the future king, then Crown Prince Fahd bin Abdul Aziz al-Saud; construction magnate Sheikh Abdullah Baroom; and others. "There were more private planes for the Saudis than many airlines have," says one pilot who flew for Salem bin Laden.[24] "It was quite an operation. Everyone had big airplanes and we flew whatever had wings."

Houston offered them a glimpse of a rapidly approaching Saudi

---

*Khashoggi made a fortune as a middleman on an estimated 80 percent of Saudi-American arms deals, including commissions of more than $100 million from Lockheed alone between 1970 and 1975.

future. As late as 1974, the tallest building in the Saudi capital, Riyadh, was a mere water tower,[25] but downtown Houston was already studded with gleaming skyscrapers. At home, the Saudis shopped in ancient markets known as souks, but in Houston, the extravagantly modern Galleria shopping mall had just opened.[26] Saudi Arabia was still a feudal desert kingdom where people lacked the professional skills and bureaucratic infrastructure to build a modern economy. Houston, by contrast, had gigantic energy-industry law firms—Baker Botts; Vinson, Elkins and Connally; Fulbright & Jaworski—that greased the wheels of America's enormous oil industry so it could easily navigate the corridors of power in Washington. In many ways, Riyadh and Houston could scarcely have been more dissimilar; yet these differences were precisely what attracted the Saudis to Texas and catalyzed a chain of events over the next three decades that would change global history.

In part, it was oil that drew the two cultures together. Its history in Texas dated to January 10, 1901, when a handful of wildcatters in Beaumont, Texas, about sixty miles from Houston, drilled away until mud mysteriously bubbled up from the ground and several tons of pipe abruptly shot upward with enormous force. A few minutes later, as workmen began to inspect the damage, another geyser of oil erupted from thirty-six hundred feet under a salt dome.[27] The wildcatters had hoped to bring in fifty barrels a day.[28] Instead, the legendary Spindle-top gusher brought in as many as one hundred thousand.[29] The Texas oil boom had begun.

Before long, Houston's Ship Channel had grown into a twenty-mile stretch of refineries constituting one of the great industrial complexes in the world, where hundreds and hundreds of towers and massive spherical tanks spewed smoke and steam, eerily illuminating the ghostly sky like a brightly lit Erector set. More than a quarter of all the oil used in the United States was refined there. Part of the complex, the Exxon Mobil plant in Baytown, is the biggest oil refinery in the world, producing more than half a million barrels a day.[30]

By contrast, oil was not even discovered in Saudi Arabia until 1938,[31] and even then, and for more than a generation afterward, control of the vast Saudi resources remained heavily influenced by the

United States thanks to lucrative concessions granted to Aramco (the Arabian American Oil Company), a consortium of giant American oil companies and the Saudis.[32]* In the early seventies, however, just before bin Laden and bin Mahfouz struck out for Texas, the world of oil underwent a dramatic change. Oil production in the United States had already peaked in 1970 and was beginning an inexorable decline at a time when more people drove more miles in bigger cars that burned more gas. Baby boomers had come of age and were driving. An elaborate suburban car culture had grown up all over the United States. There were Corvettes and Mustangs, muscle cars such as the Trans Am, and drive-in restaurants and shopping malls. The volume of America's imported oil nearly doubled—from 3.2 million barrels a day in 1970 to 6.2 million a day in 1973.[33] Saudi Arabia's share of world exports sky-rocketed from 13 percent in 1970 to 21 percent in 1972.

Saudi Arabia's transformation from an underdeveloped backwater to one of the richest countries in the world was under way. In October 1973, just after the Arab-Israeli war, OPEC—the Organization of Petroleum Exporting Countries—a heretofore impotent consortium of oil-rich nations, abruptly became a genuine cartel capable of driving the price of oil up more than 300 percent. Oil, they had discovered, could be used as a weapon. Suddenly, Saudi Arabia took on the position Texas itself had once had and became the swing oil producer for the great industrial nations of the world. The biggest transfer of wealth in human history was under way. Hundreds of billions of dollars in oil revenues poured into the Saudi kingdom.[34] The Saudis were drowning in petrodollars.

Not surprisingly, most Americans don't have fond memories of the

---

*The Saudis first granted concessions to explore for oil in Saudi Arabia to the British, thanks to Jack Philby, who is best known today as the father of the notorious British spy Kim Philby. At a time when King Abdul Aziz was hoping to find water, Philby persuaded him to let him look for oil. According to Daniel Yergin's *The Prize*, Philby was dismissed by British government officials as merely a bit player. But Standard Oil of California recognized that he had access to the king and signed him on to help acquire concessions. The initial concession agreement called for Socal to put $175,000 in gold up front, an additional loan of $100,000 eighteen months later, and still another loan of $500,000 on the discovery of oil. The concession was good for sixty years and covered 360,000 square miles. It was one of the greatest bargains in history.

Saudi ascendancy in the seventies. With the embargo, the price of gas in the United States jumped from 38 cents a gallon in 1973 to $1.35 in 1981.[35] Soaring inflation, high interest rates, and long gas lines soon followed. A nationwide speed limit of fifty-five miles per hour was imposed in the interests of fuel efficiency. Government bureaucracies were established to reduce energy consumption.

Houston, however, benefited from the newfound Saudi wealth more than any other city in the country. All over the United States, architectural firms cut back because of the recession, but in Houston, CRS Design Associates more than doubled its payroll—thanks to huge contracts from the Saudis.[36] Superdeveloper Gerald Hines built gleaming skyscrapers in downtown Houston designed by the likes of Philip Johnson and I. M. Pei—financed, it was whispered, with Saudi riyals. Petrodollars flowed into Houston's Texas Commerce Bank, thanks to Arab clients. Saudi companies bought drill bits and pipes and lubricant in Houston.[37] The price of oil was over $30 a barrel and looked as if it would never fall—and while the rest of the country had to pay the price, Texas oil producers also enjoyed the higher revenues. At last, Houston was on the map of international café society. Local socialites hung out at Tony's Restaurant on Westheimer Road, taking a prominent table with Princess Grace, Mick Jagger, fashion designer Bill Blass, or whichever well-known houseguest had flown in for the week.[38] In all, more than eighty companies in Houston developed strong business relationships with the Saudis.[39] It was even said that Houston was becoming to the Saudis what New York is to Israel and the Jews[40]—another home half a world away.

Like the Israelis, the Saudis had one overwhelming need that they sought in this new alliance-defense. For all its newfound wealth, the House of Saud was more vulnerable militarily than ever. A feudal desert monarchy that lacked the infrastructure of a modern industrial nation, the kingdom had more than fifteen hundred miles of coastline to defend. Its oil and gas facilities provided numerous high-value targets. Iran regularly sponsored riots during the pilgrimages to Mecca and provided support to Shiite extremists in Saudi Arabia.[41] Iraq, with which it shares a border, was a threat. Across the Red Sea, Sudan was a hospitable host to extremists. Other troublesome neighbors included Yemen, Oman, and Jordan. Saudi Arabia was vast—it is about a quarter the size of the United States—but it had to be defended by a population that, at the time, was under 6 million people, three-quarters of whom were women, children, and elderly.[42]

In addition, the Saudis had extraordinary internal weaknesses. As the rulers of an underdeveloped, feudal desert kingdom, they were in control of one of the most corrupt, authoritarian, undemocratic countries in the world. It was threatened by communists and Islamic revolutionaries. Women had virtually no rights. The Saudis arguably led the world in public beheadings-many of which took place in a plaza in Riyadh referred to as Chop-Chop Square.[43]

Flooded with petrodollars, the Saudis still urgently needed a partner. As a result, the kingdom began to weave a tight alliance with the United States, militarily, economically, and politically. As the petrodollars poured in over the next twenty-five years, roughly eighty-five thousand "high-net-worth" Saudis invested a staggering $860 billion in American companies-an average of more than $10 million a person and a sum that is roughly equivalent to the gross domestic product of Spain.[44] They took the United States by storm, selling crude, buying banks, building skyscrapers, buying weapons, investing everywhere.

Most important, the Saudis sought strong political ties to the United States through personal friendships with the powers that be. Education, training, and connections with American power brokers became prerequisites for the next generation of the Saudi elite. "They started sending their sons to school in the U.S.," says Nawaf Obaid, a Saudi oil analyst who himself was educated at Harvard and MIT. "They wanted to build up relationships with key people at the same time they had return on investments."[45]

The vast majority of the Saudi investments in the United States went into major banks and energy, defense, technology, and media companies. There were blue chips such as Citigroup and AOL Time Warner, and huge, secretive consortiums such as Investcorp, which put billions of Arab dollars in companies including Tiffany, Gucci, and Saks Fifth Avenue. But the House of Saud also made a handful of investments in troubled companies that were loaded with debt and regulatory problems—which just happened to be owned by men who had or might have White House ties. "The leadership in the kingdom definitely supported these activities," says Prince Turki bin Faisal al-Saud, the ambassador to Great Britain who long served as Saudi minister of intelligence and was a son of the late King Faisal's.[46]

Superlawyer Edward Bennett Williams, a roguish Washington fixer, understood exactly what the Saudis were after. According to *The Man to See,* Evan Thomas's 1991 biography of Williams, in the seventies he accompanied Clark Clifford, a perennial adviser to Democratic presidents and one of the so-called Wise Men of Washington, on a private jet after Clifford had ill-advisedly taken on billionaire Arab clients.

"Williams gleefully acted out a pantomime of a delegation of Arabs visiting Clifford in his office," wrote Thomas. "Williams, a perfect mimic, imitated Clifford gravely telling the visiting sheikhs, 'You understand, of course, that I can only get you access.'

"Then Williams imitated the Arabs winking and grinning as they shoved a bag of gold across Clifford's desk."[47]

As it happened, Edward Bennett Williams's droll account of the Arab strategy for achieving entrée to the inner sanctums of American power wasn't far from the truth. However, before approaching a man of Clark Clifford's stature, or, for that matter, wary Republican power brokers, the Saudis went to someone in Jimmy Carter's White House—someone who not only had access to the president but who also happened to be desperately vulnerable.

After taking office in 1977, Carter had appointed his close friend Bert Lance, the CEO of the National Bank of Georgia (NBG), as director of the Office of Management and Budget (OMB). Lance had played a key role in Carter's presidential campaign, but in many ways he was the polar opposite of a Beltway insider like Clifford. He was not an easy fit in Washington. The media enjoyed tweaking the rumpled, six-foot-five-inch Lance, with his syrupy Southern drawl, as something of a country bumpkin straight out of the Georgia woods. Within weeks of taking his place in the new administration, he was in trouble.

Lance had financed much of Carter's electoral campaign through overdrafts at NB G, and now that he was in the glare of the Washington political spotlight, those transactions had come under scrutiny. In addition, when he became CEO of the bank, Lance had borrowed

$2.6 million to finance the purchase of his stock in the bank under terms that required him to remain its chief executive.[48] That, however, was impossible because now that he was in the government, he was required by law to resign from the bank. Worse, bank stocks had sunk so low that Lance couldn't afford to sell his stock to pay off the loan.[49] Last, Lance was charged with having mismanaged corporate and personal financial affairs by pledging the same stock as collateral for two loans, and having improperly pledged some of the bank's assets against his loans.

An investigation and trial later found Lance innocent, but his political reputation was devastated. In September 1977, only a few months after he had taken over at OMB, he resigned. Lance was heavily in debt and unemployed.[50] He just had one thing going for him: he was still close friends with the president of the United States.

In October, just weeks after his resignation, Lance met with Agha Hasan Abedi, the Pakistani founder of the Bank of Credit and Commerce International, or BCCI. At the time, BCCI was said to be the fastest-growing bank in the world. Its assets had grown from $200 million in 1972 to more than $2 billion in 1977.[51] As a bank friendly to Muslim concerns, BCCI was perfectly positioned to take advantage of the petrodollars flowing into the Middle East in the wake of the OPEC oil embargo.

BCCI's ascendancy was also due to business practices that were highly unusual in the staid world of banking. Other banks gave toaster ovens to new depositors; BCCI provided prostitutes.[52]* Loans of millions of dollars were granted merely on the basis of a simple

---

*According to the U.S. Senate's BCCI probe, the bank's involvement in prostitution grew out of its "special protocol department" in Pakistan, which allegedly serviced "the personal requirements of the Al-Nahyan family of Abu Dhabi, and other BCCI VIPs, including other Middle Eastern rulers." The Senate report asserts that Abedi employed a woman who helped him cement his relationship with the Al-Nahyan family by providing them with Pakistani prostitutes. The report says that the woman was reputed to have first won the attention of the royal family "by arranging to get virgin women from the villages from the ages of 16 to 20. [She] would make payments to their families, take the teenaged girls into the cities, and teach them how to dress and how to act. The women were then brought to the Abu Dhabi princes. For years, [she] would take 50 to 60 girls at a time to large department stores in Lahore and Karachi to get them outfitted for clothes. Given the size of [her] retinue and her spending habits—$100,000 at a time was not unusual when she was outfitting

request. BCCI allegedly handled flight capital from countries such as India or Pakistan where currency constraints strictly prohibited the wealthy from taking their money out of the country. BCCI was luring customers away from its rivals and now had 146 branches in thirty-two countries. But it still had no presence in the biggest financial market in the world—the United States.

"You cannot be a global bank, an international bank, without some sort of presence in the United States," Lance told BCCI founder Abedi. "This is the richest, most powerful nation in the world, and this is certainly something you ought to look at."[53] Desperate to sell his stock, Lance had just the thing in mind—a modest Southern bank, namely, the National Bank of Georgia.

Abedi told Lance that Saudi billionaire Ghaith Pharaon might be just the person to take over NBG. Born in 1940, the dapper Pharaon was the son of a private physician to King Abdul Aziz[54] (as was Saudi billionaire arms dealer Adnan Khashoggi[55]). Pharaon's education included undergraduate work at Stanford and an MBA from Harvard Business School. He wore Savile Row suits and a Vandyke beard. Like his childhood friend Khalid bin Mahfouz, he was close to the House of Saud and personified the wave of "westernized" Saudi billionaires who came to the United States in the aftermath of the OPEC oil embargo.[56]

With an annual income of $300 million in 1974,[57] Pharaon had lavish homes in Saudi Arabia and Paris, and a magnificent plantation near Savannah, Georgia, that had been owned by Henry Ford. In 1975, Pharaon helped pioneer the Arab takeover of American banks by purchasing Detroit's ailing Bank of the Commonwealth at a time when Arab money was a novelty in the United States.

Negotiations to sell the National Bank of Georgia to Pharaon and BCCI began over Thanksgiving weekend in 1977, through discussions

---

... her charges—she became notorious and there was substantial competition among clothiers and jewelers for her business .... According to one U.S. investigator with substantial knowledge of BCCI's activities, some BCCI officials have acknowledged that some of the females provided some members of the Al-Nahyan family were young girls who had not yet reached puberty, and in certain cases, were physically injured by the experience. The official said that former BCCI officials had told him that BCCI also provided males to homosexual VIPs."

among Lance, Abedi, and other BCCI officials.[58] On December 20, Lance announced he was selling his NBG stock to Pharaon for $2.4 million at $20 a share—twice what it had been worth only a few weeks earlier.

Why had Saudis paid top dollar for a failing bank that was a target of federal regulators? The Senate investigation concluded that "gaining access to President Carter and the White House was ... one of the reasons the 'Arabs' were interested in having Lance represent them and in buying his interest in the National Bank of Georgia."[59]

The access Lance offered BCCI was not illusory. Through him, BCCI representatives met Jimmy Carter, the Reverend Jesse Jackson, Prime Minister James Callaghan of Great Britain, and many other officials, including Lance's attorney, the aforementioned Clark Clifford. The Senate report concluded that Carter's integrity was used by BCCI officials as the bank "went about mixing bribery and flattery to obtain access to the foreign reserves and other assets of numerous Third World countries."[60]

As for Lance, who had once been referred to as the deputy president of the United States, he returned to Georgia to work as a financial consultant. But his career in national politics was over. As for the Saudis, they had learned that they could win access to the highest levels of power in the United States.

On the Republican side, James Bath didn't have nearly the stature of Edward Bennett Williams or Clark Clifford, or for that matter, the visibility of Bert Lance. But in the seventies in Houston, for Khalid bin Mahfouz and Salem bin Laden, Jim Bath was the man to see. He counted among his friends and business associates no fewer than five Texans, four of them Republicans, who at one time or another would be considered presidential candidates.

Bath was friendly with the family of Senator Lloyd Bentsen, the lanky, distinguished Democrat who would run as vice presidential candidate in 1988* and later become secretary of the treasury. Bath had

---

*Bentsen's most memorable moment in politics came in the 1988 campaign when his youthful rival, GOP vice presidential candidate Dan Quayle, invoked President John F. Kennedy's name, to which Bentsen replied, "I knew Jack Kennedy. Jack Kennedy was a friend of mine. And, Senator, you're no Jack Kennedy."

become partners with one of his sons, Lan Bentsen, in a small real estate firm that developed an apartment complex and airplane hangars and sought investments for the senator's blind trust.[61]

While he served in the Texas Air National Guard, Bath had also befriended the young George W. Bush,[62] who had begun training in 1970 as a pilot of F-102 fighters at Ellington Air Force Base near Houston. Bush had been a member of the "Champagne Unit" of the National Guard, so-called because it was famous for serving as the vehicle through which the sons of Houston society escaped serving in the Vietnam War.

In the mid-seventies, young Bush also introduced Bath to his father. A former Houston congressman who had lost senatorial races in 1964 to liberal Democrat Ralph Yarborough and in 1970 to the more conservative Lloyd Bentsen, the elder George Bush had been a devoted Nixon loyalist even through the mire of Watergate. His steadfastness had been rewarded with appointments as U.S. ambassador to the United Nations, as chairman of the Republican National Committee, and under President Gerald Ford, as chief liaison to the U.S. mission to China. In 1976, Bush was appointed head of the CIA.

There was also Bath's duck-hunting buddy[63] James A. Baker III, then in his mid-forties. One of Houston's most powerful corporate attorneys and a true Texas patrician, Baker was a close friend and associate of George H. W. Bush's.

Finally, there was John Connally, the silver-haired, silver-tongued former Democratic Texas governor who became secretary of the treasury under Nixon in 1971 and who later switched to the Republican Party.

By 1976, Salem bin Laden had appointed Bath his American business representative.[64] Khalid bin Mahfouz drew up a similar arrangement with him as well. Bath was more than simply someone who could provide the Saudis with entrée to political power brokers. But exactly what he did beyond that, in the intelligence world and elsewhere, was shrouded in mystery. From *Time* to the *Wall Street Journal*, the press speculated about Bath's connections to the Bushes, to John Connally, to the CIA, to BCCI, and to various figures in the Iran-contra scandal of the eighties.

When asked about his career, Bath usually downplayed his importance. By his account, he was merely "a small, obscure businessman." It was often said that he was in the CIA, but Bath denied that to *Time*.[65] Later, he equivocated. "There's all sorts of degrees of civilian participation [in the CIA]," he says. "It runs the whole spectrum, maybe passing on relevant data to more substantive things. The people who are called on by their government and serve—I don't think you're going to find them talking about it. Were that the case with me, I'm almost certain you wouldn't find me talking about it."[66]

Bath's role in investing for the Saudis took various forms. "The investments were sometimes in my name as trustee, sometimes off-shore corporations, and sometimes in the name of a law firm," he says. "It would vary."[67] Bath generally received a 5 percent interest as his fee and was sometimes listed on related corporate documents.[68]

On behalf of Salem bin Laden, Bath purchased the Houston Gulf Airport, a small private facility in League City, Texas, twenty-five miles east of Houston.[69] He also became the sole director of Skyway Aircraft Leasing in the Cayman Islands, which was actually owned by Khalid bin Mahfouz.

Through Skyway, Bath brokered about $150 million worth of private aircraft deals to major stockholders in BCCI such as Ghaith Pharaon and Sheikh Zayed bin Sultan al-Nahayan, president of the United Arab Emirates. To incorporate his companies in the Cayman Islands, Bath used the same firm that later set up a money-collecting front for Oliver North in the Iran-contra affair.[70] He also served as an intermediary between the Saudis and John Connally, who, having served as Nixon's treasury secretary, began to position himself for a shot at the White House in 1980.

In August 1977, John Connally and Bath teamed up with Ghaith Pharaon and bin Mahfouz to buy the Main Bank of Houston, a small community bank with about $70 million in assets.[71] Soon, the tiny bank began obtaining more than $10 million a month in hundred-dollar bills.[72] It was highly irregular for such a tiny bank to require such large amounts of cash. Such unusual transactions can be a sign of money laundering, but bank regulators in Texas said they did not know why the bank needed the money. The transactions were not illegal and the reason for them was never uncovered.

Then, in July 1978, Khalid bin Mahfouz and forty bodyguards

took over an entire floor of the Mayflower Hotel in Washington, D.C., with John Connally there to introduce him to Texas billionaires William Herbert Hunt and Nelson Bunker Hunt.[73]* The purpose of the meeting was allegedly to get bin Mahfouz and Pharaon to participate in the Hunt brothers' quest to corner the world's silver market. The Saudis' role in the silver deal fell through—and the Hunt brothers' participation in it led to one of the great financial follies of the decade.

Nevertheless, through Main Bank, the young Saudis had established ties to Connally.[74] They were now in business with a legitimate presidential contender who seemed well positioned for the 1980 campaign. For two young men, still in their twenties, to have business partnerships with an American presidential candidate elevated them enormously in the eyes of the Saudis back home, especially the royal family.

With his lantern jaw and silver mane, his Stetson hat, cowboy boots, and bolo tie, Connally looked the part. He had movie-star good looks, and a powerful appeal to Wall Street and corporate America. He had survived close ties to the disgraced Nixon presidency and bribery charges in the so-called Milk Fund scandal of 1974. He had even survived the Kennedy assassination in November 1963. Sitting next to Kennedy in the motorcade, he too was shot that day, but emerged a wounded hero.

At the time, Connally had only one serious political rival in Texas—George H. W. Bush, a man who possessed little of Connally's charisma. Whereas Connally was festooned with the iconography of the Lone Star State, Bush was a Connecticut Yankee who constantly had to prove his Texas bona fides. Connally was a po' boy from Floresville in the Texas Hill Country—his father had been a tenant farmer—who had made his fortune through lucrative relationships with oil barons Sid Richardson and Clint Murchison and then taken on the trappings of a brash wheeler-dealer himself. By contrast, Bush

---

*In 1973, Bunker, Herbert, and Lamar Hunt, three sons of oil billionaire H. L. Hunt, began to hedge against the depreciating dollar by investing in silver at a time when gold could not be purchased in the United States. By hoarding huge quantities of the precious metal, they pushed the price of silver to more than $50 an ounce. But in 1980, the price plummeted to $9 an ounce. The Hunts never recovered from the financial debacle and eventually had to sell their art collections.

was a genuine oilman, but he was an East Coast transplant whose understated style sought to mask but only accentuated his patrician background. A partner in the huge Houston oil industry law firm of Vinson, Elkins and Connally, Connally was unabashed about being the biggest Arab-money lawyer in Texas. Bush kept his distance. Next to Connally, he seemed bland indeed.

For all that, Bush had mastered one extraordinarily important aspect of politics in a way that left Connally and scores of other wannabes in the dust. George H. W. Bush was wired. Whether it be the old-moneyed East Coast establishment or Richard Nixon's team, the rising young Turks of the new conservative movement or the power brokers of Republican Party infrastructure, Bush either knew the right people or knew how to meet them and make them his friends. He knew people who would enable him to raise campaign funds, to get the right decisions made at government agencies such as the Securities and Exchange Commission and the Export-Import Bank, people who would back his son's oil companies, who would perform favors when called on. He did not like to make decisions without knowing the outcome in advance. From the Petroleum Club in Midland, Texas to the Bayou Club in Houston to the Bohemian Grove* in California; from clubby men's institutions like the CIA and the oil industry—he had cultivated an extraordinary power base. In the long run, it was capable of taking him all the way to the White House.

And in the short run—within a few years—Saudis seeking access to the highest levels of American power soon forgot Bert Lance, Clark Clifford, and John Connally and realized that George H. W. Bush was the man to see.

---

*The Bohemian Grove has held secret meetings for a global elite since 1873 in a redwood forest of northern California. In addition to Republican presidents Eisenhower, Nixon, Reagan, and George H. W. Bush, members have included James Baker, Richard Cheney, Donald Rumsfeld, David Rockefeller, William Casey, and Henry Kissinger. Each year, the members don red, black, and silver robes and conduct a ritual in which they worship a giant stone owl.

CHAPTER THREE

The Ascendancy
of George H. W. Bush

THE SOCIAL STRUCTURE OF the United States, of course, bore little resemblance to a monarchy like that of Saudi Arabia. But within the American context, George H. W. Bush was the nearest equivalent to royalty, a member of a patrician class that was able to pass on power in both the private and public sectors from generation to generation.

Most famously, while an undergraduate at Yale, Bush had become a member of Skull and Bones, the secret society to which his father, investment banker Prescott Bush, belonged.* With its baroque and mystifying preppie voodoo rituals, Skull and Bones was where bonds were forged by men who would run the old-line banks and white-shoe law firms, men who would become the Wise Men of Washington. This was the Eastern Establishment—the Bundys, the Buckleys, the Harrimans, and the Tafts. Bonesmen counted among their ranks three presidents, several Supreme Court justices, U.S. senators, secretaries of state, national security advisers, the founders of Time, Inc., and the CIA, and more.[1]

And so, in 1948, when Bush took off for Texas with his wife, Barbara, and infant son, George W., he was not some poor immigrant striking out for the uncharted wilderness with nothing to fall back on. It was a long journey from the cosseted, leafy suburbs of Greenwich, Connecticut, where Bush grew up, to the land of barbecue and

---

*Bush's son George W. also became a Bonesman.

catfish, Dr Pepper and Lone Star beer, armadillos and the Texas two-step. But thanks to Neil Mallon, his father's best friend, Bush had already lined up a job in Odessa, Texas, with the International Derrick and Equipment Company (IDECO). Prescott Bush served on the board of directors of its parent company, Dresser Industries, had been instrumental in transforming Dresser into a public company, and was close to Mallon, its president, a fellow Bonesman and a man who was so intimate with the Bush family that he was known as Uncle Neil.[2]* Young George H. W. Bush even named his third son Neil Mallon Bush.

Bush soon found other Ivy League immigrants and elite Texans who had gone east to school. In many ways, they were reenacting a domestic version of what the British did during the Raj in India, sending out the young sons of aristocrats to mine the resources of an underdeveloped colony. Texas, with its rich oil reserves, was like a third world country ripe for development by ambitious scions of East Coast wealth. The Spindletop gusher had given birth to the mythic Texas of oil barons and *Giant,* the sprawling James Dean epic. By the forties, the state had truly begun to shift from an agrarian economy to one based on oil. It was a land where rough-hewn wildcatters won and lost fortunes overnight. Here, Bush would develop an appreciation of oil as an important strategic resource—a characteristic he would later share with his Saudi friends.

By the time Bush got there, the Midland-Odessa area of West Texas was already an oil boomtown. Bush himself described it in his memoirs, *Looking Forward,* as "Yuppieland West."[3] An incongruous quasi-prep subculture began to emerge. Newly minted millionaires lived on streets named Harvard and Princeton.[4] Oilmen sent their sons north and east to prep at the Hill School, Lawrenceville, Choate, and Andover. Preppie clotheshorses shopped at Albert S. Kelley's, Midland's answer to Brooks Brothers.[5] Bush and his circle at the Petroleum Club constituted local society.

In 1953, Bush partnered with Hugh Liedtke to form a new independent oil company, Zapata Petroleum, backed by Bush's family

---

*Dresser was later taken over by Halliburton, which was run by another Bush colleague, Dick Cheney.

connections. Bush's uncle, Herbert Walker,* whose family helped found Brown Brothers Harriman, at one time the largest private investment firm on Wall Street, raised at least $350,000. Bush's father, Prescott Bush, put in $50,000. *Washington Post* publisher Eugene Meyer put in $50,000 and again that amount in the name of his son-in-law, Phil Graham, who later succeeded Meyer as publisher.[6]

Zapata drilled 128 wells in Texas in its first year without hitting a dry hole.[7] With the company's instant success, Bush moved to Houston in 1954 and the following year founded the Zapata Off-Shore Company, which he later ran himself after spinning it off from Zapata.

At Zapata Off-Shore, Bush learned firsthand about the interaction between business and government. Crucial to the company's future was a happy resolution to a political controversy that would determine whether Zapata, or any other company, could drill offshore in the Gulf of Mexico within the twelve-mile limit. Fortunately, Bush did not have to look far to find a friendly politician happy to enter the fray on his behalf. His father, Prescott Bush, had become a Republican senator from Connecticut. Having given up investment banking for a seat in the U.S. Senate, Prescott Bush led Senate Republicans in battling efforts to take federal control of mineral deposits within the twelve-mile limit.[8] As a result, the success of Zapata Off-Shore was unsurprising. Congress tabled its attempt to federalize those waters, and George Bush's Zapata Off-Shore was able to drill off the Mississippi coast in the Gulf of Mexico.

His early success notwithstanding, Bush had never been an insatiable, dyed-in-the-wool oilman. Accumulating money for its own sake was not and had never been the driving force in his life. His father was.

At six feet four inches, Prescott Bush Sr. was a commanding figure with Hollywood good looks and athletic grace. Imposing as his physical presence was, Prescott Bush loomed even larger in the imagination

---

*The Walker family also oversaw the creation of Madison Square Garden, the Belmont Race Track, and the New York Mets, and lent their name to the Walker Cup, one of golf's most prestigious events. Walker Point in Kennebunkport, Maine, is the site of the estate to which President George H. W. Bush and his family often went for summer vacations.

of his sons. According to Herbert S. Parmet's *George Bush: The Life of a Lone Star Yankee,* he was "a leviathan of a father," a man whom his children, George included, never dared challenge. His presence inspired words such as *dignity, respect, duty, service,* and *discipline.* At home, his sons wore coats and ties to the family dinner table each night.[9] "We had a father who taught us to ... put something back in, do something, help others," Bush told the *Los Angeles Times.*[10]*

As managing partner of Brown Brothers Harriman, Prescott was a familiar figure in New York's moneyed class. He belonged to the best clubs and went on cruises with Averell Harriman, the former governor of New York, presidential adviser, and heir to the Union Pacific railroad fortune. He sang harmony on the porch after dinner with the Yalies. And yet, as much as Prescott was a part of the fabric of that world, he looked with disdain at the lives of the "economic royalists" around him whose only goal was the accumulation of money.

So to those who truly knew him, it was not surprising that Prescott Bush had gone to the Senate to serve the public; indeed, it was almost as if a Senate seat were preordained."[11] In 1962, however, for reasons of health, Prescott decided not to run for reelection. George resolved to follow in his father's footsteps—and vowed that he would go even further. He confided to his friends that he entertained presidential ambitions.

And so, in 1966, Bush sold out his position in Zapata, then worth about $1 million,[12] and was elected to his first of two stints in Congress. In saying good-bye to Zapata, Bush was leaving behind a chance at truly great wealth. In 1963, partner Hugh Liedtke had merged Zapata with Penn Oil, in the process creating Pennzoil. Having mastered the art of the hostile takeover, he then used Pennzoil to eventually gain control of the United Gas Pipeline Company, a company five times larger than his. By 1986, Liedtke's stock had gone up in value by 10,000 percent.[13]

George Bush had forsaken great riches, but he clearly had a promising political future. By the time Bush was reelected to Congress in

---

*Not everyone agreed that Prescott Bush ruled the Bush children. According to Bill Minutaglio's *First Son,* Barbara Bush once said that Dorothy Walker Bush had "ten times" as much influence on her sons as had Prescott.

1968, Richard Nixon had put the young congressman on his short list of vice-presidential candidates.[14] A Senate seat appeared to be within his grasp, and Bush thought that would be a stepping-stone to the White House. When he lost the 1970 Texas senatorial race to Lloyd Bentsen, however, he was devastated. "I feel like [General George] Custer," he told a friend, equating his campaign with Custer's disastrous loss to the Sioux Indians in the battle of Little Bighorn.[15]

Luckily, a Republican who appreciated Bush's fealty sat in the White House. In 1972, after his landslide reelection, President Nixon ordered a housecleaning based on one criterion-loyalty. "Eliminate everyone except George Bush," Nixon told his domestic affairs adviser John Ehrlichman. "Bush will do anything for our cause."[16]

Then, after Bush's stints at the United Nations, the Republican National Committee,[17]* and heading the U.S. delegation to China, in 1976 President Gerald Ford asked him to be director of the Central Intelligence Agency.

With the CIA under fire for its excesses during the Vietnam era,[†] however, being the nation's head spook was a political liability, not an asset. Bush reluctantly acceded to Ford's request to take the job, but he viewed it as a ruse by rival Republicans to keep him out of the White House. "Could that be what was happening?" Bush wrote in his memoirs. "Bury Bush at the CIA?"

Bush had other liabilities as a national candidate. His loyalty to Nixon had paid off with high-level patronage positions, but in the

---

*When Bush was chairman of the RNC, a *Washington Post* reporter asked him about a young man who had been accused of teaching political espionage and "dirty tricks" to college Republicans. According to *First Son*, a few months later, after the news stories had been forgotten, Bush hired the man, Karl Rove, as his special assistant. Part of his job was to make sure that George W. had a car whenever he came to town. Years later, Rove, of course, became known as the political strategist and image shaper behind George W. Bush.

†One of the most egregious excesses of the CIA was the Phoenix program in Vietnam. According to Vietnam Information Notes, published by the U.S. State Department in July 1969, "The target for 1969 calls for the elimination of 1,800 VCI per month .... The Phoenix program ... [has] served notice to Province Chiefs that their performance will in large part be measured by Phoenix results." In other words, under the program, the CIA required province chiefs to assassinate a quota of eighteen hundred Vietnamese per month.

aftermath of Watergate, being a protégé of the disgraced president had serious drawbacks.

And Bush had been a very real beneficiary of the Republican campaign abuses. Specifically, during his failed 1970 Senate campaign, in what became known as Operation Townhouse, Bush, assisted by campaign finance chairman Bob Mosbacher, a wealthy New Yorker who had moved to Houston in 1948,[19] and Hugh Liedtke's brother William,[20] had received $106,000 in unreported campaign funds. The money had been funneled through no fewer than fourteen different Bush campaign committees to avoid detection. Two Nixon associates, Jack A. Gleason and Herbert W. Kalmbach, later pleaded guilty to running the illegal fund-raising operation. Bush himself never faced formal charges, but the *Wall Street Journal* termed the operation "a dress rehearsal for the campaign finance abuses of Watergate."[21]*

So when Bush returned to Houston in 1978 to assess his chances for higher office, he found little enthusiasm among even his closest friends. Hugh Liedtke had warned him that the CIA job was political suicide." John E. Caulkins, a banker friend from Detroit, was taken aback when he received a call from Bush saying he planned to run for the presidency.

"Of what?" Caulkins asked.

"The United States," said Bush.

"Oh, George," Caulkins replied.[23]

Nevertheless, in late 1978, Bush met with James Baker and Bob Mosbacher and put together groups to raise funds and assess his candidacy. In addition to his father's East Coast connections, the Yalies and Bonesmen, to his CIA colleagues and his patrons in Washington and on the Republican National Committee, Bush had assembled a significant new political network in Houston—Big Oil.

For the House of Saud, of course, there was no difference between the public sector and the private sector. They owned the oil industry and ruled the country. But Bush set about transforming capital

---

*When confronted with the allegations, Bush often told reporters that special prosecutor Leon Jaworski had found no evidence of illegal activities by Bush after investigating the Townhouse fund. *As Newsweek* noted, Bush was close friends with Jaworski, a partner at the huge Houston law firm Fulbright & Jaworski.

from the oil industry into political power. With Baker and Mosbacher, he hit up executives from Pennzoil, Exxon, Houston Oil and Minerals, McCormick Oil and Gas.[24] He had oil industry contacts at the highest levels all over the world. During his days at the CIA, he had cultivated friendships with the "friendly royals" of the Middle East. In Houston, he entertained King Hussein of Jordan and Nelson Rockefeller and hung out at the exclusive Bayou Club. Bush's former partner Hugh Liedtke, as Pennzoil's president and CEO, had become an oil heavyweight in his own right. William Farish Jr., heir to the Humble Oil and Standard Oil (now ExxonMobil) fortunes, was, as Barbara Bush put it, taken in "almost like family" by the Bushes.[25]*

Bush was also tied in with the power-broker attorneys at the great law firms of the oil industry in Houston, including but not limited to Baker Botts and Fulbright & Jaworski, who lobbied the powers that be in Washington, handled international mergers and acquisitions, and mapped out strategy for multibillion-dollar pipelines for virtually every major energy firm in the world.

This was a tightly knit world. The legal department of Pennzoil, for example, was closely linked to Baker Botts, the firm founded by James Baker's great-grandfather, and which today represents ExxonMobil, ARCO, Schlumberger, BP Amoco, Halliburton, and many more top energy companies. Baker Botts had long had a special relationship with the Bush family, representing Zapata in the fifties and later providing George W. Bush with a summer job as a messenger when he was a sixteen-year-old student at Andover. The firm also played a key role in what would become the most important friendship of Bush's life, a partnership with James A. Baker III that would last a lifetime.†

---

*In 1964, Farish was the first person to whom Bush confided his presidential ambitions. A tennis partner of Bush's, he managed Bush's trust, and when Bush was elected president, Farish and his wife, Sarah, gave George and Barbara Bush a dog, Millie, that became known as the White House dog. In the election cycle of 1999-2000 alone, Farish contributed $142,875 to the Republicans. He was later appointed ambassador to Great Britain by President George W. Bush in 2001.

†James Baker was initially prohibited from working at Baker Botts because of an antinepotism rule at the firm. Eventually, the rule was changed, however, and Baker joined the firm.

* * *

Tall, trim, and athletic, Baker, who was forty-eight years old when Bush began to explore a run for the White House, brought a compelling blend of unlikely characteristics to the Bush team. He chewed Red Man tobacco and wore cowboy boots, but had polish and a certain sartorial elegance.[26] He mixed a steely-eyed toughness with an unflappable serenity. He was unyielding, but a realist—the consummate negotiator. He was also the perfect partner for George H. W. Bush.

If they had never met, Baker would likely have been merely another successful corporate lawyer, and Bush a politician with a fabulous résumé. But, like Fred Astaire and Ginger Rogers, they were more than the sum of their parts. Bush provided a genial, clubby exterior and contacts to power and capital at the highest levels in Washington and New York. Tough, decisive, and disciplined, Baker gave Bush the spine of steel he sorely needed.

Together, the two men masked their enormous ambitions under a genteel, Ivy-covered veneer that was a distinct break from the profane, cajoling, flesh-pressing, arm-twisting, bourbon-drinking Texas political style of the era dominated by Lyndon Johnson and Speaker of the House Sam Rayburn. It started, appropriately enough, as a partnership on the tennis court, with Bush's volley and net play complementing Baker's strong baseline game[27] so well that they twice took the doubles title at the Houston Country Club.[28]

Peggy Noonan, who later wrote speeches for Bush, eroticized their refined-but-ruthless ambition. "They're these big, tall, lanky, hot-as-a-pistol guys with ambition so strong it's like a steel rod sticking out of their heads," she told the *New York Times*. "But they always make a point not to show it. Steel with an overlay of tennis."[29]

Baker had captained the tennis team at the Hill School, then still a traditional private boys' school near Philadelphia, before moving on to Princeton, just as Bush had been a baseball captain at Andover before playing baseball at Yale. Likewise, Baker had been tapped by Princeton's most celebrated eating club, the Ivy, as Bush had been for Skull and Bones.[30]

The Bakers were the stuff of Texas legends. In 1872, Judge James A. Baker, Baker's great-grandfather, joined Gray & Botts,[31] a major firm that went on to represent railroad magnates and bankers such as Jay

Gould and E. H. Harriman.[32] The judge later became a name partner, and in 1900, his son, Captain James A. Baker, by then also a member of the firm, played a key role in an important part of Texas lore. He discovered that the will of a murdered client, millionaire William Marsh Rice, was fraudulent and succeeded in allowing the merchant's vast fortune to be used as intended—to establish Rice University in Houston.[33] The Bakers were not of the East Coast Establishment, but in their very Texas way, their pedigree was every bit as refined as Bush's.

Yet for all their similarities, there were important differences in the two men. Bush *seemed* guileless, his face an open book, more concerned with politeness, civility, and accommodation than substantive issues and confrontation.[34] His cousin Ray Walker, a psychoanalyst, attributed that characteristic to Bush's relationship with his father. "He always placated his father," said Walker. "Then, later on, he placated his bosses. That is how he relates—by never defining himself against authority."[35]

Bush's courtliness made for a certain protean charm. People saw in him what they wanted to see. But his agreeable exterior was so palatable to almost everyone that he risked being seen as uncertain as to his principles—"a wimp."

In contrast, Baker was all smoothness and charm, the Velvet Hammer, always proper, but a man no one wanted to cross. "Baker holds you locked in his gaze and Southern Comfort voice, occasionally flashing a rather wintry smile," the *New York Times* said. "... He is such a fox you feel the impulse to check your wallet when you leave his office."[36]

When it came to electoral politics, however, Bush and Baker had not had much success. After winning his congressional seat, Bush had lost races for the U.S. Senate in 1964 and 1970, and his name had not appeared on a ballot since. His son, George W., lost a 1978 bid for a congressional seat representing Midland, Texas. Bored by corporate law, Baker had been lured into politics by Bush, but was then relegated to relatively menial political jobs such as undersecretary of commerce in the Ford administration.[37] In 1978, he ran for attorney general of Texas, but lost to conservative Democrat Mark White.

In defeat, Baker learned a valuable lesson. Mark White, as secretary of state, had declined to extradite a murderer named Kleason, and during the campaign, an aide dug up the salacious details. "Baker was scared of [using the case] because it was so bad," the aide told the *New Republic*. "It seemed like we were making it up. It became a joke later. Baker would say, 'It's time to go with Kleason.'"[38] Baker refrained from smearing White and lived to regret it. But he was not the kind who made the same mistake twice.

By virtue of their friendship, it was a given that Baker would sign on as Bush's campaign manager-a task he did not particularly relish. Baker had played the same role in Gerald Ford's failed 1976 presidential campaign and won enormous credit in the GOP for engineering a come-from-behind campaign that barely lost to Jimmy Carter. But Baker loathed playing second fiddle, being a mere handler. He would certainly be relegated to such a role in a Bush campaign, as he had been in Bush's earlier efforts.[39]

When the 1980 season got under way in January, Bush pulled off a stunning victory over Ronald Reagan in the Iowa caucuses. But before long the Reagan juggernaut was on. In February, the affable, fatherly Reagan defeated Bush by nearly two to one in New Hampshire. In early March, Reagan won in Vermont and South Carolina, then swept Florida, Alabama, and Georgia. Then Reagan won in Illinois. Throughout the spring, Bush frantically campaigned all over the country, even resorting to an uncharacteristically biting attack during the Pennsylvania primary in which he derided Reagan's tax-cut proposal as "voodoo economics." But by June, Reagan had won twenty primaries, and Bush had defeated Reagan only four times. Baker, seeing Reagan's inevitable victory, thought about how to bring his friend's campaign to a productive end.[40]

Bush won Michigan in May, but by then, Reagan had already locked up enough delegates for the Republican nomination. Baker sent Rich Bond, a young aide who later became chairman of the Republican National Committee, to California, where Bush was campaigning, with instructions to mislead both Bush and the press into thinking Bush still had an active campaign there.[41]

Meanwhile, Baker met privately with the press. He spoke to the reporters only on background. But he made it clear that there was no way the Bush forces could continue to campaign in California when they were broke.[42] Soon, it was all over the news: Bush was dropping out.

There was just one problem. Baker had told the media, but not Bush. In effect, Baker's close friend and partner learned that his campaign was over from the press.* Later, Bush exploded at Baker. He told an associate that he had been "misserved."[43]

Baker found the clash with his longtime friend distressing. "I'll never go through that again," he later said. "That was the worst experience in my life."[44]

But soon Bush realized, as Baker had all along, that the longer he campaigned, the more likely he was to alienate the eventual winner, Ronald Reagan. Baker and Bush finally made up. Eschewing tactics and rhetoric that might have offended the gentlemanly Reagan, mending fences after Bush's "voodoo economics" gibe, Baker had adroitly managed the entire primary campaign almost as if aiming for Bush to get the vice-presidential nod.

At the last minute, during the Republican National Convention in Detroit in July, former president Gerald Ford suddenly emerged as a potential running mate for Ronald Reagan. But that "dream ticket" also raised the specter of an unworkable copresidency and soon fell through. Late at night on July 16, 1980, Reagan called George Bush in the Pontchartrain Hotel to offer him the number-two spot.[45] Finally, the Reagan-Bush campaign against Jimmy Carter and Walter Mondale could begin in earnest.

Now that he was on board as Reagan's vice-presidential candidate, a rarely seen side of George H. W. Bush emerged, at least to political insiders. In many ways, he was and would remain one of America's most misunderstood and underestimated politicians. With his genial disposition and verb-challenged, syntactical idiosyncrasies, Bush often played the amiable doofus who had an unerring instinct for the tone-

---

*In *The Politics of Diplomacy*, Baker recounts the episode: "I really had to wrestle with him to do the right thing for himself politically. 'George, it's over,' I told him. 'We're out of money, it's mathematically impossible to win the nomination, and to continue on through the last primaries would destroy any chance whatsoever you may be picked as Vice-President'"

deaf remark. On the campaign trail, he listened distractedly to an underprivileged, black ghetto youth who didn't like homework, then responded with feigned concern, "Ah, *comme ci, comme ça*."[46]

Conventional wisdom had it that Bush lacked backbone. His positions on hot-button issues such as women's rights or giving formal diplomatic recognition to mainland China flip-flopped. James Baker was the real Texan who went duck hunting and chewed tobacco. Next to that, Bush's conspicuous acts to show that he was just one of the guys-devouring pork rinds, for example—were embarrassing contrivances designed for the media. As columnist Molly Ivins put it, real Texans do not use *"summer* as a verb. Real Texans do not wear blue slacks with little green whales all over them. And real Texans do not refer to trouble as 'deep doo-doo.'"[47]

But in fact, Bush's perceived weakness—his accommodation to his superiors—was not so much spinelessness as a powerful political weapon. He was a consummate pragmatist capable of changing positions when political demands called for it. As Reagan's running mate, he had shown how far he would go to be a team player, reversing his stands on Reagan's "voodoo economics" and on the Equal Rights Amendment.[48] Accommodation was a means of achieving goals. Bush got what he wanted.

However, Bush was not just flexible and open to compromise as all politicians must be. His genial disposition disguised it well, but when he engaged in combat, he could be cunning and devious. As early as 1960, the elder Bush won success for Zapata Off-Shore that was partially attributable to a dubious deal in Mexico in which Bush used third-party fronts to disguise his presence in the transactions.[49]*

---

*At the time, Mexican law required that all oil drilling contracts be controlled by Mexican citizens. But according to *Barron's,* in 1960 Bush and Zapata Off-Shore teamed up with a prominent Mexican businessman, Jorge Diaz Serrano, a longtime friend of Mexican president Lopez Portillo, to circumvent that law. Diaz Serrano later served five years in jail for defrauding the Mexican government of no less than $58 million.

The financial magazine reported that Bush and his Zapata Off-Shore colleagues owned about half the stock in Perforaciones Marinas del Golfo, better known as Permargo, but made it appear as if Permargo was 100 percent Mexican-owned. Zapata's shareholders were never told of the company's part ownership of Permargo. When asked why the American participation in the company was kept secret, Bush press

During his tenure as U.S. representative to the United Nations, as chief of the U.S. liaison office in China, and as director of the Central Intelligence Agency, he had also mastered the arts of compartmentalization and secrecy, and some of the more unsavory practices of political combat.

As head of the Republican National Committee, Bush had served on the front lines during the Watergate scandal. He had benefited from the Republicans' scandalous campaign practices through Operation Townhouse, but did not suffer politically. At the CIA, Bush had not initiated the Agency's use of Panamanian president Manuel Noriega, but he was kept apprised of Noriega's role in narcotics traffic, met with the dictator,[50]* and still continued to use him as an intelligence asset.[51] Bush's great talent was that he regularly employed such practices to their fullest, but managed to do so without leaving fingerprints. He always emerged unscathed.

Just a few years earlier, in the wake of Watergate and investigations into the overzealous practices of the CIA, Bush's credentials would have been a serious campaign liability. But in November 1979, Iran had seized fifty-two American hostages. With the crisis still ongoing and the theme of America held hostage an endless drumbeat dominating the news, it was a particularly propitious time for the Republicans to have someone with Bush's experience in intelligence on the ticket.

... aide Steve Hart said, "An American firm could not do business directly in Mexico without having Mexican partners."

After Bush became vice president in 1981, the Securities and Exchange Commission destroyed SEC filings for Zapata for 1960 to 1966, the years during which Bush was involved with Zapata and Permargo. According to SEC officer Suzanne McHugh, "The records were inadvertently placed in a session file to be destroyed. It does occasionally happen."

*Noriega once boasted, "I've got Bush by the balls." He told the *Washington Post's* Lally Weymouth that Bush "is my friend. I hope he becomes president."

Bush had been warned about using Noriega as an asset by the legendary head of French intelligence, Count Alexandre de Marenches, who warned him with regard to Noriega, "My own philosophy has always been that when you have something particularly dirty to do, you hire a gentleman to do it. If the gentleman is persuaded that what we are contemplating is an act of war, and by extension an act of patriotism, then we will find some very good people to work for us. By contrast, if we hire a thug, then eventually we will be compelled to kill the thug in one way or another because eventually we would be blackmailed by him."

Certainly the CIA itself saw Bush as a favorite son. Jimmy Carter's appointment of Stansfield Turner as CIA director had angered hundreds of agents. In October 1977, Turner eliminated 820 surplus CIA personnel, many of whom had been counterintelligence officers. "You can't imagine the tremendous anger against the Carter administration in the military and intelligence apparatus," says Susan Clough, Carter's personal secretary. "Emotions had been boiling for years."[52]

Widely hailed as the most popular director of Central Intelligence since Allen Dulles, Bush had enormous support within the Agency. As the campaign got under way, Reagan-Bush posters appeared all over CIA headquarters in Langley, Virginia, many cut in the middle with only the right side, the Bush side, on display.[53]

During the campaign, Bush would allow the tradecraft of intelligence to work for the Republican ticket, again without leaving fingerprints. On July 15, 1980, while the Republican Convention was still taking place in Detroit, Reagan-Bush campaign manager William J. Casey announced that an "intelligence operation" was "already in germinal form" to monitor the Carter administration.[54]

Republican officials insisted that these efforts did not suggest "clandestine information gathering."[55] And many of the activities were simply aggressive but legitimate campaign practices, such as getting Jimmy Carter's schedule so that Reagan-Bush teams could spin the press at Carter's appearances.[56]

But a 1984 congressional investigation determined that the Reagan-Bush campaign's "information gathering efforts were *not* [emphasis in the original text] limited to seeking materials that could be acquired through public channels."[57] The report, sometimes referred to as the Albosta Report, after its chairman, Congressman Donald Albosta, a Democrat from Michigan, added that there was "credible evidence" that crimes had occurred.[58] Specifically, as the election approached, the Republican campaign operation attempted to get internal Justice Department documents on an investigation into the president's brother, Billy Carter,* confidential reports on the Iranian hostage

---

*In the scandal that became known as Billygate, President Carter's brother, Billy, registered as a Libyan agent and accepted $220,000 from Libya, thereby precipitating a congressional investigation.

crisis from the Justice Department and Carter's National Security Council, and more.[59] The most famous of these Reagan-Bush operations later became known as Debategate and involved the apparent theft of Carter's briefing papers by Republicans before the October 1980 presidential debates.[60†]

On November 4, 1980, Reagan and Bush swept to a landslide victory over Jimmy Carter and Walter Mondale, winning the electoral vote by 489 to 49. In the two and a half months before the new administration took office, Bush spent his time putting together his staff and bolstering his relationships with Reagan's team. Reagan appointed Bush's Yale friend and Connecticut campaign chairman Malcolm Baldrige as secretary of commerce.

More important, James Baker's adroit political footwork during the campaign and his success at getting Bush to bow out of the race before dealing any unseemly blows to Reagan had so impressed Ronald Reagan's circle that he was the surprise choice for the powerful position of chief of staff. Thanks in part to lobbying on his behalf from the new CIA director, Bill Casey, Baker was now gatekeeper to the president of the United States.

A new era was beginning. The juxtaposition was stark. The Carter administration had been characterized by economic stagflation, hostages being seized, and a period of national embarrassment and humiliation. Now, a glamorous Hollywood royalty was replacing the dowdy Georgia rubes. Nancy Reagan breezed into the White House wearing Reagan Red—her own color!—in gowns by Galanos, Bill Blass, and Adolfo.[61] There was a sense of style not seen since the Kennedys. The inauguration was going to be a coronation.

On January 18, 1981, just two days before the Reagan inauguration, the Carter administration finally reached an accord with Iran about returning the fifty-two hostages, who had then been in captivity for 442 days. All that remained before signing the agreement was a final translation of the terms into three languages, English, French, and Farsi.[62] Senator Charles Percy, chairman of the Senate Foreign Relations

---

†For a detailed look at Debategate and the intelligence operation behind the Reagan-Bush campaign in 1980, see note 60.

Committee, said, "I'm certain a deal will be made public before we go to bed tonight."

President Carter desperately hoped he would be able to welcome home the released hostages before his administration ended. But the next day, as negotiators fiddled with the final wording of the translations, Tehran Radio asserted that Carter would not get his wish.[63] "He certainly will not have the opportunity to engage in such clowning acts, because he has to be present outside the White House tomorrow to hand over his shameful office to his successor."

There seemed no reason for the Iranians to delay-except to further humiliate Carter. As January 20 approached, one of the Iranian negotiators bragged that "we have managed to rub the nose of the biggest superpower in the world in the dust."[64]

Two hours before sunrise on Inauguration Day, Carter at last announced the final agreement for the hostages to be released. As Carter left the White House, and Reagan took the oath of office, the television networks cut furiously back and forth from their inauguration coverage to images of the hostages returning.*

Meanwhile, the Saudis had been closely watching their connections climb the political ladder and had taken on the services of former secretary of defense Clark Clifford. That spring, Clifford began lobbying on behalf of a group of Arabs, led by Sheikh Kamal Adham, the former chief intelligence officer of Saudi Arabia, to acquire Financial General Bankshares, a Washington, D.C.–based bank holding company.[65] In the banking world at least, the Saudis were moving up the ladder.

In addition, the Saudis were now particularly visible in Houston. Just three months after Bush and Baker began to settle down in the nation's capital, the *Washington Post* published a long article by Dan

---

*According to Heinrich Rupp, a pilot who worked for Salem bin Laden, at the behest of Vice President-elect George Bush, one of the bin Laden planes, a BAC-111, was made available to pick up the hostages in Tehran and take them back to the United States. "When they were liberated, he [Salem bin Laden] offered it, and he had the airplane. I was sitting in Tehran airport [as the plane's pilot] when we got called off." Rupp is a highly controversial source whose credibility has been questioned by a congressional investigation. The author has been unable to corroborate or refute Rupp's account.

Balz on "Houston as the Mecca for the Saudis."[66] The piece went on about how the Saudis had become Houston's number-one trading partner. It discussed the mysterious Khalid bin Mahfouz, living in his stone mansion in the exclusive River Oaks section, sealed off from the neighborhood by a daunting iron fence, a sea of azaleas, and a burly guard poised to ward off intruders. It mentioned John Connally's involvement with bin Mahfouz and Ghaith Pharaon in buying the Houston Main Bank.

Two prominent Houstonians, Vice President George Bush and White House chief of staff James Baker, however, were nowhere mentioned in the article. The Bush family had pretty much steered clear of the Saudis—or so it seemed.

But indirectly, bin Mahfouz had managed to get closer to James Baker. According to his attorney, Cherif Sedky, bin Mahfouz and his brothers joined forces with Houston developer Gerald Hines in developing the Texas Commerce Tower, the seventy-five-story I. M. Pei-designed home of Texas Commerce Bancshares, which was completed in 1982.[67]* The building (now known as JP Morgan Chase Tower) was under construction by the time Baker and Bush got to Washington.

Sedky says neither he nor bin Mahfouz recalls who the other partners were in developing Houston's tallest building. But, according to the *American Banker,* the other major partner was the Texas Commerce Bank itself,[68] which had been founded by James Baker's grandfather.[69] According to the *New York Times,* as of December 31, 1980, just before he became chief of staff, Baker owned or controlled 111,428 shares of the bank company, worth $7,242,820 at the time. When he entered the Reagan administration, Baker put his stock into a blind trust to avoid potential conflicts of interest. There is no reason to believe he engaged in wrongdoing.[70]

But from the Saudi side, bin Mahfouz had accomplished something of a coup. Just thirty-two years old, the young Saudi billionaire now had shared business interests with the chief of staff to the president of the United States, the gatekeeper to the White House—something that

*When it was founded by Captain James A. Baker, it was known as South Texas Commercial Bank.

was bound to win approval at the highest levels of Saudi royalty. "Bin Mahfouz is a shrewd banker. He is not a risk taker," says a Saudi analyst who knows the royal family. "When he did that transaction, he had to have the complete authorization of the Saudi royal family." (James Baker declined requests to be interviewed for this book.)

To many Americans, the Saudi investments with politicians seemed unsavory, though it was not always precisely clear why. The most obvious assumption was that the Saudis were trying to buy access to the White House or to influence policy toward Israel—or rather against it.

But in fact, even the Texans who had met the bin Ladens and the bin Mahfouzes knew little about them. Few had been to Saudi Arabia. Few knew anything about the House of Saud. Few understood the nature of the Saudi monarchy and its hierarchy. Few knew anything about its culture, about what was taught in Saudi schools. They did not know that the kingdom was a theocratic monarchy, that there was no separation of church and state, nor did they understand the first thing about Wahhabi Islam and its fundamentalist and puritanical nature.

For the most part, Texans interpreted the Saudis in American terms, in terms they understood, ones that had to do with money and oil and huge homes and multimillion-dollar business deals. The Saudis were so rich they could fly their own private commercial-size jets halfway around the world to see famous heart surgeons like Denton Cooley and Michael DeBakey at the Houston Medical Center.

Even those who were somewhat more knowledgeable thought the new generation of Saudis appeared thoroughly westernized and that perhaps the rules had changed. "As Americans trying to do business in Saudi Arabia, we'd always had lots of problems," says one oil executive who had been going to Riyadh for decades and knew the royal family firsthand. "Back then, you had to wear Arab clothes. And the Wahhabis were always reluctant to do business with the infidel. But now they came over dressed in Western clothes and looked real good. They were good businessmen. They did due diligence and hired good people."

Yet enormous differences between the Saudis and the Americans lay hidden beneath the surface. The American pilots who flew for the bin Ladens and the bin Mahfouzes and saw how they lived in Jeddah were among the few who actually got to glimpse the Saudis on their home turf. On one occasion in the mid-seventies, Gerry Auerbach, a pilot from Texas who worked for Salem bin Laden, noticed a tall, lanky, rather dour teenage Saudi boy, who was one of Salem's many half brothers, and inquired who the young lad might be.

"Oh," he was told. "That's Osama. He's praying."[71]

CHAPTER FOUR

Three-Dimensional Chess

THE FORTUNES OF NEWLY elected presidents are always subject to the deeper forces of history, and the Reagan-Bush administration was no exception. By the time George Bush and James Baker moved into Washington in January 1981, a powerful wave of Islamic fundamentalism had already begun transforming the Middle East. The implications were staggering. The Islamic revolution threatened America's ability to slake its unquenchable thirst for oil, its support for Israel, and its geostrategic position in the Cold War vis-à-vis the Soviet Union.

The humiliation of America by the Shiite regime of Iran's Ayatollah Khomeini in 1979 was just the beginning. Islamic terrorism was an increasingly brutal reality. Each assertion of American and Israeli interests in the Middle East was parried by a dramatic, forceful, and violent response. Arab leaders too close to the United States now risked the same fate as the deposed Shah of Iran—or worse.

In 1979, Egyptian president Anwar Sadat signed the historic Camp David Peace Accords with Israel. In October 1981, nine months after the Reagan-Bush administration had taken office, Sadat was assassinated by members of the Al Jihad movement.[1]* Israeli troops moved

---

*Thousands of suspected terrorists were rounded up and jailed, among them Sheikh Omar Abdel Rahman, who, in the wake of the 1993 World Trade Center bombing, was convicted of conspiring to blow up New York City landmarks, and Ayman al-Zawahiri, who became known as one of Osama bin Laden's two top lieutenants.

into southern Lebanon. In retaliation, Hezbollah, an Iranian-supported paramilitary group of Shiite militants, went into action. The militant Muslim Brotherhood, which had been banned since the fifties, continued to defy Egypt's West-leaning government.* Islamic militants spread throughout the region, planting the seeds of the militant Hamas, to arise later on the West Bank and Gaza Strip,[2] and Al Qaeda, in Saudi Arabia.

By and large, the response of American politicians was to demonize Islamic fundamentalism and rally public opinion against the militants in Iran who had seized American hostages. Reagan and Bush owed their 1980 electoral victory to a campaign charging President Jimmy Carter with being "weak and vacillating" in dealing with Iran.[3] Bush said that the American people regarded Iran with "hatred." Then he added, "I feel that way myself."[4]

But the political realities were far too complex to lend themselves to such a reductionist approach. The United States was entering a bizarre and perplexing game of three-dimensional chess complicated by not one but two regional war—between the Soviet Union and Afghanistan, on the one hand, and between Iran and Iraq, on the other. In both cases, the United States played an enormous but low-profile role, waging covert war by proxy, and ironically, funding and financing Islamic fundamentalists whom, in other contexts, the U.S. government demonized. In the Afghanistan War, the United States supplied weapons, training, and billions of dollars to forces aiding the mujahideen rebels fighting the pro-Soviet Afghan government. In the Iran-Iraq War, short-term realpolitik considerations and factionalism within the administration led the United States to tilt toward Iran, then Iraq, back and forth again and again while secretly arming both sides.

A vital factor in these stratagems was that Saudi Arabia had begun to replace Iran as the United States's primary regional ally. The United States had long had "a special relationship" with Saudi Arabia, but with

---

*The fundamentalist Muslim Brotherhood's history in Egypt dated back to the twenties. For decades it had gone through various periods of acceptance and harassment, as it became increasingly militant.

the Cold War still ongoing, and Iran no longer a friend, it became increasingly important in geostrategic terms as well.[5]*

The subtext behind the new relationship could be explained in two words that are the eternal and defining pillars of American policy in the Middle East: *oil* and *Israel*. During OPEC's oil embargo in the after-math of the 1973 Arab-Israeli war, the United States had learned about the wrath of the Arab oil-producing countries when it leaned too far toward Israel. Now, by arming the Saudis, the United States would ensure the stable flow of oil at reasonable prices.

The process began with the sale of just five airplanes. Reagan had come into office with the reputation of being pro-Israel, but to the dismay of the Israeli lobby, one of his first decisions was to sell five AWACS (airborne warning and control system) planes to Saudi Arabia, as part of a $5.5-billion package with associated technology and infrastructure.[6] This was the first crucial foreign policy test of the Reagan era. Dashing young Prince Bandar, who, at thirty-two, had just earned his master's degree at Johns Hopkins University, led the Saudi lobby in a fierce battle against its Israeli counterpart by getting Vice President Bush to push Reagan on the arms sale,[7] and then dazzling senators with his wit and charm.

Behind that charm was a driving psychological need to succeed on a grand scale. Bandar was the grandson of Abdul Aziz, the founder of modern Saudi Arabia, and Hassa bint Ahmed al-Sudairi, one of the most honored and respected women in Saudi history. But he had little contact with his father, Prince Sultan, who was the governor of Riyadh and still in his early twenties at the time of Bandar's birth. The reason was that Bandar's mother, Khizaran, was a dark-skinned sixteen-year-old from southern Saudi Arabia and a commoner who, as Bandar himself put it, served as Prince Sultan's concubine. Bandar grew up living with his mother and hoping to legitimize himself in the eyes of his father. "It taught me patience, and a defense mechanism, if you want,

---

*Secret agreements between the Saudis and various U.S. presidents dated back to the early postwar era and continued into the twenty-first century. Thanks to a pact between President Harry Truman and King Ibn Saud in 1947, the United States vowed to come to Saudi Arabia's defense if it was attacked. Likewise, in 1963, President Kennedy sent a squadron of fighter jets to protect Saudi Arabia when Egypt's Gamal Abdel Nasser attempted to kill members of the Saudi royal family.

to not expect anything," he told the *New Yorker*. "And the way I rationalized it to myself was if I don't expect anything and I don't get anything, I don't get disappointed. So nobody can hurt my feelings."[8] Bandar's great success in the AWACS lobbying effort not only enhanced his standing with his father and the House of Saud, it also won him the coveted position of Saudi ambassador to the United States, an extraordinarily powerful post.

Just before Congress was to vote on the package, the Pentagon told *Washington Post* reporter Scott Armstrong that the AWACS planes cost about $110 million each. When Armstrong first did the math, he mistakenly thought that five times $110 million must be $5.5 billion. Then he realized that a decimal point was misplaced, which meant that the AWACS sale was about far more than just five airplanes.[9] What had been announced as a small arms deal was the start of something big. Where was all the money going? "This was ... the linchpin to an elaborate electronic communications system that would be the equivalent of the heart of what we have in NATO, for example," Armstrong said in a PBS *Frontline* documentary. "It was creating a new theater of war."[10]

On October 28, 1981, the Senate narrowly approved the AWACS package, 52 to 48.[11] Four days later, Armstrong's front-page article in the *Washington Post* outlined a secret plan that had never been confronted in the congressional debate.[12]* An unwritten agreement lay behind what had been framed as merely the sale of five airplanes. In return for an integrated package of highly sophisticated military technology, Saudi Arabia would build a massive network of naval and air defense facilities that could sustain U.S. forces should they ever be needed to protect the region or wage war against an aggressor.[13]

The Saudis had no problem footing the bill. By 1981, Saudi oil rev-

---

*In late October 1981, four days before the Senate vote, Armstrong prepared an explosive article for the *Washington Post* asserting that the AWACS sale was just the beginning of a secret $50-billion plan to build surrogate military bases in Saudi Arabia.

But on Friday, October 23, just a few days before Armstrong's article was to run, Pentagon officials called the *Post*. As General Richard Secord recounted it, they said, "'You know, this guy's preparing this cockamamy story.' You know, 'You've got to give us a break on this. This is crazy,' you know? And that's why the story was published after the vote, not before."

enues had reached $116 billion a year. The Saudi monetary agency was charged with the task of investing nearly $320 million a day.[14] Over the next decade, the Saudis bought $200 billion in American arms and built nine major new ports and dozens of airfields all over the kingdom. A beneficiary of the military buildup was the Saudi Binladin Group, which built facilities for the Al Salaam Aircraft Company.[15] They have now hundreds of modern American fighter planes and the capability of adding hundreds more," said Armstrong.[16]

More than a massive military buildup, the U.S.-Saudi alliance constituted a major shift in American foreign policy in the Middle East that took place with virtually no public debate in the press or in Congress. "It's absolutely phenomenal, a two-hundred-billion-dollar program that's basically put together and nobody's paying attention to it," said Armstrong. "... It is the ultimate government-off-the-books."[17]

Even more secretive was the new understanding that Saudi Arabia would become a U.S. partner in covert operations, not just in the Middle East but all over the globe. As a monarchy without the constitutional constraints that burdened the CIA, the Saudis had enormous flexibility to help the Reagan administration execute covert operations prohibited by Congress. Not long after the AWACS sale was approved, Prince Bandar thanked the Reagan administration for the vote by honoring a request by William Casey that he deposit $10 million in a Vatican bank to be used in a campaign against the Italian Communist Party.[18] Implicit in the AWACS deal was a pledge by the Saudis to fund anticommunist guerrilla groups in Afghanistan, Angola, and elsewhere that were supported by the Reagan administration.[19]

And so, Saudi-American relations were becoming an ever more complex web of international defense and oil deals, foreign policy decisions, covert operations, and potentially compromising financial relationships between Saudis and American politicians who shuttled back and forth between the public and private sectors.

Increasingly, Bandar, who was appointed ambassador in 1983 just after Fahd became king, was at the heart of these operations. He was learning to love politics. "When I first got to America, I didn't understand politics," he said. "I was confused by it. Then it became like a game, like a drug. I enjoyed the game. It was exotic and exciting.

There was no blood drawn. It was physically safe, but emotionally tough."[20]

Officially, the United States was neutral in the Iran-Iraq War. But from the onset, two factions within the Reagan-Bush administration battled over which country posed the greater threat to U.S. interests. That struggle became the most acrimonious foreign policy conflict within the administration during the entire Reagan-Bush era. One bloc, which was led by National Security Adviser Robert "Bud" McFarlane and two members of his National Security Council staff, Howard Teicher and Oliver North, argued in favor of arming Iran. Their rationale was a variation on the old saw that the enemy of my enemy is my friend. In this case, since Israel's biggest enemy was Iraq, and Iraq's enemy was Iran, the McFarlane faction proposed moving toward Iran to enhance Israeli stability. As early as 1979, Teicher had written a highly classified study endorsing Israel's view that Saddam's Iraq, not Iran, would ultimately pose the greatest threat to the Gulf region.[21]* History would prove him right.

The other faction, led by Secretary of Defense Caspar Weinberger and Secretary of State George Shultz, was virulently opposed to Ayatollah Khomeini's fundamentalist regime in Iran. After all, failure to oppose it could allow Islamic fundamentalism to spread throughout the region, endangering pro-West governments in Kuwait and Saudi Arabia, and thus America's oil supplies. "It was insanity," said Weinberger. "How could you send arms to the ayatollah when he was sworn to destroy us?"[22]

But if arming Iran to support Israel was insane, the flip side of the policy, in the long run at least, was truly demented: Weinberger and Shultz favored defending Saudi Arabia and the enormous U.S. oil interests there by secretly bolstering the brutal Iraqi dictator Saddam Hussein. As a result of their efforts, billions of dollars in aid and weapons were funneled to Saddam's regime.

From the outset, the Reagan administration had promised to take a tough, uncompromising policy against Islamic fundamentalists, and

---

*Some of the material in this chapter is adapted from "In the Loop" by Murray Waas and Craig Unger, which appeared in the November 5, 1992, *New Yorker*.

just eight days after it took office, Reagan's first secretary of state, Alexander Haig, spelled it out unequivocally: "Let me state categorically today that there will be no military equipment provided to the government of Iran."[23] Officially, Iran was a terrorist state and an arms embargo was in place.

Nevertheless, a secret strategy to arm Iran got under way almost immediately. Within a few months, Haig had told Israel that "in principle" it was okay to send weapons to Iran, but only for spare parts for F-4 fighter planes, an aging, technologically obsolete warhorse from the Vietnam era, and that the United States had to approve specific arms sales lists in advance.

By early 1982, however, the U.S. government was aware that Israel was providing U.S. arms to Iran that went far beyond that agreement. In the *New York Times,* Seymour Hersh later reported that "Israel and American intelligence officials acknowledged that weapons, ammunition, and spare parts worth several billion dollars flowed to Iran each year during the early 1980s."[24]

Ultimately, the secret arms sales to Iran became enmeshed with another covert policy of the administration-its attempt to overturn the left-wing government of Nicaragua by subsidizing right-wing rebels known as the contras. This was the scandal known as Iran-contra. It was striking that in trying to shape the future of a tiny Latin American country, the Reagan-Bush administration would go to the other side of the world for help.

The Saudis had no particular interest in Nicaragua; they didn't even have diplomatic relations with this small country half a world away. But at the time, congressional opposition to the administration's policy was so strong that on December 8, 1982, the House of Representatives voted *unanimously* to prohibit the use of U.S. funds to overthrow the government of Nicaragua.

However, even the Boland Amendment, as the bill was known, was not an insurmountable obstacle to a National Security Council that was prone to macho covert operations, bravado, and cowboy-style adventurism. It considered a variety of options to fund the contras, including obtaining funds from other countries and skimming profits from arms deals with Iran. Finally, in the spring of 1984, National Security Adviser Robert McFarlane raised the possibility of approaching Prince Bandar for the money. If the Saudis were to accede to the request, clearly they would gain favor from the Reagan administration. On June 22, 1984, Bandar and McFarlane agreed that the Saudis would give $1 million a month to the contras.

But the gambit was like playing political Russian roulette and had to be approved by the White House before it could proceed. What would happen if Congress found out? On June 25, 1984, a special meeting of the National Security Planning Group was called to discuss the issue. The highest officials in the country were present—Ronald Reagan, George Bush, George Shultz, Caspar Weinberger, William Casey, and Robert McFarlane, among others. According to minutes taken at the meeting, James Baker, ever the vigilant attorney, argued that actively soliciting money from third countries—such as Saudi Arabia—could be an impeachable offense.

But Vice President Bush took issue with that position and said there was nothing wrong with encouraging third parties to help the anti-Sandinistas so long as there was no explicit quid pro quo. "The only problem that might come up is if the United States were to promise these third parties something in return so that some people could interpret this as some kind of exchange," he said.[25]

Bush, after all, had been director of the CIA. The way to do it, he seemed to be saying, was for the United States to let the Saudis finance the contras. Afterward, the United States could then reward the Saudis for their loyalty, but the two events would have to happen without being explicitly tied to each other.

And so, Bandar deposited $8 million in a Swiss bank. Over time, the amount given by the Saudis to the contras reached $32 million.[26]* No explicit promises had been made to the Saudis, so the administration could assert there was no quid pro quo, and therefore no impeachable offense had taken place. And yet the Saudis did not go away empty-handed. After all, tens of millions of dollars had changed hands. At the time, King Fahd and Bandar wanted several hundred Stinger missiles from the United States, which had put restrictions on the sale of such weapons. To help the Saudis out, President Reagan invoked emergency measures to bypass Congress and four hundred Stingers were secretly

*Salem bin Laden was said to be involved in this effort.

flown to Saudi Arabia. The Saudis had received their payoff. To put it baldly: in exchange for doing something that had been explicitly prohibited by the House of Representatives by a vote of 411 to 0, Saudi Arabia received lethal, state-of-the-art American weaponry it would not have been allowed under normal conditions. The Saudis had come a long, long way from their first few airplane deals with James Bath. But in many ways their dealings with the House of Bush had just begun.

The Reagan-Bush administration and the Saudis were not just helping the contras. Early on, the administration also used Prince Bandar as an intermediary to meet Saddam Hussein, and soon Bandar told the United States that Iraq was ready to accept American aid.[27] Even though Congress would never have approved arms transfers to Iraq, the Reagan administration secretly began allowing Saudi Arabia, Kuwait, and Egypt to transfer U.S. weapons, including howitzers, helicopters, and bombs, to Iraq. These shipments may have been in violation of the Arms Export Control Act.[28]*

U.S. support for Saddam Hussein could be traced all the way back to 1959, when the CIA hired him as a twenty-two-year-old assassin to shoot Iraqi prime minister General Abd al-Karim Qasim. Saddam fired too soon, however, and as a result he killed Qasim's driver and only wounded the prime minister.[29] In the ensuing two decades, the Agency saw him as a cutthroat and a thug, but at least he was their thug—one

---

*In some small measure, support for both Iran and Iraq may merely have been a continuation of a policy started by President Carter. According to classified documents uncovered by Robert Parry, a Washington, D.C., investigative reporter, after meeting with Prince Fahd, Alexander Haig briefed President Reagan in April 1981 that Fahd had explained that Iran was receiving spare parts for U.S. equipment from Israel. Haig's notes had another astonishing assertion: "It was also interesting to confirm that President Carter gave the Iraqis a green light to launch the war against Iran through Fahd." In other words, Haig had been told by the future Saudi king that Jimmy Carter had given clearance for Saddam to invade Iran and begin the Iran-Iraq War. According to former Iranian president Bani-Sadr, even though the United States did not officially have relations with Iraq, the Carter administration used Saudi channels to send Iraq secret information that exaggerated Iran's military weakness. By encouraging Iraq to attack, the United States hoped to set the stage for a solution to the Iranian hostage crisis with a possible arms-for-hostages deal.

who could be called on to fight Soviet expansion in the Middle East. In 1963, that meant that CIA officers in Baghdad provided Saddam with lists of "communists" whom he then assassinated.[30]

In 1979, Saddam began his rule by purging his political opponents with a slew of show trials and executions designed to maximize terror and establish his authority. Meanwhile, thanks to the high price of oil in the seventies, Iraq had become relatively prosperous, and Saddam saw it as a propitious time to make a play for regional leadership. In September 1980, he invaded southwestern Iran,[31] hoping to keep the Shiite fundamentalist revolution in Iran from spreading to Iraq, which is largely Shiite. Initially supported by the United States, the Soviet Union, most of Europe, and many Arab countries, including Saudi Arabia, Saddam had plenty of backing for a long war.

The single most powerful reason for U.S. support of Saddam was to protect the Saudis and, of course, their oil reserves. Ayatollah Khomeini's Islamic fundamentalist revolution in Iran had repercussions throughout the entire Arab world and represented a grave threat to the House of Saud. Khomeini's appeal extended beyond his Shiite constituency. Other fundamentalist Muslim groups began emulating him, and the House of Saud was panicked. Rich with petrodollars but with no military to speak of, the Saudis could not risk confronting Iran directly. Instead, they bankrolled Saddam's war against Iran with $30 billion.[32] Likewise, the United States feared that a new, Middle East version of the domino theory was in play. Saddam would have to act as a bulwark against Shiite extremism to prevent the fall of pro-American states such as Saudi Arabia, Jordan, and Kuwait.

As the Iran-Iraq conflict wore on, evidence of Saddam Hussein's ruthless ways became increasingly apparent. Iranian diplomats came to the United Nations armed with horrific photos of Iranian soldiers whose bodies had been burned by chemical weapons.[33] Key members of the Reagan administration, including Vice President Bush and James Baker, repeatedly reacted to these revelations of Saddam's atrocities largely as if they posed a delicate public relations problem rather than a genuine moral issue. The Reagan administration knew that Iraq was using mustard gas, sarin, VX, and other poisons. In public, the United States condemned such actions. But privately, senior officials supported a covert program in which the Defense Intelligence Agency provided Saddam with detailed planning for battles, air strikes, and bomb-damage assessments.[34]

The architect of these covert operations aiding Saddam was William Casey, and according to Howard Teicher, a National Security Council staffer who leaned toward Iran, one of the people Casey confided in was Vice President Bush. As recounted in *Spider's Web*, a book by British journalist Alan Friedman about the arming of Iraq, Bush also made it clear that he was open to aiding Iraq.[35] "I attended meetings where Bush made clear he wanted to help Iraq," said Teicher. "His door was always open to the Iraqis. If they wanted a meeting with Bush, they could get it."

In fact, Bush had leaned toward Iraq from the start.[36] Early on in the administration, on June 7, 1981, Bush articulated his sympathy for Iraq when Israel bombed Saddam Hussein's nuclear reactor in Osirak. The power plant was considered Iraq's first step toward making a nuclear weapon. "Reagan went around the room and asked each of us to give our opinion on the Osirak raid," recalled Alexander Haig, who felt strongly that Israel had done the right thing. "I remember Bush and then Baker making it very clear that they thought Israel needed to be punished."[37]

By November 1983, a State Department memo confirmed Iraqi chemical weapons producers were buying materials "from Western firms, including possibly a U.S. foreign subsidiary," and added that "it is important that we approach Iraq very soon in order to maintain credibility of U.S. policy on CW [chemical weapons] as well as to reduce or halt what now appears to be Iraq's almost daily use of CW."[38]

But in another memo just three weeks later, the State Department decided not to press the issue because it did not want to "unpleasantly surprise" Iraq. As a result, the administration's policy against chemical weapons was confined to "close monitoring."[39]

One of the key people in carrying out U.S. policy toward Baghdad during this period was Donald Rumsfeld, who had been Gerald Ford's secretary of defense and later took the same post under President George W. Bush. In December 1983, when Iraq continued to use chemical weapons "almost daily," Rumsfeld traveled to Baghdad as a special presidential envoy to meet with Saddam and pave the way for normalization of U.S.-Iraqi relations.[40]

In 2002, Rumsfeld told CNN that during that visit "I cautioned [Saddam Hussein] about the use of chemical weapons." However, a "Secret" memo of that 1983 meeting, which has since been declassi-fied, contradicts Rumsfeld and indicates that there was no mention of chemical weapons whatsoever during that discussion.* Far from con-fronting Saddam, Rumsfeld warmly assured the Iraqi dictator that America's "understanding of the importance of balance in the world and in the region was similar to Iraq's."[41]

As the United States continued to criticize the use of chemical weapons, the administration wanted to make certain that Saddam knew such pronouncements were merely for public consumption. So in March 1984, Rumsfeld returned to Baghdad. According to a cable from Secretary of State George Shultz, Rumsfeld was to tell Iraqi for-eign minister Tariq Aziz that the recent U.S. statement on chemical weapons, or CW, "was made strictly out of our strong opposition to the use of lethal and incapacitating CW." The cable added that the statement was not made to imply a shift in policy, and the U.S. goal of improving "bilateral relations, at a pace of Iraq's choosing" remained "undiminished." The cable further advised Rumsfeld, "This message bears reinforcing during your discussions."[42] In other words, Rumsfeld was to assure Saddam that U.S. concerns about chemical weapons were nothing more than posturing.

And so it went—a double policy. Throughout the entire Reagan-Bush era, the United States publicly denounced Iraq's use of chemical weapons, but secretly it supported Saddam. In an April 5, 1984, "Top Secret" National Security Decision Directive, the Reagan administra-tion condemned chemical weapons use, but also called for the prepa-ration of "a plan of action designed to avert an Iraqi collapse."[43] As a result, the United States allowed programs to go forth that may have aided Iraq's development of biological and chemical warfare. Beginning in 1984, the Centers for Disease Control began providing Saddam's

---

*Rumsfeld did raise the issue in his subsequent meeting with Iraqi official Tariq Aziz, but addressing the issue at a lower level was indicative of the administration's priorities.

Iraq with biological materials—including viruses, retroviruses, bacteria, fungi, and even tissue that was infected with bubonic plague. Among the materials that were sent were several types of West Nile virus and plague-infected mouse tissue smears.[44]

The exchange may have been initiated in the spirit of an "innocent" transfer of scientific information. But it is not difficult to argue against giving bubonic-plague-infected tissues to Saddam Hussein. "We were freely exchanging pathogenic materials with a country that we knew had an active biological warfare program," said James Tuite, a former Senate investigator. "The consequences should have been foreseen."[45]

Initially at least, Vice President Bush played a low-profile role in the Reagan administration, his position circumscribed by the stigma he bore from being perceived as the lone "moderate" in a conservative revolution.* As he saw it, his mandate was to display his unfettered loyalty to Reagan. Even before he took office, in the fall of 1980, Bush's stated goal was to be as innocuous as possible. "I've thought a lot about it," he said. "I know I'm not gonna have much input on policy, nothing substantive to do at all .... And I've decided I can be happy with that."[46]

Over time, however, Bush played a bigger role, albeit an ambiguous one. Most figures within the Reagan-Bush administration tilted to one side or the other with regard to Iran or Iraq. But Bush played both sides. "He was good at conducting diplomatic dialogue," said Teicher. "He knew the style, the diction. He was good at having diplomatic discussions. But he could be swayed by personal relationships with foreign leaders. Regarding Iraq, he and Casey both had great naïveté, thinking you could be friends with Saddam Hussein, which was not unlike a lot of government officials at that time. And he saw the geostrategic logic in new relationships with Iran. Bush's goals were contradictory because our policy was full of contradiction .... He thought talking to both sides was good."[47]

---

*Though he was often viewed with suspicion by Reagan conservatives as a "moderate," such perceptions were more a reflection of Bush's roots in the Eastern Establishment than of his own deeply held political convictions. As early as 1964, Bush had endorsed conservative Barry Goldwater for president over the liberal Republican candidate Nelson Rockefeller.

Such duplicity had always been characteristic of Bush and had long served his ambitions. As ambassador to the United Nations, Bush had observed Henry Kissinger, who as national security adviser kept him in the dark about his secret diplomacy. Now, in the morass of American foreign policy in the Middle East, Bush was a player.[48]

In 1984, that meant helping Iraq construct a new oil pipeline to the Jordanian port of Aqaba to circumvent the Iranian blockade of Iraq's ports in the Persian Gulf.[49] To support the Aqaba pipeline, the administration had to tacitly accept Iraq's ongoing use of chemical weapons, but it also had a second problem. The Export-Import Bank, a U.S. government agency that covers loans for American companies if foreign customers default, had determined that war-ravaged Iraq was not creditworthy enough to merit a loan for the pipeline. As a result, the Reagan administration had to lobby to get the bank to overlook its own guidelines. On June 12, 1984, Charles Hill, executive secretary to Secretary of State George Shultz, sent a confidential memo to Vice President Bush, suggesting Bush call William Draper, chairman of the Export-Import Bank, and pressure him to provide the okay for the loan.[50]

Bush was a logical choice for this task, not only because he had such a high office, but because Draper and he were old friends. Draper had been at Yale when Bush was there; he had been cochairman of the Bush Financial Committee for the 1980 presidential race[51] and had invested in young George W. Bush's first oil company, Arbusto.[52]

The talking points that were prepared for Bush suggested he tell Draper that the loan affected America's vital interests and that America's goal in the Iran-Iraq War was "to bring the war to a negotiated end in which neither belligerent is dominant."[53] Almost immediately after the call from Bush, Draper reversed the previous position of the Export-Import Bank and agreed to provide the financing.* Bush's lobbying of the bank marked the point at which he began to take an active role in the covert policy to support Saddam Hussein's Iraq.

In November 1984, the Reagan-Bush team won reelection, and in Reagan's second term the internal struggle over the two covert strate-

*Because of unrelated problems about obtaining insurance, the Aqaba pipeline was never built.

gies exploded. The United States had been trying a variety of policies including both incentives and punitive measures against Iran. Secretly, CIA director William Casey worked with Prince Bandar to execute the harshest measures of all toward Iranian-backed fundamentalists: assassination. As reported in Bob Woodward's *Veil*, in early 1985, Prince Bandar invited Casey to his home in Virginia just after the Iranian-supported Hezbollah had bombed American facilities in Beirut and kidnapped CIA station chief William Buckley. Casey and the Saudis agreed it was time to strike back. The target: Sheikh Fadlallah, leader of the Party of God, Hezbollah. Control of the operation was given to the Saudis. If anything went wrong, they would deny CIA involvement.

According to Woodward, the Saudis laundered $3 million through various bank accounts and found an operative from Britain's elite special forces to handle the operation. Vice President Bush was apparently left out of the loop. On March 7, 1985, he was in Sudan, meeting with Sudanese president Jaafar Numeiry to discuss the plight of starving refugees and whether the United States would resume food aid. The next day, a car packed with explosives blew up about fifty yards from Fadlallah's high-rise residence in Beirut. Eighty people were killed and two hundred injured. Fadlallah, however, escaped unharmed. To cover their tracks, the Saudis provided Fadlallah with incontrovertible information leading to the operatives they had hired. "You suspect me and I turn in my chauffeur and say he did it," Bandar explained. "You would think I am no longer a suspect."[54] The bombing was widely blamed on Israel.

Meanwhile, others in the administration argued vociferously that it was time to try a policy of incentives toward Iran. Perhaps the most forceful case was made by Graham Fuller, the CIA's national intelligence officer for the Middle East, in two memos he wrote in May 1985. "Our tilt to Iraq was timely when Iraq was against the ropes and the Islamic revolution was on a roll," Fuller wrote to CIA director William Casey in May 17, 1985. "The time may now have come to tilt back." Fuller argued that the United States should once again authorize Israel to ship U.S. arms to Iran.[55]

Fuller's rationale was the mirror image of the argument that Secretary of Defense Caspar Weinberger had made in favor of supporting Iraq three years earlier. To counter the effects of one covert policy, another one was needed. This time, however, another factor had to be taken into consideration. In the preceding year and a half, seven Americans had been taken hostage in Beirut by Hezbollah, the Shiite fundamentalist group backed by Iran.[56]

Meanwhile, the Iran-Iraq War escalated. A wave of Iranian assaults against which the Iraqis used chemical weapons left twenty thousand Iranians and fourteen thousand Iraqis dead. At roughly the same time, Hezbollah took two more American hostages in Beirut. President Reagan angrily charged that Iran was a member of a "confederation of terrorist states ... a new, international version of Murder, Incorporated." He pledged, "America will never make concessions to terrorists."

But secretly, the White House was already preparing to send weapons to Iran in an arms-for-hostages deals.[57] On June 11, 1985, just two days after Thomas Sutherland, a dean at the American University in Beirut, was kidnapped, the National Security Council drafted a presidential directive advocating that the United States help Iran obtain selected weapons. The opposing faction in the administration—principally Secretary of State George Shultz and Secretary of Defense Caspar Weinberger—was irate. "This is almost too absurd to comment on," Weinberger wrote in a memo. "It's like asking Qadaffi to Washington for a cozy chat."[58]

Nevertheless, on August 30, Israel sold more than five hundred U.S.-origin TOW missiles (Tube-launched, Optically tracked, Wire-command) to Iran. Just over two weeks later, on September 15, 1985, the Reverend Benjamin Weir, who had been kidnapped in Beirut more than a year earlier, was released.

The administration hoped that other hostages would be released, too, but none were. The problem: Iran didn't need more weapons. Now, something else had to be done.

Over time, Bush had begun to win over key members of the Reagan administration. Even William Casey, the brilliant spymaster who Reagan had named to head the CIA, had initially distrusted Bush, but grew to admire him. "Casey knew there was no one in government who could keep a secret better," says one former high-level CIA official.[59] "He knew that Bush was someone who could keep his confidences and be trusted. Bush had the same capacity as Casey to receive a briefing and give no hint that he was in the know."

That such qualities went hand in hand with Bush's patrician background won him the highest compliment of all from Count Alexandre de Marenches, the legendary godfather of French intelligence. A crusty Cold Warrior who had nothing but contempt for most players on the world stage, de Marenches found Bush to have the perfect pedigree for covert operations: he was a gentleman. All through Bush's political life, journalists and colleagues have spoken of him as if he were two people. One was the gracious and courtly George Bush who was so acquiescent to those who had higher rank and power. The other was George Bush the ruthless politician, who would go into campaign mode to do whatever it might take to win. Casey confided to his colleagues that he felt that the two sides of Bush were really one and the same. Bush had the capacity to act on the judgment of others, to live within the constraints of their agendas. This philosophy had served him well in the long line of appointive offices he had won. Casey, according to his colleagues, understood that Bush's compliant nature, like his merciless side, served a higher ambition. As a result, he chose Vice President Bush to carry out his secret mission to break the impasse that had stalled the release of the remaining hostages.

Casey, according to two aides who worked with him at the CIA, reasoned that if Iraq escalated the air war, Iran would have a renewed need for U.S. weapons and that would force it to conclude the stalled arms-for-hostages deal on acceptable terms.[60]

In the past, the United States had turned to the Saudis to help out on such matters. In February 1986, to induce Iraq to carry out more bombing operations, the Reagan administration had secretly authorized Saudi Arabia to transfer U.S.-origin bombs to Iraq and encouraged the Saudis to provide Saddam with British fighter planes as well. Later that month, according to classified reports, Saudi Arabia sent Iraq fifteen hundred MK-84 bombs, nonguided two-thousand-pound devices designed for operations where maximum blast and explosive effects are desired.*

---

*Ironically, during the Gulf War the United States delivered the same bomb to Iraq through other means. During Operation Desert Storm, the United States dropped more than twelve thousand MK-84s on Iraq.

But to the dismay of U.S. officials, because the Iraqis were afraid to lose planes and sometimes did not even know where they should be striking, Saddam failed to make full use of the U.S. bombs.[61] Vice President Bush would have to intercede.

On Friday, July 25, 1986, Bush left for Israel and the Middle East to meet with the heads of state of Jordan and Egypt. More than a dozen reporters accompanied him. Bush said the purpose of the trip was to "advance the peace process," but exactly what that meant was unclear. The day before the trip, the Bush aide said, "I don't think it is sensible to talk in terms of dramatic initiatives. In fact, I would play that down."[62]

A Bush adviser discussed the agenda in terms that seemed to have been cribbed from Chauncey Gardner, the hero of Jerzy Kosinski's comic political novel *Being There*. "It's like tending a garden," he told the *Times*. "If you don't tend the garden, the weeds grow up. And I think that there are a lot of weeds in that garden."[63]

Once the trip got under way, in Israel alone there were thirty-five opportunities to shoot photos of the vice president as a world leader advancing the peace process in the Middle East. When Bush got to Jordan, aides tried to arrange to have a photo of him peering through binoculars at enemy territory—until it was pointed out that the territory in question was Israel's. At one point, Bush turned to Jordan's commander in chief.

"Tell me, General, how dead is the Dead Sea?" the vice president asked.

"Very dead, sir," the general replied.[64]

Secretly, however, Bush was pursuing a very different agenda from the one written about in the media: the former CIA director was now actually working as an intelligence operative on a mission from William Casey to facilitate the arms-for-hostages deal with Iran and to set in motion the delivery of military intelligence to Saddam Hussein.

Now the feverish double-dealing began in earnest. On July 29, Israeli counterterrorism adviser Amiram Nir briefed Bush at the King David Hotel in Jerusalem and told him that Iran had agreed to release the American hostages in exchange for four thousand missiles.[65]

The next day, Bush went to Jordan to perform the most delicate part of his mission, initiating the transfer of military intelligence to Saddam. According to two Reagan administration officials, Bush told King Hussein that Iraq needed to be more aggressive in the war with Iran and asked that Saddam Hussein be urged to use his air force against targets inside Iran.[66]

A few days later, on August 4, Bush met in Cairo with President Hosni Mubarak and asked him to pass on to Saddam Hussein the same message he had given King Hussein of Jordan. Saddam had previously rejected U.S. advice to escalate the bombing, but now, because of the cost of the war, he desperately needed American money and weapons. In addition, CIA officials began directly providing the Iraqi military both with highly classified tactical intelligence and technical equipment to receive satellite intelligence so Iraq could assess the effects of its air strikes on Iran.

During the forty-eight hours after Bush's meeting with Mubarak, the Iraqi air force flew 359 missions. Over the next few weeks, Iraqi planes struck deep into Iran and bombed oil refineries, including for the first time the loading and storage facilities on Sirri Island, 460 miles from the border—a daring feat for the Mirage pilots, who risked running out of fuel.

On August 5, Bush returned to Washington and was debriefed by Casey. "Casey kept the return briefing very close to his vest," one of his aides said. "But he said Bush was supportive of the initiative and had carried out his mission."

Meanwhile, the covert arms sales to Iraq almost came undone. Low-level American officials at the U.S. embassy in Riyadh had become aware of the Saudi transfer of U.S. MK-84 bombs to Iraq earlier that year. Unaware that the Reagan administration had secretly authorized the deal, the officials went so far as to question Prince Bandar, who assured them the transfer had been accidental and small. The White House forwarded a similar message to Republican senator Richard Lugar, chairman of the Senate Foreign Relations Committee. But in fact, fifteen hundred bombs had been sold to Iraq with the authorization of the Reagan administration, and Bandar had played a far bigger role than Congress realized. He had even played the middleman in making sure that Iraq obtained highly sensitive satellite information about Iranian troop movements from the CIA.[67]

If Bush's team seemed like characters in a Kosinski novel, perhaps it was because American Middle East policy had taken on such an astonishingly dark, surreal cast that was so utterly at odds with what was being reported in the American press. Bush's trip was widely touted as a peace mission. But in fact he had gone to the Middle East as a spy, an operative whose cover was that he was trying to advance the peace process. His real mission, however, was to give strategic military intelligence to a murderous dictator, Iraq's Saddam Hussein, so that he might kill more Iranians. After Iran had seized more American hostages and President Reagan had termed it "Murder, Incorporated," the United States had promised a harsh response. But instead the United States sold Iran four thousand missiles. And Bandar had asserted that he so loved the game of politics because "there was no blood drawn." But he had launched an operation that had killed eighty innocent people in Lebanon.

In November 1986, the Lebanese newspaper *Al Shirra* broke the story about the Reagan administration's arms sales to Iran. As the ensuing Iran-contra revelations unfolded, Robert McFarlane, Oliver North, and most of the key officials who had advocated tilting toward Iran left the White House in disgrace, giving their rivals a clear field. Consequently, the Reagan administration, in its closing days, leaned strongly toward Iraq.

When the Iran-contra disclosures broke, Bush told the *Washington Post* that he had not been aware that Shultz and Weinberger had raised serious objections to selling weapons to Iran. "If I had sat there and heard George Shultz and Cap express it strongly, maybe I would have had a stronger view. But when you don't know something, it's hard to reach .... We were not in the loop," he said.

On August 6, 1987, the day the *Post* story appeared, Weinberger telephoned Shultz, incredulous that Bush had denied knowledge. "He was on the other side," Weinberger said. "It's on the record! Why did he say that?"[68]

The answer may have lain in Vice President Bush's ambitions. By early 1988, he had been all but anointed Reagan's successor as the Republican presidential nominee and began positioning himself for a run against the eventual Democratic candidate, Michael Dukakis.[69]* He was in an exceptionally strong position. Inflation had plummeted from 13.5 percent in 1980, the last year of the Carter administration, to about 4 percent in 1988. The price of oil now fluctuated between $15 and $20 a barrel, less than half its peak in the early eighties.[70] Gas was so cheap that Detroit auto manufacturers were reveling in the success of a new kind of car called the minivan, the precursor of the gas-guzzling SUV.

American participation in both the Iran-Iraq War and the Afghanistan War, taking place simultaneously, did not register at all on the radar screen of the American electorate. By contrast, the Vietnam War had led to more than fifty thousand American deaths, endless coverage on the nightly news, and a powerful antiwar movement that affected the course of national politics. To be sure, there were hundreds of thousands of deaths in each conflict. But these were wars by proxy, and in the United States, American participation was virtually invisible. Osama bin Laden was unknown to the American people. Only those few who followed the Afghanistan War closely might be aware that he had achieved a nearly heroic status among Islamic militants. As for Saddam Hussein, he was widely seen as a heavy-booted but reliable American ally in the fight against both the Soviets and militant Islamic fundamentalism. There was no domestic political pressure to change American foreign policy in the Middle East.

It might appear that the Saudis' role in the Iran-Iraq War was confined to their shared interest with the United States in protecting Saudi oil fields and participating in a few covert operations. But in fact they performed another function that was both highly secretive and utterly essential. BCCI had played a key role in American operations in Iraq since the early eighties, when CIA director William Casey met every few months at the Madison Hotel in Washington, D.C., with Hasan

---

*One thing that was not easy for Bush during his successful presidential campaign in 1988 was his relationship with his longtime friend James Baker, who confided that when he traveled with Bush, he was at times left playing the role of the "goddamn butler." "Do you think I enjoyed leaving the office of secretary of treasury, being fifth in line to the presidency, to come over here to be called a handler?" he said. When he saw his picture on the cover of *Time,* under the headline "The Year of the Handlers," he told his aides he felt like retching.

Abedi, the bank's founder.[71] Though Abedi was Pakistani, increasingly BCCI had become a Saudi operation with major investors such as Kamal Adham and Ghaith Pharaon. In fact, in the spring and summer of 1986, Khalid bin Mahfouz, the Saudi banker who had gone to Texas in the seventies, spent nearly $1 billion to become BCCI's biggest shareholder.

Because it offered many services not available at Citibank or Chase, such as providing phony documentation and letters of credit to facilitate the purchase of weapons,[72] BCCI was the bank of choice for illegal arms sales to Saddam Hussein's regime in Iraq as well as other CIA covert operations.

To understand BCCI, it is helpful to think of the institution as something other than merely a bank. *Time* once described it as "a vast, stateless, multinational corporation that deploys its own intelligence agency, complete with a paramilitary wing and enforcement units, known collectively as the Black Network."[73] The bank maintained relations with foreign countries through its own "protocol officers" and traded such huge amounts of commodities like grain, rice, coffee, and, of course, oil that it became a major factor in international markets.

In short, it was everything William Casey had ever dreamed of. "What [BCCI founder] Abedi had in his hand [was] magic—something [Saudi intelligence chiefs] Kamal Adham or even Prince Turki didn't have," said a BCCI official. "Abedi had branches and banks in at least fifty third-world countries. The BCCI people ... were on a first-name basis with the prime ministers, the presidents, the finance ministers, the elite in these countries—and their wives and mistresses."

If Casey wanted to know a political leader's secrets, the official continued, Abedi could tell Casey "how much he's salted abroad and how much money he gives to his girlfriend."[74] Meanwhile, the bank created a template with which to finance covert operations all over the world for an international network of terror. As a senior U.S. investigator put it, "BCCI was the mother and father of terrorist financing operations."[75] Not only were many of these BCCI deals illegal, at times they obscured the U.S. goal of solidifying its position in the Middle East.

Meanwhile, as the Iran-Iraq War continued, even Saddam's most brutal atrocities could not weaken U.S. support of Iraq, in part because the Iran-contra scandal had stirred a deep Saudi concern.

The Saudis asserted that in selling arms to Iran the United States was not doing enough to support its ally Iraq, so the United States redoubled its efforts.

In March 1988, Saddam Hussein dropped chemical bombs on Halabja, an Iraqi town in Iranian-held territory, killing five thousand of his own people, Iraqi Kurds.[76]* "It was life frozen," said an Iranian photographer who came upon the scene. "Life had stopped. It was like watching a film and suddenly it hangs on one frame. It was a new kind of death to me."[77]

U.S. intelligence sources told the *Los Angeles Times* that the poison gas was sprayed on the Kurds from U.S. helicopters, which had been sold to Iraq for crop dusting.[78] The Halabja attack was condemned throughout the world and was later used as a reason by President George W. Bush to invade Iraq in 2003.

According to Peter W. Galbraith, the senior adviser to the Senate Foreign Relations Committee who exposed Saddam's gassing of the Kurds, two men who were key players in the Reagan-Bush era and later became principal figures in George W. Bush's administration helped kill the Prevention of Genocide Act, a bill that would have imposed sanctions on Iraq for its genocidal campaign. The bipartisan bill passed the Senate unanimously just one day after it was introduced. But thanks

---

*Various accounts have blamed the Iranians for the gas or have suggested that both Iran and Iraq were using chemical weapons at Halabja. But according to Joost R. Hiltermann in the *International Herald Tribune,* the U.S. State Department instructed its diplomats to blame Iran as well to mute the condemnation of Iraq for using chemical weapons. "The deliberate American prevarication on Halabja was the logical outcome of a pronounced six-year tilt toward Iraq .... Sensing correctly that it had carte blanche, Saddam's regime escalated its resort to gas warfare, graduating to ever more lethal agents. Because of the strong Western animus against Iran, few paid heed. Then came Halabja. Unfortunately for Iraq's sponsors, Iran rushed Western reporters to the blighted town .... In response, the United States launched the 'Iran too' gambit. The story was cooked up in the Pentagon, interviews with the principals show. A newly declassified State Department document demonstrates that United States diplomats received instructions to press this line with United States allies ... the UN Security Council['s] choice of neutral language (condemning the 'continued use of chemical weapons in the conflict between the Islamic Republic of Iran and Iraq' and calling on 'both sides to refrain from the future use of chemical weapons') diffused the effect of its belated move. Iraq proceeded to step up its use of gas until the end of the war and even afterward."

to Colin Powell and Dick Cheney, it never became law. "Secretary of State Colin Powell was then the national security adviser who orchestrated Ronald Reagan's decision to give Hussein a pass for gassing the Kurds," Galbraith wrote. "Dick Cheney, then a prominent Republican congressman, now vice president and the administration's leading Iraq hawk, could have helped pass the sanctions legislation, but did not."[79]

On August 20, 1988, a cease-fire went into effect between Iran and Iraq. Just five days later, Saddam Hussein again staged poison-gas attacks against his own people in villages in Iraqi Kurdistan. None of this, however, changed the administration's policy.

By the time Bush became president in January 1989, the Iran-Iraq War had ended in a stalemate; there was no longer a reason to arm Saddam.* Nevertheless, BCCI's role in arming Iraq continued. Arms dealer Sarkis Soghanalian, who sold billions of dollars' worth of weapons to Saddam,[80] banked there. BCCI regularly loaned billions in short-term, often overnight, loans to the Banca Nazionale del Lavoro, an Italian bank that in turn backed Saddam.

But now that he was president, Bush overlooked BCCI's excesses and actually increased U.S. aid to Saddam in an effort "to bring him into the family of nations."[81] Incredibly, Bush's policy would facilitate Iraq's development of ballistic, chemical, and even nuclear weapons. Bush implemented it despite repeated warnings from his own administration about Saddam's massive military buildup, human-rights violations, use of chemical weapons, and continued support for terrorism.†

---

*According to Hadi Qalamnevis, director general of the Statistics and Information Department at the Islamic Revolution Martyrs Foundation, 204,795 Iranians lost their lives in the Iran-Iraq War, including 188,015 military and 16,780 civilians. Earlier, Mohsen Rafiqdust, the former head of the Iranian Revolutionary Guard Force, estimated that 400,000 were wounded during the war. According to Iranian health officials, about 60,000 Iranians were exposed to Iraqi chemical-weapons attacks during the war. More than 15,000 war veterans suffering from chemical-weapons syndrome reportedly died in the twelve years after the end of the Iran-Iraq War, according to Abbas Khani, the head of the Legal Office for War Veterans.

†In May 2003, after the Iraq War, the magnitude of Saddam's crimes became more apparent when mass graves were found throughout the country. According to columnist Ureib Al-Rintawi in the Jordanian daily *Al-Dustour,* the remains of over fifteen thousand Iraqis were found on the outskirts of the city of Basra, making "the

In March 1989, State Department officials told Secretary of State James Baker that Iraq was working on chemical and biological weapons and that terrorists were still operating out of Iraq. In June, the Defense Intelligence Agency sent a Top Secret report to thirty-eight Bush administration officials, warning that it had uncovered a secret military procurement network for Iraq operating all over the world.[82]

That included the United States. In September 1989, the Defense Department discovered that an Iraqi front company in Cleveland was funneling American technology to Iraq's nuclear weapons program, but the Bush administration allowed the company to operate—even after the invasion of Kuwait in August 1990, nearly a year later. On September 3, 1989, a Top Secret CIA assessment informed Baker that Iraq had a program to develop nuclear weapons.

In spite of all these warnings, on October 2, 1989, President Bush signed a National Security Directive authorizing even closer relations with Iraq, giving Saddam yet more aid. Four days later, James Baker met with his Iraqi counterpart, Tariq Aziz, and promised that the Bush administration would not tighten restrictions on high-technology exports to Iraq. Baker gave these assurances despite the CIA warning he had received the previous month alerting him that some of the "dual-use" technology might be used in Iraq's nuclear weapons development program.

By this time, international bankers had cut off virtually all loans to the Iraqi dictator. But on October 31, 1989, James Baker called the secretary of agriculture, Clayton Yeutter, and pressed for a billion dollars in new agricultural loan guarantees for Iraq. State Department officials were aware that Iraq was diverting some of its dual-use technology to its nuclear weapons program, yet it decided not to tighten export licenses. In January 1990, President Bush waived congressional restrict-

---

... story of Halabja seem like a minor episode in the bloody game experienced by the Iraqi people under Saddam Hussein." Films were later discovered that showed the execution of victims by remote control with explosives stuffed into their pockets, followed by executioners applauding as the victims flew into the air. Columnist Hazem Saghiya wrote in the Arabic-language London daily *Al-Hayat* that the number of those murdered by Saddam was between 1 million and 1.5 million, and Arab observers began to say that Saddam's atrocities were on the level of the mass murders that took place in the killing fields of Cambodia under Pol Pot.

tion on Iraq's use of the Export-Import Bank and in doing so over-looked new evidence that Iraq was testing ballistic missiles and stealing nuclear technology.

All told, the Reagan and Bush administrations ended up providing Saddam Hussein with more than $5 billion in loan guarantees. In the end, American support had enabled the repressive dictator to become a major military force in the Persian Gulf. Saddam had chemical weapons and a nuclear arms program.

There were now a million men in the Iraqi army. Those members of the Bush administration who worried that Shiite revolutionaries would sweep through the Middle East could rest assured that such an event was highly unlikely. The United States had helped build Iraq into the strongest military force in the Middle East. Little did Bush and the Saudis dream that they would soon be at war with the man they had helped create.

CHAPTER FIVE

The Double Marriage

THROUGHOUT THE ROARING EIGHTIES, the U.S.-Saudi marriage continued to thrive. It wasn't just that the United States got billions of dollars of reasonably priced oil and the Saudis were able to arm themselves with American weapons. In addition, the covert operations in Afghanistan and Iraq were beneficial to both parties. For all its success, however, there was just one problem with the arrangement: if one thought of the U.S.-Saudi activities as a steady relationship, the Saudis were already married to someone else.

More specifically, the House of Saud's political legitimacy was based on its allegiance to the sect of Sunni Islam known as Wahhabism and dated back three hundred years. It was at the core of the kingdom's existence. Since many Wahhabis saw the United States as the Great Satan, that meant the Saudis had vital relationships essential to their survival—a double marriage of sorts—with partners who were mortal enemies.

Perhaps the Italian prime minister Giulio Andreotti best explained the Saudis' high comfort level with such extraordinary contradictions and duplicity. "For an Islamic person to be polygamous is not unusual," he once told Jimmy Carter. "They can have four wives, for example. So forget it when it comes to foreign policy."[1]*

* * *

*Higher-ranking Saudis often had far more than just four wives. According to Said Aburish's *The House of Saud*, it is estimated that the forty-two sons of Abdul Aziz married more than fourteen hundred women, an average of more than thirty-three wives for each son.

The ascendancy of the House of Saud's power dates to 1747,* when the Arab clan of al-Saud established a rudimentary government in league with the family of Ibn Abd al-Wahhab, the prophet of Wahhabism. Marriages between the two families cemented the alliance, and the two families agreed that power would be handed down from generation to generation.[2]

The piety of al-Wahhab gave legitimacy to the dubious religious credentials of the al-Sauds, who were essentially a violent bandit tribe. Likewise, the political muscle of the al-Sauds gave al-Wahhab a means to spread his unusual theological views. What emerged over the next 250 years has been characterized by neoconservative author Stephen Schwartz in *The Two Faces of Islam* as "a unique fusion of religious and political control, a system in which faith and statecraft would be run as a family business."[3]

Over time, the Wahhabi-Saudi alliance spread, in part out of conviction, in part out of fear. Those who accepted Wahhabism swore allegiance to the leadership of the alliance and were expected to fight for it and contribute *zakat* (an Islamic tax to the leader of the religious community). Those who resisted it risked raids that threatened their livelihood.[4]

Schwartz and many neoconservatives who are scathing critics of the House of Saud argue that this synthesis of religious and political control in service to these extreme beliefs gave birth to a new kind of totalitarian "Islamo-fascist" regime, a theocratic monarchy espousing a radical fundamentalist form of Islam.[5] Other scholars argue that the physical and intellectual environments that shaped Saudi Arabia—an ancient and conservative desert culture imbued with Islam—have produced a way of life that Westerners like Schwartz all too easily misinterpret.[6]

In many ways, the extremely puritanical teachings of Wahhabism broke sharply with more traditional Islam by promulgating a wide range of practices that were heresy to traditional Muslims. For example, Wahhabis downgraded the status of Muhammad. They condemned those who did not observe all the prescribed times of prayer. They believed in an anthropomorphic God. They insisted on various

---

*Various texts differ on the date. According to Madawai Al-Rasheed's *A History of Saudi Arabia*, the alliance began in 1744.

specific bodily postures in prayer. And they required that their adherents profess faith in Wahhabism in a manner not unlike the practices of born-again Christian fundamentalists.[7]

Whereas American democracy was predicated in part on the separation of church and state, Saudi Arabia was based on their unification. Such a notion is antithetical to Western culture, much of which has long characterized Saudi Arabia as a moderate Arab state. But the unification of this extreme Islamic sect with political power meant that the Koran and the teachings of the Prophet Muhammad were regarded as the country's constitution, that fundamentalist interpretations of Islamic law ruled civil life, that such laws were enforced by religious police, that militant clerics had enormous political power. Wahhabi clerics repeatedly issued fatwas that were not necessarily in keeping with traditional Islam. There were fatwas against women driving, fatwas opposing the telephone, fatwas declaring that the earth was a flat disk and ordering the severe punishment of anyone who believed otherwise.[8]*

Some of the more puritanical Wahhabi practices led to violence and bloodshed. Shortly after Ibn Abd al-Wahhab began his campaign to "reform" Islam, he staged the public stoning of a woman accused of "fornication."[9] During a hajj in the early nineteenth century, Wahhabi fighters slaughtered forty members of an Egyptian caravan to prevent them from defiling the holy sites with false idols.[10] In 1926, Wahhabi militia, who had never heard music before, were so inflamed by hearing pilgrims coming toward Mecca accompanied by musicians that they began gunning down the numerous "unbelievers" who played music or appeared to enjoy it.[11]

Even in recent times, extreme interpretations of Islamic codes have resulted in senseless tragedies. In March 2002, for example, at least fourteen students at a girls' public intermediate school in Mecca died in a fire. According to *Human Rights News*, several members of the Committee for the Promotion of Virtue and the Prevention of Vice

*In 1985, the blind Wahhabi imam Abdul Aziz bin Baz retracted his fatwa punishing people who believed the earth was round after a conversation with Prince Sultan bin Salman bin Abdul Aziz al-Saud, the grandson of Ibn Saud. The prince had just been a passenger in the American space shuttle *Discovery* and told the imam that having been in outer space, he could personally attest that the world was round.

obstructed rescue attempts because the fleeting students were not wearing the obligatory public attire (long black cloaks and head coverings) for Saudi girls and women. "Women and girls may have died unnecessarily because of extreme interpretations of the Islamic dress code," said Hanny Megally, executive director of the Middle East and North Africa division of Human Rights Watch.[12]

At the same time that the Wahhabi clerics were developing their extraordinary version of Islam, the al-Saud family, the more political half of the Wahhabi-Saud marriage, had begun a rich history of violence and brutality. As recounted in *The Rise, Corruption and Coming Fall of the House of Saud,* by Palestinian author Said Aburish, in 1902 Ibn Saud retook Riyadh by terrorizing the general population and decapitating many of his enemies, displaying their heads on the gates of the city.[13] Between 1918 and 1928, the al-Sauds repeatedly massacred rival tribes, executing hundreds of people, including women and children. Members of the al-Saud family personally beheaded many of them.[14]

These executions were only a small part of the al-Sauds' legendary reputation for brutality. In the Saudis' successful campaign to conquer the Arabian peninsula in the twenties, it was not unusual for the al-Sauds to execute all their enemies even *after* they surrendered, to amputate the arms of the poor for stealing bread, and to brutally settle old tribal scores. By the time they subdued the country, they had staged public executions of 40,000 people and carried out 350,000 amputations—this in a population of 4 million.[15]*

Decades later, with the influx of hundreds of billions of petrodollars, the al-Sauds' penchant for violence became just one ingredient in a rich stew that included extraordinary extravagance, unimaginable corruption, and fanatic religious fundamentalism—all at levels unri-

---

*Even in the modern era, the Saudi fondness for harsh punishment persisted. In June 2003, a BBC interview with Riyadh's leading executioner, Muhammad Saad al-Beshi, gave Westerners a taste of exactly how commonplace beheadings are in Saudi Arabia. "It doesn't matter to me: two, four, ten—as long as I'm doing God's will, it doesn't matter how many people I execute," said Beshi, a forty-two-year-old father of seven children. Beshi said he kept his executioner's sword razor sharp and sometimes allowed his children to help him clean it. "People are amazed how fast it can separate the head from the body," he added.

valed the world over. For all practical purposes, the House of Saud saw the kingdom's oil as a family business. Tens of billions of dollars were siphoned off into the al-Sauds' treasury. The top princes took as much as $100 million a year each—this in an enormous extended royal family in which there were thousands of princes. (An ordinary prince, with two wives and ten children, was paid $260,000 a month.[16]) As a result, despite its huge oil income, the kingdom ran an increasingly big budget deficit and had a huge disparity between rich and poor. And with many princes having dozens of wives and scores of children, the situation could only worsen.

Personal excess was unparalleled. King Fahd married one hundred women. His palace cost $3 billion. He regularly lost hundreds of thousands of dollars a night gambling and once, in 1962, dropped nearly $8 million in one night in Monte Carlo.[17] For decades, reports filled the tabloids about extravagant Saudi binges, partying with prostitutes, and other gross excesses. In the eighties, Fahd and his entourage spent up to $5 million a day on visits to the palace in Marbella, Spain.[18] On a private holiday, his fleet consisted of eight aircraft, including five Boeing 747s, and he brought with him four hundred retainers, two hundred tons of luggage, and twenty-five Rolls-Royces and limos.[19] In a PBS *Frontline* interview, Prince Bandar acknowledged that his family had misappropriated tens of billions of dollars. "If you tell me that building this whole country ... we misused or got corrupted with fifty billion, I'll tell you, 'Yes.'... So what? We did not invent corruption, nor did those dissidents, who are so genius, discover it."[20]

Years later, the National Security Agency began electronically intercepting conversations of the royal family that specified exactly how corrupt they were. According to an article by Seymour Hersh in the *New Yorker*, in one call, Crown Prince Abdullah complained about billions of dollars being diverted by the House of Saud from a huge state-financed project to renovate a mosque. In another call, a powerful Saudi Minister told a subordinate not to give police a prostitute's "client list" that presumably included members of the royal family.[21] As recently as the fall of 2003, according to one of their retainers, members of the royal family and their entourage while on a trip to Los Angeles carried packets stuffed with ten thousand dollars to the pharmacy to buy huge quantities of Viagra, then picked up some strippers and prostitutes. Corrupt, rich, and brutal, this was one of America's most powerful friends, the ally on whom much of the American economy depended.

Titillating as such reports of corruption might be, they did not represent a national security threat to the United States. If a peril was hidden in the alliance with the House of Saud, it had to do with the royal family's alliance with the Wahhabi clerics and their growing extremism. One elemental distinction between the Wahhabis and other Muslims was in the interpretation of the Islamic term *jihad*. In some contexts, *jihad* refers to the inner struggle to rid oneself of debased actions or inclinations, to achieve a higher internal moral standard. In the Koran, it also refers to a larger duty, outside the boundaries of the individual, "to enjoin good and forbid evil."[22] The Prophet Muhammad referred to both meanings of the term when he returned from a military campaign and is said to have told his companions, "This day we have returned from the minor jihad [war] to the major jihad [self-control and betterment]."[23]

Islam allows the use of force to fulfill these duties so long as there is no workable alternative. The more radical neo-Wahhabis, however, especially those under the sway of the militant Muslim Brotherhood, strongly emphasized a much more extreme interpretation of jihad. Far from confining the meaning of jihad to the defense of Islamic territory, the Muslim Brotherhood advocated waging a holy war against the enemies of Islam. Not all Wahhabis were so radical, particularly those close to the House of Saud, which looked upon extreme militants as an aberration. Nevertheless, many Middle East scholars see Saudi Arabia as bearing considerable responsibility for the rise of such violence. According to F. Gregory Gause III, a University of Vermont professor and a member of the Council on Foreign Relations, "It is undoubtedly true that the extremely strict, intolerant version of Islam that is taught and practiced in Saudi Arabia created the milieu from which Osama bin Laden and his recruits emerged."[24]

As the House of Saud entered the modern era, there were bitter disagreements within the royal family on exactly how close to the West it was acceptable to be. But to even the most westernized Saudis, modernization—incorporating new technology, becoming part of the global economy—did not mean buying into secular, libertine Western culture. Even though their extravagant behavior may have suggested otherwise, as Wahhabis they were profoundly opposed to becoming "westernized."

That included even the most powerful and pro-West branch of the royal family, the Sudairis. The Sudairis consisted of the descendants of the favored wife of the late king Abdul Aziz. Cosmopolitan and sophisticated world travelers who lived lavishly and loved the night life, they held the reins of power and most of the highest-ranking positions in the government and were known to favor engagement with the United States. Officially, they were rigorously observant of Islamic law, but as a result of their worldly ways many Islamic purists saw them as hypocrites—*munafageen*.[25]

Bandar, whose father, Prince Sultan, was one of the Sudairi Seven,* was a case in point. He had palatial estates in Aspen, in Virginia near the CIA, and in the English countryside. No one enjoyed the fruits of Western civilization more than he.[26] But in the end, Bandar knew as well as anyone that the House of Saud was a theocracy and must heed the call of Islam. He was fond of pointing out that the Iranian Revolution had shown that no regime could adopt secular Western customs without considering the consequences. He once told the *New York Times* an anecdote about the shah of Iran's writing King Faisal a letter before he was deposed in 1979, saying, "Please, my brother, modernize. Open up your country. Make the schools mixed, women and men. Let women wear miniskirts. Have discos. Be modern, otherwise I cannot guarantee you will stay in your throne." To which King Faisal responded, "Your Majesty, I appreciate your advice. May I remind you, you are not the shah of France. You are not in the Élysée, you are in Iran. Your population is ninety percent Muslim. Please don't forget that."[27]

---

*King Abdul Aziz, the founder of modern Saudi Arabia, had forty-three sons, and the Sudairi Seven refers to the seven sons by his favored wife. They include King Fahd, Defense Minister Prince Sultan, Riyadh governor Prince Salman, Interior Minister Prince Nayef, business leader Prince Abdulrahman, Prince Ahmed, and Prince Turki bin Abdul Aziz, who is not to be confused with onetime intelligence chief Prince Turki bin Faisal. It was Fahd who permitted U.S. forces to be stationed on Saudi soil during the Gulf War. Sultan's son Prince Bandar had, of course, been the most prominent Saudi in the United States for decades.

History proved Faisal right. As Bandar explained, "Intangible social and political institutions imported from elsewhere can be deadly—ask the shah of Iran .... Islam for us is not just a religion but a way of life. We Saudis want to modernize, but not necessarily westernize."[28]

So as King Faisal called for Saudi Arabia to modernize—that is, to import technology and renew the economy—he also made clear that he did not mean the country should westernize, as, say, Turkey had.[29] As part of Faisal's "reforms," the ulema, the senior Islamic clerics, became civil servants, part of the state bureaucracy. If anything, the alliance between the House of Saud and Wahhabi fundamentalism became more formalized than ever before. Wahhabi Islam was still the most fundamental part of the Saudi identity. This was irrevocable policy at the highest level of the kingdom. When necessary, the House of Saud did what it had to do to placate the Wahhabi clerics. Always.

Meanwhile, from the eighties on, U.S. oil consumption grew from 15 million barrels a day to nearly 20 million a day.[30] Imported oil as a percentage of U.S. consumption continued to soar, and U.S. policy makers and oil executives alike overlooked the more disagreeable practices of their supplier.

That had always been the case. For decades, most of what Americans knew about Saudi Arabia came courtesy of Aramco, the Arab-American oil consortium that was granted the spectacularly lucrative long-term concession to bring Saudi oil to U.S. markets. As economic historian J. B. Kelly, the author of *Arabia, the Gulf and the West,* explained it, "Because there were no other sources of information about that country open to the American public, Aramco could put across its version of recent Arabian history and politics with almost insolent ease .... Naturally, little prominence was accorded in Aramco's publicity to the fanatic nature of Wahabbism, or to its dark and bloody past."[31]

One family that lived with these contradictions was the bin Ladens. A devout Muslim who enforced strict religious and social codes in raising his children, Mohammed bin Laden, Osama's father, kept all of his children in one residence so he could preside over their discipline and religious upbringing.[32] He took pride in having fathered twenty-five sons for the jihad.

To Westerners, Mohammed's piety may have seemed incongruous in a cosmopolitan family of jet-setters with private planes, giant homes all over the world, and all the accoutrements of modern Saudi billionaires. But in the Saudi context, his great wealth and global business interests in no way contradicted his piety.* Thanks to his private planes, on at least one occasion he fulfilled his dream of saying morning prayers in Jerusalem, midday prayers in Medina, and evening prayers in Mecca—the three holiest cities in the Arab world.[33] He deeply supported the Palestinian cause. At one point, he even attempted to convert two hundred of his company's bulldozers into military tanks for the Palestinian insurgents. "He wanted to use them to attack Israel," Osama told a Pakistani journalist. "However, his technicians told him it would be impossible and he gave up the idea."[34]

Osama learned Islam at his father's knee and by the age of seven was studying with fundamentalist Islamic groups.[†] He took enormous pride in his father's having rebuilt the holy mosques in Mecca and Medina. These were no ordinary mosques; they were the Islamic equivalents of Notre Dame and the Vatican. "Allah blessed him and bestowed on him an honor that no other contractor has ever known," Osama later told Aljazeera television.[35]

In 1968, Mohammed bin Laden was killed when his private jet crashed into the mountains of southern Saudi Arabia, leaving Osama, who was ten years old at the time, a fortune estimated at $30 million to $60 million—roughly $200 million to $400 million in 2003 dollars. By the time he was a teenager, Osama was an unusually self-possessed and gentle young man. "He was singularly gracious and polite and had a great deal of inner confidence," recalled a man who taught English to bin Laden when Osama was about thirteen years old, around 1970. "[In his work, bin Laden was] very neat, precise, and conscientious. He

---

*The Saudi Binladin Group was so comfortable with infidel culture that it actually played an important role in bringing Disney-like theme parks to the Arab world. In 1998, SBG contracted to build the Dreamland megamarket, a shopping complex of megastores adjacent to Dream Park, Cairo's answer to Disney World.

†Reports differ as to the exact number of children sired by Mohammed bin Laden—but it is generally agreed to be at least fifty-four. In addition, various accounts place Osama bin Laden as his seventeenth son while others say he was the last of twenty-five sons.

wasn't pushy at all .... If he knew the answer to something, he wouldn't parade the fact. He would only reveal it if you asked him."[36]

Older brother Salem, who took over the family business after Mohammed's death, bought huge homes in Texas and Florida, jetted around the globe, and flew private planes up the Nile.[37] Educated at Millfield school, Somerset, he married an upper-class Englishwoman, Caroline Carey, whose stepfather was the Marquess of Queensberry.[38]

But Osama led a more insular and ascetic existence. The only bin Laden child to be educated solely in the Middle East, he had far less contact with the West than his siblings and was perhaps the only one who did not travel to the United States. In 1971, Osama and twenty-two other members of the family went to Falun, Sweden, where the family had business with Volvo. But such jaunts to the West were rare for Osama. Given his family's high status, Osama was allowed to socialize with royalty, but even as a teenager, he preferred the company of the ulema.[39] Moreover, to the extent he related to the West, his antipathy was such that he pretended that he could not speak English—even though several sources, his English teacher and journalists among them, say he learned the language fluently.[40]*

As a teenager, Osama may have briefly strayed from the devout path he followed most of his life. Bin Laden, a controversial biography of Osama by the pseudonymous Adam Robinson, asserts that while he attended Broumanna High School in Lebanon, Osama played the part of a debonair Saudi playboy, driving a canary yellow Mercedes, wearing handmade suits, and drinking Dom Pérignon and Johnnie Walker Black Label at the Crazy Horse and the Casbah.[41]

But bin Laden was redeemed, the book says, in 1977 when he and his brother Salem joined the masses to perform the demanding series of rituals of the hajj near Mecca. Afterward, Osama visited the cave at Mount Hira, near Mecca, where Muhammad is said to have received the revelations from God. According to Robinson, Osama was pro-

---

*In 1989, journalist Edward Girardet of the Christian Science Monitor encountered bin Laden in Afghanistan and had a heated forty-five-minute conversation with him in English. In addition, a man named Brian Fyfield-Shayler claims to have taught English to bin Laden and thirty other wealthy Saudis around 1970.

foundly moved by the experience, sold his Mercedes, grew a beard, and threw himself into Islamic studies as never before.[42]

At Jeddah's King Abdul Aziz University* bin Laden's religious training began in earnest, at a time when thinking at the university was dominated by two of the leading voices of the Muslim Brotherhood, Egyptian scholar Sayyid Qutb, an intellectual hero and principal theoretician of the Islamist revolution, and Sheikh Abdullah Azzam, the creator of the First International Jihadist Movement, who was a stirring speaker and a powerful figure raising funds and recruiting for the jihad.[43]

Qutb had been a secular Egyptian scholar and literary critic—he discovered Egyptian novelist Naguib Mahfouz, who was later awarded the Nobel Prize—but a sojourn to the United States in 1949 left him appalled at American insensitivity to spiritual matters.[44] A student at what was then Colorado State Teachers College in Greeley, Colorado—ironically, a conservative, religious town—Qutb wrote about Greeley in his book *The America I Have Seen* as materialistic and soulless, finding evidence of America's greed in conventions and possessions that seem quite ordinary to most Americans, such as the green lawns in front of their homes.[45] Qutb attacked American jazz music and dress, and most of all, the American concern with sexuality, especially among women. "The American girl ... knows seductiveness lies in the round breasts, the full buttocks, and in the shapely thighs, sleek legs—and she shows all this and does not hide it," he wrote.

Shocked when he witnessed a priest encourage young men and women to dance together at a party, Qutb saw a church social as evidence of America's debased attitude toward sexuality—and wrote about it with the salaciousness of a romance novelist: "They danced to the tunes of the gramophone, and the dance floor was replete with tapping feet, enticing legs, arms wrapped around waists, lips pressed to lips, and chests pressed to chests. The atmosphere was full of desire ..." Qutb returned to Saudi Arabia a militant Muslim, determined to forge a vision of Islam purged of the vulgar influences of the West.

*It is widely agreed that bin Laden attended King Abdul Aziz University, but there are conflicting reports as to when or if he graduated and which field he studied—economics, engineering, or public administration.

One of Qutb's books, *Signposts Along the Road,** argued that Western civilization had led to "corruption and irreligion" and that jihad should be waged not just defensively to protect Islamic home-lands, but offensively against enemies of Muslims.[46] Qutb asserted that the United States was especially dangerous precisely because, unlike the Saudis, the Americans insisted on separating church and state. As a result of this, he argued, the West was trying "to confine Islam to the emotional and ritual circles, and to bar it from partici-pating in the activity of life." In the end, as he saw it, this amounted to "an effort to exterminate this religion."[47]

By the early sixties, Qutb had become the most prominent funda-mentalist theoretician in Islam, and his suffering in prison in Egypt and his execution in 1965 became the stuff of legend.[48] The more moderate Islamists saw Qutb's analyses as valuable but flawed by his bitterness at having been jailed and tortured. Wahhabis influenced by the House of Saud scorned his followers as a sect they labeled Qutbites.[49]

Nevertheless, Qutb's ideas lived on. They were promulgated by both the militant Wahhabi scholar Sheikh Abdullah Azzam and Ayman al-Zawahiri, an Egyptian surgeon who later became notorious as the man behind Osama bin Laden. Azzam became particularly effective in persuading masses of Muslims all over the world to wage an international jihad.[50] By the late seventies, Osama, six feet five inches, lean, bearded, and dour, had imbibed such strong anti-American feelings from Azzam at the university that he began to boycott American goods. When Muslims bought American, they were contributing to the repression of Palestinians, he said.[51]

At the time, the notions of Islamic fundamentalism had begun spreading through Saudi Arabia. Sayyid Qutb's views had become important to the organization now known as the World Assembly of Muslim Youth (WAMY), which had been founded by Abdullah bin Laden, a relative of Osama's, in 1972. Omar bin Laden, another relative, was also a director of WAMY.

In addition, Mahrous bin Laden, one of Osama's older brothers, became friendly with Syrian members of the militant Muslim Brother-

---

*The title of the book, *Ma'allim fi al-tariq*, is sometimes also translated as *Milestones.*

hood in exile in Saudi Arabia.[52] In late 1979, the Muslim Brotherhood asserted that the House of Saud had lost its legitimacy through "corruption, ostentation, and mindless imitation of the West."[53] Not much later they mounted their most daring operation ever.

On November 20, just a month before the Soviet invasion of Afghanistan, more than a thousand members of the Muslim Brotherhood invaded Mecca and seized control of the Grand Mosque in a desperate attempt to rid the country of the House of Saud. The Grand Mosque, of course, is the spectacular place of worship to which 2 million Muslims make their pilgrimage during the hajj each year. It is the site of the Kaaba, one of the holiest icons in all of Islam, a rectangular stone room with black silk and cotton sheaths embroidered in gold with verses from the Koran.

At the time of the uprising, the Saudi Binladin Group was rebuilding the mosque, and its trucks carried permits allowing them to enter and depart without having to be inspected. An investigation by Saudi intelligence revealed that the militants had taken advantage of Mahrous to use the bin Laden family's trucks without his knowledge.[54] The episode, which became known as the Mecca Affair, was the most serious attack on the House of Saud in its three-hundred-year history.

The siege led to a two-week battle that left the Saudi Arabian National Guard (SANG), a praetorian guard of sorts whose primary mission was to defend the royal family, battling the fundamentalists to the death. One hundred twenty-seven Saudi troops and 117 rebels were killed.[55] Fighting was so fierce that the Vinnell Corporation, an American company that trained the Saudi National Guard, was called in to help out.[56]*

The battle marked a rare moment in which both the covert nature

---

*Vinnell, which had trained the Saudi National Guard since 1975, was widely said to have been a CIA front. In the Vietnam era, the company did everything from construction of military bases to military operations, and a Pentagon source termed it "our own little mercenary army in Vietnam." When one of Vinnell's men in Riyadh was asked if he saw himself as a mercenary, however, he had a slightly different characterization. "We are not mercenaries because we are not pulling the triggers," he told *Newsweek*. "We train people to pull the triggers. Maybe that makes us executive mercenaries."

of the Saudi-American relationship and the contradictions of the marriage between the House of Saud and militant Islamic fundamentalism erupted. To the Brotherhood, the House of Saud were nothing more than corrupt, pro-Western hypocrites—*munafageen*—who were paying lip service to the clerics while they were really in bed with the decadent Great Satan, the United States. For this reason, the Brotherhood asserted that the Saudi regime had lost its legitimacy.[57]

The members of the Muslim Brotherhood suffered the ultimate penalty: no fewer than sixty-three rebels were publicly beheaded. Mahrous, though arrested for his connection with the group, was released and later became manager of the Saudi Binladin Group's offices in Medina.[58]

The House of Saud's gentle treatment of Mahrous strongly suggests that the bin Ladens' ties to the royal family had paid off. However, this would not be the last time a member of the bin Laden family would be at odds with the House of Saud.

CHAPTER SIX

Another Frankenstein

WHILE THE UNITED STATES was aiding Iraq throughout the eighties, the CIA's campaign in Afghanistan was also well under way, becoming the biggest and most successful covert operation in the Agency's history. The entire program cost virtually no American casualties and a mere $3 billion for American taxpayers. Yet it dealt a devastating blow to the Soviet Union and was deemed a major factor in winning the Cold War for the United States.

The seeds of the campaign had been planted even before the Reagan-Bush administration took office, through a bold but clandestine strategy designed by the Carter administration. Better known for his innocence and naïveté than for audacious foreign policy ploys, President Carter nevertheless had a few tricks up his sleeve. On July 3, 1979, on the advice of his brilliant and hawkish national security adviser, Zbigniew Brzezinski, Carter signed the first directive to secretly aid Afghan rebels known as the mujahideen who were fighting the pro-Soviet regime in Kabul. Soon, the CIA began to provide weapons and money to the mujahideen through Islamic fundamentalist warriors. This was a war by proxy. The aid was intended to bait the Soviets into committing more troops and weapons to defending their newly embattled allies. If everything went according to plan, ultimately the Soviets would become ensnared in a brutal, expensive, futile, and endless war that would lead to the disintegration of their entire empire.

On December 26, less than five months later, the USSR took the bait, and Soviet troops marched into Afghanistan to confront their emboldened foes. To Brzezinski, the architect of the plan, the Soviet invasion offered the United States an unrivaled geopolitical opportunity. As soon as the Soviets crossed the border, he wrote President Carter, "We now have the opportunity of giving to the USSR its Vietnam War."[1]

The policy was a delicious new rendering of the so-called Great Game, made famous in Rudyard Kipling's novel *Kim,* in which the British used indigenous Islamic forces to keep the Russians out of Afghanistan. But now the Americans were updating it for the Cold War. On the grand global chessboard, Brzezinski's strategy was a gambit worthy of Kasparov and when the Reagan-Bush administration took office, they eagerly embraced it. Soon, aid to the Afghan rebels was a centerpiece of what the administration called the Reagan Doctrine. The intention of the policy was to make Soviet support for third world governments too costly to be sustainable.

A student of the American Revolutionary War, CIA director William Casey said the key to the American victory in 1776 was that they used "irregular partisan guerrilla warfare."[2] That was the methodology of the Afghan mujahideen, and Casey liked it that way. Early on, he was buoyed by reports that covert aid to the mujahideen was paying off. According to a declassified CIA intelligence assessment in late 1982, the Agency believed that the rugged terrain of Afghanistan and the resourcefulness of the mujahideen would prevent the Soviets from winning. The report concluded that even an extra fifty thousand Soviet troops would be unlikely to break the logjam.[3]

By this time, Prince Bandar had become King Fahd's trusted point man in Washington. When William Casey approached Bandar about Saudi Arabia's funding an escalation of anti-Soviet forces, the two men flew to Jeddah with Bandar serving as Casey's translator for the meeting with Fahd.[4] Casey met a receptive audience. This campaign was uniquely appealing to the Saudis. Not only would it enable them to cement their ties to the United States, it would also help the royal family deal with domestic unrest. And so, the House of Saud eagerly joined in, matching "America dollar for dollar supporting the mujahideen," as Prince Turki, longtime head of Saudi intelligence, puts it.[5]

In the U.S. Congress, the Afghan rebels were championed by Democratic congressman Charlie Wilson, the colorful six-foot-seven-inch, skirt-chasing Texan whose role in America's biggest covert operation was celebrated in George Crile's book *Charlie Wilson's War*. At dinner parties in Houston and in Washington, Wilson would bring together the likes of Henry Kissinger, White House chief of staff James Baker, and Prince Bandar along with a glittering assortment of senators, astronauts, diplomats, Texas oil barons, and military men in celebration of the mujahideen.

"Allah will not be pleased if the king abandons his freedom fighters," Wilson teased Bandar.[6] To which Bandar replied, "Allah will soon be smiling, Charlie. You will see." For his part, Wilson played an important role in seeing to it that Congress provided the $3 billion in covert aid for the mujahideen.[7]

The Saudis were a key part of the equation. Thousands of young warriors calling themselves Afghan Arabs streamed out of Saudi Arabia, Jordan, Yemen, and all over the Middle East to aid the mujahideen. Neither the United States nor the Saudis seemed to mind that the crusading young Muslims could not have cared less about helping America win the Cold War. They were motivated by religious fervor and passion. This was a people's war, a noble crusade against an infidel superpower that had invaded Muslim lands, a fight to avenge the martyrdom of their Afghan brothers being crushed by Moscow. It was a time to demonstrate faith and courage. For many Muslims, the liberation of Afghanistan became a very personal jihad.

In sharp contrast to the Mecca Affair, the Afghanistan War was a mission that could be embraced by the gamut of Saudi society, from the wealthy merchant families and the House of Saud to the militant clerics and the fundamentalist masses. For the royal family, the war was not just part of the cornerstone of the burgeoning Saudi alliance with the United States, but served other purposes as well. Contributing to the war effort placated the militant clerics and helped accommodate the growing unrest and the more radical elements of society. In the wake of the Iranian revolution, there was a new determination on the part of Saudi Muslims to outdo their Iranian counterparts, to create a "new Islamic man."[8]

Instead of focusing their anger at the House of Saud or the United States, the militants could now zero in on the atheistic Soviets. A missionary zeal spread through every layer of society. "There was a sense that every penny you sent in made a difference," says Armond Habiby, an American lawyer who has practiced in Saudi Arabia for many years. "It was a very noble movement. The poor gave away prayer rugs, embroidered tablecloths. It established a monumental footprint that went across all levels of society."[9]

As the war got under way, with the United States, the Saudis, and the Pakistanis secretly supporting the Afghan rebels, the Pakistani Inter-Services Intelligence (ISI) hoped that Prince Turki bin Faisal, then head of Saudi intelligence and a member of the House of Saud, would bring an actual member of the royal family to the front to demonstrate the commitment of the House of Saud to the jihad.[10] But no Saudi prince wanted to or needed to brave the Afghan mountains. Osama bin Laden, a protégé of Prince Turki's, was the next best thing.

At twenty-two, Osama bin Laden could easily have become a wealthy Saudi businessman, like his father, Mohammed, or his older brother Salem. Thanks to his family's vast fortune and close ties to the royal family, he was perfectly positioned to join the Saudi elite. Instead, incensed by the Soviet invasion, he went straight to Afghanistan.[11] "I was enraged and I went there at once," he said.[12] He arrived before the end of 1979, just a few days after Soviet troops had crossed the border.

For bin Laden, the war was not only a historic turning point during which he would emerge as a leader, it was also a momentous time in Muslim history. He and his fellow Afghan Arabs were stirred by the plight of Muslims from a medieval society besieged by a twentieth-century superpower.[13] "One day in Afghanistan," Osama said, "counted for more than a thousand days praying in a mosque."[14]

Bin Laden's action carried extraordinary weight in large part because of his family's unique place in Saudi society.* Their ties to the royal family were so crucial that both sides made certain the relationships transcended generations. Many of the twenty-five bin Laden boys attended school with the sons of King Abdul Aziz and his successor, Faisal, at Victoria College in Alexandria, where they had classmates such as King Hussein of Jordan, the Khashoggi brothers (of

*Mohammed bin Laden was so close to the royal family that in the sixties, he played a vital role in persuading King Saud to abdicate in favor of his brother Faisal.

whom Adnan* was the preeminent Saudi arms dealer of the Iran-contra era), and Kamal Adham, the billionaire who ran Saudi intelligence before Prince Turki.[15] The boys earned reputations as discreet chaperones for the young royals.

In 1968, when Mohammed bin Laden was killed in a plane crash, King Faisal said his "right arm" had been broken[16] and rushed to the support of the bin Ladens, who, at the time, did not have anyone old enough to take the helm of the family business. Faisal appointed the highly regarded head of his own construction company to make sure the Saudi Binladin Group was in good hands until Salem, Osama's older half brother, was old enough to take over.[17] Later, when King Fahd took the throne in 1982, Salem became one of his two best friends.[18]

Closely tied as they were to both the royal family and the United States, at this point the bin Ladens had only indirect connections to the Bush family and its allies. James Bath, the American business representative of Salem bin Laden, knew both George W. Bush and George H. W. Bush. Khalid bin Mahfouz, who was close to both the bin Ladens and the royal family, had helped finance the Houston skyscraper for the Texas Commerce Bank, in which James Baker had a significant stake. He also had ties to Bath.

But these Bush–bin Laden "relationships" were indirect—two degrees of separation, perhaps—and at times have been overstated. Critics have asserted that money may have gone from Khalid bin Mahfouz and Salem bin Laden through James Bath into Arbusto Energy, the oil company started by George W. Bush, but no evidence has ever been found to back up that charge, which appears to be unfounded.[†]

More to the point, now, in the Afghanistan War, Vice President Bush's interests and Osama bin Laden's converged. In using bin

---

*Adnan Khashoggi was also the uncle of Dodi Fayed, who died in a Paris automobile crash with Princess Diana in 1997.

†Bath had fronted for Saudi billionaires Salem bin Laden and Khalid bin Mahfouz on other deals, but in this case he says, "One hundred percent of those funds were mine. It was a purely personal investment." Bin Laden and bin Mahfouz, he insists, had nothing to do with either the elder George Bush or his son. "They never met Bush," Bath says. "Ever. And there was no reason to. At that point Bush was a young guy just out of Yale, a struggling young entrepreneur trying to get a drilling fund."

Laden's Arab Afghans as proxy warriors against the Soviets, Bush advocated a policy that was fully in line with American interests at that time. But he did not consider the long-term implications of supporting a network of Islamic fundamentalist rebels.

Specifically, as vice president in the mid-eighties, Bush supported aiding the mujahideen in Afghanistan through the Maktab al-Khidamat (MAK) or Services Offices, which sent money and fighters to the Afghan resistance in Peshawar. "Bush was in charge of the covert operations that supported the MAK," says John Loftus, a Justice Department official in the eighties. "They were essentially hiring a terrorist to fight terrorism."[19]

Cofounded by Osama bin Laden and Abdullah Azzam, the MAK was the precursor to bin Laden's global terrorist network, Al Qaeda. It sent money and fighters to the Afghan resistance in Peshawar, Pakistan, and set up recruitment centers in over fifty countries including Egypt, Saudi Arabia, Pakistan, and even the United States to bring thousands of warriors to Afghanistan to fight the Soviet Union.[20] The MAK was later linked to the 1993 bombing of the World Trade Center in New York through an office in Brooklyn known as the Al-Kifah Refugee Center. It is not clear how much contact he had with bin Laden, but Sheikh Omar Abdel Rahman, the "Blind Sheikh," who masterminded the 1993 bombing of the World Trade Center, also appeared in Peshawar on occasion.[21]

Throughout the eighties in Saudi Arabia, Prince Turki oversaw bin Laden's efforts aiding the mujahideen. Prince Bandar also met bin Laden, but many years later said he was not impressed. "At that time, I thought he couldn't lead eight ducks across the street," he said.[22]

And yet Osama now played a vital role for the House of Saud. Not merely a trophy to show how committed the royal family was to this noble cause, he helped the House of Saud celebrate the American commitment to the mujahideen's efforts. "Bin Laden used to come to us when America ... [was] helping our brother mujahideen in Afghanistan to get rid of the communist, secularist Soviet Union forces," recalled Prince Bandar. "... Osama bin Laden came and said, 'Thank you. Thank you for bringing the Americans to help us to get rid of the secularist, atheist Soviets.'"[23]

Between 1980 and 1982, bin Laden went back and forth repeatedly between Saudi Arabia and the front, bringing donations from the Saudis. In Jeddah, his family enthusiastically endorsed his commitment to the cause.[24] Working closely with Turki[25] and with Prince Salman, the governor of Riyadh,[26] bin Laden played a key role in financing, recruiting, and training Arabian volunteers.

Finally, in 1982, Osama settled in Peshawar, the command headquarters of the jihad near the Khyber Pass, known as the Dodge City of the Afghan rebels, bringing with him engineers and heavy construction equipment from the Saudi Binladin Company to build roads and depots for the mujahideen. "In those years, there was no Al Qaeda," says Prince Turki. "Bin Laden gave money, equipment, and construction material from his family's company."[27]

Abdullah Azzam, the professor-cleric-mujahid who had taught at the university in Jeddah when Osama was there, had by this time become a spiritual leader of the mujahideen. "Azzam was the man who developed the idea of jihad in a complete way," said Mukahil ul-Islam Zia, a professor at the Islamic Center at Peshawar University. "Azzam enshrines the need for armed struggle as part of daily life."[28] Azzam helped many Arabs just off the plane take part in the jihad by starting the Jihad Training University. With Azzam as his mentor, bin Laden began recruiting warriors for the jihad. "Osama would have been nothing without Azzam," said one expert on the Taliban. "Before he came to Peshawar, Osama was a kind of playboy, a dilettante, not serious, not what we see today."

Some Western publications have characterized bin Laden as merely having used his family fortune to bankroll the mujahideen. Given his wealth, it was tempting for critics to dismiss him as a "Gucci terrorist." But according to a Pakistani who fought with him, he "was a hero to us because he was always on the front line, always moved ahead of everyone else. He not only gave of his money, he gave of himself."[29]

All of which served U.S. interests at the time—in a way the CIA had only dreamed of. In 1985, a CIA assessment estimated that there had already been ninety-two thousand combined Soviet and Afghan casualties—more than twice that of the rebels—and that the Soviets were "no closer than they were in 1979 to achieving their goals." The report concluded that the Soviets were "unlikely" to quell the rebels' insurgency.[30]

To CIA chief William Casey, the success was inspiring. A longtime Cold Warrior who believed not in containment of the communists but what in the late forties and early fifties had been called rollback, Casey saw that he could push all the way across the Soviet border by escalating the war. Casey had told John N. McMahon, the CIA's deputy director of operations, how he felt about Afghanistan. "This is the kind of thing we should be doing—only more. I want to see one place on this globe, one spot where we can checkmate them and roll them back. We've got to make the communists feel the heat. Otherwise, we'll never get them to the negotiating table."[31]

And so, the United States escalated. By 1987, well into the second term of the Reagan-Bush administration, the United States began to provide the rebels with nearly $700 million in military assistance a year. In addition, the CIA began supplying the mujahideen with intelligence, training, and equipment that allowed them to make scattered strikes against factories, military installations, and storage depots that were actually *inside* the Soviet Union. They gave the Islamic rebels satellite reconnaissance data, intercepted Soviet intelligence, and provided sniper rifles, timing devices for tons of C-4 explosives for urban sabotage, antitank missiles, and other sophisticated equipment.[32]

Most coveted of all were the Stinger missiles, portable, shoulder-fired antiaircraft guided missiles with infrared seekers for downing low-flying helicopters and planes,[33] missiles so sophisticated that, as one CIA officer put it, "a nearsighted, illiterate Afghan could bring down a few million dollars' worth of Soviet aircraft."[34] With a hit rate of 89 percent, the Stingers downed an average of one plane every day. Soon, the Afghan air force was depleted, and for the Soviets, the cost of the war soared.[35]

Meanwhile, bin Laden built a major arms storage depot, training facility, and medical center for the mujahideen at Khost in eastern Afghanistan. Peshawar became the center of a burgeoning pan-Islamic movement. More than twenty-five thousand Islamic militants, from the Palestinians' Hamas, from Egypt's Al Gama'a al-Islamiya and Al Jihad, from Algeria's Islamic Salvation Front, from the Philippines'

Moro Liberation Front, from countries all over the world, made the pilgrimage through Peshawar to the jihad.[36]

"You can sit at the Khyber Pass and see every color, every creed, every nationality, pass," a Western diplomat said. "These groups, in their wildest imagination, never would have met if there had been no jihad. For a Moro* to get a Stinger missile! To make contacts with Islamists from North Africa! The United States created a Moscow Central in Peshawar for these groups, and the consequences for all of us are astronomical."[37]

A new network of charities grew into a formidable infrastructure to support the growing pan-Islamic movement. Money flowed into the Services Offices in Peshawar. A new leadership emerged that included Sheikh Azzam and his best friend, the rotund, blind Sheikh Omar from Egypt. CIA forces in Peshawar saw him as a valuable asset, letting pass his militant anti-Western sentiments because he was such a powerful force in uniting the mujahideen.[38]

Bin Laden became a leader himself. His identity was truly forged in this period. "If you really want to understand Osama, you have to understand Afghanistan in the 1980s," said his younger brother Abdullah bin Laden, who last saw Osama at the funeral of their brother Salem in 1988. "His views do not come from his childhood or upbringing, but from prolonged exposure to war against a non-Islamic force.

"Look to that period of history for your answers. In the West, people do not understand the incensing brutality of the Soviet war in Afghanistan. It had a severe effect on him. It seemed to change him completely. I believe it fomented his radical feelings and it scarred him. At least, this is how I try to understand my brother and come to terms with what he has done."[39]

Arab journalists who covered him then spoke of him in dark, romantic terms. "He is a man that seeks the afterlife and who truly feels that he has lived more than enough," said Abd-al-Bari Atwan, editor of *Al-Quds al-Arabi*. "You feel there is a sadness in him—which he did not express—that he was not martyred when he was fighting the Soviet arm .... You feel like he's saying: Why am I alive?"[40]

*The reference is to the Islamic separatist movement in the Philippines.

Years later, bin Laden rhapsodized about those days as a great romantic spiritual adventure. "Those were the prettiest days of our lives," he said. "... What I lived in two years there, I could not have lived in a hundred years elsewhere."[41]

Bin Laden was not the only one who could savor the bittersweet qualities of the war against the Soviets. In May 1984, Vice President George H. W. Bush visited the region and peeked across the border into Afghanistan from the Khyber Pass in Pakistan. Armed with a $14-million check for humanitarian relief, Bush told the refugees, "Across the border, a brutal war is being waged against the people of Afghanistan. I know your resistance will continue until the Soviets realize they cannot be able to subjugate Afghanistan."[42]

We do not know exactly where bin Laden was at that moment, but during this period he was nearby in Afghanistan and had begun working with Azzam to build up the Services Offices.[43] Chances are, this is the closest that Osama bin Laden and George H. W. Bush ever got physically. They were in the same region at roughly the same time. And most important, they were fighting for the same cause.

By February 1987, a CIA assessment reported that the war was crippling the Soviet Union. "General Secretary Gorbachev has referred to the war as a 'bleeding wound,'" the report read. It had led to censure of the Soviets within the UN, impinged on Soviet relations with China and nonaligned third world nations, caused domestic social unrest, and diverted energies from pressing economic problems.[44] What the report did not say, but the Soviets felt, was that tens of thousands of Soviet youths were dying on killing fields in a foreign land, fighting for a cause they didn't believe in, detested by the local populace they allegedly fought for, bleeding the crippled economy of their own country dry.

For the Americans, the Afghanistan policy was so successful that as the 1988 presidential election neared, Bush saw it as proof of his bona fides as a Cold Warrior during his campaign against Massachusetts governor Michael Dukakis. On October 18, 1988, Bush stopped at Westminster College in Fulton, Missouri, the site of Winston Churchill's 1946 historic speech warning that an "Iron Curtain" of communism was descending across the European continent. Bush seized the propitious occasion to comment on what Reagan had famously labeled "the evil empire."

It was Bush's most dramatic speech of the campaign, perhaps of his entire life, and it commemorated what was unquestionably the greatest accomplishment of the Reagan-Bush era, the end of the Cold War. "The Iron Curtain still stretches from Stettin to Trieste," Bush said. "But it's a rusting curtain. Shafts of light from the Western side, from our side, the free and prosperous side, are piercing the gloom of failure and despair on the other side.

"The truth is being sought as never before," he added. "And the peoples of Eastern Europe, the peoples of the Soviet Union itself, are demanding more freedom, demanding their place in the sun."

Seventy years after the Russian Revolution, Bush said, Marxism is finally "losing its luster." At last, in the age of Mikhail Gorbachev's glasnost (openness) and perestroika (transformation), the Cold War was thawing and there was a sense of a new flexibility. One key reason for such historic changes, Bush said, was that "the price of aggression was too high, because we supported the mujahideen in Afghanistan."[45]

By the time George Bush moved into the White House in early 1989, having easily beaten Dukakis, the Soviet troops were already withdrawing from Afghanistan. At CIA headquarters, William Webster—who had succeeded Bill Casey as director—and his euphoric "Afghan Team" toasted the success of the multibillion-dollar covert operation to support the Muslim Afghan rebels. The Cold War was over. The Afghan campaign had been the coup de grâce.[46]

As the Soviets withdrew, however, the many unintended consequences of the war became increasingly apparent. The arms pipeline set up by the CIA had unwittingly become a drug pipeline as well. As first reported by the *Herald*, an English-language magazine in Pakistan, the main conduit through which weapons reached the Afghan rebels was now one of the principal routes for the transport of heroin to Karachi for shipment to Europe and the United States.

"It is really very simple," the *Herald* reported in January 1987. "If you control the poppy fields, Karachi, and the road which links the two, you will be so rich that you will control Pakistan." The article added that the drugs came down by truck from Peshawar with "sacks [containing] packets of heroin .... This has been going on now for about three and a half years."[47]*

An even bigger issue, however, was that the United States was still pouring billions of dollars in funding and sophisticated weaponry to build a vast pan-Islamist army. "During the war, if there was any thought of postwar complications from this stuff, it wasn't much expressed," says Frank Anderson, chief of the CIA's Afghan Task Force from 1987 to 1989. "Everyone was busy getting the Soviets kicked out of Afghanistan. The Muslim world was excited by this stuff, and at the time we knew nothing of these activities being related to terrorism."[48]

"We set up the very system [of Islamist terrorism] we are now trying to dismantle," says a senior investigator who participated in the Senate probe into BCCI. "People forget that we invented this shit, that Bill Casey was getting the Saudi fundamentalists to assemble all these kooks and go out and kill the Russians. No one asked what would happen when it was over."[49]

Throughout the eighties most of the American media, with a few rare exceptions, such as Edward Girardet of the *Christian Science Monitor*, simply ignored the war in Afghanistan. And yet, as Steve Galster, project director of the National Security Archive's Afghanistan archives, has observed, "This was the longest war in Soviet history, the largest CIA paramilitary operation since Vietnam, and with one million dead Afghans, the bloodiest regional conflict in the world at the time."[50]

Even America's most heralded investigative reporters missed the story. In *Veil*, his 1987 account of the CIA's secret wars of that era, Bob Woodward devotes several pages to the Afghanistan operation, but he

*At the time he visited the war-ravaged region in May 1984, Vice President Bush was also serving as the head of the National Narcotics Border Interdiction System, a national network designed to stop the flow of drugs into the United States. A vigorous critic of drug use, Bush later vowed to tell drug dealers, "Your day is over. You're history."

The CIA later insisted it had no knowledge of the heroin running. But according to the Financial Times, the CIA not only had knowledge, it actually started a special cell that "promoted the cultivation of opium and the extraction of heroin in Pakistani territory as well as in the Afghan territory under Mujahadeen control for being smuggled into the Soviet-controlled areas in order to make the Soviet troops heroin addicts."

does not mention the mujahideen, Wahhabism, BCCI, or in any way suggest that billions of American dollars were going to arm and finance a global network of militant Islamic fundamentalists.

On rare occasions, starting as early as 1983, these concerns did make their way up the policy ladder in Washington. That year, the CIA suspected the mujahideen had gotten so many weapons that they were selling the extras to third parties, so they sent CIA deputy director of operations John McMahon out to investigate. When he got to Peshawar, McMahon brought together eight different mujahideen from eight different tribes who ran the supply operation and confronted them.

"Finally, I brought up our main concern," said McMahon. "We'd given them enough land mines to mine the whole goddamn country. So I just laid it out. I said, 'We have a feeling that all the weapons we're giving you aren't showing up on the battlefield. What's going on? Are you cashing them in?'"

A tribal chief named Khalis gave McMahon an unexpectedly candid response: "Yes, we are. We do sell some of your weapons. We are doing it for the day when your country decides to abandon us, just as you abandoned Vietnam and everyone else you deal with."[51]

For all that, Washington actually responded by sending more and more sophisticated weapons. By 1986, the Reagan administration was supplying hundreds of the sought-after Stinger missiles to the mujahideen. The two premises behind the decision were, one, that the transactions would remain secret and, two, that the Islamic rebels would not use them for terrorist activities. Soon enough, however, Reagan's decision was widely reported in the news, and one Republican aide on Capitol Hill pointed out the risks of arming the mujahideen.

"Some of these guys are a lot closer politically, religiously, and philosophically to [Iran's Ayatollah Ruholla] Khomeini than they are to us," the aide said. "There is concern that one of these guys could show up in Rome aiming a Stinger at a jumbo jet."[52]

Nor was that the only sign that the groundwork was being laid for a national security catastrophe. "In Saudi Arabia I was repeatedly ordered by high-level State Department officials to issue visas to unqualified applicants," Michael Springman, the head of the American visa bureau in Jeddah from 1987 to 1989, told the BBC. "People who had no ties either to Saudi Arabia or to their own country. I complained there. I complained here in Washington to Main State, to the inspector general, and to Diplomatic Security, and I was ignored.

"What I was doing was giving visas to terrorists—recruited by the CIA and Osama bin Laden to come back to the United States for training to be used in the war in Afghanistan against the then Soviets."[53]

This was blowback. "Afghanistan provided a place where these guys could hang out in a subculture for people who wanted to be warriors," says the CIA's Frank Anderson. "It built up the craft of giving money to people like this that undoubtedly continued past when it should have."[54]

By the late eighties, the CIA finally approached the Saudis about whether the Muslims' enthusiasm for the battle was getting out of control. "The Saudis said, 'We can't modulate this,'" recalls Anderson. "They said, 'We can either turn [the flow of money] on—or off.'" Funding for the Afghan War was by this time widespread among prominent Saudi families. In 1988, for example, Khalid Bin Mahfouz was approached for a contribution to the Afghan resistance movement by his close friend, Salem Bin Laden, Osama Bin Laden's eldest brother, and made a donation of approximately $270,000 for Osama's cause in early 1988.*

By February 1989, the last Soviet soldier had left Afghanistan, but the pro-Soviet government continued to hold power in Kabul. On February 12, President Bush approved continuing U.S. military aid to the rebels resisting the Soviet-imposed government in Afghanistan.[55] With the prospect that the puppet government would soon fall, the United States was exuberant. At last, America had learned how to achieve its foreign policy goals without incurring massive casualties or costs. It was an extraordinary bipartisan achievement. Even a decade later one of the principal architects of the policy, Zbigniew Brzezinski, evinced few regrets. "What is most important to the history of the world?" he asked the French weekly the *Nouvel Observateur*. "The Taliban or the collapse of the Soviet empire? Some stirred-up Moslems or the liberation of Central Europe and the end of the Cold War?"[56]

Brzezinski and the Reagan-Bush administration were right about the extraordinary value of supporting the mujahideen. But they had resolved the past by endangering the future. They vastly underesti-

*http://www.binmahfouz.info/faqs_5.html#submenu10. and *Guardian* 31.03.04.

mated the price America would pay in the long run. Thanks to the United States, Osama bin Laden had learned an important lesson: mujahideen warriors fighting for Islam could bring a superpower to its knees.

Not long after he took office in 1989, President Bush was warned about exactly this possibility by someone in a position to know. Displeased that the president continued to support extremist radical Muslims, Pakistani prime minister Benazir Bhutto let him know about the dangers. Arming the mujahideen might initially have been the right thing, she told Bush. But, she explained, "The extremists so emboldened by the United States during the eighties are now exporting their terrorism to other parts of the world to the extent that they use heroin trafficking to pay for their exploits."

It had gone too far, she said. By aligning the United States with the most extremist mujahideen groups, she told him, "You are creating a veritable Frankenstein."[57]

By this time, Bhutto's "Frankenstein" had set up a vast infrastructure capable of financing a global operation for years to follow. At this time not yet a terrorist network, it was becoming known as Al Qaeda—the Base. Osama bin Laden was now seen as a heroic figure in the Afghanistan War. Money poured into his operations from the mosques, the House of Saud itself, Saudi intelligence, the Saudi Red Crescent, the World Muslim League, various princes, and the kingdom's merchant elite.[58]

Perhaps the greatest insight into the origins of Al Qaeda came after a March 19, 2002, raid by Bosnian authorities on the Sarajevo offices of the Benevolence International Foundation, a multimillion-dollar Islamic charity, yielded a computer with a file marked "Tareekh Osama," Arabic for "Osama's History."[59] The contents included the key founding documents of Al Qaeda—including photographs and scanned letters, some in Osama bin Laden's own handwriting. One 1988 document tells how Al Qaeda evolved from the Afghan resistance and how "we took very huge gains from the country's people in Saudi Arabia ... gathering donations in very large amounts."[60]

One document asserted, "The only solution is the continuation of the armed jihad."[61] Notes discussed training with Kalashnikov rifles and showed how the group began to take the battle that had begun in Afghanistan on to Chechnya, Bosnia, Sudan, and Eritrea. An extraordinary network of global terrorism was taking shape.

Another item discovered was a document that bore a verse from the Koran—"And spend for God's cause"—followed by a list of twenty wealthy Saudis known as the Golden Chain and identifying large sums of money in relation to each of them. After each name, the translator had written a second name in parentheses.[62] One of the names, Usama—Osama bin Laden—appeared seven times.

The names on the Golden Chain list were not just wealthy Saudis—they were members of the crème de la crème of the great Saudi industrial and merchant elite.* Among them, they owned sixteen of the hundred biggest Saudi companies,[63] which had more than $85 billion in assets in 2003.[64] There were three billionaire bankers, a former government minister, and leading Saudi merchants and industrialists, including the bin Laden brothers who ran the Saudi Binladin Group.[65]

By the late 1980s, bin Mahfouz had taken over the National Commercial Bank from his father and effectively become the banker for the House of Saud, and the most powerful banker in Saudi Arabia. As a result, over the next decade, his name was on many, many wire transfers to Muslim charities. "He was the banker for the royal family," says Robert Baer, a former CIA case officer in the Middle East, and the author of *Sleeping with the Devil.* "If someone in the royal family ordered money to be transferred, he would have no choice. That's the way the relationship works."[67]

In addition, by then bin Mahfouz had also become the biggest investor in BCCI.[68] Not only did BCCI finance arms deals in both the Afghanistan War and the Iran-Iraq War, it also continued to pursue U.S. political contacts, just as it had lured Bert Lance and Clark Clifford a decade earlier. In 1987, one company in particular that interested some BCCI shareholders was a troubled Texas oil company called Harken Energy. Loaded with debt, having drilled dry hole after dry hole, beset by accounting irregularities, barely subsisting during a period in which the price of oil was plummeting, Harken seemed like a particularly unlikely investment for the Saudis—especially in light of Saudi Arabia's vast oil riches. Nevertheless, Harken had one asset that BCCI truly knew how to appreciate: one of its investors and directors was a forty-one-year-old businessman named George W. Bush.

CHAPTER SEVEN

Friends in High Places

BREEZILY LIKABLE, SEEMINGLY UNCOMPLICATED, George W. Bush once said that the difference between him and his father was that his dad "attended Greenwich Country Day and I went to San Jacinto High School in Midland."[1] He was right.

Dubya, as he was known in Texas, shared much of his father's legacy—Andover, Yale, Texas, and the oil business. But, culturally speaking, he was more of a real Texan than his dad—much more. The elder George Bush was very much at home in the East Coast sanctums of Old Money. By contrast, Dubya was profoundly uncomfortable when he was surrounded by the "intellectual arrogance" he encountered at Yale and Harvard Business School at the height of the counterculture in the sixties and early seventies.

For George H. W. Bush, it was always a stretch to make nice with the Republican Party's powerful Christian right, which, in turn, viewed him as suspect, an interloper who sometimes said the right things but didn't really believe them. By contrast, Dubya was a genuine born-again Christian who had "accepted" Jesus Christ as his personal savior in 1985 and read the Bible and prayed daily. The elder Bush loved the family's summer retreat on Walker's Point in Kennebunkport, Maine, and all that it suggested—golfing, lobster, the rugged Maine shore, and a rich family heritage that was deeply embedded in the Eastern Establishment. By contrast, Dubya's home away from home was not Maine, the Hamptons, or Nantucket, but Crawford, Texas, in the hardscrabble dry plains near Waco. Located right in the middle of Texas's Baptist-dominated Bible Belt, its history was bereft of Yankee railroad barons and the like and was instead studded with Ku Klux Klan marches and incidents such as the FBI assault on David Koresh's Branch Davidians, who became martyrs of the right-wing militia movement.[2] Not exactly a likely oasis of choice for a scion of the East Coast elite.

Finally, Dubya had one political advantage over his father. The elder Bush so embodied the image of a spoiled and privileged son of the Eastern aristocracy that in 1988 when Ann Richards, who was soon to become governor of Texas, delivered her famous sound bite about the elder Bush at the Democratic National Convention, the words resonated throughout the United States and made Richards a national figure. "Poor George," she had drawled, "he can't help it. He was born with a silver foot in his mouth."

By contrast, Dubya cast a figure that could be powerfully evocative of the cowboys who once strode Texas's wide-open spaces. At a time when most Texans lived in air-conditioned suburbs, but still longed for its rich and powerful mythic imagery of wide-open spaces and the Old West, he understood and appealed to rural Texas archetypes that were an amalgam of male-bonding rituals forged on the ranch, in the oil fields, and in the locker room. These were ideals that celebrated the virtues of toughness, self-reliance, and neighborliness, all generously larded with Marlboro Country-type cowboy imagery. At their best, these values were democratic in the true sense of the word, recognizing no social barriers separating the ranch hand from the millionaire. This was in large part a source of Dubya's appeal that enabled him to win support that crossed class barriers.

But the reality was wildly at odds with the imagery. Dubya was still very much a child of privilege himself. He accepted his high station in life so unquestioningly that detractors often said he had been born on third base and thought he had hit a triple. After graduating from Yale, Bush returned to Houston to join the Texas Air National Guard in 1968.[3] In addition to aircraft broker James Bath, Bush's unit consisted of several members of the River Oaks and Houston country clubs, and Lloyd Bentsen III, a son of the Texas senator. According to the *Washington Post,* Bush's political connections helped him get into the unit, a highly sought-after refuge for young men seeking to avoid service in Vietnam. Dubya gained admission to the guard only after

Ben Barnes, the powerful Speaker of the House in Texas, intervened to get him a pilot's slot.[4]

Even after he got into the guard, Bush's stint was marked by controversy. In 1972, orders had required Bush to report to a lieutenant colonel with a Dickensian name, William Turnipseed, in Montgomery, Alabama. But, according to Turnipseed, Bush "never showed up."[5]

In the end, Bush's National Guard record was something less than distinguished—and it created issues that would haunt his electoral future. In 1972, Bush was suspended from flying for "failure to accomplish annual medical examination."[6] As it happened, that was the year drug testing became part of military medical exams, and political opponents later accused Bush of avoiding the exam so as to escape detection of cocaine use.[7]*

During his sojourn at Harvard Business School, Bush made it clear exactly where his heart was. Classmate Marty Kahn's first memory of Bush was "sitting in class and hearing the unmistakable sound of someone spitting tobacco. I turned around and there was George sitting in the back of the room in his [National Guard] bomber jacket spitting in a cup. You have to remember this was Harvard Business School. You just didn't see that kind of thing."[8] Coming as it did during the height of the Vietnam War, in hippie-infested Cambridge, Massachusetts, the East Coast epicenter of the tie-dyed, Birkenstocked, long-haired antiwar movement, chewing tobacco was a defiant fashion statement that loudly proclaimed George W. Bush would have absolutely nothing to do with the counterculture.

If Dubya received favored status in the National Guard as a result of his powerful father, it was nothing compared to the help he got in his business career. In 1977, Bush had decided to follow in his father's

---

*According to Bill Burkett, a former lieutenant colonel in the Texas National Guard, when Bush was governor of Texas and beginning plans to run for the presidency in 2000, his aides visited National Guard headquarters "on numerous occasions" to make sure that public records about his military service squared with his official autobiography's version of his service in the guard. Bush's military records read, somewhat mysteriously, "Not rated for the period 1 May 1972 through 30 April 1973. Report for this period not available for administrative reasons." A website at www.awolbush.com/ offers readers many of the relevant documents.

115

footsteps and moved to Midland, Texas, where his father had started out, to launch his first oil company, Arbusto Energy.

Arbusto, which means "bush" in Spanish, was founded as a one-man outfit that Bush hoped would grow into a company that could drill for oil all over the country. Thanks to help from his uncle Jonathan Bush, a Wall Street financier, and his grandmother Dorothy Bush, Dubya, then thirty-one, put together a $4.7-million partnership consisting largely of relatives and powerful family friends to launch Arbusto. There was venture capitalist William Draper* and Celanese Corporation CEO John Macomber, each of whom would serve as chairman of the Export-Import Bank during the Reagan-Bush era; Prudential Bache CEO George Ball; multimillionaire New York Republican Lewis Lehrman; and George H. W. Bush fund-raiser Russell Reynolds among others.[9] Also among the investors was Dubya's National Guard friend James Bath, who put up $50,000 for 5 percent of the stock.

According to the *Washington Post*, Bush immediately put Arbusto on his résumé to use as a credential in his unsuccessful 1978 congressional race—even though it didn't start operations until March 1979, several months after he lost the election.[10] When it did get going, Arbusto struggled financially, forcing Bush to seek new investors to save the day. In January 1982, just a year after his father had become vice president, Dubya managed to find such an angel, New York investor Philip Uzielli, a Princeton classmate[11] and longtime friend of James Baker's. What was particularly astonishing about Uzielli's participation in Arbusto was the exorbitant price he paid—$1 million in exchange for 10 percent of Bush's tiny company. According to *Time*, the entire company was then worth only $382,000.[12] In other words, Uzielli had paid twenty-six times market value for his share of the company's equity.

Bush rationalized the high price by saying, "There was a lot of romance and a lot of upside in the oil business." But at the time, the international oil market was collapsing, with the price per barrel

*Readers may recall that as head of the Export-Import Bank in 1984, Draper, in response to lobbying from Vice President George H. W. Bush, reversed bank policy and guaranteed loans to Saddam Hussein's Iraq.

plummeting from $38 in 1981 to $11 in 1986.[13] The situation was so bad that Vice President Bush flew to Saudi Arabia to persuade King Fahd that the oil glut had made oil too cheap and was decimating West Texas oil companies.[14] Arbusto continued to drill one dry hole after another. Its name became such a subject of mockery—with detractors derisively emphasizing the second syllable—that Bush changed it to Bush Exploration.

In 1984, in need of more financing, Bush merged Arbusto into another oil company, Spectrum 7. But even that wasn't enough. In the rapidly deflating boomtowns of Houston and Dallas, this was the era of real estate busts, see-through skyscrapers, and so-called glass prairies—gleaming, new skyscrapers built during that boom that were almost entirely empty because of the recession. Banks were folding. Oil giants faced huge layoffs. The prospect for small independent oil companies in West Texas was even worse.[15]

Bush's problem was not just that Spectrum had drilled too many dry wells. As the price of oil fell, even the value of its productive wells plummeted. Investors were nowhere to be seen. In 1985, Spectrum lost $1.6 million. Altogether, it owed more than $3 million,[16] and Bush had little hope of paying it off. "We lost a lot of money," said Philip Uzielli, who had become a director of Spectrum 7. "... Things were terrible. It was dreadful."[17]

By this time, Bush's father, then vice president, was the odds-on favorite to be the next president of the United States. But Dubya, who was about to turn forty, had accomplished almost nothing. One by one, his oil companies in their various incarnations—Arbusto, Bush Exploration, and Spectrum 7—slid toward the brink, even after getting generous help from his father's and James Baker's powerful friends. The normally optimistic Bush was despondent. "I'm all name and no money," he said.[18]

But, in 1986, another savior came to Bush's rescue. A Dallas-based energy firm owned partially by Harvard University and international investor George Soros, Harken Energy, then known as Harken Oil and Gas, gave Bush a spectacular deal and bought his failing company for $2.25 million in stock. Bush got roughly $600,000 out of the deal,[19] a seat on the board, and a consultancy paying between $50,000 and $120,000 a year.[20] Now he didn't even have to work full-time and could help his father pursue the White House, where he was rapidly becoming a trusted adviser to the president.

As for why his benefactors were so generous, Harken founder Phil Kendrick was to the point: "His name was George Bush. That was worth the money they paid him."[21]

"You'd have to be an idiot not to say [that's] impressive," added Alan Quasha, a Harken shareholder.[22]

Meanwhile, Harken had problems. Loaded with debt and a history of drilling dry wells, Harken had almost nothing going for it. In 1989, it lost more than $12 million. The next year, it lost $40 million. Even these losses vastly understated the gravity of Harken's crisis. *New York Times* columnist Paul Krugman has since charged that Harken created a front company that seemed independent but was really under Harken's control solely to concoct phony transactions and to buy some of the firm's assets at high prices—all to falsely inflate revenues.[23] "Mr. Bush profited personally from aggressive accounting identical to recent scams that have shocked the nation," Krugman wrote, referring to the Enron and Arthur Andersen scandals.

Phil Kendrick, who had sold most of his stock but was still a small shareholder, best characterized Harken's incomprehensible business practices. "Their annual reports and press releases get me totally befuddled," he said. "There's been so much promotion, manipulation, and inside deal-making. It's been a fast-numbers game."[24]

And yet, with the Bush name now on its marquee, suddenly all sorts of marvelous things started to happen to Harken—new investments, unexpected sources of financing, serendipitous drilling rights in faraway countries. All thanks to people who now found Harken irresistible—many of them close to BCCI, the Saudi-dominated bank that had political connections all over the world and whose biggest shareholder was Khalid bin Mahfouz. It was a kind of phantom courtship.

Even if Harken had not had its liabilities, for Saudi billionaires, whose wealth came from the biggest oil reserves in the world, investing in Harken was at best truly a case of selling coals to Newcastle, ice to the Eskimos. "Think about it," explains Bush's friend and business partner James Bath. "It doesn't make sense. What we would consider a big oil drill here [in Texas] would be laughable to them."

"You had this terribly complicated dance," recalls a former senior Senate investigator into BCCI. "It was not just that the Saudis used BCCI to buy power. There were people in the United States who saw the opportunity to make scads of money. They weren't exactly raping the system. It was more like consensual sex."

Neither George W. Bush nor Harken, it should be said, had any direct contact of any kind with bin Mahfouz or BCCI. Bin Mahfouz professed no knowledge of any intention to create a special relationship with Bush or Harken[25] and, according to his attorney, "does not recall that the matter of BCCI's relationship with Harken" was brought up at BCCI board meetings or "in any other fashion."[26] Likewise, Harken officials, including George W. Bush, said they were unaware of their new investors' links to BCCI. On paper, there was no relationship whatsoever between the two institutions or their principals.

But like so much of what went on with BCCI, this elaborate dance often took place through convoluted financial transactions and third parties. It was not essential for the key players in this aspect of the Saudi-Bush drama even to know each other to have productive relationships. In fact, for many of the participants, the less they knew the better.

In particular, in later years George W. Bush would very much *not* want to know bin Mahfouz. According to his associates, bin Mahfouz was a moderately devout Muslim who eschewed excess—at least by the standards of Saudi billionaires.[27] That meant that in addition to his Texas properties, he had, or would acquire, a large estate in Buckinghamshire, England, and homes in Jeddah, Cairo, New York, Paris, London, and Cannes.[28] Bin Mahfouz's greatest extravagance was his preferred mode of transportation. He flew his own Boeing 767, a Boeing 737, and in later years, a Bombardier Global Express, one of the hottest ultra-long-range, high-speed business jets on the market.[29] An observer who boarded one of his 767s in 2003 said that $40 million had been spent on the interior to outfit it with gold-plated bathroom fixtures, magnificent wood paneling, a drop-down movie screen with surround sound, and a bedroom with emergency medical equipment.[30]

In decades past, the Saudis had put constraints on the international ambitions of the bin Mahfouz family and National Commercial Bank, in part because Islamic tradition had outlawed the charging of interest. But with petrodollars flooding into the country and the globalization of the financial markets, such antiquated practices no longer made practical business sense. In addition, such strictures might interfere with the kind of political ties the Saudis could create through BCCI, as they had with Bert Lance and Clark Clifford when Jimmy Carter was in the White House.[31]

In 1987, when Vice President George H. W. Bush was positioning himself to succeed Reagan, several people close to BCCI began to approach Harken Energy. One of them was Arkansas investment banker Jackson Stephens, a principal in Little Rock's Stephens, Inc., one of the biggest investment banks outside of Wall Street. Stephens was so politically wired that he had access to the White House from the Carter administration through the Reagan-Bush era and into the Clinton administration. A classmate of Jimmy Carter's at the U.S. Naval Academy, Stephens was also an associate of Bert Lance, the first casualty of the BCCI scandal. But Stephens's political affiliations were not merely Democratic. Though he had been a contributor to Jimmy Carter, Stephens also gave $100,000 to George H. W. Bush's presidential campaign in 1988 and his company put in another $100,000. In addition, his wife, Mary Anne, was Arkansas cochairman of the Bush for President Campaign that year.

In the late seventies, Stephens had suggested to BCCI that it try to take over Washington, D.C.'s biggest bank, First American Bankshares, and he subsequently became a defendant in a suit aimed at preventing the takeover. He was the man who had introduced Bert Lance to BCCI founder Agha Hasan Abedi. His proximity to the corrupt bank notwithstanding, there is no evidence that Stephens was anything but an innocent bystander or a victim in the BCCI scandal.

And so, not long after he joined forces with Harken, George W. Bush found himself in Little Rock with Jackson Stephens, who began to put a rescue plan in motion by raising $25 million from the Union Bank of Switzerland to invest in Harken in exchange for equity. What happened next was reported in a 1991 article by Thomas Petzinger, Peter Truell, and Jill Abramson in the *Wall Street Journal* that detailed the links between BCCI and Harken after George W. Bush became a board member of the struggling oil company.

From the start, the deal Stephens put in play was far-fetched: for one thing, the Union Bank of Switzerland didn't ordinarily put money in small U.S. firms. For another, UBS was linked to BCCI through a joint-venture partnership in a Geneva-based bank.[32]

Before a deal could be finalized, the financing ran into difficulties and fell apart. As a result, still another financier was needed to rescue Harken.[33] This time, Stephens introduced Harken to a new investor, Abdullah Taha Bakhsh, a real estate magnate from Jeddah, whose subsequent injection of capital resulted in his ownership of 17.6 percent of Harken's stock.

A well-known Saudi investor, Bakhsh had been a founding member of the board of Investcorp, the enormous global investment group.[34] Bakhsh had had business dealings with the most prominent people in Saudi Arabia, including members of the Saudi royal family.[35] He also had two ties to BCCI. According to the *Journal*, he had been chairman of the Saudi Finance Co., a holding company partly controlled by BCCI shareholders. In addition, he was well acquainted with bin Mahfouz.[36]

All parties concerned—bin Mahfouz, Bakhsh, and Harken—have denied that Bakhsh's role in Harken had anything to do with BCCI or his relationship to bin Mahfouz.[37] "Mr. Bakhsh was not in any way representing Khalid bin Mahfouz's interests in any investment by Mr. Bakhsh in Harken Energy," says Cherif Sedky.[38]

Certainly other Saudis may have been involved with Bakhsh. They could allow companies such as BCCI to engage indirectly in major transactions for them. "In general, there are two sorts of investment mechanisms that wealthy Saudi businessmen do in the U.S.," says Saudi oil analyst Nawaf Obaid, "those in which they act on their own behalf, and those done on behalf of a group or consortium."[39]

Or, as the 1992 Senate investigation into BCCI put it, BCCI's principal mechanisms for doing business included "shell corporations, bank confidentiality and secrecy havens, layering of corporate structure, front men and nominees, back-to-back financial documentation among BCCI-controlled entities, kickbacks and bribes, intimidation of witnesses, and retention of well-placed insiders to discourage governmental action."[40]

In their group investments, the Saudis at times made the identities of their investors intentionally opaque. When Salem bin Laden and Khalid bin Mahfouz had first come to Houston in the seventies, they had taken on James Bath as their representative to do business deals in which they were not always visible as investors. A knowledgeable Saudi source speculates that the Harken investment may have been part of the same strategy the Saudis had of investing in U.S. companies that were connected to powerful politicians.

Moreover, this serendipitous infusion of capital was not the only windfall for Harken that was tied to BCCI. In January 1990, by which time the elder George Bush had become president, Harken came into another stroke of unexpected good luck. The beleaguered oil company had had no offshore drilling experience whatsoever and had never even drilled outside the borders of the United States. Nevertheless, tiny Harken stunned industry analysts by beating out giant Amoco to win exclusive offshore drilling rights in Bahrain—thanks to yet another BCCI stockholder, the prime minister of Bahrain, Sheikh Khalifa bin Salman al-Khalifa.

By all accounts, George W. Bush was against the Bahrain deal and argued that Harken was too inexperienced to undertake such a costly and sophisticated venture on the other side of the globe.[41] "I thought it was a bad idea," he said, adding that he "had no idea that BCCI figured into Harken's financial dealings."[42]

But because he was the son of the president of the United States, people were lining up to do business with him. In the end, the Harken board found the prospects irresistible. Bush went along with it when the final vote came. Striking oil was never a sure thing, but if Harken got lucky, the payoff could be enormous. "This is an incredible deal, unbelievable for this small company," Houston energy analyst Charles Strain told *Forbes*.[43]

No one in the oil industry doubted that the Bahrain deal happened solely because Bush's father was president. Moreover, George W. Bush was one of its greatest beneficiaries and profited handsomely from it. Harken was hemorrhaging money at the time and the prospects of the Bahrain deal kept the stock price reasonably high. And since George W. had a far more grandiose business deal on his mind, the timing could not have been more fortuitous. On May 17, 1990, Bush attended a special meeting of the Harken board of directors that was called during a crisis. According to internal documents from Harken obtained by the *Boston Globe*, the board was told that Harken was expected to run out of money in just three days.[44]

At the time, one of Harken's biggest investors, the endowment fund of Harvard University, had engineered a plan to stave off bankruptcy by spinning off two of Harken's most troubled divisions.[45]* According to a Harken memo, if the plan did not go through, the company had "no other source of immediate financing."[46]

Five days later, on May 22, Harken issued an announcement about the plan to spin off its divisions, but it expressly stated that terms of the offering were still being formulated. Meanwhile, Bush had taken out a $500,000 loan to buy into the Texas Rangers baseball team—an investment that would later bring him $15 million—and was thinking of selling his Harken stock to pay off the loan. In early June, he asked Harken's general counsel for advice.[47] In response, Bush was given a nine-page memo dated June 15, 1990, and titled "Liability for Insider Trading and Short-Term Swing Profits."

It explicitly cautioned Bush about trading so soon after the meeting the previous month: "The act of trading, particularly if close in time to the receipt of the inside information, is strong evidence that the insider's investment decision was based on the inside information .... The insider should be advised not to sell."[48]

On June 22, just a week after the memo was written, Bush ignored the warnings given to him in it and sold 212,140 shares of stock for

---

*For decades, the most influential person overseeing Harvard's endowment was Robert Stone Jr., an oilman who has been described as "the driving force behind its energy investments." The *Wall Street Journal* reported that it was not clear if the Bush and Stone families were friends, but they were politically aligned and both had been residents of Greenwich, Connecticut, and Houston, Texas. "Mr. Stone was a financial supporter of the senior Mr. Bush when he ran for president in 1979, as were his father, siblings, and executives at his oil and gas company," the *Journal* reported. "Mr. Stone and his wife, Marion, also contributed to the senior Mr. Bush's successful 1988 run."

$848,560. It was just in time: about two months later, Harken announced soaring losses for the second quarter of $23 million. Before the year was out, the stock had plummeted from $4 to $1.25.

Not long afterward, the Securities and Exchange Commission began to consider whether to bring insider-trading charges against Bush. According to a July 1991 SEC memo, Bush declined to turn over many documents to the SEC, claiming they were private correspondence between him and his lawyer. "Bush has produced a small amount of additional documents, which provide little insight as to what Harken nonpublic information he knew and when he knew it," the memo said.[49]

It is not difficult to make a case that the SEC had close ties to the Bushes. At the time, Bush's father was president of the United States. The chairman of the SEC was Richard Breeden, a former lawyer from James Baker's firm, Baker Botts, and a good friend of the Bush family's who had been nominated to the SEC by President George H. W. Bush.[51] In addition, the SEC's general counsel at the time of the investigation was James Doty, another Baker Botts attorney, who had represented George W. Bush earlier when he negotiated to buy an interest in the Texas Rangers.[52] (Doty recused himself from the investigation.) Bush himself was represented in the SEC case by Robert Jordan, who had been law partners with both Doty and Breeden at Baker Botts and who later became George W. Bush's ambassador to Saudi Arabia.[53]

On August 21, 1991, however, the SEC ruled that it would not charge Bush with insider trading. Not until the next day did Bush's attorney finally turn over the memo warning Bush against insider trading.[50] California securities lawyer Michael Aguirre told the *Boston Globe* that he was surprised the SEC did not probe more deeply into the case. "It appears that Mr. Bush had insider information," he said, "that he was told that such insider information could be considered material, [and] was given express warnings about what the consequences could be."

Insider-trading allegations aside, Harken was also under fire because of its ties to BCCI. Criticism went all the way to the Bush White

House, which repeatedly denied that anything underhanded was going on. "There is no conflict of interest, or even the appearance of conflict, in these business arrangements," said presidential press secretary Marlin Fitzwater.[54]

The younger Bush was not the only figure close to the president who appeared to benefit from BCCI. In August 1991, President George H. W. Bush's political director, Ed Rogers, was leaving the White House. Rogers, who had only briefly practiced law, accepted a $600,000 contract to be a lawyer for BCCI's American representative, Sheikh Kamal Adham.[55] Likewise, the deputy manager of the 1992 Bush reelection campaign, James A. Lake, won a lucrative contract as an adviser with another BCCI-associated company.[56] One by one, BCCI hired government officials, federal prosecutors, and Federal Reserve attorneys.*

The elder George Bush deftly deflected charges about BCCI. "I would suggest that the matter is best dealt with by asking [Ed Rogers] what kind of representation he is doing for this sheikh," he told a press conference. "But it has nothing to do, in my view, with the White House."

Yet there is evidence that Saudi favors to Bush interests had begun to pay off. In August 1990, Talat Othman, a Chicago investor of Arab descent who represented the interests of Abdullah Taha Bakhsh on the board of Harken Energy, was granted unusual access to the president and attended White House meetings with him to discuss Middle East policy—at a time of crisis during which the Gulf War was brewing.† The White House, George W. Bush, and Harken all denied that Othman's presence was related to Bakhsh's investment.

---

*According to the Senate investigation, other high-level Washington officials hired by BCCI and its various fronts were a former secretary of defense (Clark Clifford), former senators and congressmen (John Culver, Mike Barnes), former federal prosecutors (Larry Wechsler, Raymond Banoun, and Larry Barcella), a former State Department official (William Rogers), and former Federal Reserve attorneys (Baldwin Tuttle, Jerry Hawke, and Michael Bradfield). In addition, BCCI solicited the help of Henry Kissinger, who chose not to do business with BCCI but made a referral of BCCI to his own lawyers.

†In 2002, during the presidency of George W. Bush, Othman again won access to the White House and met with Secretary of the Treasury Paul O Neill to discuss U.S. government raids on Muslim charities that were allegedly funding terror.

In addition, according to the 1992 Senate BCCI investigation, the Bush Justice Department went to great lengths to block prosecution of BCCI. The Senate probe determined that federal officials repeatedly obstructed congressional and local investigations into BCCI, and for three years thwarted attempts by Manhattan district attorney Robert Morgenthau to obtain critical information about the bank.

The Senate investigation concluded that in 1990 and 1991 the Bush Justice Department, with Assistant Attorney General Robert Mueller* leading the way, consistently put forth the public impression that it was aggressively moving against BCCI. But, in fact, the Senate probe said the Justice Department was actually impeding "the investigations of others through a variety of mechanisms, ranging from not making witnesses available, to not returning telephone calls, to claiming that every aspect of the case was under investigation in a period when little, if anything, was being done."[57]

Specifically, among other charges, the Senate report alleged that a federal prosecutor lied to Morgenthau's office about important material; that federal prosecutors failed to investigate serious allegations that BCCI laundered drug money; and that Justice Department personnel in Washington, Miami, and Tampa actively obstructed and impeded congressional attempts to investigate BCCI in 1990, and this practice continued to some extent until William P. Barr became attorney general in late October 1991.

There were many possible explanations for the Justice Department's failures—bureaucratic rivalries and ineptitude among them. But BCCI had also shown it could undermine the judicial process in many countries. In the media, the *Washington Post, Time,* and many others speculated that that was exactly what was happening in the Bush Justice Department.

Given the international scope of BCCI's crimes, however, even the White House could not keep investigators away from BCCI forever. On July 5, 1991, in Great Britain, the Bank of England finally shut the bank down, letting it collapse under $12 billion of debt, and opening the way for charges in the United States and Europe against people involved with BCCI.

*Mueller became the director of the FBI under President George W. Bush.

On July 1, 1992, Morgenthau indicted bin Mahfouz and others for allegedly having wrongfully obtained $300 million from BCCI depositors. BCCI's Ponzi schemes and unorthodox accounting procedures had created an insolvent bank that had defrauded depositors of between $5 billion and $15 billion. It was the biggest fraud in banking history. In England, the *Observer* described it as "the Gulf sheikhs' version of Robin Hood: robbing the poor to help the rich."[58]

A spokesman for bin Mahfouz says the indictment was "completely unwarranted."[59] Bin Mahfouz immediately resigned his position as chief operating officer of the National Commercial Bank in Saudi Arabia, in order to devote his time to defending himself. To settle the charges against him, in 1993 he jointly agreed with another defendant to pay $225 million in restitution without admission of guilt. As part of the settlement agreement, bin Mahfouz was forbidden to engage in banking in the United States in perpetuity. "It was a very painful experience," bin Mahfouz said, "... I'm glad it's nearly over. You are an example of your family. You have to be strong in front of your customers and in social life, but inside you are personally shattered."

As for BCCI's links to the Bush family, when political opponents suggested something was amiss, as Ann Richards's campaign did in the 1994 Texas gubernatorial race, it often blew up in their faces. "George W. Bush did not take proper precautions in choosing his business partners," says Jason Stanford, a former aide to Ann Richards, who lost the gubernatorial race to Bush. "Your average small-town preacher had better sense. These BCCI guys had some pretty bad criminal problems at the time, so there was a hint of trying to buy favors. Maybe they were hoping for a pardon—who knows?"[60]

However, when the Richards campaign attacked Bush on the issue, they were assailed as conspiracy nuts. "Ann Richards has dragged her campaign into the gutter," said Bush spokeswoman Karen Hughes. "We have no response to silly conspiracy theories."[61]

The strongest critique of the Bush family's relationship with BCCI came from the 1991 *Wall Street Journal.* "An investigation by this paper has not revealed evidence of wrongdoing or influence-peddling by George W. Bush or anyone else connected with Harken," the *Journal* reported. "Yet what does emerge is a complex pattern of personal and financial relationships behind Harken's sudden good fortune.

"The mosaic of BCCI connections surrounding Harken Energy may prove nothing more than how ubiquitous the rogue bank's ties were. But the number of BCCI-connected people who had dealings with Harken—all since George W. Bush came on board—likewise raises the question of whether they mask an effort to cozy up to a presidential son."[62]

With regard to this tantalizing but murky relationship between the Bushes and the Saudis, the *Journal* could not possibly have known two things. One was that BCCI would later be seen by U.S. counterterrorism analysts as one of the key conduits for the growing global terror network. And the other was that George W. Bush would become far more than just another presidential son.

CHAPTER EIGHT

War Drums

GIVEN THAT JAMES BAKER and George H. W. Bush later compared Saddam Hussein to Adolf Hitler, why did they support the Iraqi dictator for more than seven years after they first learned of his atrocities? In his 1995 memoirs, *The Politics of Diplomacy,* a somewhat chagrined James Baker looks back on his years as secretary of state and attempts to explain his role in forging this munificent policy toward such a brutal monster. The strongest argument Baker makes is that initially the United States needed Saddam's Iraq to contain the emerging threat of Iran's Islamic fundamentalism. He also asserts, less persuasively, that Iraq was "a potentially helpful Arab ally" in the Middle East peace process.[1] Even less convincingly, Baker argues that giving Saddam incentives might "stem nuclear proliferation, bring economic benefits, and enhance prospects for Arab-Israeli peace."[2] Finally, Baker cites banal domestic economic and political considerations. The Department of Agriculture loan guarantees to Iraq, he says, were extremely popular with American agricultural interests. If the Bush administration had not supported these programs, Baker adds, "we would surely have been castigated" by Democratic congressmen.

By the late eighties, however, neoconservative Republican policy makers such as Richard Perle and Paul Wolfowitz had begun voicing their discontent with the Bush administration's pro-Saddam policies. A militant hawk sometimes referred to by critics as the Prince of Darkness, Perle was a fellow at the American Enterprise Institute, later chaired the Defense Policy Board, and was often a supporter of policies endorsed by the Likud, Israel's largest right-wing political party. Even during the Iran-Iraq War, Perle had been uncomfortable with supporting Saddam and felt that "the right course immediately after the end of that war would have been to say to Saddam, now we've had enough of you too, and we're not gonna tolerate it."[3]

By the spring of 1990, Saddam Hussein's love affair with the White House had survived ten years of the Reagan-Bush era, but thanks to Saddam's overreaching, Richard Perle was about to get his wish. As a rule, in the Arab world it didn't hurt to lash out at Israel. But on April 2, Saddam made the kind of slip of the tongue of which diplomatic catastrophes are borne, boasting that he had chemical weapons and would use them to "make fire eat up half of Israel."[4] James Baker's State Department immediately issued a statement saying the remarks were "inflammatory, irresponsible, and outrageous."[5]

Saddam was so stunned by the angry reaction from Washington that he promptly got on the phone to King Fahd of Saudi Arabia and demanded that Fahd send someone to Iraq immediately to act as a go-between with the United States. The best man for the job was Fahd's nephew Prince Bandar.[6]

It was the kind of task at which Bandar excelled. By now a specialist in back-channel operations, Bandar had so assiduously cultivated the powers that be in Washington that he lived in a realm far above any other mere "diplomat." Bandar was close to James Baker, National Security Adviser Brent Scowcroft, Secretary of Defense Dick Cheney, and Chairman of the Joint Chiefs of Staff Colin Powell.[7] Between 1984 and 1987, he met or talked to Defense Secretary Caspar Weinberger at least sixty-four times.[8] Colin Powell noted with distress that the Saudi billionaire functioned as if he were a cabinet officer within the Bush administration.[9] Even that was an understatement: Bandar was free from the congressional oversight that constrained cabinet officers.

But his relationship with President Bush was what truly set Bandar apart. During Reagan's first term, Bandar had lunched with Vice President Bush several times a year. In 1985, when Bush was just beginning to be derided as a wimp by the media, Bandar staged a huge party for him with entertainment by singer Roberta Flack.[10] Bandar said he regarded the president "almost like a buddy."[11]

The relationship went both ways. From the administration's point of view, Bandar was important because he was both a confidant of

King Fahd's and had had close contact with Saddam Hussein. As reported by Bob Woodward in *The Commanders,* on April 5, just after Saddam's remarks about Israel, Bandar flew to Iraq in his own private jet. When Bandar sat down with Saddam, the Iraqi dictator insisted that he had been misinterpreted. "I want to assure President Bush and His Majesty King Fahd that I will not attack Israel," he said.[12]

Four days later, Bandar met with Bush in the Oval Office and relayed news of the conversation. Bush was stunned. If Saddam didn't mean to attack Israel, then why had he said it? Even though Bush was skeptical about trusting Saddam, he resumed his generous policies toward Iraq. The Commerce Department tried to stop the flow of U.S. technology to Iraq, but its efforts were stymied by the White House. In May 1990, the Bush administration continued to share military intelligence with Saddam. In July, the White House pushed for additional agricultural loans to Iraq and rebuffed efforts by the Defense and Commerce departments to restrict the export of dual-use technology. And at the end of July 1990, Bush opposed congressional efforts to impose sanctions on Iraq—all in an effort to bring Iraq "into the family of nations."[13] Bush and Saddam had kissed and made up.

Or so it seemed. Meanwhile, the State Department joined Defense and Commerce in becoming increasingly concerned about Saddam. On July 19, State sent a memo to Baker advising stricter controls because Saddam was developing chemical and biological weapons and was working on nuclear weapons. "Iraq has been attempting to obtain items to support these proliferation activities from U.S. exporters, in some cases successfully," said the memo, which was initialed by Baker to acknowledge that he had read it.[14] According to the memo, a review had uncovered seventy-three export licenses for goods sent to Iraq that were "probably proliferation related," including seventeen licenses for bacteria that could be used with biological weapons and computers for chemical and weapons programs.

Finally, Baker changed course. On July 25, he asked Commerce secretary Robert Mosbacher for new controls over exports. "Iraq's extraordinarily aggressive weapons proliferation efforts make this situation urgent," wrote Baker.

That same day, the U.S. ambassador to Iraq, April Glaspie,* was summoned to a rare meeting with Saddam Hussein. For years, Iraq had nursed a grudge with Kuwait concerning the oil-rich border shared by the two countries. Earlier that month, Iraq had accused Kuwait of stealing Iraqi oil and engaging in an "imperialist-Zionist plan" to depress oil prices through overproduction.[15] According to *Al Jumhuriya,* a government-controlled newspaper in Baghdad, Kuwait had seized Iraqi territory and stolen $2.4 billion of oil from disputed oil fields along their border.[16]

On July 27, 1990, Bandar told the administration that Saddam had assured Arab leaders that he was not going to invade Kuwait.[17] But Saddam was lying. By then he had already sent thirty thousand troops to the Kuwaiti border. By July 31, the number had risen to one hundred thousand.[18] On August 1, a CIA assessment reported, "Baghdad almost certainly believes it is justified in taking military action to reclaim its 'stolen' territory and oil rights."[19] The very next day, Iraqi troops invaded Kuwait. By the middle of August, the total number of Iraqi troops in Kuwait and the nearby region was more than two hundred thousand.[20] Worse, the Iraqis were within striking distance of Saudi Arabia. According to Dick Cheney, another forty thousand Iraqi soldiers had been deployed in southern Iraq, near Saudi Arabia.[21]

This was Bush's worst nightmare. To defend the biggest oil fields in the world, he had helped build Saddam into a powerful military force as a bulwark against the Islamic fundamentalist threat. But now Saddam himself had become the threat. Iraq already had enormous oil reserves. If he won the Saudi oil fields as well, with the oil from Iraq, Kuwait, and the Saudis, Saddam would control about 40 percent of the world's known oil reserves.[22] To President Bush, also an oilman, such a prospect was horrifying. Saddam would be able to manipulate

---

*Glaspie was widely criticized for supposedly leaving Saddam with the impression that the United States was giving a green light to his invasion of Kuwait. But Tariq Aziz, who was present at the meeting between Saddam and Glaspie, told ABC-TV's *Good Morning America* that she did nothing of the kind. "No, she didn't do that," said Mr. Aziz. "... We didn't have that false illusion that the United States would watch and would not react severely to any move towards Kuwait." He said Iraq knew before the invasion that there would be serious repercussions, including a harsh American reaction. "We knew that there would be a conflict."

oil prices at will and would have the American economy at his mercy. The Reagan and Bush administrations had created a monster.

Now the Bush team dramatically switched course. On August 5, President Bush stepped off Marine One on the White House lawn and, referring to the Iraqi invasion, uttered the most famous words of his presidency: "This will not stand, this aggression against Kuwait."

The spontaneous remark meant one thing: war.[23] But before that could happen, the United States had to build an international coalition; it had to make sure the Saudis would allow the use of American troops on Saudi soil; and it had to build domestic support. As the United States began to deploy forces to the Middle East, James Baker brought the Soviets on board, worked the United Nations Security Council, and lined up $15 billion each in promises from the Saudis and Kuwait.

That was just the beginning. On November 3, 1990, Baker left Washington and visited twelve countries on three continents over the next three weeks. According to his memoirs, the day after Thanksgiving, "I had set a personal record with a thirty-seven-hour day that took me from Jeddah, Saudi Arabia, to Bogotá, Columbia, to Los Angeles, then home to Housto .... I met personally with all my Security Council counterparts in an intricate process of cajoling, extracting, threatening, and occasionally buying votes." A coalition was coming together.[24]

But Saudi cooperation was still an open question. Close as Bush was to them, he could not be certain what course of action they might take. In fact, Bush and Bandar had wildly different views about Kuwait. Bush's relationship with Kuwait went back thirty years. When he was head of Zapata Off-Shore, he had built Kuwait's first offshore oil well with the approval of the ruling al-Sabah family of Kuwait.[25] The Kuwaitis were his benefactors and he was forever indebted to them. By contrast, Bandar had only contempt for Kuwait, which he derided at every opportunity, even stooping to bathroom humor. When Bandar excused himself to go to the men's room, he was known to say, "I've got to go to Kuwait."[26]

In addition, the royal family was divided. On the one hand, the House of Saud was outraged by Saddam. "[Saddam] doesn't realize that the implications of his actions are upsetting the world order," Fahd told Bush. "He is following Hitler in creating world problems ... I believe nothing will work with Saddam but the use of force."[27] On the other hand, the House of Saud would face fierce opposition from puritanical Islamic clerics if American "infidels" used the holy lands to attack Iraq.[28]

As a result, it was essential that the House of Saud see that Saddam was an imminent threat to their survival. On August 3, Cheney called Bandar to his office for a meeting with Colin Powell, Undersecretary of Defense Paul Wolfowitz, and National Security Council staffer Richard Haass. The purpose was to convince Bandar that Saddam intended to attack the House of Saud as well. Cheney and Powell took out overhead photos that showed three Iraqi divisions moving through Kuwait, one of them directly toward the Saudi border.[29] The other divisions might follow, and Riyadh was just 275 miles away.

When Cheney arrived in Saudi Arabia a few weeks later and asked permission for American troops to use Saudi bases, King Fahd had clearly gotten the message. The Saudis "didn't just want [Saddam] ejected from Kuwait; they wanted him destroyed," said Secretary of State James Baker. "For them, the *only* solution was an American-led war that would annihilate Saddam's military machine once and for all."[30]

Having convinced the House of Saud, the Bush administration still had to win the hearts and minds of Americans. In the United States, one of the most effective lobbyists was Bandar. Again and again, he persuaded even the most unlikely allies in the United States—thanks to an approach that was extraordinarily ecumenical for one of the preeminent custodians of an Islamic theocracy that reviled the West. At a memorable private breakfast in late October 1990, one could enjoy the spectacle of the most prominent Arab in America wooing over the capital's staunchest supporters of Israel, including Representatives Stephen J. Solarz of New York, Tom Lantos of California, and Robert G. Torricelli of New Jersey.[31] Bandar even sent out Christmas cards to influential Washingtonians with the message: "Behold, the angels said: 'O Mary, God giveth thee glad tiding of a Word from Him: his name will be Christ Jesus, the son of Mary, held in honour in this world and the Hereafter and of [the company of] those nearest God."[32]

Winning over the public at large, however, required more convincing. The problem was no matter how evil Saddam may have been, Americans seemed to find him more palatable than Iran's Ayatollah Khomeini, who referred to the United States as the "Great Satan." True, as villains go, Saddam was straight out of a textbook. He had killed hundreds of thousands of Iranians, thousands of his own citizens, used chemical weapons, and committed atrocity after atrocity. But because Saddam had long been an ally of the Reagan and Bush administrations, such heinous crimes had gotten little attention in the media and few Americans thought of him as a dangerous enemy.

Given that Saddam's atrocities against Iran and the Kurds had not stirred the American populace, why should his invasion of Kuwait cause more than a ripple? Few Americans even knew where the tiny emirate was. Even if they did, why should Americans go to war over this particular border dispute? If this was about defending democracy, Kuwait certainly didn't make the cut. Only sixty-five thousand people out of a population of about 2 million were given the privilege of voting—males who could prove Kuwaiti ancestry dating back to 1920.[33] Women had no political rights whatsoever. Executive power was in the hands of the emir, who was chosen by and was a member of the ruling al-Sabah family. Senator Daniel Patrick Moynihan had described Kuwait as "a poisonous enemy of the United States" famous for its "singularly nasty" anti-Semitism.[34]

And since most Americans thought oil was not a good enough reason to go to war, both Bush and Baker floundered for a rationale to put soldiers in harm's way. "If you're [trying] to get me to say that low gasoline prices are worth American lives, it's not something I'm going to say," said Baker.[35]

"The fight isn't about oil," Bush asserted. "The fight is about naked aggression that will not stand."

All of which meant that Americans suddenly had to buy into the notion of Saddam's villainy, even though it was a villainy their government had secretly supported for many years. To that end, the Kuwaiti government swiftly poured millions of dollars into twenty public relations agencies, lobbying groups, and law firms to rally U.S. public opinion against Saddam.[36] On August 11, just nine days after the invasion, Hill & Knowlton agreed to represent Citizens for a Free Kuwait, a front group funded almost entirely by the Kuwaiti government.[37]* The vast majority of the budget of Citizens for a Free Kuwait went to Hill & Knowlton.

Hill & Knowlton was not just the world's largest PR firm, it was also the most politically wired firm in the country. The firm's chairman, Robert Gray, had been a key aide in both of Ronald Reagan's presidential campaigns. On the Democratic side, the firm relied on Vice Chairman Frank Mankiewicz, who had worked for both Robert F. Kennedy and George McGovern.

In this case, however, the most important politico on the Hill & Knowlton staff was the man running its Washington office, Craig Fuller, a friend of President George H. W. Bush's who had served as his chief of staff when Bush was vice president. With Fuller on the Kuwaiti account from day one,[38] Hill & Knowlton went into overdrive, putting 119 executives in twelve offices across the country on it. According to *Second Front,* John R. MacArthur's account of U.S. censorship and propaganda during the Gulf War, Hill & Knowlton organized a Kuwait Information Day on twenty college campuses on September 12. On Sunday, September 23, churches across the country observed a national day of prayer for the embattled emirate. The next day, Americans celebrated Free Kuwait Day. There were tens of thousands of bumper stickers and T-shirts, as well as media kits on Kuwaiti history. Hill & Knowlton's Lew Allison, a former news producer for CBS and NBC, created two dozen video news spots about Kuwait for the evening news.[39] All over the country, there were full-scale press conferences showing torture by the Iraqis. As the end of 1990 approached, the American media, which had largely ignored Saddam's atrocities against Iran and the Kurds when they took place, again and again broadcast reports of his mayhem.

Then, on October 10, Hill & Knowlton was granted a forum to present its evidence against Iraq before the congressional Human Rights Caucus. Their chief witness was a fifteen-year-old Kuwaiti girl who was said to have firsthand knowledge of Iraqi atrocities. She went only by

---

*The Kuwaiti government channeled $11.9 million dollars to Citizens for a Free Kuwait, whose only other funding totaled $17,861.

her first name—Nayirah. Her last name was withheld, presumably in the interests of preventing reprisals against her or her family.[40]

As recounted in *Second Front,* Nayirah cried as she testified about her time as a volunteer at the al-Addan hospital. "While I was there, I saw the Iraqi soldier come into the hospital with guns and go into the room where fifteen babies were in incubators," she said. "They took the babies out of the incubators, took the incubators, and left the babies on the cold floor to die."[41]

After the hearing, Congressman Tom Lantos said that "we have never had the degree of ghoulish and nightmarish horror stories coming from totally credible witnesses that we have at this time." President Bush said that he was happy that the atrocities in Kuwait had been highlighted on CNN.[42] Bush referred to the incubator story at least five more times during the next five weeks.[43] Amnesty International published the story with only a minor qualification, saying that over three hundred premature babies had been left to die.[44] Repeated again and again, it spread quickly across the globe.

As MacArthur pointed out, it is difficult to overstate the significance of the incubator story. Saddam had done many horrible things, but Nayirah's testimony suddenly enabled the press to compare him to Hitler. Here you had a guileless teenage girl's tearful account of a dictator so depraved he would have his soldiers kill innocent babies. Even though he had long supported Saddam, President Bush himself fueled the Hitler analogy, asserting that Saddam's troops had performed "outrageous acts of barbarism .... I don't believe that Adolf Hitler ever participated in anything of that nature."[45]

Over the next three months, the "baby killer" story made its way along the media food chain. It was referred to again and again in speeches by President Bush and Vice President Dan Quayle. It was in the *New York Times* and the *Sunday Times* of London, on CBS and CNN, in *Time,* on the wires and in countless newspapers across the country from the *Los Angeles Times* to the *St. Louis Post-Dispatch.*

But it wasn't true.

While the story was in the news, Middle East Watch, a New York-based human rights organization, was also following up on it, but unlike most of the American press, it did not simply repeat previously published reports without verifying them. It sent an investigator named Aziz Abu-Hamad to hospitals in Kuwait, where he found many doctors who refuted the incubator story. In a January 6, 1991, memo, less than two weeks before the war began. Abu-Hamad noted, "I have yet to come across the name of one family whose premature baby was allegedly thrown out of an incubator." He added that while he could not irrevocably refute the charges about the incubators, he had found many bogus stories about Iraqi atrocities in Kuwait. "Many prominent Kuwaitis had been reported dead before I left for Saudi Arabia, but I was surprised to find them alive and well."[46]

On March 15, 1991, after the Gulf War was over, ABC News's John Martin finally sorted out the mess. In his news report, he quoted Dr. Mohammed Matar, the director of Kuwait's primary health care system, and his wife, Dr. Fayeza Youssef, chief of obstetrics. "No, [the Iraqis] didn't take [the babies] away from their incubator .... To tell the truth ... [there were] no nurses to take care of these babies, and that's why they died."[47]

Martin again specifically asked if Iraqi soldiers had left the babies on the floors to die. "I think this is something just for propaganda," replied Matar. Even Amnesty International, the highly respected human rights organization that had helped publicize the story, now issued a retraction of sorts, asserting that its team had "found no reliable evidence that Iraqi forces had caused the death of babies by removing them or ordering their removal from incubators."[48]

How had such a false but provocative story become part of the conventional wisdom that created the war-frenzied support of the Gulf War? For that, one must go back to the original source of the story, Nayirah, the fifteen-year-old Kuwaiti girl who had testified before Congress. After all, what better source for reporters across the country than congressional testimony, even though it was not under oath, from a tearful teenage girl—even though she declined to give her full name.

But who really was Nayirah? At the time of her testimony, her full name had been kept secret to protect her family from reprisals in occupied Kuwait. But, as John MacArthur revealed a year after the war was over, there was a better reason to keep her name secret. She was the daughter of the Kuwaiti ambassador to the United States, Saud Nasir al-Sabah. "Such a pertinent fact might have led to impertinent demands for proof of Nayirah's whereabouts in August and September of 1990, when she said she witnessed the atrocities, as well as corroboration of her charges," MacArthur wrote.[49]

It is worth adding that Nayirah was not just the ambassador's daughter, but as such was a member of the ruling family of Kuwait, the same family that had granted oil concessions to George H. W. Bush's Zapata Off-Shore company thirty years earlier.

At the same time that Nayirah was telling Americans about Iraqi atrocities, the Pentagon began telling Americans about the looming Iraqi military threat. By mid-September, even before Nayirah's testimony, the Bush administration claimed that 250,000 Iraqi troops were in Kuwait and the surrounding region. But there was compelling evidence that the Iraqi military threat to the Saudis had either been vastly overstated by the United States or that Iraq had withdrawn its troops. In August, a Japanese newspaper approached Peter Zimmerman, a fellow with the U.S. Arms Control and Disarmament Agency, with photos of Kuwait taken by a Soviet commercial satellite company. Zimmerman showed the photos to various other experts and "all of us agreed we couldn't see anything in the way of military activity."[50]

The media, however, was too cautious to run with a story saying that the Pentagon had exaggerated the Iraqi military threat. Nevertheless, ABC News pursued the story and bought a set of five Soviet satellite pictures of eastern Kuwait and southern Iraq, which were taken on September 13, at a time during which the United States asserted that the Iraqi military force was at full strength.[51] According to Zimmerman, the photos were "astounding in their quality."[52] But when he reviewed them with another expert, both of them were shocked not by what they saw, but by what they didn't see. "We turned to each other and we both said, 'There's nothing there,'" said Zimmerman. Nothing suggested an Iraqi military presence anywhere in Kuwait. "In fact," *Newsweek* reported, "all they could see, in crystal-clear detail, was the U.S. buildup in Saudi Arabia."[53] Where were the Iraqi soldiers? The evidence strongly suggested that Cheney's presentation to Prince Bandar six weeks earlier vastly overstated the Iraqi threat—or that the Iraqis had retreated.

ABC News, however, had neglected to obtain a photo showing one thirty-kilometer strip of land in Kuwait. Perhaps all the Iraqi troops were hiding in that sector. But an enterprising reporter in Florida named Jean Heller got her newspaper, the *St. Petersburg Times,* to purchase the missing photo. It too showed no sign of the missing Iraqi troops. "The Pentagon kept saying the bad guys were there, but we don't see anything to indicate an Iraqi force in Kuwait of even twenty percent the size the administration claimed," Zimmerman told Heller.[54]

As the story spread, the Pentagon's PR machine shifted into damage-control mode. A spokesman said the military "sticks by its numbers," then went to work discouraging ABC, CBS, and the *Chicago Tribune* from pursuing the story. ABC News's Mark Brender explained that the network dropped it partly because the photos were inconclusive, but also because there was "a sense that you would be bucking the trend .... If you're going to stick your neck out and say that the number of Iraqi forces may not be as high as the administration is saying, then you better be able to say how many there are."[55]

One of the few major newspapers to suggest that Iraq never really showed up for battle en masse was *Newsday,* which, after the Gulf War was under way, reported that American troops had encountered a "phantom enemy." It noted that most of the huge Iraqi army, which was said to have half a million troops in Kuwait and southern Iraq, simply was nowhere to be seen. In addition, as if foreshadowing the Iraq War of 2003, Saddam Hussein's supposed chemical warfare never materialized.

One senior American commander told a *Newsday* reporter that the information about the Iraqi defenses put out before the war was highly exaggerated. "There was a great disinformation campaign surrounding this war," he said.[56]

Later, after America's overwhelming military superiority quickly defeated Iraq, only one serious criticism of George H. W. Bush's triumphant policy emerged—and that came from within his own administration. Why on earth had he not allowed American troops to march all the way to Baghdad?

In *A World Transformed,* the book he and his national security adviser Brent Scowcroft published in 1998, Bush explained that he allowed Saddam to stay in power because "trying to eliminate Saddam ... would have incurred incalculable human and political costs. Apprehending him was probably impossible .... We would have been forced to occupy Baghdad and, in effect, rule Iraq .... There was no viable 'exit strategy' we could see, violating another of our principles. Furthermore, we had been self-consciously trying to set a pattern for handling aggression in the post-Cold War world. Going in and occupying Iraq, thus unilaterally exceeding the United Nations' mandate, would have destroyed the precedent of international response to aggression that we hoped to establish. Had we gone the invasion route, the United States could conceivably still be an occupying power in a bitterly hostile land."[57]

That response was persuasive, but it did not satisfy everyone, particularly Paul Wolfowitz, the rising young policy maker in the neo-conservative camp who was then undersecretary of defense. In 1992, just after the Gulf War but while Bush was still in office, Wolfowitz oversaw the drafting of a policy statement on America's mission in the post-Cold War era. Called "Defense Planning Guidance," the forty-six-page classified document, which was coauthored by I. Lewis Libby, who later became Vice President Dick Cheney's chief of staff, circulated at high levels in the Pentagon. After it was leaked to the press and met a hostile reaction, the White House ordered Secretary of Defense Dick Cheney to rewrite the highly controversial document. The policy paper was never implemented during the administration of George H. W. Bush, and soon Bill Clinton was in office.

Nevertheless, a decade later, Wolfowitz's original draft became extraordinarily relevant. It outlined several scenarios in which U.S. interests might be threatened, focusing specifically on North Korea and Iraq, where the greatest dangers were the proliferation of weapons of mass destruction, terrorism, and a sudden shock to the global supply of oil. The policy paper also asserted, somewhat patronizingly, that coalitions of the type Bush and Baker had put together for the Gulf War "hold considerable promise," but that in the end they were not necessarily the answer. The United States, Wolfowitz insisted, would have to be prepared to take unilateral military action.[58] Wolfowitz's policies suggested a new sort of militaristic idealism in which preemptive strikes were justifiable if they took out a brutal dictator. If such actions alienated America's longtime allies, he seemed to be saying, so be it. That was the price we must be prepared to pay. As to whether the new policy might commit the United States to enormous costs both in terms of human life and in dollars, or whether it might lead to even greater dangers, Wolfowitz had no answer.

CHAPTER NINE

The Breaking Point

FOR ALL THEIR ANTI-AMERICANISM, even the most militant Islamists agreed that something had to be done about Saddam Hussein, a secular ruler who was seen as bent on destroying Islam. Immediately after Iraq invaded Kuwait in August, one of their leaders went to Riyadh to meet with Defense Minister Prince Sultan and to present him with an alternative way of going after Saddam without having to rely on the U.S. military. That militant leader was Osama bin Laden.

By this time a battle-hardened thirty-three-year-old, bin Laden told Sultan that the kingdom did not have to allow American infidels on Saudi soil to fight Saddam's troops.[1] Fresh from driving the Soviets out of Afghanistan, Osama was ready to take on another superpower. Armed with maps and a detailed ten-page plan, he asserted that his family's construction and engineering equipment could be used to quickly build fortifications.[2] Thanks in part to U.S. support for the Afghanistan campaign, bin Laden already had a global network of Islamic warriors ready to bolster Saudi forces. If the Islamic forces could defeat a true superpower like the Soviet Union, he argued, they could certainly take on Saddam Hussein. As Muslims, Iraqi soldiers could not possibly be deeply committed to someone as secular as Saddam and would not resist the jihad.

Stunned by bin Laden's proposal, Prince Sultan warned Osama that Saddam had four thousand tanks. "There are no caves in Kuwait," he said. "You cannot fight them from the mountains and caves. What will you do when he lobs the missiles at you with chemical and biological weapons?"[3]

"We [will] fight him with faith," bin Laden replied. He said he could lead the fight himself and promised to put together one hundred thousand former warriors from the Afghanistan War.[4] Still devoted to the House of Saud, bin Laden warned the royals that if they allowed U.S. soldiers near the holy mosques of Medina and Mecca, militant Islamists, not just in Saudi Arabia but throughout the entire Muslim world, would not overlook "Riyadh's transgressions of the sacred principles of Islam."[5] In its search for military security, he said, the royal family risked losing its religious legitimacy.

According to one report, for reasons that are unclear, bin Laden left his meeting with Prince Sultan thinking that the House of Saud agreed with him and was going to accept his offer.[6] But soon, he received the news that would transform his life: King Fahd was going to allow U.S. forces into the kingdom.[7]

To bin Laden, this development was "a backbreaking calamity." For decades, the secretive House of Saud had maintained its two different realities. In the West, it proudly paraded its alliance with the United States as evidence of its security and the Saudi entry into the modern world. But within Saudi Arabia, the House of Saud had downplayed any ties to the United States so as not to provoke militant Islamists. Now, however, the double marriage between the two mortal enemies was out in the open. When King Fahd asked the senior Islamic clerics who oversaw the Saudi judiciary to endorse the idea of allowing U.S. troops in Saudi Arabia, at first they refused.[8] Allowing American soldiers on sacred Saudi soil was so abhorrent that it called into question the very legitimacy of the House of Saud as the custodian of Islam. Throughout all of Saudi Arabia, Islamists could talk of nothing else but the schism between the royal family and the ulema.

Meanwhile, on August 7, 1990, the United States began sending the most sophisticated and powerful fighting machine in the history of the world into the ancient desert kingdom of Saudi Arabia. First, there were paratroopers of the 82nd Airborne Division; then F-15 fighter jets and B-52 bombers.[9] The Saudi port town of Khafhi on the Persian Gulf near the Kuwait border was transformed overnight into a bustling garrison. Transport planes laden with soldiers and equipment arrived every ten minutes.

Tens of thousands of American soldiers—blacks, Asians, Christians, Jews, even women—made their way into a tribal, male-dominated

Arab culture that had never seen anything of the like. Soon, the most awesome display of high-tech aerial firepower ever assembled straddled the entire Islamic world from east to west. There were aircraft carrier battle groups in the Indian Ocean and the Red Sea. Radar-dodging Stealth F-117 bombers moved into the area. F-111 bombers headed for Turkey and B-52s to the Indian Ocean island of Diego Garcia, both within striking distance of Iraqi targets. There were F-15 Eagles armed with Sparrow and Sidewinder missiles; the F/A-18 Hornet with missiles, laser-guided bombs, and cluster bombs; the A-10 Thunderbolt and A-6 Intruder ground-attack planes, armed with Hellfire missiles; and the AH-64 Apache missile- and cannon-bearing helicopter.

To Americans, the imminent war had the makings of a patriotic but antiseptic spectacle that carried no more risk than a video game. In addition, the Saudi and American leadership had never been on better terms. When George and Barbara Bush visited American troops in Saudi Arabia during the Thanksgiving holiday in 1990, the *New Yorker* reported, Bush called Bandar, who was in the country at the time. The Bushes were staying in the royal palace, and when Bandar arrived at their quarters, the president told him how much his recently divorced daughter, Dorothy, appreciated the friendship of Bandar's family. Dorothy had been alone at the White House with her children when Princess Haifa, Bandar's wife, invited her and the rest of the family over for Thanksgiving. The gesture so deeply touched the president that he was moved to tears.[10] The first lady began to call him Bandar Bush.

But poignant as the friendship was between Bandar and Bush, within the Arab world at large there was little warmth toward the United States. True, James Baker had forged a coalition that had significant backing from the leadership of the Arab world.[11] But on the so-called Arab "street," the arrival of U.S. troops ripped open bitter wounds within the Islamic world that dated back to the Crusades. As hundreds of thousands of U.S. troops began flooding into Saudi Arabia in August, fundamentalists in Iran called for a boycott of the hajj so long as U.S. forces were in Saudi Arabia.[12] In November, a Saudi F-15 pilot defected to Sudan with his aircraft in protest of the U.S. military presence.[13] A sermon in the Grand Mosque in Mecca by a prominent academic asserted that a U.S. "occupation" of the region was part of a long-range plan. The message was stark: "If Iraq has occupied Kuwait, then America has occupied Saudi Arabia. The real enemy is not Iraq. It is the West."[14] Tape recordings of it circulated throughout the kingdom. For millions of Muslims, the U.S. presence was a humiliation of Islam that called forth visions of invading Christians and Jews.

A rising tide of anti-Americanism and animus against the House of Saud swept through the kingdom. Repeatedly using language that evoked images of the medieval holy war against Islam, bin Laden asserted that King Fahd had "sided with the Jews and Christians" and had committed an "unforgivable sin."[15] "The American government has made the greatest mistake in entering a peninsula that no religion from the non-Muslim states has entered for fourteen centuries," he said. He declared that the arrival of U.S. troops constituted a grave and unprecedented threat to Islam, a Crusader attack that marked "the ascendance of Christian Americans over us and the conquest of our lands."[16] For the first time since the annunciation of the Prophet Muhammad, bin Laden said, the three most sacred places of Islam—Mecca, Medina, and Jerusalem—were "under the open and covert control of non-Muslims."[17]

Still, bin Laden refrained from challenging the House of Saud directly, as many militant Islamists did, and directed his anger toward the United States. He called for a boycott of all American products. "When we buy American goods, we are accomplices in the murder of Palestinians," he said, asserting that American tax dollars ended up funding Israel, which then killed Palestinians.[18] But this was just the beginning. He and his acolytes were prepared to go much further.

Early in the evening of November 5, 1990, in New York City, it became clear exactly how far bin Laden and his associates were prepared to go. Three months had passed since bin Laden's meetings with Prince Sultan and a huge invading armada of American soldiers and matériel had landed in Arab lands, poised for attack. Rabbi Meir Kahane, the fiery founder of the militant Jewish Defense League, was appearing at a meeting at the New York Marriott Hotel on West Forty-ninth Street in Manhattan. Kahane, who referred to Arabs as "dogs" and whose slogan was "Every Jew a .22," had been characterized by author Robert I. Friedman as a "Pied Piper of confused Jewish youth" who had "a knack for convincing youngsters that violence in the name of Greater Israel or Soviet Jewry is heroic in the tradition of the Bible."[19] Elected to the Knesset, the Israeli parliament, in 1984 by advocating the expulsion of all Arabs from Israel, Kahane had subsequently been barred from elective office in Israel after a new law banned parties that had racist platforms. As Kahane took questions from the audience, a man of Arab descent with an odd smile on his face suddenly approached and shot Kahane dead with a silver-plated .357 handgun.[20]

The man who pulled the trigger, El Sayed Nosair, was a thirty-four-year-old New York City air-conditioner repairman originally from Egypt. Nosair was just one of dozens of young Arabs who spent time at the Al-Kifah Refugee Center in Brooklyn, New York,[21] where the CIA had once recruited prospects to join the cause of the mujahideen in the Afghanistan War in the eighties.* It was there that Nosair had become mesmerized by Abdullah Azzam, the hypnotic Islamic orator, scholar, and colleague of bin Laden's who frequently left Peshawar to raise funds in the United States for the mujahideen.[22]

At Nosair's apartment, police discovered bomb-making materials and instruction manuals on special warfare. They also found a list of potential assassination targets, and maps and photos of many of New York's landmarks—including the World Trade Center.[23] Some of the materials tied Nosair to the famous Blind Sheikh from Egypt, Omar Abdel Rahman, who preached jihad against America, and who, it was later revealed, had ordered Nosair to kill Kahane.[24] Nosair, it became clear, stood at the center of an Islamist cell intent on waging war against America.

But thanks to bungling from both the CIA and the FBI, a serious investigation was not in the cards. The Blind Sheikh had been tied to the 1981 assassination of Egyptian president Anwar Sadat, but later in the eighties the CIA saw him as a recruiting tool for the mujahideen and may have protected him so that his shady past did not set off alarms among U.S. authorities.[25] According to Peter Bergen's *Holy*

---

*Despite the testimony of several eyewitnesses who said he pulled the trigger, Nosair was acquitted of shooting Kahane in a verdict that Judge Alvin Schlesinger said was "devoid of logic and common sense." The judge sentenced Nosair to seven and one-third to twenty-two years in jail for shooting two men and trying to hijack a taxi after the murder.

War, Inc., even though the Blind Sheikh was known to be a leader of Egypt's militant Islamic Group, he had been issued a visa in 1987 and again in 1990.[26]

On the night of the Kahane assassination, Edward Norris, a detective with the New York Police Department's Seventeenth Precinct, thought two Arab cabdriver friends of Nosair's might be involved. But after briefly detaining the two men, the police were ordered to release them. "They really were anxious at that time to get on to the press and say, 'We have a murder. We have a gunman. The case is solved. There's no reason to be afraid,'" said John Miller, coauthor, with Michael Stone and Chris Mitchell, of *The Cell*.[27]*

FBI officials also insisted "that Mr. Nosair had acted alone and was not part of a larger conspiracy."[28] Worse, they didn't even bother to examine the contents of Nosair's filing cabinets thoroughly once they took them from the police. When they finally got around to translating the Arabic documents in the files more than two years later[29]—after the 1993 bombing of the World Trade Center—they found that the papers included a sermon urging Muslims to attack America and "blow up their edifices." There were videotapes of the electrifying speeches of Abdullah Azzam.[30] They even discovered a document that appears to be one of the very first bearing the name of bin Laden's new organization: Al Qaeda.

The relevance of that term would, of course, later become clear. But at the time, Kahane's murder appeared to have been an isolated event, an assassination of one extremist by another. America was poised to go to war with Saddam Hussein and was alive with patriotic fervor. When the Gulf War began on January 16, 1991, much of the country stood behind President Bush. Night after night, millions of people were spellbound by the high-tech spectacle on CNN, unaware that Osama bin Laden's jihad against America had begun. In Meir Kahane, Al Qaeda had already claimed its first casualty on American soil.

* * *

*In the late nineties, Miller went to Afghanistan and became one of the few American journalists to interview bin Laden. He opened his conversation with the master terrorist by telling the translator, "For a guy who comes from a family known for building roads, he could sure use a better driveway up this mountain."

The bin Laden family on a 1971 visit to Falun Sweden, where the family did business with Volvo. Osama, who is thought to be the second from the right, was then about fourteen years old.

The magnificent Great Mosque in Mecca, which is visited by 2 million Muslim pilgrims during the hajj each year. Renovated by the Saudi Binladin Group, it was also the site of a violent siege by Islamic militants in 1979 that involved Mahrous bin Laden.

In the mid-seventies, Houston businessman James R. Bath represented the interests of Salem bin Laden and Khalid bin Mahfouz. Bath was also friendly with George W. Bush, his father, James Baker and other prominent Texas politicians.

Shown here during George H. W. Bush's failed 1980 presidential campaign, James Baker and George H. W. Bush had complementary strengths that made them a potent duo. 'They're these big, tall, lanky, hot-as-a-pistol guys with ambition so strong it's like a steel rod sticking out of their heads,' said speechwriter Peggy Noonan. 'But they always make a point not to show it. Steel with an overlay of tennis.'

In 1983 and 1984, Donald Rumsfeld served as presidential envoy to Saddam Hussein's Iraq. He privately assured Iraqi leaders that even though the United States was publicly protesting against Iraq's use of chemical weapons, America's goal of improving relations with Iraq remained undiminished.

Bin Laden, shown here training in Afghanistan in 2001, in a still taken from a video-tape. He was backed by both Saudi Arabia and the United States to lead the 'Afghan Arabs' against the Soviets during the eighties.

Prince Bandar thought of George H. W. Bush as 'a buddy'. Here he meets with President Bush in 1991 after their Gulf War victory.

A devotee of the Dallas Cowboys, Prince Bandar visits Texas Stadium to see his friend team owner Jerry Jones, shown here with quarterback Troy Aikman in 1993.

Former Prime Minister of Great Britain John Major and former President Bush both served the Carlyle Group, the giant private equity firm, in Saudi Arabia. In late January 2000, they met with Saudi businessman Khaled al-Ibrahim, a nephew of King Fahd's, at his palace in Riyadh.

*****PAX Manifest for the B727 trip: LEX to London, England Toda

NAME	DATE OF B	NATIONALITY	PASSPORT No
1— H.R.H. PRINCE AHMED BIN SALMAN BIN ABDULAZIZ	1958	SAUDI	50A
2— AHMAD O.H. ALBIEBI	8 DEC 1961	SAUDI	C 163782
3— HASHIM ABDELMAGID BASHIR	1952	SUDANI	322632
4— ALI BEN MOHANED AOUNI	9 APRIL, 1970	TUNISIENNE	M422989
5— JESUS CALDA	17, APRIL 1946	PHILPINO	22 044436
6— JACK RUSBRIDGE	22, NOV, 1932	BRITISH	740063374
7— SALAH AL —HAMMADI	18, SEPT, 1959	SAUDI	C466336
8— EHAB ABUAGLAH MOHAMMED	1, FEB, 1968	SAUDANI	A 322606
9— AHMAD A.M. ALHAZMI	22 NOV, 1981	SAUDI	B 805019
10— TALAL M.M. ALMEJRAD	10, JUNR, 1983	SAUDI	8513500
11— ANTHONY JHON STAFFORD	4, MARCH, 1946	BRITISH	002220165
12— MOHANED OSMAN AHMED ELMARAZKI	28, JULY, 1939	EGYPT	71296
13— ABOULSALAM A.M. ALHADDAD	6, NOV, 1964	SAUDI	C 364366
14— FAHAD A.A. ALZEID	24, NOV, 1980	SAUDI	C549295
15— H.R.H. PRINCE SULTAN BIN FAHAD BIN SALMAN BIN ABDULAZIZ	1982	SAUDI	406 A

The passenger list drawn up by the Saudi embassy for the flight out of Lexington, Kentucky, en route to London showed Prince Ahmed bin Salman at the top of the list, which included other high-ranking Saudis. Comparable flights have since come to light.

Flight attendants remember Prince Ahmed bin Salman boarding the lavishly customized Boeing 727 in Lexington during the White House-sanctioned evacuation of Saudis that began just after 9/11. In May 2002, his racehorse War Emblem won the Kentucky Derby. During a controversial interrogation, an Al Qaeda operative said Ahmed served as an intermediary between Al Qaeda and the House of Saud and knew in advance that Al Qaeda would attack on 9/11.

Not long afterwards, the prince died in Saudi Arabia of a heart-attack at the age of forty-three.

Campaigning in Tampa, Florida, in March 2000, George W. Bush made an aggressive push to win the Muslim-American vote, courting Islamic militants such as Sami Al-Arian, to the right of Bush. Al-Arian was later arrested on dozens of charges, among them conspiracy to finance an organisation accused of terrorist attacks that killed more than a hundred people. Al-Arian denies the charges and is awaiting trial.

Prince Bandar, shown here at the president's ranch in Crawford, Texas, in August 2002. Bandar was not as close with the younger Bush as he was with Bush senior, yet the prince remained very much a friend of the family.

Counter-terrorism czar Richard Clarke drew up plans to retaliate for Al Qaeda's October 2000 bombing of the USS *Cole*, which killed seventeen American sailors, but the Bush administration never acted on them.

U.S. Navy/Sipa

Robert Tripper/Sipa

After working for George H. W. Bush, Richard Clarke resigned as counter-terrorism czar in February 2003. 'I already don't miss it,' he said later. 'You know that great feeling you get when you stop banging your head against a wall?'

The attack on New York City's World Trade Center, September 11, 2001.

Spencer Platt/Getty Images

As bin Laden's popularity grew, the House of Saud became increasingly threatened by him. At first, Saudi officials warned that they would seize his property and take punitive measures against the Saudi Binladin Group.[31] Soon, relations between bin Laden and the royal family reached the point where he had to leave the country. In April 1991, after the end of the Gulf War, he first traveled to Pakistan[32] and later to Sudan, a paradise for militant fundamentalists ruled by a former member of the Muslim Brotherhood, the Sorbonne-educated Hassan al-Turabi.[33] Arriving with about $30 million from his inheritance, bin Laden launched a series of businesses to provide a cash flow for terrorist operations. There was the Islamic al-Shamal Bank, the al-Hijra construction company, a bakery, a tannery, a cattle-breeding firm, and several other companies.[34] He also built a coalition with the local jihadists.

Having defeated the Soviet Union, the Afghan Arabs saw themselves as triumphant warriors who were now immersed in one international struggle after another. The disintegration of Yugoslavia that year led to the killing of thousands of Bosnian Muslims. Ironically, one of the seminal moments in bin Laden's campaign against the United States would come in reaction against what was probably the most altruistic foreign venture by the administration of George H. W. Bush. In December 1992, U.S. troops landed in Somalia to work with the United Nations humanitarian mission to provide relief in the famine-ravaged country. No U.S. foreign venture was more devoid of ulterior motives. But as bin Laden saw it, "famine relief" was merely a pretext for an American attempt to control not just Somalia, but Sudan, Yemen, and Eritrea—the entire Horn of Africa.[35]

In a rare interview, however, bin Laden denied that he had any plans for a global jihad. "The rubbish of the media and the embassies," he said. "I am a construction engineer and an agriculturalist. If I had training camps here in Sudan, I couldn't possibly do this job."[36] But in fact bin Laden had already decided that Al Qaeda should take on U.S. forces in Saudi Arabia, Yemen, and Somalia.[37]

One by one the attacks began. On December 29, 1992, a bomb exploded in a hotel in Aden, Yemen, where U.S. troops had been staying before going on to Somalia. The U.S. soldiers had left already, and two tourists were killed.[38]

In February 1993, in Jersey City, New Jersey, Ramzi Ahmed

Yousef began assembling a host of restricted chemicals such as lead nitrate, phenol, and methylamine with magnesium, aluminum, ferric oxide, and nitric acid into a fifteen-hundred-pound bomb.[39] On February 26, Yousef, who was said to have been a houseguest of Osama bin Laden's in Pakistan,[40] and Ismail Najim, an associate who had flown up from Texas to take part in the operation, drove a rented white Ford Econoline van to the World Trade Center and parked it in the B-2 level of the underground garage.[41]

At 12:17 p.m., the device exploded. It killed six people and injured more than a thousand others, but failed to accomplish its intended mission of knocking down both of the Twin Towers. The terrorist cell behind the bombing included Kahane's assassin El Sayed Nosair* and his accomplices, Mohammed Salameh and Mahmoud Abouhalima—the two men who had briefly been detained by police but then released after the Kahane murder.[42] Also involved was the Blind Sheikh, Omar Abdel Rahman.[43] The Al-Kifah Refugee Center in Brooklyn was not just a hub for the conspirators, it was now the New York outpost of Osama bin Laden and Al Qaeda's operation.[44]

Seven months later, in October 1993, came the episode that inspired the movie *Black Hawk Down*. Relying on Yemenite "Afghan Arabs" who had fought with him against the Soviets, and financing the operation with businesses he owned in Yemen, bin Laden backed the ambush that killed eighteen U.S. Army Rangers who were trying to capture two aides to a Somali warlord. By early 1994, bin Laden had set up at least three Al Qaeda training camps in northern Sudan with Islamic rebel trainees from six countries. In June 1995, bin Laden tried, unsuccessfully, to assassinate Egyptian president Hosni Mubarak.[45]

Now that bin Laden's jihad was under way, even his own family finally took action against him. In February 1994, Bakr bin Laden, who had succeeded Salem as head of the extended bin Laden family, sought to dissociate himself, his family, and the Saudi Binladin Group from his terrorist half brother. He sent a faxed message to the Saudi press that expressed the family's "regret, denunciation, and condemnation of all acts that Osama bin Laden may have committed, which

---

*Astonishingly, Nosair had been acquitted of Kahane's murder in a state trial. Only later was he convicted of the crime in a 1995 federal terrorism case.

we do not condone and which we reject."[46] Two months later, the Saudi government moved to revoke bin Laden's citizenship and freeze his Saudi assets because of his militancy. His passport was seized. In 1994, there was even a botched attempt by the Saudis to assassinate bin Laden.[47]

In many ways, the Saudis appeared to be taking aggressive action against bin Laden and the growing terrorist threat. But mere bureaucratic measures against bin Laden carried little weight against a demographic time bomb that was inexorably ticking away. In the early seventies when it was first awash in petrodollars, the Saudis had imported millions of foreign workers to do low-level jobs that most Saudis thought beneath them. By the mid-nineties, however, immigrants filled nearly 70 percent of all jobs in Saudi Arabia,[48] and unemployment in the kingdom had risen to 25 percent.[49] At the same time, the soaring birthrate meant that a growing population of Saudi youths was joining the labor market with few technical skills or employment options. To strengthen its frayed relationship to the ulema, the House of Saud funded the madrassas, schools with a strong Islamic fundamentalist ideology scattered throughout Muslim countries in the Middle East. The schools taught a new generation that Allah turned Jews and Christians into apes and pigs, that Judgment Day will not come "until the Muslims fight the Jews and kill them." As a result, many Saudi graduates had training that was more appropriate for joining Al Qaeda than for entering the professional world.[50]

At the same time, per capita income in Saudi Arabia had dropped to just one-third of what it had been during the oil boom of the seventies.[51] Even that understated the problem. Since many princes had scores of wives and even more children, the House of Saud itself was growing at a fantastic rate. Now thousands of princes expected huge monthly stipends. Given the grotesque disparity between the wealth of the royal family and the unemployed masses, it was not surprising that increasingly thousands of Saudis saw bin Laden as a powerful voice articulating the anger against the House of Saud and the United States.

The rise of militant Islam was just one factor in shaping a new era in U.S.-Saudi relations. In 1992, Bill Clinton won the presidency from

George H. W. Bush. Bandar took Bush's defeat as a personal loss. The night before the election, at two in the morning, he wrote a letter to Bush expressing his feelings. "You are my friend for life, one of my family. Tomorrow you win either way. If you win, you deserve it, and if you lose you are in good company," he wrote, referring to Winston Churchill's having lost reelection after winning the war.[52]

When the results came in, Bandar was so despondent he told King Fahd that he wanted to resign. "It was like I lost one of my family, dead," he said.[53] But he stayed on and took solace in adding onto his thirty-eight-room home in McLean, Virginia,[54] with one extravagant addition after another to the house. An ardent fan of professional football, Bandar also followed the fortunes of the Dallas Cowboys, who were having an excellent season, and whose owner, Jerry Jones, had hosted Bandar at Cowboys' games.[55]*

*Bandar's relationship with the Dallas Cowboys football team and their head coach was one of the most bizarre but revealing episodes in the Americanization of this sentinel of Wahhabi Islam. Having been trained as a jet fighter pilot in Texas in 1970, Bandar grew to love American football and immediately became a devoted fan of "America's Team," as the Dallas Cowboys were known. After the Cowboys won the Super Bowl in 1993, to cement his close friendship with team owner Jerry Jones, Bandar gave Jones a platinum-and-sterling-silver Dallas Cowboys football helmet in a display box, inscribed, "You said you would do it, and you did it." It was signed, "Bandar."

An independent oilman from Arkansas, Jones no doubt was aware of Bandar's role in the royal House of Saud. Certainly, he also saw that Bandar was close friends with President George H. W. Bush. To the dismay of Cowboys coach Jimmy Johnson, Jones treated Bandar accordingly. At a time when Johnson had led the Cowboys from a 1–15 record to the Super Bowl championship, Jones became so attached to Bandar that he gave the prince the rare privilege of being allowed on the team's sidelines during the game, even though he had as many as thirty bodyguards. Johnson was irate. When Bandar was allowed into the team's locker room as well after the game, that only made matters worse between Jones and his coach.

In December 1992, after the Cowboys fumbled the ball in a game against the Chicago Bears, Coach Johnson looked up to see Bandar and his entourage nearby on the sidelines. Enraged by the distraction, Johnson marched up to the owner's box and erupted at Jones for allowing the Saudi prince to intrude on his turf. A year later, a similar event happened. After beating the Washington Redskins, Johnson closed the locker room and kept both Jones and Prince Bandar waiting outside. When they finally gained entrance, Johnson left as fast as possible. A month later, the Cowboys won their second consecutive Super Bowl with Johnson as coach. But by then the relationship between Johnson and Jones was frayed so badly that Johnson was forced out and resigned—even though he had won two consecutive championships. Jerry... Jones repeatedly denied that his friendship with Bandar had been a factor, but it was widely reported as a major irritant between the two men. In any case, for the Dallas Cowboys, the Jimmy Johnson era was over.

Now that the House of Bush had been remanded to the private sector, the Saudis did not forget its members. Prince Bandar was quite-candid about how the game was played. "If the reputation then builds that the Saudis take care of friends when they leave office," he said, "you'd be surprised how much better friends you have who are just coming into office."[56]

The Saudis were also taking the long view. They reasoned that sooner or later, the Republicans would be back in office and one of the promising sons of George H. W. Bush or his allies might be elevated to power. In the meantime, there was money to be made. As it happened, the Carlyle Group, a new private equity firm in Washington, D.C., was becoming a home away from home for some of the leading figures of the Reagan-Bush era. It was just the kind of place where the Saudis would be able to give them their due.

CHAPTER TEN

Masters of the Universe

TODAY, THE CARLYLE GROUP is such a well-known player in global commerce, boasting a roster of talent studded with world leaders, that it is easy to forget that the company was once merely a prescient idea. On a bright summer afternoon in 2003, David Rubenstein, the creator of that idea, sits behind his desk at 1001 Pennsylvania Avenue in Washington.[1] As founding partner and managing director of Carlyle, one of the world's biggest private equity firms, the fifty-two-year-old Rubenstein works out of an elegant but Spartan office. A scale model of a fancy corporate jet someone is trying to sell him occupies an otherwise barren and nondescript conference table. But it has been left there as an oversight, not to impress. Rubenstein's office is a study in anonymity. It has virtually no personal effects on display—not even the requisite photos of his wife and three children. He inhabits it, and his somewhat rumpled pin-striped suit, as a driven man, an ascetic workaholic. He does not golf. He works. The Carlyle Group is not just his job. It is his life.

Rubenstein is now rich and powerful—though he bristles at such notions—but in some ways he has not changed much since he was a lowly $48,000-a-year domestic policy adviser in Jimmy Carter's White House.[2] Back then, Rubenstein was the subject of one profile after another in which he was consistently characterized as the archetypal Beltway grind who was legendary for putting in eighteen-hour days and subsisting on vending-machine cuisine. He still uses his most famous quote from back then with reporters today: "Machine food is underrated."[3]

But the days of being a modestly-paid, junk-food-ingesting policy wonk are long gone for Rubenstein.[4] For more than a decade, he has been consorting with multibillionaires and world leaders daily. In some measure, geography is metaphor, and as a result Rubenstein is deeply chagrined about the location of Carlyle's Washington offices midway between the White House and the Capitol, close to the center of power of the Western world. The reason is simple. Carlyle, a company that didn't even exist until 1987, in an industry that, in this form at least, is relatively new, has gone from zero to $16 billion in assets under management, making it one of the fastest-growing companies in the world. The people tied to Carlyle as partners, advisers, counselors, or directors of its companies have included the most powerful people in the world: former president George H. W. Bush, former secretary of state James Baker, former prime minister John Major of Great Britain, former secretary of defense Frank Carlucci, and former head of the Office of Management and Budget Richard Darman. There are or have been former heads of state from the Philippines, South Korea, and Thailand, former cabinet officials, ambassadors, heads of government regulatory agencies such as the Securities and Exchange Commission and the Federal Communications Commission, directors of stock exchanges, and the like. Even the forty third president of the United States, George W. Bush, was a director of a Carlyle company at one time.

All of which has led critics to conclude what may seem woefully obvious: Carlyle is spectacularly well-connected politically. Yes, the firm has made lots of smart business decisions, but ultimately it is Carlyle's seemingly unfettered access to power that makes it so distinctive. Carlyle has what everyone wants: the luxury of being able to make decisions—multibillion-dollar decisions, at that—with a reasonable certainty that it knows the outcome of its decisions in advance. If defense companies are on sale at depressed prices, for example, Carlyle knows there is a good chance that it can line up billions of dollars of military contracts for them. As a result, it can parlay its political connections into vast amounts of equity.

That's the conventional wisdom about the Carlyle Group. David Rubenstein abhors it. And when he meets the press, he goes to Herculean lengths to put that conceit to rest. Rubenstein once even invited a *Washington Post* reporter into the wood-paneled den of his Bethesda,

Maryland, home and fairly shouted at him, "We're not that well connected!" At the time, Rubenstein was surrounded by candid photos of himself and his buddies, including one of him on a plane with George W. Bush; another of him with former president George H. W. Bush and his wife, Barbara; another with Mikhail Gorbachev; with Jimmy Carter; and of course, Rubenstein with his close personal friend the Pope.[5]

On this particular day, however, Rubenstein tries a softer sell. "By focusing on Bush, James Baker, and John Major, the press has missed the real story about Carlyle," he says. "They would have you believe that James Baker is sitting in his office calling the chairman of General Motors and saying Carlyle wants you to buy this or buy that. It just doesn't happen that way."

What has really happened and continues to happen merits a chapter somewhere in the history of capitalism and the darker arts of influence peddling. Before Carlyle came along, the so-called revolving door in Washington worked something like this: As every new administration moved into Washington, a coterie of powerful Beltway politicians would move out from the public sector into the private sector, where they cashed in by renting their access to power for $500,000 a year or so as lawyers or lobbyists at huge law firms like Williams & Connolly or Akin Gump Strauss Hauer & Feld, and PR firms like Hill & Knowlton. Everyone did it—Democrats and Republicans alike.

But after laboring over multibillion-dollar defense contracts, certain politicians began to realize that they could do rather better than a mere half million dollars or so a year. Much better. In an era of trillion-dollar federal budgets, half a *million* was chump change, proverbial shoe-shine money. How come the guys on Wall Street were Masters of the Universe when the men on Capitol Hill managed so much more money?

As a result, through Carlyle, the most powerful figures of the Reagan-Bush era decided not just to rent their access to the White House, to the Pentagon, to the regulatory agencies, but to transform it into corporate assets—real equity in publicly held corporations—stocks worth hundreds of millions of dollars. Carlyle was on its way to perfecting the art of what might be called "access capitalism."[6]*

---

*The term *access capitalist* was first used in a 1993 *New Republic* piece by Michael Lewis that was one of the first serious critiques of Carlyle.

To pull it off, Rubenstein first assembled a critical mass of great international icons in the eighties to form a shadow government of sorts that gave it political clout that was unparalleled among investment firms. These politicians who had forged political power out of capital, particularly in the energy and defense sectors, now could reverse the process and transform their political clout into capital.*

Named after the elegant hotel on New York's fashionable Upper East Side, the Carlyle Group began modestly enough in 1987. Its first success was referred to half-jokingly as the Great Eskimo Tax Scam. At the time, an unusual tax loophole allowed companies in Alaska that were owned by Eskimos to sell their losses to other U.S. companies needing tax write-offs. According to the *New Republic,* in less than a year Carlyle "shuffled between $1 billion and $2 billion of dubious Eskimo losses into profitable American companies," taking fees of between $10 million and $20 million.[7]

But Rubenstein had more on his mind than Eskimo tax losses. This was the go-go era of leveraged buyouts, and for a couple of years in the late eighties, he participated in the zeitgeist of the LBO frenzy with mixed results. Ultimately, his real goal was far more grandiose— to create a world-class merchant bank in Washington that could compete with the big Wall Street firms such as the Blackstone Group, Kohlberg Kravis Roberts, and ultimately, even the legendary Goldman Sachs.

As Rubenstein saw it, Carlyle would be different from the flash-and-dash of the eighties leveraged-buyout firms. It would be an institution. For the most part, the LBO firms of that heady era were run by men afflicted with the Master of the Universe Syndrome, men whose egos had become inflated after doing too many $10-billion deals, men who chortled with delight over having their own private Gulf-stream G5 jets, or in being a member of Augusta National, the legendary Georgia golf course where the Masters is played each year.

Moreover, many of these firms were almost completely dependent

---

*Baker became a full partner in Carlyle, but former president George H. W. Bush did not. He was paid by the appearance—at what was reported to be $80,000 to $100,000 per speech. He was allowed to reinvest his earnings in Carlyle funds, though his investments did not end up in companies that do business with the U.S. government.

on two or three superstars—but they tended to disintegrate once those stars left. "Most people who start these firms are essentially deal-doers who are not building institutions that will survive them," says Rubenstein. "So most private equity firms don't outlast the founders. We want to build an institution that would survive. Then, we will have created something significant."[8]

In terms of its distinctive corporate culture, Rubenstein admired the intensely competitive white-shoe firm of Goldman Sachs, whose ethos of sobriety and levelheadedness had helped it avoid some of the excesses of the eighties. But Rubenstein wanted to take Carlyle a step further than Goldman Sachs. His idea was to create a great reputation like Goldman's, a brand, but then to do something Goldman Sachs had never done, to market its brand and put its label on other funds.

It could create real estate, venture-capital, and high-yield funds, then do the same in Europe and Asia. This had been done with mutual funds, but never in the world of private equity, investments for rich clients. Carlyle would be the first. In the end, it assembled an astoundingly diverse international empire consisting of seventy thousand employees at 165 companies worth $16 billion. It created buyout, venture, and real estate funds in Asia, Europe, and North America. It had investments in aerospace and defense, energy and power, telecommunications and media, financial services and technology. Carlyle owned hotels, soft drink companies, trucking, health care, and real estate. There were holdings in Air Cargo, Inc., the Chicago Marriott hotel, Dr Pepper beverages, United Defense, Vought Aircraft, and much, much more. In defense and aerospace alone, it completed twenty-seven transactions worth $5.8 billion.[9]

Carlyle's first step was to hire former government officials who could help the firm make its reputation in sectors that were tied to the federal government. A company brochure put it best: "We invest in niche opportunities created in industries heavily affected by changes in governmental policies."[10] Its investment strategy was to focus "on industries we know and in which we have a competitive advantage," in particular "federally regulated or impacted industries such as aerospace/defense."[11] Later, once the company made its name, it would move into automotive, health care, transportation, technology, and other industries.

One of Carlyle's first big hires, at a time when it was still a tiny firm with about ten people, was Fred Malek.[12] A classic Washington insider, Malek had met the elder George Bush when Bush was a congressman in 1970. They became close when Bush ran the Republican Party during the Watergate scandal.[13] Malek worked as an aide to President Nixon at a time when the paranoid president suspected a Jewish cabal was working against him in the Labor Department. At Nixon's request, he had counted up the number of Jews employed in the Bureau of Labor Statistics. Malek had worked on George H. W. Bush's presidential campaign in 1988 but was forced to resign when the Jew-counting scandal finally became public. Malek then became part owner of the Texas Rangers baseball team with, among others, George W. Bush, who had just sold his interest in Harken Energy.

Malek's relationship with the elder Bush had lasted more than twenty years, and Bush stood by Malek even through the Jew-counting scandal, speaking to him several times a week. Through Malek, Carlyle began to bring in people who had real political connections.

The strategy of bringing in politically connected businessmen didn't always work. In 1989, Carlyle acquired Caterair, an airline catering company.[14] "[Malek] came to me and said, 'Look, there is a guy who would like to be on the board,'" Rubenstein told a group of Los Angeles investors. "'He's kind of down on his luck a bit .... He'll be a good board member and be a loyal vote for the management.'"[15]

Rubenstein was not particularly impressed by Malek's friend, but as a favor, he agreed to put him on the board anyway. The new board member came to meetings for about three years and told a few corny jokes, but showed no interest whatsoever in the company. Finally, Rubenstein confronted him. "I'm not sure this is really for you," he said. "Maybe you should do something else .... You don't know that much about the company."

"I'm getting out of this business anyway," the board member replied. "And I don't really like it that much. So I'm probably going to resign from the board." Rubenstein thanked him and didn't expect to see him again. His name was George W. Bush.[16]*

---

*At the time, Caterair was carrying an enormous amount of debt financing and trying to cope with unexpected changes in the airline industry that had already led to

Carlyle had better luck when another Republican colleague of Malek's came on board, former secretary of defense Frank Carlucci, who had served during the Reagan administration. Carlucci had one of the most wildly mixed reputations in all of Washington. As the *Times* of London put it, he was regarded by some Beltway insiders "as honest, loyal, and extraordinarily efficient ... and by others to be a cunning, devious former CIA operative who was involved in lots of Third World skullduggery."[17] He told the reporter that he had been accused of plotting the 1961 assassination of Patrice Lumumba, who won independence for the Congo; the overthrow of Chilean president Salvador Allende; coups in Brazil and Zanzibar; and numerous other covert actions. Carlucci has denied all the accusations and none have been proven.

A collegiate wrestler at Princeton, class of 1952, with his slight frame and competitive spirit, Carlucci was, in the words of his father, "a tough little monkey." On the Princeton wrestling team, he met Donald Rumsfeld, with whom he forged a longtime friendship. Another classmate was none other than James Baker.[18] Both Carlucci and Rumsfeld went on to become secretaries of defense, Carlucci after having been brought in by Ronald Reagan as assistant to the president for national security affairs to clean up the Iran-contra scandal.

By the time Carlucci joined Carlyle in 1989, the Cold War was drawing to a close and the entire defense industry was contracting rapidly, thereby earning the disfavor of Wall Street. Dozens of large firms were for sale, their stock prices weak. Even Carlyle's critics acknowledge that Carlucci's decision to move into the defense sector at this time was a brilliant piece of contrarian strategy. Still, Carlyle was not the only firm bidding for defense companies, and if a buyout firm really wanted to make money, it had to avoid getting caught up in Wall Street feeding frenzies with lots of bidders jacking up the price. "Get into auctions—that's the way to lose a lot of money," Rubenstein explained.[19]

Fortunately for Carlyle, Carlucci sat on the boards of no fewer than thirty-two companies and organizations[20] and thus enjoyed the inside track over an ordinary executive to reach a CEO interested in selling

---

... more than $263 million in operating losses. As a result of its poor performance, the company became known as Craterair, and when Bush ran for governor of Texas in 1994, he dropped his board membership from his official campaign résumé.

parts of his company. "Frank gave us the credibility to avoid full-scale auctions," Rubenstein says.[21] Thanks to the influential friends of Carlucci, Baker, and Darman, more than 60 percent of Carlyle's transactions through 1998 were handled on a proprietary basis rather than through auctions.[22] Whether it was as a board member, a friend, or a former customer, Carlucci had had a close relationship with many of the companies in question. As Frank Gaffney, a former Defense Department official, put it, "The one thing that people like Frank Carlucci know how to do is to work the system."[23]

And so, over the next decade, with Carlucci leading the way, one by one Carlyle began wolfing down bargains in the defense industry. In 1990, Carlyle bought BDM, a McLean, Virginia, military consulting firm that was run by a close friend of Carlucci's named Earle Williams, for $115 million in cash and $15 million in notes and other securities.[24] In 1992, while still under Carlyle's ownership, BDM bought the Vinnell Corporation, a professional and technical services company that, among other things, trained the seventy-five-thousand-man Saudi Arabian National Guard to protect the royal family and its oil installations.

In August 1992, Carlyle bought Vought Aircraft, which makes parts for the B-2 bomber and the C-17 transport plane, for $215 million. Two months later, Carlyle bought the electronics division of General Dynamics, GDE. Less than a year after that, Carlyle purchased the military electronics division of Phillips, Magnavox, for $400 million. In 1997, it bought United Defense, the enormous manufacturer of combat vehicles, artillery, naval guns, missile launchers, and munitions, for $850 million, and in 2000, Northrop Grumman's jet parts unit.[25]

Carlyle had come from nowhere to become one of the largest defense contractors in the world. By 1993, each of its partners was

---

*Readers may recall that Vinnell was called in to help put down the uprising known as the Mecca Affair in 1979.

†According to Chris Ullman, a spokesman for Carlyle, the firm's most recent evaluation, in 2001, put Carlyle's worth at approximately $3.2 billion. Ullman added that the firm's three founding partners, owned substantially more than 50 percent but less than 75 percent of that. Using the 2001 evaluation, that would mean that the *average*

making $2 million to $3 million a year.[26†] And along the way, David Rubenstein and two other founding partners, Dan D'Aneillo and William Conway, were becoming enormously wealthy.

But that was just the beginning. Now that the Reagan-Bush era had come to an end, David Rubenstein had his eyes on another highly prized acquisition: James A. Baker III. Carlucci had brought great stature to Carlyle, but Baker was in another league altogether. Whether it was heads of state or CEOs, there wasn't a person in the world who would refuse a call from Baker. "I admired Jim Baker," says Rubenstein. "I thought since World War II, he was one of the two most successful people in a nonelective position—the other being Henry Kissinger. He had held three jobs and he had done all of them spectacularly well. I knew he could give us credibility overseas, so we approached him."[27]

As a former White House chief of staff, secretary of the treasury and secretary of state, statesman, and confidant of George H. W. Bush, Baker was assessing what he was going to do for his next act. If he signed on, Carlyle could go global. It could take what it had done in defense and replicate it in other sectors, on other continents.

And so, in early 1993, not long after Baker left office, Rubenstein met him at his home in the exclusive Foxhall section of Washington. Even though Carlyle had come a long way with Carlucci, it was still a small firm with only about twenty-five people. "I'd say Baker was skeptical," Rubenstein recalls. "His attitude was, 'Who are you guys? You're not exactly Goldman Sachs.'"

If Baker was reticent about joining Carlyle, it was not because he was averse to cashing in on the Gulf War. At roughly the same time, in April 1993, he accompanied former president Bush and two of his sons, Marvin and Neil, on a trip to Kuwait. According to an article by Seymour Hersh in the *New Yorker*, Baker stayed in Kuwait for meet-

---

... share for each of the three founding partners would be worth between $533 million and $800 million.

The remaining equity in Carlyle, if divided equally among the twenty other partners, would yield an average of $40 million to $80 million per partner. Ullman points out, however, that the shares are *not* divided equally among the partners, and he notes that Carlyle is highly illiquid.

ings in which he represented Enron, the Houston oil company, which was bidding to rebuild a Kuwaiti power plant.* Even though Enron's bid was characterized as "fatally flawed," the article said, it was taken seriously by the powers that be in Kuwait because of "pressure" from the ruling al-Sabah family to compensate Baker for his services during the Gulf War.[28]

The trip demonstrated the kind of cachet Baker had that an ordinary businessman didn't. To woo the former secretary of state, Rubenstein went first to Richard Darman, who had served as Baker's deputy when Baker was Reagan's chief of staff and at the Treasury Department when Baker was its secretary. After one of the most dazzling non-elective careers in the history of American politics, Baker became one of just seven partners at Carlyle. "I have run five presidential campaigns," he told the *Financial Times*. "I have run the Treasury. I have run the White House twice, and I have run the State Department. I don't want to manage."[29] As usual, Baker took full advantage of his new opportunity: not only did he join Carlyle, but his law firm, Baker Botts, also won Carlyle as a prized client.[30] Darman was so entranced with the possibilities that Carlyle offered that in the end he joined the firm as well.

Carlyle was not the only investment firm to bring in high-powered politicians, of course. In 1988, David Stockman, Ronald Reagan's budget director, had joined the Blackstone Group. Years later, Henry Kissinger joined the firm of Hicks, Muse, Tate & Furst, which itself was closely connected to George W. Bush. But Carlyle was developing the practice of access capitalism into an art form.

Getting James Baker on board had been an extraordinary coup, but in 1995, Rubenstein topped even that by persuading former president George H. W. Bush to join Carlyle as a senior adviser. Later, former prime minister John Major joined as well. For good measure, Carlyle added prominent Democrats such as former Speaker of the House

---

*Marvin Bush was representing a company selling electronic fences to Kuwait, and Neil was selling antipollution equipment to Kuwaiti oil contractors. All parties concerned insisted there was no conflict of interest. But another hero of the Gulf War, General Norman Schwarzkopf, shied away from business with Kuwait that could be characterized as war profiteering. "I told them no," he said. "... American men and women were willing to die in Kuwait. Why should I profit from their sacrifice?"

Tom Foley and Arthur Levitt, former head of both the Securities and Exchange Commission and the American Stock Exchange.[31]*

Rubenstein argues that the role played by these high-profile officials in Carlyle has been wildly exaggerated by the press. Carlyle, he points out, has 320 deal makers—nearly three times as many as the next largest firm. And once they had joined the firm, as Rubenstein tells it, these high-profile statesmen didn't really do that much. "We would have lunches or dinners with prospective investors," he says. "We would talk to investors and Baker would talk about the world and that would be it. He didn't negotiate deals. He would meet with prospective investors and not ask for money."

Likewise, Rubenstein says Bush was not directly involved in fundraising. "Bush's speeches are about what it's like to be a former president, and what it's like to be the father of a president. He doesn't talk about Carlyle or solicit investors."

Of course, just showing up was all that was necessary[†]—particularly when Bush and Baker went to visit the House of Saud in Saudi Arabia on behalf of Carlyle.

Rubenstein takes umbrage when asked about the firm's relationship with the Saudis, which he characterizes as virtually nonexistent. "The implication is that we have so much Saudi business," he says. "Actually, we have no investments in Saudi Arabia and never have."[32]

Maybe. But a look at the many defense companies Carlyle has bought and sold shows that the investment firm has had a long and

---

*Carlyle's formula was so successful that several of its key figures left to start similar investment firms on their own. One of Carlyle's cofounders, Stephen Norris, left the firm to start Appian Group, with former secretary of state Lawrence Eagleburger as an adviser. Fred Malek went on to chair Thayer Capital Partners, and Alton Keel, the former NATO ambassador, left Carlyle to start Atlantic Partners.

†Carlyle also had an advantage over its rivals when it came to pitching portfolio managers from state funds—given that two governors were members of the Bush family. In March 1995, the University of Texas Board of Regents voted to invest $10 million in one of the Carlyle Group's funds, Carlyle Partners II, at a time when George W. Bush was the governor of Texas and had direct power over the board. In addition, the Florida State Board of Administration had placed a $200-million investment in Carlyle that had begun before Jeb Bush became governor of Florida, a relationship that continued during his administration.

lucrative history with the Saudis. The Carlyle Group was not just the most prominent outpost for Bush and his allies in the private sector, it was also where the House of Saud and the House of Bush *really* did business.

Carlyle's first major transaction with the Saudis took place in 1991 when Fred Malek steered Prince Al-Waleed bin Talal, a flamboyant thirty-five-year-old Saudi multibillionaire,[33]* to the firm for a deal that would enable him to become the largest individual shareholder in Citicorp, which had seen a sharp fall in its stock price. At the time, Carlyle's partners said they were selected by Al-Waleed because they knew the right people in the right places. Suddenly, Carlyle, a nonentity compared to the huge Wall Street firms, had a name. "Little-Known Carlyle Scores Big," read the headline in the *New York Times*.[34]

Al-Waleed's investment would prove enormously profitable. By 1998, his $590 million in stock was worth as much as $7 billion.[35] Soon, the amity between the House of Saud and Carlyle became a two-way street. In bringing together Baker, Darman, Carlucci, and later, former president Bush, Rubenstein had reassembled the team that had helped set up the AWACS deal with Bechtel and Saudi Arabia in the early days of the Reagan-Bush era. A decade earlier they had turned on the spigot for tens of billions of dollars of arms sales to the Saudis.

Carlyle's companies still had to compete with rivals for Saudi defense contracts, but now they had extraordinary advantages. In addition to its familiarity with the corridors of power, Carlyle's trump

---

*Shortly after 9/11, Al-Waleed offered to give $10 million to the World Trade Center victims' fund, but his gift was rejected by New York mayor Rudy Giuliani when Al-Waleed suggested the United States reexamine its policy toward the Palestinians.

Al-Waleed had also been the subject of an earlier debacle. After taking his huge position with Citicorp, of which Diners Club was a subsidiary, he distributed Diners Club credit cards to his relatives, which is to say, the House of Saud. According to *The Rise, Corruption and Coming Fall of the House of Saud*, by Said K. Aburish, a few months later Diners Club was faced with $30 million in charges it refused to honor. The reason was typical of the thinking of the House of Saud, asserted Aburish, in that "the recipients proceeded to use [the credit cards] without knowing that they had to pay for their purchases." As a result, the Diners Club ceased to operate in the kingdom of Saudi Arabia.

card was that it could offer members of the royal family or other wealthy Saudis equity in the Carlyle funds that owned defense companies. That way, the Saudis could share in the profits instead of seeing the money leave the kingdom to go to the Bechtels of the world or to rival defense companies. "They knew that the Saudis were tired of relying on foreigners and having all their money leave the country," says an American oil executive with ties to the Saudi royal family. "That's where Carlyle made its claim to fame."[36]*

As world leaders who had defended the Saudis during the Gulf War, Bush, Baker, and Major were soon becoming star rainmakers for Carlyle, and the firm's practices allowed them to do so without sullying their hands by asking for money directly. On several occasions, Bush, Baker, and Major flew to Saudi Arabia on behalf of Carlyle to meet with and speak before members of the royal family and wealthy merchants such as the bin Ladens and the bin Mahfouzes.[37] "Carlyle wanted to open up doors," one observer told the *Financial Times,* "and they bring in Bush and Major, who saved the Saudis' ass in the Gulf War. If you got these guys coming in ... those companies are going to have it pretty good."[38]

As elsewhere, it was standard procedure for former president Bush to give speeches before potential investors.[39] After Bush's speeches, in which he never mentioned investing in Carlyle, CEO David Rubenstein and his fund-raising team went in for the money. The Saudis could not have been more receptive.

According to a source close to the Saudi government, the royal family viewed investing in the Carlyle Group as a way to show their deep gratitude to President Bush for defending the Saudis in the Gulf War. "George Bush or James Baker would meet with all the big guys in the royal family," the source says. "Indirectly, the message was, 'I'd appreciate it if you put some money in the Carlyle Group.'" From the Saudi point of view, the source adds, "There is nothing wrong with this. You are basically marketing the relationship you have developed."[40]

---

*The Carlyle Group also participated in what was called the Economic Offset Program, through which American defense companies selling arms to the Saudis gave back some of their revenues through contracts to Saudi businesses, many of which were connected to the House of Saud.

And so Carlyle became the vehicle through which the highest officials of the Reagan-Bush era reaped their rewards. Prince Bandar himself, the *Washington Post* reported, was among those who invested.[41] In 1995, the bin Ladens joined in, investing $2 million in the Carlyle Partners II Fund, a relatively small sum that was widely reported to be part of a larger package. And according to Cherif Sedky, Abdulrahman and Sultan bin Mahfouz, two sons of Khalid bin Mahfouz's, became investors that year as well by making an investment "in the neighborhood of $30 million."[42]* Carlyle put a first cousin of the bin Mahfouzes, a Saudi investment manager named Sami Ba'arma who oversaw their finances, on one of its boards.[43]

Now that key Saudis, who had the blessing of the royal family, shared in the profits, it was not difficult for Carlyle's defense companies to win contracts in Saudi Arabia. In the wake of the 1991 Gulf War, while under Carlyle ownership, defense contractor BDM won contracts for technical support services for the Royal Saudi Air Force[44] and computer systems in Kuwait.[45] In 1993, BDM opened an office in Riyadh and expanded its presence to support its growing interests in the kingdom.[46] In 1994, it won lucrative new contracts to provide technical and logistics support to the Saudi Air Force.[47]

In 1995, after a visit to the kingdom by Carlucci, Vinnell won a $163-million contract to modernize the Saudi Arabian National Guard.[48] According to Associated Press accounts, under a new contract with the Saudis, Vinnell, which was serving as part of the personal bodyguard unit for Crown Prince Abdullah bin Abdul Aziz, the designated heir to King Fahd, agreed to "share the proceeds, taking on a brother-in-law of the crown prince as a joint-venture partner. Saudi Arabia's princes often make government contracts a family affair."[49] In July 1995, BDM announced its earnings per share had increased 46 percent, in large measure due to the company's expansion in Saudi Arabia.[50] In all, BDM alone had more than $5 billion in contracts with the Saudis over two decades.[51]

---

*The Carlyle Group categorically denied that Prince Bandar or the bin Mahfouz family ever invested in Carlyle. When apprised of Carlyle's denial, Cherif Sedky stood by his original statement. "I assume that Carlyle has records of investments from somebody on the bin Mahfouz side, whether it is with Sami Ba'arma as a nominee or someone else," he said, in an e-mail to the author.

In 1994, the Saudis spent $6 billion on fifty U.S.-made commercial airliners, the tail sections of which were made by Carlyle's Vought Aircraft.[52] United Defense, which Carlyle had bought in 1997, quietly operated joint ventures in Saudi Arabia.[53] Among many other items, United Defense manufactured the Bradley Fighting Vehicle, which forms the core of American mechanized forces, two thousand of which were used in the 1991 Gulf War.* Through a joint venture with the Saudi government, United Defense provided training and maintenance for the Bradleys that were purchased by the Royal Saudi Land Forces after the Gulf War.[54]

As a private equity firm, Carlyle's goal was not long-term profits for the companies it acquired. Rather, its strategy was to buy companies cheaply, rebuild them to the highest levels of profitability possible, and sell them within three to five years—at huge margins. Thanks in large part to the Saudi contracts, its defense portfolio performed handsomely. When they were sold off, the defense deals Carlucci had brought in to the firm reaped some $2 billion in profits.[55] This for a company that, according to Rubenstein, had no investments in Saudi Arabia.

---

*United Defense also manufactured another weapons system named, astonishingly enough, the Crusader, as if they were oblivious to the implications of sending Crusaders into battle in the Islamic world. Given that United Defense had made billions of dollars selling tanks to the Saudis, it was not exactly a wise marketing ploy.

CHAPTER ELEVEN

A House Divided

LUCRATIVE AS THE HOUSE of Bush's relationship was with the Saudis through Carlyle, it did not come without a price. After all, the ruling Saudis were still the custodians of Wahhabi Islam, and now its most militant adherents, led by Osama bin Laden, were on the warpath. At precisely 11:30 a.m. on November 13, 1995, just before the midday call to prayers in Riyadh, a car bomb exploded outside the offices housing the Military Cooperation Program, a nondescript structure just off Thirty Street, which has been described as Riyadh's answer to Rodeo Drive.[1] The explosion killed seven people—five of them Americans—and wounded sixty others, among them several American advisers with Vinnell, the mysterious military consulting firm that trained the Saudi Arabian National Guard (SANG). The rather anonymous-looking building was staffed in part by nonuniformed Americans and its offices were shared by SANG and Vinnell.

The bombing could not definitively be pinned on bin Laden, but his fingerprints were everywhere. The techniques behind it—a powerful car bomb with smaller antipersonnel devices, the types of fuses and explosives—were identical to those used in his terrorist training camps in Sudan and in Pakistan.[2] Bin Laden himself described the attack as "praiseworthy terrorism."[3] Several militant Islamic fundamentalist groups—apparently using bogus names—claimed credit for it and cited him as their major influence.

In striking their most serious blow against the House of Saud since the Mecca Affair in 1979, militant Islamists had hit a target of extraordinary symbolic value—an American-staffed, private military facility at the heart of the supposedly impregnable al-Saud family, a building that represented the ties between the House of Saud and its mighty American defenders. And in addition, knowingly or not, the bombers had attacked a company linked to George H. W. Bush and James Baker, who had sent the infidel Americans to Saudi Arabia in the first place.

In response to a terrorist attack so pregnant with meaning, both the House of Saud and the House of Bush took the same course of action: they acted as if it had no significance whatsoever. Prince Bandar categorically declared that Saudi "dissidents did not cause the car bombing."[4] Later, he explained, "Islamic radicals are very, very small and looked upon in this country as outcasts .... Islamic extremists are not a threat to the stability of the country."[5] Likewise *al-Hayah*, a Saudi publication owned by another son of Prince Sultan, Khalid bin Sultan, and something of a mouthpiece for the defense minister, asserted, "No one believes that the blast has internal connotations."[6]

The House of Bush took the same tack. In an appearance on CBS's *This Morning*, James Baker blandly told newscaster Paula Zahn, "You see a lot of terrorism in that part of the world, but very little of it in Saudi Arabia .... We'll just have to wait and see who's responsible."[7] Baker was interviewed because of his weighty experience in the Middle East. But strikingly, in his CBS appearance, he was not identified as a partner in Carlyle, which owned Vinnell's parent company, BDM. Nor did he acknowledge any relationship to the employees of company who had been bombed. Likewise, Carlyle itself refrained from issuing a statement or an expression of condolences to the families of the victims, even though several of Vinnell's employees had been wounded in the attack.[8] Carlyle's companies had billions of dollars in business with the Saudis. Its interests were best served by keeping a low profile. Discretion was the order of the day.

The Clinton administration, however, did not have the luxury of ignoring the Riyadh bombing. For nearly two decades, America had quietly served as the military guardian of Wahhabi Islam. But how could that protection continue now that the more militant neo-Wahhabis had declared war on America?

In fact, the Clinton administration's fight against terrorism had actually begun even before the Riyadh bombing. In June 1995, Clinton signed a presidential directive reorganizing the management of federal agencies in the event of a terrorist attack.[9] In October, he ordered the Departments of Justice, Treasury, and State, the CIA, and the National Security Council to integrate their efforts against money laundering for terrorists.[10] And immediately after the attack in Riyadh, President Clinton sent a dozen FBI agents to Saudi Arabia and insisted on being informed of the investigation into "this hideous act."[11]

Initially, Clinton counterterrorism officials naively saw bin Laden as merely a financier of terror.[12] "At first we thought that by watching him we would find out who the real bad guys were, because they would be coming to him for money," says Steven Simon, the senior director for transnational threats on the National Security Council in the Clinton administration.[13]

But the attacks escalated. Just six days after the Riyadh bombing, on November 19, 1995, the Egyptian embassy in Pakistan was bombed, killing sixteen people and wounding sixty.[14] The bombing was said to have been the handiwork of bin Laden's Egyptian colleague Ayman al-Zawahiri. A year earlier, Pakistani prime minister Benazir Bhutto had extradited Ramzi Yousef, a conspirator in the 1993 World Trade Center bombing, and more than a dozen Egyptian militants, to the United States and Egypt respectively.[15] Authorities believe that Bhutto's campaign against terrorism was the motive behind the bombing.

On June 25, 1996, a truck bomb with five thousand pounds of explosives rocked the Khobar Towers military housing complex in Dharhan, Saudi Arabia, killing dozens of people, including nineteen American soldiers, and wounding more than five hundred others. The blast left a crater thirty-five feet deep and eighty-five feet across. Again, bin Laden was suspected.[16]*

Soon the Clinton administration realized that bin Laden had radically redefined the way terrorism worked. He was not just underwriting bombings, he was also running huge training camps for terrorists and had set up a network to finance them. With his Al

---

*By this time, the extended bin Laden family clearly had interests on both sides of the terrorist wars. The family profited from the attacks when the House of Saud gave the Saudi Binladin Group a $150-million contract to rebuild the Khobar Towers facility.

Qaeda operatives, he could ship massive quantities of arms across international borders and use suicide bombers to engage in sophisticated feats of asymmetrical warfare. He was even trying to obtain materials for nuclear weapons and to develop chemical arms.[17] Moreover, he and his network embodied a new, transnational entity, an Islamic fundamentalist army that was state-free. With bin Laden in the saddle, no longer were terrorists dependent on state sponsors. In Sudan, and later in Afghanistan, it was he who helped out the government financially—not the other way around.

As a result, the administration's approach to fighting terrorism changed dramatically. "Clinton immediately understood the transnational nature of terrorism," says Will Wechsler, who served as director for transnational threats on Clinton's National Security Council.[18] The CIA, which heretofore had focused solely on a country-by-country approach to terrorism, created its first "virtual" station, the UBL* station, targeting Osama bin Laden and Al Qaeda.[19] Richard Clarke, a career civil servant with a rare facility for navigating difficult bureaucracies, was appointed chairman of the Coordinating Sub-group (CSG) to centralize control of various interagency groups—in effect becoming the nation's first counterterrorism czar. National Security Council "threat" meetings were held three times a week. Clinton put billions into stockpiling antidotes and vaccines against a possible bioterrorism attack.

In early 1996, the Clinton administration pulled the U.S. embassy staff out of Sudan and urged all other Americans to leave the country. It demanded that the Sudanese turn over information on bin Laden's finances, give it access to terrorist training camps, and that the Sudanese expel bin Laden. Conservative critics often attack the Clinton administration for missing an opportunity to capture bin Laden when the Sudanese allegedly offered to turn the terrorist over to the United States in March 1996. But in fact, the Sudanese had offered to send him back to Saudi Arabia, not to the United States. However, as Daniel Benjamin and Steven Simon, both of whom served on Clinton's National Security Council, report in *The Age of Sacred Terror*, there was absolutely no likelihood that the Saudis would take him. "Riyadh

*UBL = Usama (Osama) Bin Laden.

had stripped bin Laden of his citizenship in 1994 for a reason. It would do everything it could to keep him out of the kingdom, where he would have become a magnet for opponents of the monarch. As the scion of one of Saudi Arabia's wealthiest clans, bin Laden was untouchable. U.S. officials approached the Saudis, but were turned down cold .... The issue came up again several times over the next few years, but the kingdom's aversion to taking custody of bin Laden remained a stumbling block."[20] Bin Laden ended up leaving Sudan in 1996 for Afghanistan, where the Taliban served as his host.

But Clinton was up against more than just Osama bin Laden. At times, partisan resistance from Republicans and Saudi Arabia's lack of cooperation thwarted crucial counterterrorism measures. An early example was the administration's bill to bar foreign countries and banks from U.S. financial markets unless they cooperated with investigations into money laundering. The legislation was bitterly opposed by the banking industry, which objected to the new constraints it would impose on financial institutions, and as a result it was killed by the chairman of the Senate Banking Committee, Phil Gramm, a Republican from Texas, who called the counterterrorism efforts "totalitarian."[21] The right-wing Gramm added that he killed the bill because he was a "civil libertarian," a label that was wildly incongruous with his political history.

Worse, Clinton never had the warm relationship with the Saudis that Bush enjoyed, especially once he began pressuring them to clamp down on terrorism.[22]* Wary of having a visible American presence on

---

*The Saudi-Clinton relationship began with, and was typified by, a halfhearted, last-minute attempt by Prince Bandar to win over Clinton even before he entered the White House. In 1989, Clinton, then the governor of Arkansas, tried to help the University of Arkansas raise $23 million to launch a Middle East studies program and approached Prince Turki, who had been a classmate of his at Georgetown University. Turki came up with $3 million. But that still left $20 million, so in 1991 Clinton approached Prince Bandar.

However, at the time Bandar was preoccupied with the Gulf War and twice canceled appointments with the little-known Arkansas governor. At a third appointment, Bandar saw Clinton, but gave him short shrift, and for two years there was no response to Clinton's request. Bandar had other things on his mind. Then, suddenly, in the summer of 1992, Clinton emerged as the Democratic presidential nominee. As

the streets of Riyadh after the November 1995 bombing, the Saudis conducted their investigation behind closed doors. Five months later, they announced that four suspects had been arrested. But before American authorities could interrogate them, the Saudis beheaded the four men.[23]

After the Khobar Towers bombing in 1996, Clinton's national security adviser, Sandy Berger, repeatedly met with Prince Bandar to press for better Saudi cooperation with the FBI.[24] But the Saudis still refused to allow the FBI access to the suspects or relevant materials and tried to blame Iran for the bombing. Berger got nowhere. According to Benjamin and Simon, Bandar's unending evasions were so frustrating that Berger described them as *"Groundhog Day"* rituals, a reference to the Bill Murray movie in which one day repeats itself endlessly.

At the same time Prince Bandar was stalling Berger, however, he had secretly established a back channel to FBI director Louis Freeh. A 1993 Clinton appointee, Freeh had never enjoyed a good relationship with the White House, partly because of the bureau's disastrous failure in counterterrorism.[25] According to Benjamin and Simon, Bandar eagerly exploited Freeh's well-known antipathy toward Clinton to "undercut U.S. efforts to pursue the investigation."[26]

Notwithstanding Berger's repeated efforts to get Saudi help, Bandar told Freeh again and again that the White House had absolutely no interest in the investigation whatsoever. But President Clinton kept after the Saudis. When he met with Saudi Crown Prince Abdullah in 1998,* Clinton warned Abdullah that Saudi-American relations would suffer if the Saudis did not cooperate on the Khobar Towers investigation.[27] Nevertheless, Bandar continued to tell Freeh that he was the only one in Washington who cared about the Americans who had died in Khobar Towers.

... the economy soured, incumbent George H. W. Bush began plummeting in the polls. In October, just a few weeks before Clinton won the presidency, Bandar got word that the $20-million request had been approved.

*King Fahd collapsed in August 1998, and as his health deteriorated, Crown Prince Abdullah, already Fahd's designated heir, gradually became the de facto ruler of Saudi Arabia.

In response, Freeh did something highly irregular. He reached out to former president Bush, knowing full well how Bush was revered by the Saudis, and asked Bush to be his secret emissary to get the Saudis to cooperate with the investigation.[28] Later, Bandar invited Freeh to his estate in northern Virginia and told him the FBI would be allowed to watch through a one-way mirror while Saudis interrogated the suspects. According to Elsa Walsh of the *New Yorker,* Freeh credited this sudden breakthrough not to the Clinton administration's efforts, but to former president George H. W. Bush.[29]

Whether it was Bush's phone call or pressure from Clinton that actually triggered the Saudi cooperation is not entirely clear. But one thing was certain: the House of Saud preferred Bush, not Clinton, in part because the Democratic administration was violating the unwritten rule about Saudi-American relations: Don't ask any questions about what really goes on in Saudi Arabia.[30]

As subsequent events and revelations have made clear, the Saudis had reason to fear the inquiries of the Clinton administration. There was a lot to hide. In the eighties, the House of Saud had encouraged donations to charities that funneled tens of millions of dollars to bin Laden's Afghan Arabs during the Afghanistan War. But over the years, as Al Qaeda evolved from Afghan Arab freedom fighters into sophisticated anti-American terrorists, Osama bin Laden had effectively hijacked countless millions to fund terrorism. As a report sponsored by the Council on Foreign Relations later put it, "These widely unregulated, seldom audited, and generally undocumented practices have allowed unscrupulous actors such as Al Qaeda to access huge sums of money over the years."[31]

The funds regularly flowed through Saudi Arabia's biggest bank, the National Commercial Bank. According to court documents filed in a $1-trillion lawsuit by more than four thousand relatives of the victims of 9/11 against hundreds of wealthy Saudis and others who had allegedly aided bin Laden, "A bank audit of NCB in 1998 showed that over a ten year period, $74 million was funneled by its Zakat Committee to the International Islamic Relief Organization, a

Muslim charity headed by Osama bin Laden's brother in law."[32] Congressional testimony by Vincent Cannistraro, former chief of operations for the CIA's Counterterrorism Center, which was also cited in the court case, adds that much of "the money is paid as 'protection' to avoid having the enterprises run by these men attacked" by Al Qaeda terrorists.[33]

The court documents also contain allegations that funds were transferred through another institution tied to the bin Mahfouz family, the Muwafaq (Blessed Relief) Foundation. In 1991, Khalid bin Mahfouz was the principal donor to Muwafaq, hoping, according to a spokesman, "to establish an endowment like the Rockefeller Foundation to give grants for disaster relief, education, and health."[35] His son, Abdulrahman bin Mahfouz, had become a director of it. However, there is no evidence either man was aware that Muwafaq funds were being used for terrorism and in response to allegations that the bin Mahfouz family had supported terrorism, Cherif Sedky, an attorney for the family, issued a statement: "The entire Bin Mahfouz family categorically and unreservedly condemns terrorism in all of its manifestations. At no time has any member of the family contributed to any terrorist organization, nor has the family ever had reason to believe that funds it has given over the years to a wide variety of charities, including Muwaffaq (Blessed Relief), have been used other than for the charitable purposes intended."[36]*

Even though the bin Laden family claimed to have cut off ties with their errant terrorist sibling, that was not clearly the case for the entire extended family. According to Carmen bin Laden, an estranged sister-in-law of Osama's, several members of the family may have continued to give money to Osama.[37] As mentioned, at least one member was a central figure in Al Qaeda and was widely reported to be linked to the 1993 World Trade Center bombing.

Two other relatives were key figures in a charitable foundation linked to Osama, which was cited by the Philippine military and Indian officials for funding terrorism in Kashmir and the Philippines.

*Cherif Sedky, an attorney for the family, and http://www.binmahfouz.info/faqs_2.html.

Members of the charity have denied that the organization has been involved in terrorist activities. FBI documents marked "Secret" and coded "199," indicating a national security case, show that the two Saudis were under investigation by the FBI for nine months in 1996 and that the file was reopened on September 19, 2001, eight days after the 9/11 attacks.[39]

Then there was the Saudi royal family itself. According to court documents in the 9/11 families' lawsuit, after the Gulf War in 1991, Saudi defense minister Prince Sultan, the father of Prince Bandar, supported and funded several Islamic charities, including the International Islamic Relief Organization, that allegedly provided funds to Osama bin Laden and Al Qaeda totaling at least $6 million.[40] Sultan's attorneys acknowledge that for sixteen consecutive years he approved annual payments of about $266,000 to the International Islamic Relief Organization, a Saudi charity whose U.S. offices were raided by federal agents.[41] In response to charges that Prince Sultan had knowingly funded terrorists, Casey Cooper, an attorney for Prince Sultan at James Baker's law firm, Baker Botts, says, "The allegations have no merit." He adds that Prince Sultan authorized the grants as part of his official governmental duties and did not knowingly fund terrorism.

Finally, there was Prince Bandar. Saudi royalty, including Bandar and his wife, frequently came to the aid of Saudis who had financial trouble when they were abroad. As first reported by Michael Isikoff of *Newsweek,* in 1998 a Saudi living in California, pleaded for financial assistance from the Saudi embassy in Washington because his wife was suffering from a thyroid condition, Prince Bandar wrote a check for $15,000. In addition, his wife, Princess Haifa bint Faisal, began sending the couple a stipend of roughly $2,000 a month.[42] According to the *Baltimore Sun,* over a four-year period the sum given by Bandar and his wife came to roughly $130,000.[43] As it turned out, the Saudi, said to be an Al Qaeda sympathizer, signed the money over to Omar al-Bayoumi, another Saudi who had moved to the United States. Bayoumi, the report of the 9/11 Commission states, was called a 'ghost employee' by a colleague at San Diego based Ercan, who noted Bayoumi was one of the many Saudis on the payroll not obliged to work. From there the money was used to help out two other newly arrived Saudis, Nawaf Alhazmi and Khalid Almidhar, two of the men who helped hijack American Airlines Flight 77, which crashed into the Pentagon on September 11. What had happened was undeniable: funds from Prince Bandar's wife had unintentionally ended up in the hands of the hijackers.

In all these instances, the Saudi royals and the Saudi merchant elite argue, sometimes persuasively, that they did not knowingly aid terrorists or their sympathizers. Given Osama bin Laden's hatred of the royal family and their wealthy merchant allies, it would be counterintuitive to think they would do so. "Who do you think Osama bin Laden really wants to destroy most?" argues Saudi oil analyst Nawaf Obaid. "It's the royal family and billionaires like bin Mahfouz. It's laughable to think that they would intentionally aid bin Laden."[44]

"People say we pay [Al Qaeda] off, but that's simply not the case," adds Nail al-Jubeir, a spokesman for the Saudi embassy in Washington, D.C. "Why would we support people who want to overthrow our own government?"[45] The problem, al-Jubeir explains, was in not having tough regulatory measures to govern the flow of money through these charities, a task that was especially difficult as money circulated through international channels. It was, he adds, essentially a case of innocent contributions gone wrong.

It should certainly be said that the allegations against the Saudi merchant elite and various members of the House of Saud are precisely that—allegations. Charges that many of them *knowingly* facilitated the transfer of funds to terrorists have been brought in court and have not been proven.

In fact, in November 2003, the suits against Prince Turki and Prince Sultan were thrown out when U.S. District Court judge James Robertson ruled that there was not sufficient evidence to suggest that the Saudi princes had intentionally funded 9/11. "Plaintiff's allegations that Prince Turki or Prince Sultan funded those who carried out the September 11th attacks would stretch the causation requirement ... not only to the farthest reaches of the common law but perhaps beyond, to terra incognita," Robertson wrote.[46]

"My own view is that extraordinary claims require extraordinary evidence," says Will Wechsler. But, he adds, "The search for the sin of commission makes people overlook the vast sin of omission, which is definitely true. These guys did not pay any serious attention to this issue. They did not give us all the cooperation we needed. There was no real political will to stop this. That's clear."[47]

In fact, whenever the United States tried to investigate these charitable donations or looked at financial institutions, the House of Saud performed a well-rehearsed rendition of Captain Renault in *Casablanca* proclaiming himself "Shocked! Shocked!" that funds were flowing to terrorists. According to counterterrorism czar Richard Clarke, when U.S. counterterrorism officials tried to trace terrorist funding through Islamic charities, the Saudis inevitably came back with one of two answers. "They said we need more information from you, or that they had looked and hadn't found anything."[48]

Clarke suggests that the lack of cooperation from the Saudis occurs because they have responded to Al Qaeda in different ways. Some actively support the terrorists while some cooperate with Al Qaeda in the hope that the group will leave them alone. Others merely resent American interference in what they see as their own domestic issues. "Some of them were clearly sympathetic to Al Qaeda," Clarke says.[49]

But the larger point is that the complex, impenetrable, and unregulated system of Islamic charities actually enabled Saudis to have it both ways. Through their generous charitable donations, they could both establish their bona fides as good Muslims and even buy "protection" from militants. And thanks to the unregulated nature of the charities, they could do so in a way that gave them plausible deniability to the West.

In addition, many things suggest that the House of Saud was not nearly so naive as it professed to be. Despite its pronouncement that the 1995 Riyadh attack was not the work of dissidents, some Saudis clearly knew better. Privately, Minister of Intelligence Prince Turki had even told Egyptian authorities that bin Laden's Afghan Arabs were behind the attack, probably with the help of accomplices who had infiltrated the Saudi National Guard.[50]

In fact, a few days after the bombing, threatening letters had been faxed to the private fax numbers of several high-level Saudi officials, including Prince Turki and Interior Minister Prince Nayef.[51] The implications were staggering. The fax numbers were for the exclusive use of the highest-ranking members of the royal family. The National Guard's sole mission was to protect the House of Saud. Terrorists had penetrated the House of Saud's last line of defense—and the royal family clearly knew it. Moreover, there were thousands of princes in the family, and many of them were said to be privately delighted by the bombings. "A lot of the royal princes remained sympathetic to bin Laden, even after his citizenship was stripped," says Robert Baer, a former CIA case officer in the Middle East and the author of *Sleeping with the Devil.* "Quite a few of the junior princes hate the U.S."[52]

According to one author, it was widely speculated that a powerful member of the royal family had advance knowledge of the 1995 bombing and allowed it to take place to solidify his political position, hoping to use the growing Islamist violence and his putative ability to control it to advance his fortunes—perhaps even all the way to the throne.[53]

When it came to dealing with the West, of course, the House of Saud revealed none of this internecine complexity, preferring to project the image of a stable monarchy that ruled a patriotic populace that honored its legitimacy and authority. Despite pressure from Clinton, in the end the Saudis simply declined to press any charges whatsoever against bin Laden for the 1995 Riyadh bombing and the Khobar Towers bombing in 1996. On November 5, 1998, Saudi interior minister Prince Nayef bin Abdul Aziz said, "It has been reported that the two explosions in Riyadh and Khobar were planned by Osama bin Laden. This is not true."

Nayef went further, asserting, with astonishing logic, that because the kingdom had revoked his citizenship, bin Laden was no longer a Saudi and therefore the Saudis no longer had any interest in the activities masterminded by the world's most wanted terrorist. "He does not constitute any security problem to us and has no activity in the kingdom," said Nayef. "Regarding his external activity, we are not concerned because he is not a Saudi citizen."

The House of Saud failed to have bin Laden extradited from Afghanistan, where he was a guest of the Taliban, and declined to prosecute him legally.[54]

And so, the double game continued—though by now, through his repeated bombings, bin Laden had upped the ante. Through the late nineties, cash flowed virtually unrestricted into bin Laden's and Al Qaeda's coffers as they escalated their jihad against the West. In counterterrorism circles, it was widely said that the Saudis had made deals with militant groups such as the Muslim Brotherhood and Hamas, agreeing to fund them in return for a promise not to wreak havoc on Saudi soil.[55]* It was not unreasonable to ask if they were doing the same with Al Qaeda. This was the Saudi veil that the Clinton administration had to penetrate if it was to get a handle on terrorist funding.

Over time, the Clinton administration slowly began to decipher the web of international Islamic religious foundations funneling money to Al Qaeda.[56]

Richard Clarke pounded the table in National Security Council meetings demanding to know about Islamic charities and foundations that may have been funding Al Qaeda.[57] But the administration was not able to move fast enough.

At 5:30 a.m. on August 7, 1998, Bill Clinton was awakened unexpectedly by National Security Adviser Sandy Berger.[58] It was the eighth anniversary of the arrival of U.S. troops in Saudi Arabia leading up to the Gulf War—or, as bin Laden would have it, the occupation of Islam's holiest sites by the Jewish and Christian Crusaders. To mark the occasion, Osama bin Laden had struck his most violent blows yet against the United States, setting off massive car bombs in front of the U.S. embassy in Dar es Salaam, Tanzania, at 10:30 a.m. local time, and then at the U.S. embassy in Nairobi, Kenya, 450 miles away, just five minutes later.

The carnage was unparalleled in the history of terrorism. In Nairobi, the explosion gutted half the U.S. embassy, leveled a nearby

---

*The House of Saud was not merely paying lip service to the Palestinian jihad. In fact, the Popular Committee for Assisting the Palestinian Mujahideen, headed by Prince Salman bin Abdul Aziz, the governor of Riyadh, gave over $4 billion to Palestinian groups fighting Israel.

secretarial school, incinerated dozens of people in buses passing by, and left more than a dozen pedestrians dismembered. In Dar es Salaam, the entrance to the U.S. embassy was in ruins. Altogether, about 260 people were killed. Roughly five thousand people were wounded in the twin attacks. Many of the victims were African Muslims.

The magnitude of the explosions and the fact that they had taken place simultaneously suggested an operation of enormous complexity and sophistication. Nearly a ton of military-type explosives was used in each bombing. This huge quantity had been shipped from Pakistan to Tanzania and Kenya, where it was stored in safe houses. Scores of people were involved in a highly compartmentalized operation.[59] Counterterrorism analysts knew immediately who was behind it. For the first time, the eyes of the world turned on Osama bin Laden as master terrorist and public enemy number one.

The operation was extraordinary not just because of the increased ferocity and sophistication of the bombings. There was now a grandiose scope and extraordinary clarity to bin Laden's hallucinatory vision, a paranoid fantasy straight out of the Crusades that called forth the image of heroic Muslims battling a Judeo-Christian alliance to control the holy places of Mecca, Medina, and Jerusalem. In 1996, bin Laden had issued a declaration of jihad specifying that in response to "one of the greatest disasters in the history of Islam,"[60] his goals were to drive American forces from the Arabian Peninsula, overthrow the House of Saud, liberate Muslim holy sites, and support Islamic revolution all over the world.[61] In 1998, bin Laden had elaborated on his ruling by issuing another fatwa in the spirit of the Crusades. "We—with God's help—call on every Muslim who believes in God and wishes to be rewarded to comply with God's order to kill the Americans and plunder their money wherever and whenever they find it," he declared.[62]

His philosophy mandated that all Muslims take part in brutal terrorist acts. It rationalized the killing not just of American soldiers, but of civilians as well; the killing of not just Americans, but of devout Muslims as well; and the killing not just of Muslim soldiers, but of civilians, women and children included. As bin Laden explained it, the duty of Muslims was "to kill the Americans and their allies—civilian and military ... in any country in which it is possible."[63]

If necessary, he added, he would even sacrifice the lives of his own children. "Imagine it was my own children [who] were taken hostage," bin Laden said. "And that shielded by this human shield, Islam's enemies started to massacre Muslims. I would not hesitate, I would kill the assassin even if to do that I had to kill my children with my own hand .... Sometimes, alas, the death of innocents is unavoidable. Islam allows that."[64]

Clinton vowed to strike back. "These acts of terrorist violence are abhorrent, they are inhuman," he said. "We will use all the means at our disposal to bring those responsible to justice."

Less than two weeks after the attacks on the U.S. embassies in East Africa, on August 20, 1998, Clinton launched a two-pronged strike against Al Qaeda targets in Afghanistan and Sudan. The rationale for attacking Afghanistan was incontrovertible. Bin Laden had been encamped there, escaping not long before the U.S. attack. The justification for attacking Sudan was more tenuous. The Clinton administration asserted that Khartoum, which was swarming with Al Qaeda operatives, still had Bin Laden operations, including the El-Shifa pharmaceutical factory.[75] The Americans said that tests conducted on a soil sample from Khartoum suggested the presence of a rare chemical which has no commercial use, but can be used for the fabrication of XV—a lethal chemical weapon, a single drop of which can cause death within fifteen minutes of being placed on the skin.[66]*

As a result, Clinton ordered a devastating Cruise missile attack which destroyed the El-Shifa factory, which was in fact owned by a Mr Saleh Idriss. Accusing him of association with terrorism, the Clinton Administration froze his U.S. assets. This mistaken claim, however, was not pursued when Idriss hired George Salem, a promi nent Arab American atorney and Republican fund-raiser, and sued the U.S. government.*

Clinton's strike against bin Laden also came while the president

---

*Further reasons for the decision lay in the testimony of Jamal Ahmed al-Fadl, the first witness for the prosecution in the trial for the bombings of the two embassies in East Africa in 1998. Al-Fadl, a Sudanese Islamist who joined Al Qaeda in 1989 and was one of its first members, testified that Al Qaeda manufactured chemical weapons in Khartoum.[67]

enmeshed in the Monica Lewinsky sex scandal. Just three days before he struck El-Shifa, on August 17, the president had appeared before a grand jury investigating his sexual relationship with the young intern. Caught in a political whirlpool, Clinton was weakened further by a cultural event: several months earlier *Wag the Dog*, a movie starring Robert De Niro and Dustin Hoffman, had been released, about a foreign war fabricated by the White House to cover up a presidential sex scandal.

Whether or not politics was imitating art, the juxtaposition of the movie and Clinton's dilemma was irresistible. Partisan politicians and the press had a field day. From right-wing talk radio hosts to the toniest magazines in the land, virtually every media outlet in the English-speaking world picked up the *Wag the Dog* theme. Radio talk-show host Rush Limbaugh demanded to know how many innocent people were killed in bombing "an aspirin factory."[68] Christopher Hitchens of *Vanity Fair* and the *Nation* alone raised the subject in more than half a dozen columns he wrote.[69] Republican senator Dan Coats of Indiana accused Clinton of "lies and deceit and manipulations and deceptions."[70] Former CIA officials criticized the legitimacy of El-Shifa as a target.[71] Thousands of articles asserted that the administration had destroyed an innocent target, a factory that made medication for poor people, not deadly nerve gas, that the factory was struck not for reasons of national security, but to distract the public from the Lewinsky affair.

These were not just partisan attacks; they spanned the political spectrum and included supposedly liberal icons in the media such as the *New Yorker,* the *New York Times,* and CBS's Dan Rather.[72] A profile in the *Washington Post* characterized the owner of the El-Shifa factory, Saleh Idriss, as a rags-to-riches son of a tailor who "wasn't making nerve gas for terrorists, just ibuprofen for headaches"[73]*

---

*The article also described him as a protégé of Khalid bin Mahfouz's. According to bin Mahfouz's attorney, Cherif Sedky, Idriss served as deputy general manager of the National Commercial Bank from 1996 to 1998. Sedky adds, "Mr. Idriss was involved in coordinating the activities of the various lawyers representing KBM (Khalid bin Mahfouz) and the bank during the BCCI litigation." Idriss had other ties to the bin Mahfouz family. He was a shareholder in a company called WorldSpace and introduced it to the bin Mahfouz family. Subsequently, bin Mahfouz's sons, through a company called Stonehouse Capital, held a large amount of

A large measure of the failure of Clinton's battle against terrorism was the fault of the president himself. By getting involved with Monica Lewinsky, he had given his enemies exactly what they were looking for. The ensuing impeachment hearings provided a ready-made, ongoing forum for an epic circus that far, far surpassed any concerns Americans had for national security. Next to the lascivious spectacle of a search for a semen-stained dress, the terrorist threat of Al Qaeda was nothing more than a weak sideshow starring an unfamiliar and bizarrely dressed Arab with a weird and exotic name. At a time when Wall Street was euphoric over dot-com mania, and the economy was booming as never before, the American zeitgeist had no room for faraway fears.

Worse, now that Clinton's attempt to protect Americans from chemical weapons had been ridiculed, his counterterrorist efforts, however noble their intentions, were crippled. The Lewinsky affair had so depleted Clinton's political capital that there was no support for strong military measures in Afghanistan. At a time when national security was a genuine issue, the administration was also widely criticized for trying to get bin Laden, because in doing so, they had "mythologized" him and helped build him into a hero among Muslims. Yet Clinton continued to fight bin Laden. He cut off relations with the Taliban government in Afghanistan that harbored bin Laden. He pressured the Saudis to negotiate with the Taliban to extradite bin Laden, and he pressured the Saudis to audit the National Commercial Bank's funding of terrorism. But as a result of Monicagate, few Americans understood the nature of the terrorist threat.

The House of Saud was clearly none too happy with the Clinton administration's efforts to probe Saudi ties to terrorism, and the Sauds much preferred their longtime American friends the House of Bush. Their relationship now spanned roughly two decades, in both the private and public sectors, and neither side had any reason to think that their close ties would not continue for years to come.

... debt in WorldSpace. "Saleh Idriss and KBM are business acquaintances and have done together from time to time, although the El-Shifa plant in Sudan was not a matter in which KBM had any interest," says Sedky.

In the summer of 1998, for example, just before the East African embassy attacks, Bandar visited George H. W. Bush and his family at Walker's Point in Kennebunkport, on the peninsula jutting out from the rugged Maine coast.[76] For former first lady Barbara Bush, the visit was an unexpected but delightful surprise, with Bandar cooking up a storm in the kitchen.

By this time, the Bushes could provide Prince Bandar with a ray of hope that his frustrations with the Clinton administration would soon be over. The president's son, Texas governor George W. Bush, was positioning himself as the leading Republican presidential candidate for 2000. Karl Rove, once his father's aide, was putting together one of the most efficient fund-raising machines ever. Within a month of getting started, Bush had raised hundreds of thousands of dollars, two of the primary big contributors being the massive oil giant Enron and Baker Botts, James Baker's law firm.

Bandar's visit was soon followed by the carnage in Kenya and Tanzania. But for former president Bush and Baker, it was business as usual. In November, Bush flew to Saudi Arabia and met with members of the bin Laden family representing the Saudi Binladin Group. Likewise, in January 2000, Bush again met with Crown Prince Abdullah and the bin Laden family, not long after the United Nations had passed sanctions against their terrorist sibling Osama. At the time, Carlyle was working with SBC Communications, the Texas-based communications giant, in an unsuccessful attempt to nail down the acquisition of 25 percent of the Saudi phone system. In addition, during his trips to Saudi Arabia, James Baker met with Khalid bin Mahfouz on several occasions.[77]

Officially, Bush was not really doing business with the Saudis—or so a spokeswoman said. "President Bush has never conducted business with Saudi citizens or government officials on behalf of anyone, including the Carlyle Group," says Jean Becker, chief of staff to former president Bush. "He has delivered some speeches at Carlyle functions in Saudi Arabia and other countries, but has not engaged in private business conversations with anyone in Saudi Arabia or elsewhere."[78] As for whether Bush had concerns about doing business with the Saudis in light of all the terrorist bombings, a spokesman for the Carlyle Group said that Bush had "no responsibilities for investor relations." But in fact, what that meant was that Carlyle had created an elaborate deniability mechanism for Bush. The relationship was such that in the end, with Bush and Baker making appearances before potential Saudi investors, the Saudis placed $80 million in the firm.[79] It is unclear how much of that sum was raised following meetings attended by Bush or James Baker.

Meanwhile, as Bill Clinton's second term was coming to an end, the House of Saud was eagerly looking forward to a Bush restoration. If that happened, it could be fairly said that their friends in the House of Bush would be unlikely to probe too deeply into the Saudi role in the terrorist threat.

CHAPTER TWELVE

The Arabian Candidate

IN THE PRESIDENTIAL RACE of 2000, George W. Bush had the advantage of instant name recognition across the land. His birthright included a spectacular Republican fund-raising apparatus.* And, as heir to an extraordinary brain trust, he had the ultimate Washington insiders and oil industry executives at his side—his father, a former president; James Baker, one of the most powerful nonelected officials in American history; Donald Rumsfeld, a former secretary of defense; Condoleezza Rice, who had served on the elder Bush's National Security Council and was a director of Chevron;† and Dick Cheney, the former secretary of defense who had become CEO of Halliburton, the giant oil services company.

But for all its advantages, the Bush political legacy was also a mixed blessing. It carried the liability of being a nationally known political brand that had failed. Among the senior Bush's chief contributions to the American political lexicon was a solemn declaration that had come to be synonymous with broken political promises—"Read my lips—no new taxes." Who else had been derided on the cover of national magazines as a "wimp"?

---

*Giant energy-industry law firms such as Vinson & Elkins and Baker Bous put in $202,850 and $116,121 respectively; high-flying Enron, the corrupt oil giant, contributed $113,800. The oil and gas industry contributed $1,929,451 to Bush—thirteen times as much as it gave to Democratic nominee Al Gore. Altogether, the energy sector contributed $2.9 million to Bush and only $325,000 to Gore.

†During her tenure at Chevron, Rice even had an oil tanker named after her. When Bush appointed her to be national security adviser, Chevron quietly renamed the ship *Altair Voyager*.

To make George W. Bush's task more complicated, the 2000 campaign was taking place at the end of a prosperous eight-year Democratic reign. The Monica Lewinsky sex scandal, as embarrassing and damaging as it was for Clinton, had played out during a mood of national economic euphoria. It was an era of dot-com millionaires, bulging 401 Ks, frenzied online day traders, and SUVs driven by soccer moms. Twenty-two million new jobs had been created during the Clinton years. Unemployment had fallen to its lowest levels in decades. The Dow Jones average was flirting with 12,000. Nasdaq had broken 5,000. It was a period of unparalleled peace and prosperity. America seemingly ruled the world as never before. With Vice President Al Gore the uncontested Democratic nominee, the challenge for the GOP was clear. Bush had to make the case, as one Republican media consultant joked, that because things had never been better, it was time for a change.[1]

The task of reinventing and marketing this flawed brand fell to Karl Rove, Bush's longtime friend, confidant, and handler who had earned the sobriquet Bush's Brain. His solution was to create a Rorschach test candidate so that moderates, conservatives, and independents would see in Bush exactly what they wanted to see. Bush's theme of "compassionate conservatism" meant whatever one wanted it to mean. To Wall Street Republicans, who couldn't care less about social issues crucial to the antiabortion, antigay, progun Christian right, Bush was his father's son, a genial and appealing moderate who would be good for business. To the powerful cadres of the radical Christian right, Bush's vow to restore honor and integrity to the White House, his promise that his deepest commitment was to his faith and his family, meant that he was unmistakably one of them.

But few voters realized, for example, how dissimilar the Texas governor was from his father. Not content merely to bring back the ancien régime of the Reagan-Bush era, George W. wooed key conservative constituencies that the elder Bush had failed to bring into his camp. One was the powerful Christian right.[2] Given his difficulties winning the trust of born-again evangelicals during the 1988 presidential campaign, the elder Bush had given his son the task of working with the campaign's liaison to the Christian right, an Assemblies of God evangelist named Doug Wead.[3] When evangelists asked Vice President Bush trick questions designed to reveal whether he was really one of the flock, he almost always stumbled. But his son was a natural. According to Wead, if asked what argument George W. would give to gain entry to heaven, he would say, "I know we're all sinners, but I've accepted Jesus Christ as my personal savior."[4]

Bush had become so attuned to all the nuances of the evangelical subcultures that virtually no one questioned the sincerity of his acceptance of Christ. But even if one did, as author Joan Didion has noted, it did not matter.[5] The larger point was that Bush had replaced his father's visionless pragmatism with the Manichaean certitudes of Good and Evil. Where the elder Bush was, as one colleague put it, "utterly devoid of conviction" on almost any subject,[6] his son was forging a neo-Reaganite vision that jibed with an evangelical sense of destiny. Dubya's bond with the Christian right was a crucial part of what distinguished him from his father.

As Bush contemplated his candidacy, he repeatedly met with evangelical leaders, and in October 1999, he addressed the powerful but secretive Council for National Policy, a body that had attracted the who's who of the evangelical movement.[7]* The organization's founding president was Dr. Tim LaHaye, author of the best-selling *Left Behind* series of novels, prophetic military-religious thrillers that extol the Rapture, the moment when true believers in Christ will be "raptured" into heaven.

At the time, the Christian right had focused largely on domestic issues concerning values and morality—abortion, homosexuality, gun control, prayer in the schools, and so on. But LaHaye and his millions of followers—the eleven books in his series have sold 55 million copies—added a new foreign policy dimension to its agenda, specifically with regard to the Middle East. According to LaHaye, the armies of the Antichrist would soon have their final battle with Christ and "witness the end of history" after a series of conflicts in the Mid-

---

*Members included Senator Jesse Helms; Congressmen Dick Armey and Tom DeLay; the Reverend Jerry Falwell; Oliver North; Phyllis Schlafly of the Eagle Forum; the Reverend Donald Wildmon of the American Family Association; the Reverend Pat Robertson of The 700 Club and the Christian Coalition; Ralph Reed of Century Strategies; and Christian Reconstructionist Rousas John Rushdoony.

dle East—not unlike those taking place today.[8] This belief that the events in the Middle East were part of God's plan, that Christ would return only after Israel truly controlled the Holy Land, put the Christian right on course for a low-profile liaison with a highly unlikely political ally—hard-line, pro-Israeli, neoconservative defense policy intellectuals.

The neocons, who had also bedeviled his father, were the other constituency with whom Bush quietly mended fences. In the late eighties and early nineties, one may recall, defense policy makers Richard Perle and Paul Wolfowitz, who had close ties to the Israeli right, had criticized George H. W. Bush first for his pro-Saddam policies and later for not ousting Saddam after the Gulf War. In 1992, the notorious Defense Planning Guidance paper written by Wolfowitz argued for military action in the Middle East as part of a larger plan to rid the world of rogue states—but the Bush White House had rejected it as too militaristic.

In 1998, Perle and Wolfowitz, along with sixteen other prominent neoconservatives from a group called the Project for a New American Century (PNAC), lobbied President Clinton to remove Saddam Hussein and his regime from power.[9] But rather than overthrow Saddam, Clinton continued a policy of containment through periodic air strikes.

By the time George W. Bush put together his team of advisers in 1999, however, several of its key members, including his brother, Florida governor Jeb Bush, Dick Cheney, and Donald Rumsfeld, as well as Perle and Wolfowitz, had signed on to the Project for a New American Century. Untutored as he was in foreign policy, Bush's own positions on crucial issues in the Middle East were not yet fully formed. But now the hard-line neocons had his ear—and picking up from Wolfowitz's Defense Planning Guidance paper, they put forth a grandiose vision for American foreign policy of the next century. The language used in their reports was the language of world domination. One such PNAC report referred admiringly to Wolfowitz's infamous work as a "blueprint for maintaining global U.S. preeminence, precluding the rise of a great power rival, and shaping the international security order in line with American principles and interests,"[10] and asserted that its judgments were still sound.

That Bush was amenable to some of the same Middle East policies that his father had rejected was not widely known to the public—but it was not entirely secret either. In November 1999, Perle, by then an adviser to Bush, told the *Pittsburgh Post-Gazette* that the candidate was drafting a speech calling for Saddam Hussein's removal from power. He added that Bush's speech would be critical of Clinton and would say, "it's time to finish the job. It's time for Saddam Hussein to go."[11] According to Perle, Bush also planned to say that it was understandable that his father's administration had underestimated the Iraqi leader's ability to stay powerful. When the presidential race got under way in 2000, however, no such statements about Iraq were forth-coming.

For all the firepower behind Bush's candidacy, his nomination was not a foregone conclusion. On February 1, 2000, insurgent Arizona senator John McCain won the crucial opening primary in New Hampshire, beating Bush by an astonishing 19 percentage points. An authentic Vietnam war hero who had been a longtime prisoner of war, McCain had cast himself as a crusading pied piper leading his horde of McCainiacs around the country on a bus he called the Straight Talk Express.

McCain's challenge brought out Bush's true colors. The next major primary state was South Carolina, one of the most conservative in the Union, and Bush retaliated aggressively by painting the conservative McCain as a liberal. He blitzed the state with brutal attack ads on TV, on radio, in print, and by telephone. He appeared before thousands of evangelicals at Bob Jones University, the fundamentalist college that had banned interracial dating. He declined to endorse the Republican governor's opposition to flying the Confederate flag above the statehouse.[12]

Thousands of voters got phone calls asserting that McCain's wife had mob ties, that McCain had illegitimate children, that he had a "black" child, that there had been an abortion in the McCain family.[13] A group of Bush supporters called Republicans for Clean Air spent $2.5 million on commercials attacking McCain and distorting his record on the environment. Ads went out saying McCain opposed breast cancer research even though his sister was fighting the disease.*

Astonished by the ferocity of the attacks, McCain told a reporter, "They know no depths, do they? They know no depths."[14] But Bush's tactics proved successful. On February 19, he trounced McCain 53 percent to 42 percent in South Carolina. Three weeks later, on the March 7 "Super Tuesday" primaries, Bush won California, Ohio, Georgia, Missouri, and Maryland to all but lock up the Republican nomination.

If the vitriol from the Bush campaign did not poison the body politic across the United States, it was because when it came to the care and feeding of the press, no candidate that season surpassed George W. Bush. As he traveled about the country by bus, plane, and train, Bush joshed with reporters about their romances, handed out nicknames to pet journalists, put his arm around them, slapped them on the back, and passed out cookies and treats. In a documentary she did for HBO, *Journeys with George,* NBC television producer Alexandra Pelosi said that after the Bush staff bought her four birthday cakes, and her network bought her none, "I started to wonder, who am I working for?

She wasn't the only journalist who was being wooed. "We were writing about trivial stuff because he charmed the pants off us," explained Richard Wolffe, who covered the campaign for London's *Financial Times.*[15] Whenever Bush journeyed to the back of the press bus, explaining earnestly how much he loved a good bologna sandwich, making corny jokes, giving a young woman an orange and telling her, "You are the orange of my eye," reporters "went weak in the knees," Wolffe added. Thanks to such warm relations with the media, Bush repeatedly turned his liabilities into assets. A poor public speaker who made one verbal gaffe after another, Bush played the self-deprecating common man under fire by the know-it-all intellectuals.[16]† Intimate with the Wise Men of Washington since childhood,

*McCain had voted against a cancer research project as part of a larger spending bill that he said contained wasteful spending, but he had supported many other bills funding cancer research.

†Bush became something of a laughingstock among East Coast liberals for endless gaffes that became known as Bushisms—all of which only endeared him further to his constituency. "I know how hard it is for you to put food on your family," he told

scion to one of the greatest political dynasties in American history, Bush was even able to sell himself as an outsider to power. "My zip code is 78701," Bush said on *Face the Nation*, referring to his Austin, Texas, address. "It's not Washington, D.C. If you were to call me on the telephone, it would be area code 512, not 202."[17]

At one campaign stop after another, Bush delivered the same canned speeches asserting that his priorities were his faith and his family—and reporters dutifully did his bidding. "I have not learned one single thing about his policies or him," said Wayne Salter, a *Dallas Morning News* reporter who had covered Bush for years in Texas and followed him during the primaries. "We are lemmings. We follow [the Bush campaign] like lemmings and do exactly what they say."[18]

On the rare occasion that they did not obey and dared to probe beneath the surface, reporters learned the hard way the high price to be paid: they would be denied access to the candidate—access that was the lifeblood of a Washington journalist's career. When Alexandra Pelosi asked Bush if he was certain that every prisoner executed on his watch as Texas governor was guilty, Bush, who had coyly flirted with her throughout the campaign, suddenly became brusque, gave a terse answer, and later chastised her for violating the rules of engagement. "I'm not answering your questions," he told her afterward. "You came after me the other day. You went below the belt."[19]

And so Pelosi backed off. "All of our careers are tied to George Bush," she said. Like the rest of the press corps, she had realized that tangling with him was bad for business. "If I throw him a hardball, he'll push me into the outfield. And it's my job to maintain my network's relationship to the candidate."[20]

As a result, the scripted, fabricated reality put together by Rove

... New Hampshire voters. In South Carolina, he asserted, "Rarely is the question asked: Is our children learning?" and "We must all hear the universal call to like your neighbor just like you like to be liked yourself." He referred to Kosovars as Kosovian, Greeks as Grecians, and the East Timorese as East Timorians.

When it came to economics, Bush asserted, "A tax cut is really one of the anecdotes to coming out of an economic illness." And in Iowa, he explained to voters the dangers of foreign policy: "When I was coming up, it was a dangerous world, and you knew exactly who they were. It was us versus them, and it was clear who them was. Today, we are not so sure who the they are, but we know they're there."

and his team was disseminated by the media virtually unchallenged. In the bright lights of the mass media, tens and tens of millions of Americans saw Bush as the candidate of the common man, a Washington outsider, a moderate, a centrist, a compassionate conservative. The more complex reality wasn't part of the picture. Few saw him as he was, a candidate of Big Oil, the ultimate insider, and a radical conservative who was closely tied both to the evangelical right and to hawkish neoconservative defense policy makers. In *Harper's,* Joe Conason raised compelling questions about Bush's rise to riches and his ties to the oil industry. A handful of small liberal publications followed suit. And the *Intelligence Newsletter,* a tiny publication with a keen eye on the intelligence community but a weaker grasp of what animates American politics, reported on Bush's close ties to the Saudis.[21]*

But those were rare exceptions. Even the bombings in Kenya and Tanzania had not put terrorism on the radar screen of the American electorate. No major media outlet asked about Bush's ties to the Saudis or the Carlyle Group† and how that might affect dealing with the forces of terror.

If the Saudis had been happy with the presidency of George H. W. Bush—and they were—they must have been truly ecstatic that his son was the Republican candidate for president. Indeed, the relationship between the two dynasties had come a long way since the seventies when Khalid bin Mahfouz and Salem bin Laden had flown halfway around the world to buy a secondhand airplane from James Bath, George W. Bush's old friend from decades before. Even bin Mahfouz's subsequent financing of the Houston skyscraper for James Baker's family bank or the bailout of Harken Energy by other Saudis that helped George W. Bush make his fortune were small potatoes compared with what had happened since.

---

*It included a comment on his connection with bin Mahfouz.

†According to a search on the Nexis-Lexis database, only three articles in the entire country raised the issue during the whole campaign, one by Gene Lyons in the *Little Rock Democrat-Gazette,* one by John Judis in the *American Prospect,* and one by David Corn and Paul Lashmar in the *Nation.*

The Bushes and their allies controlled, influenced, or possessed substantial positions in a vast array of companies that dominated the energy and defense sectors. Put it all together, and there were myriad ways for the House of Bush to engage in lucrative business deals with the House of Saud and the Saudi merchant elite.

The Saudis could give donations to Bush-related charities. They could invest in the Carlyle Group's funds or contract with one of the many companies owned by Carlyle in the defense sector or other industries.

James Baker's law firm, Baker Botts, represented both the giant oil companies who did business with the Saudis as well as the defense contractors who sold weapons to them. Its clients also included Saudi insurance companies and the Saudi American Bank. It negotiated huge natural gas projects in Saudi Arabia. It even represented members of the House of Saud itself. And the firm's role was not limited to merely negotiating contracts. When global energy companies needed to devise policies for the future, when government bodies required attention, Baker Botts was there.

And the Saudis were also linked to Dick Cheney through Halliburton, the giant Texas oil exploration company that had huge interests in the kingdom.[22]*

How much did it all come to? What was the number? Where did the money go? With the understanding that the sums were paid by both individuals and entities to both individual and entities, for diverse purposes at different times, it is nonetheless possible to arrive at a reckoning that is undoubtedly incomplete but which by its very size suggests the degree and complexity of the House of Bush-House of Saud relationship.

In charitable contributions alone, the Saudis gave at least $3.5 million to Bush charities—$1 million by Prince Bandar to the George H. W. Bush Presidential Library and Museum, $1 million by King Fahd to Barbara Bush's campaign against illiteracy, $500,000

---

*The Saudis did contribute to George H. W. Bush's presidential library, but on that score they were truly bipartisan, having made donations to every presidential library created over the last thirty years.

by Prince Al Waleed to Philips Academy, Andover, to finance a newly created George Herbert Walker Bush Scholarship Fund, and a $1-million painting from Prince Bandar to George W. Bush's White House.[23]

Then, there were the corporate transactions. As mentioned earlier, in 1987, a Saudi investor bailed out Harken Energy, where George W. Bush was a director, with $25 million in financing. At the Carlyle Group, investors from the House of Saud and their allies put at least $80 million into Carlyle funds. While it was owned by Carlyle, BDM, and its subsidiary Vinnell, received at least $1.188 billion in contracts from the Saudis. Finally, Halliburton inked at least $180 million in deals with the Saudis in November 2000, just after Dick Cheney began collecting a lucrative severance package there.

In all, on a conservative estimate, $1.476 billion had made its way from the Saudis to the House of Bush and its allied companies and institutions.* It could safely be said that never before in history had a presidential candidate—much less a presidential candidate and his father, a former president—been so closely tied financially and personally to the ruling family of another foreign power. Never before had a president's personal fortunes and public policies been so deeply entwined with another nation.

And what were the implications of that? In the case of George H. W. Bush, close relations with the Saudis had at times actually paid dividends for America—certainly in terms of the Saudi cooperation during the Gulf War, for example. But that carried with it a high price. The Bushes had religiously observed one of the basic tenets of Saudi-American relations, that the United States would not poke its

---

*For a more complete breakdown of Saudi investments, contracts, and contributions to companies, foundations, and charities owned by the Bushes and their associates, see Appendix C on page 295. It should be noted that the above number is an estimate of the total business done between the Saudis and companies related to the interests of the Bush family and their associates. The figure does not include undisclosed legal fees for deals with the Saudis done by Baker Botts, nor does it include contracts between large publicly held companies, such as the major oil companies, and the Saudis. The actual total will never be known and may well be substantially greater.

nose into Saudi Arabia's internal affairs. That might have been fine if the kingdom was another Western democracy like, say, Great Britain or Germany or Spain. By the late nineties, it was clear that Saudi Arabia, more than any other country in the world, was responsible for the rise of Islamic fundamentalist terrorism. Now that Islamic terrorists acting on Osama's orders were killing Americans in the Khobar Towers bombing and in Kenya and Tanzania, America's national security was at stake. What had previously been considered a purely domestic issue for the Saudis—the House of Saud's relationship to Islamist extremists—was now a matter of America's national security. Hundreds had already been killed by Saudi-funded terrorists, yet former president Bush and James Baker continued their lucrative business deals with the Saudis apparently without asking the most fundamental questions.

Now, of course, George W. Bush was closing in on the White House. It remained to be seen how, if elected, he would deal with the Saudis and the global terrorist threat. Federal election laws prohibit foreign nationals from funding American political candidates. But the Saudis were not like last-minute holiday shoppers. They had begun buying their American politicians years in advance.

The close relationship between the two great dynasties was not the only factor that might interfere with Bush's acting against the growing terrorist threat. Republicans had just woken up to the fact that there were roughly 7 million Muslims in America[24]*—a huge pool of voters who had largely been ignored by both political parties. To remedy that, Bush campaign strategist Grover Norquist came up with an aggressive plan to win them over by making alliances with groups run by Islamic fundamentalists. He invented the notion of a Muslim-American electoral bloc.

A bearded, stocky, Harvard-educated intellectual who described himself as a "winger" of the radical right, Norquist gained notoriety

---

*There is considerable disagreement as to how many Muslims there are in the United States. Some estimates place the number as low as 3.5 to 4 million, while others go as high as 12 million. A report by the Council on American-Islamic Relations and other organizations in April 2001 put the number at 7 million, and a Cornell University study also came up with the same figure.

in the nineties as the right-hand man of Speaker of the House Newt Gingrich when Gingrich's power was at its zenith. When Gingrich's star fell, Norquist moved on and hitched his wagon to two of the most powerful conservatives in Washington, Tom DeLay, the House majority whip, and Dick Armey, the majority leader. Norquist's secret was that he had managed to link the moneymen of the big lobbying groups on K Street in Washington to the hard-core ideological right.

As the president of Americans for Tax Reform, Norquist was a founding member of the Islamic Institute, a nonprofit foundation promoting Muslim political movements. His Muslim partner, Khaled Saffuri, was deputy director for the American Muslim Council (AMC) and had an extensive network of contacts with other Muslim-American leaders.

On the surface, Norquist's stratagem to win the Muslim-American vote had a powerful political appeal. Muslims had voted two to one for Clinton in 1996,[25] but Norquist argued that they could easily be won over to the Republican side. It is axiomatic that come election time, every American presidential candidate rallies wholeheartedly behind Israel. But the Republicans could make the case that Bush's ties to the oil lobby made him more receptive to Arab and Muslim concerns. In addition, his father had been relatively tough on Israel and had in 1991 threatened to suspend loans to Israel in an effort to stop ongoing Israeli settlements in Palestinian territories.[26] "That was a sense the Bush people played up: 'I'm my father's son,' and people liked that," said James Zogby, the head of the Arab American Institute, who served as a Gore adviser during the campaign. Finally, and perhaps most important, when Al Gore picked a Jewish running mate, Joe Lieberman, Muslims became much more receptive to Republicans.

One problem with Norquist's strategy, however, was that Muslim Americans are not a homogeneous ethnic group. Many are African Americans who converted to Islam. Many are immigrants from Pakistan, India, Iran, Africa, and the Middle East. Less than 20 percent of American Muslims are of Arab descent. Among Arab Americans there are Arabs who immigrated before the rise of Islamic fundamentalism and who are usually moderate, and there are Muslims who came recently and are more likely to be Islamic fundamentalists. There are many different Islamic sects, and each has a different agenda. Finally, even though the vast majority of Muslim Americans are moderates who are well integrated into American society, many of the biggest and most powerful Muslim organizations in the United States are run by Wahhabi Islamic fundamentalists.

The inordinate influence of Wahhabi Islam in the American Muslim community dates back to the eighties, when the Saudis saw an opportunity to gain sway over the burgeoning new Islamic community in the United States by establishing what author Steven Schwartz calls the "Wahhabi lobby." In many ways, Schwartz says, to win political power in America, the Saudis chose to replicate the model created by influential Jewish and Israeli lobbying groups. With Saudi backing, American Muslims started organizations like the Council on American Islamic Relations (CAIR), which was similar to the Anti-Defamation League; the American Muslim Council (AMC), which was modeled on the American Jewish Committee; the Muslim Public Affairs Council (MPAC), which was similar to the American Israel Public Affairs Committee, and so on.[27]

As Schwartz pointed out in congressional testimony, the generous Saudi support of Islam in the United States could easily be documented on the official website of the Saudi embassy.[28]* In 1995, the Saudi government reported $4 million in donations to construct a mosque complex in Los Angeles, named after Ibn Taymiyyah, one of the forefathers of Wahhabism. The same year, the website reported a $6-million donation for a mosque in Cincinnati, Ohio. In 1999, the Saudis helped CAIR buy land for its Washington, D.C., headquarters. In 2000, the kingdom contributed to Islamic centers and mosques in Washington, Los Angeles, Fresno, Denver, and Harrison, New York. In all, Schwartz estimated that over many years the Saudis have given at least $324 million to mosques and Islamic groups in the United States. As a result, out of thousands of mosques in the United States—estimates range from twelve hundred to as high as six thousand—as many as 80 percent have come under Wahhabi control.[29] According to Schwartz, that means having authority over property, buildings, appointment and

---

*The information on Saudi funding of mosques in the United States has since been removed.

training of imams, the content of preaching, the distribution of Friday sermons from Riyadh, and of literature distributed in mosques and mosque bookstores.

Innocent as such charitable contributions may sound, in fact many were effectively an extension of the same global flow of money that had created and funded Al Qaeda. Far from being confined to the Middle East, such charitable funding went to Muslims all over the world—including the United States. This was money that went not just to fund terrorist activities but to support thousands of mosques, schools, and Islamic centers that were dedicated to the jihad movement in non-Muslim countries.

Just how rigorous Schwartz was in arriving at his figure of $324 million in Saudi funding is unclear, but other sources suggest his estimate is not an exaggeration. According to *U.S. News and World Report*, since 1975, the Saudis have allocated a total of $70 *billion* to this international campaign.[30] That makes the Saudi program, according to Alex Alexiev of the Center for Security Policy, a Washington think tank, the biggest worldwide propaganda campaign in history—far bigger than Soviet propaganda efforts at the height of the Cold War.

As Schwartz noted, even in the United States the money went to charities "many of which have been linked to or designated as sponsors of terrorism."[31] Al-Kifah Refugee Center, the Brooklyn branch of which was the locus of the 1993 World Trade Center bombing conspiracy, was effectively such a U.S. outpost for Al Qaeda. Even events sponsored by mainstream national Muslim groups could be overtly anti-Jewish. At a 1998 rally sponsored by CAIR and the American Muslim Council, for example, a considerable number of people sang a song with questionable lyrics.

As a result, Norquist's Muslim strategy was sometimes criticized—usually from the right—for giving credibility to Muslim groups that seemed harmless, but were in fact supporting extremist interests.* Out-

---

*Subsequent to 9/11, through Operation Greenquest, an attempt to stop the flow of money to terrorists, the U.S. Treasury Department took action against a number of Islamic charities accused of funneling money to terrorists, including the Global Relief Foundation, the Benevolence International Foundation, and the Holy Land Foundation for Relief and Development.

spoken critics of the policy included conservative writers and commentators such as Frank Gaffney, Cal Thomas, Michelle Malkin, Kenneth Timmerman, and David Keene.[32] According to Mona Charen, "The names of the Saudi fronts are benign, but a cursory examination of the leaders reveals their radicalism. The leader of one group "refused to denounce any terror group practicing suicide bombing in the Middle East and has even declined to denounce Al Qaeda, calling it a 'resistance movement.'"[33] If there were any doubt, the group's website made its position about Islamist terrorism quite clear, warning its Muslim readers that when the Feds came to investigate terrorism, 'Don't talk to the FBI.'"[34]

According to Mustafa Elhussein, secretary of a center for Muslim intellectuals known as the Ibn Khaldun Society, "There is a great deal of bitterness that such groups have tarnished the reputation of mainstream Muslims" because "self-appointed leaders ... spew hatred toward America and the West and yet claim to be the legitimate spokespersons for the American Muslim community."[35] Elhussein believes not only that they should "be kept at arm's length from the political process, but that they should be actively opposed as extremists."

Nevertheless, with Norquist working behind the scenes, Bush aggressively pursued the Islamists in hopes of winning their endorsements. In appearances on TV, Bush and fellow campaign staffers referred not just to churches and synagogues as places of worship, but to mosques as well. Again and again, Governor Bush sought out meetings with Muslim leaders—often without looking into their backgrounds. He invited the founder of the American Muslim Council, Abdurahman Alamoudi, to the governor's mansion in Austin. In the mid-1990s, Alamoudi had played an important role in recruiting as many as a hundred "Islamic lay leaders" for the U.S. military. The *Wall Street Journal* reported that he had arranged for "an arm of the Saudi government" called the Institute of Islamic and Arabic Sciences to train "soldiers and civilians to provide spiritual guidance when paid Muslim chaplains aren't available." The *Journal* queried whether the school disseminated the fundamentalist "strain of Islam espoused by the [Saudi] kingdom's religious establishment." A self-proclaimed supporter of Hamas and Hezbollah, Alamoudi reportedly attended a terrorist summit in Beirut later in 2000 with leaders of Hamas, Hezbollah and Al Qaeda.[36]* But such a militant background did not keep Alamoudi away from Norquist and Bush. According to an article by Frank Gaffney, Alamoudi wrote two checks for $10,000 each, one an apparent loan, to help found Norquist's Islamic Institute.[37]†

On March 12, 2000, Bush and his wife, Laura, met with more Muslim leaders at a local mosque in Tampa, Florida.[38] Among them was Sami Al-Arian, a Kuwaiti-born Palestinian who was an associate professor of engineering at the University of South Florida. George and Laura Bush had their photo taken with him at the Florida Strawberry Festival. Laura Bush made a point of complimenting Al-Arian's wife, Nahla, on her traditional head scarf and asked to meet the family. Nahla told the candidate, "The Muslim people support you." Bush met their lanky son, Abdullah Al-Arian, and, in a typically winning gesture, even nicknamed him Big Dude.[39] In return, Big Dude's father, Sami Al-Arian, vowed to campaign for Bush—and he soon made good on his promise in mosques all over Florida.

But Al-Arian had unusual credentials for a Bush campaigner. The founder and chairman of the board of World and Islam Enterprise (WISE), a scholarly Muslim think tank, Al-Arian had nonetheless been under investigation since 1995 by the FBI for his associations with Islamic Jihad, the Palestinian terrorist group.[40] Al-Arian had

---

*In September 2003, Alamoudi was arrested after arriving from a trip to the Middle East in which he allegedly tried to transport $340,000 from a group tied to Libyan leader Muammar Qaddafi. Prosecutors also said Alamoudi was at the center of several northern-Virginia-based Islamic charity groups, including the International Relief Organization, under investigation for allegedly financing terrorism. In December 2003, the *Wall Street Journal* reported that Alamoudi had helped back a program to train Islamist imams for the U.S. military and that even well after 9/11, in 2002, the Pentagon had hired them. The website of the IIASA appears no longer to be functioning. As part of a plea-bargain, Alamoudi is said to have alleged that at a meeting in June 2003 Mr Qaddafi told him: "I want the crown prince killed either through assassination or through a coup." When they met again in August Mr Qaddafi asked why he had not seen "heads flying".

†Alamoudi was welcomed at the White House by both President Bill Clinton and George W. Bush for his work for Muslim causes.

brought in Ramadan Abdullah Shallah, the number-two leader in Islamic Jihad, to be the director of WISE.[41]

Al-Arian also brought to Tampa as a guest speaker for WISE none other than Hassan Turabi, the powerful Islamic ruler of Sudan who had welcomed Osama bin Laden and helped nurture Al Qaeda in the early nineties.

Al-Arian has repeatedly denied that he had any links to Islamic terrorism. But terrorism experts have a different view. "Anybody who brings in Hassan Turabi is supporting terrorists," said Oliver "Buck" Revell, the FBI's former top counterterrorist official, now retired and working as a security consultant.[42]

Nor were those Al-Arian's only ties to terrorists. According to *American Jihad* by Steven Emerson, in May 1998 someone known to Al Arian personally traveled to Afghanistan to deliver a satellite telephone and battery to Osama bin Laden.[43] In addition, *Newsweek* reported that Al-Arian had further ties with terrorist organisations."[44]

There were also Al-Arian's own statements. In 1998, he appeared as a guest speaker before the American Muslim Council.[45] According to conservative author Kenneth Timmerman, Al-Arian referred to Jews as "monkeys and pigs" and added, "Jihad is our path. Victory to Islam. Death to Israel. Revolution! Revolution! Until victory! Rolling, rolling to Jerusalem!"

That speech was part of a dossier compiled on Al-Arian by federal agents who have had him under surveillance for many years because of suspected ties to terrorist organizations. In a videotape in that file, Al-Arian was more explicit when he appeared at a fund-raising event, Timmerman says.[46] In an article in the *Tampa Tribune*, Al-Arian later explained, "In the heat of the moment, one may not use the best expressions, especially during impromptu presentations. I had such regrettable moments. However, on many occasions, some of my speeches were mistranslated or totally taken out of context."

Finally—a fact that Bush could not have known at the time—Al-Arian would be arrested in Florida in February 2003 on multiple charges, among them conspiracy to finance an organisation suspected of terrorist attacks that killed more than one hundred people—including two Americans. The indictment alleged that "he directed the audit of all moneys and property of the PIJ [Palestinian Islamic Jihad] throughout the world and was the leader of the PIJ in the United States."[47] The charges refer to the Islamic Jihad as "a criminal organization whose members and associates engaged in acts of violence including murder, extortion, money laundering, fraud, and misuse of visas, and operated worldwide including in the Middle District of Florida."*

Astonishingly enough, the fact that militant Islamists like Al-Arian were campaigning for Bush went almost entirely unnoticed. Noting the absence of criticism from Democrats, Bush speech-writer David Frum later wrote, "There is one way that we Republicans are very lucky—we face political opponents too crippled by political correctness to make an issue of these kinds of security lapses."[48]

Those who were most outraged were staunch Bush supporters and staffers like Frum. "Not only were the al-Arians *not* avoided by the Bush White House—they were actively courted," Frum wrote in the *National Review* more than two years later. "Candidate Bush allowed himself to be photographed with the Al-Arian family while campaigning in Florida .... The Al-Arian case was not a solitary lapse .... That outreach campaign opened relationships between the Bush campaign and some very disturbing persons in the Muslim-American community."[49]

Nevertheless, Norquist continued to build a coalition of Islamist groups to support Bush. On July 31, 2000, the Republican National Convention opened in Philadelphia with a prayer by a Muslim, Talat Othman, in which Othman offered *a duaa,* a Muslim benediction.[50] It was the first time a Muslim had addressed any major U.S. political gathering. A third-generation American and a businessman from Chicago of Muslim-Arab descent, Othman was chairman of the

---

*In December 2003, clerks at a federal courthouse in Tampa accidentally destroyed search warrants in the Al-Arian case. The documents contained affidavits from federal agents that supported 1995 searches of Al-Arian's home and offices and were among thousands of documents shredded sometime between 1998 and 2002. There were serious questions as to whether the destruction of the documents might affect his prosecution.

Islamic Institute. He had also been the board member of Harken Energy representing the interests of Abdullah Taha Bakhsh, the Saudi investor who had helped Bush make his fortune by bailing out Harken in the late eighties.

When the convention ended on August 3, after George W. Bush had formally been nominated for president, between his family's extended personal and financial ties to the House of Saud and his campaign's ties to Islamists, it could be said that he was truly the Arabian Candidate.

Not that Bush was alone in pursuing Muslim voters. Gore occasionally mentioned Muslims as well and met with Muslim leaders at least three times. But because of their unshakable ties to Israel, the Democrats rarely got more than a mixed reception. Hillary Clinton, who was then running for Senate, had won goodwill for endorsing a Palestinian state in 1998. But when she returned a $50,000 donation from the American Muslim Alliance, saying their website had offensive material, Muslims saw her as pandering to Jewish voters in New Yorks.[51] Later in the summer, the Democrats invited Maher Hathout, the senior adviser at the Muslim Public Affairs Council, to give a prayer at the Democratic National Convention. But the Gore team was always a step behind.[52]

Meanwhile, Norquist associate Khaled Saffuri had been named national adviser on Arab and Muslim affairs for the Bush campaign. In September, Saffuri joined Karl Rove in his car as Rove was catching a ride to the airport and explained to him that the vote of Arab Americans—both Muslims and Christians—was still within Bush's grasp if he just said the right things.[53] Rove, apparently, was happy to listen to Saffuri's suggestions.

As the campaign headed into the homestretch, the two candidates were neck and neck, but Bush, with his disarming, self-deprecating charm, was winning on issues of style. "I've been known to mangle a syll-obble or two," he told reporters. By contrast, Gore was stuffy and self-conscious. Mocked for repeatedly using the term *lockbox* to suggest that funding for Social Security and Medicare should be untouchable, Gore was caricatured, not without reason, as a finicky policy wonk. But the level of American political discourse was such that the media obsessed over trivial questions such as whether a character in the movie *Love Story* had been based on Gore and whether he was concealing a bald spot.

On Tuesday, October 3, 2000, the first debate with Gore was a triumph over expectations for Bush, with his reputation for verbal missteps. Next to the vice president, who came off as a stiff, self-conscious, supercilious pedant, Bush appeared charming and at ease with himself. Afterward, thousands of articles appeared all over the country criticizing Gore for making irritating sighs and winces while Bush was speaking.

Two days after the debate, on October 5, Bush was in Michigan to meet with GOP activist George Salem and several other Arab Americans to help him prepare for the second debate with Gore.[54] Along with Florida, Michigan was one of two crucial swing states with a big Muslim electorate. An attorney at the politically wired law firm of Akin Gump Strauss Hauer & Feld, Salem had played key roles for the 1984 Reagan-Bush campaign and the 1988 Bush-Quayle campaign, and helped Bush raise $13 million from Arab Americans for the 2000 presidential campaign. In addition to being active in Arab-American affairs, Salem was the lawyer for Saleh Idriss in his lawsuit against the U.S. government.* Now he was advising the son as he had once advised the father.

Salem made clear to Bush that two issues that would animate Muslim-American voters were the elimination of racial profiling at airports to weed out terrorists and the use of "secret evidence" against Muslims in counterterrorism investigations. The campaign against secret evidence—i.e., the use of classified information in a court case— was a pet project of Sami Al-Arian, the Florida Islamist campaigning for Bush,[55] in part because Al-Arian's brother-in-law, Mazen Al-Najjar, had been detained on the basis of secret evidence for nearly four years.†

---

*Salem also represented the Holy Land Foundation for Relief and Development.

†INS judge R. Kevin McHugh ultimately ruled in Al-Najjar's favor, asserting, "Although there were allegations that the ICP and WISE [the two organizations in question] were fronts for Palestinian political causes, there is *no* evidence before the Court that demonstrates that either organization was a front for the Palestinian

On Wednesday, October 11, the second presidential debate took place in Winston-Salem, North Carolina. The topic was foreign policy, a field in which Gore was thought to have a major advantage over a Texas governor who had rarely ventured abroad. The first questions had to do with when it would be appropriate to use American military force, especially with regard to the Middle East.

One might surmise that Bush's answers would be congruent with policy papers being drawn up by his advisers. Just a few weeks earlier, in September, the Project for a New American Century, with which so many key Bush advisers were associated,* had released a new position paper, "Rebuilding America's Defenses," which dealt with precisely those questions and articulated a bold new policy to establish a more forceful U.S. military presence in the Middle East. The PNAC plan acknowledged that Saddam Hussein's continued presence in Iraq might provide a rationale for U.S. intervention, but it also asserted that it was desirable to have a larger military presence in the Persian Gulf—whether or not Saddam was still in power and even if he was not a real threat. "The United States has for decades sought to play a more permanent role in Gulf regional security. While the unresolved conflict with Iraq provides the immediate justification, the need for a substantial American force presence in the Gulf transcends the issue of the regime of Saddam Hussein,"[56] the paper said.

The policy was so radical that even its authors realized that it would be impossible to implement "absent some catastrophic and catalyzing event—like a new Pearl Harbor."[57] In the pre-9/11 world, voters had not exactly been demanding war in the Middle East or any such radical change in foreign policy. As the presidential campaign

---

... Islamic Jihad. To the contrary, there is evidence in the record to support the conclusion that WISE was a reputable and scholarly research center and the ICP was highly regarded" (emphasis added). This same ruling was upheld by a three-judge panel in Washington, D.C., and Attorney General Janet Reno, who all had access to the secret evidence.

*PNAC signatories who became key figures in the administration of George W. Bush included Vice President Dick Cheney, Secretary of Defense Donald Rumsfeld, Deputy Secretary of Defense Paul Wolfowitz, National Security Council staffer Elliott Abrams, and Zalmay Khalilzad, special presidential envoy for Afghanistan.

neared its last stages, such issues had not even been put before the American electorate. Nor was such a policy likely to play well with the Muslim voters Bush was courting. So when it was Bush's turn to answer, he gave a far more moderate response. He repeatedly asserted that it was essential for the United States to be "a humble nation." "Our nation stands alone right now in the world in terms of power," he said. "And that's why we've got to be humble and yet project strength in a way that promotes freedom .... If we're an arrogant nation, they'll view us that way, but if we're a humble nation, they'll respect us."

More specifically, Bush dismissed the prospect of toppling Saddam because it smacked of what he called "nation building." He chided the Clinton administration for not maintaining the multilateral anti-Saddam coalition that his father had built up in the Gulf War.[58]*

To the tens of millions of voters who had their eyes trained on their televisions, Bush had put forth a moderate foreign policy with regard to the Middle East that was not substantively different from the policy proposed by Al Gore, or, for that matter, from Bill Clinton's. Only a few people who had read the papers put forth by the Project for a New American Century might have guessed a far more radical policy had been developed.

After the Middle East had been discussed, moderator Jim Lehrer asked the two candidates a follow-up question from the previous presidential debate about whether they would support laws to ban racial profiling by police. The question referred to recent instances of racism directed at African Americans, but Bush saw his opening. "There is [sic] other forms of racial profiling that goes on in America," he said. "Arab Americans are racially profiled in what's called secret evidence. People are stopped, and we got to do something about that."

Bush was apparently somewhat confused. He had conflated two

---

*Bush reasserted this point of view in the final presidential debate. "It's going to be important to rebuild that coalition to keep the pressure on [Saddam]," he said. "There may be some moments when we use our troops as peacekeepers, but not often. I'm not so sure the role of the United States is to go around the world and say, 'This is the way it's got to be.'" Cheney echoed Bush's position, saying that the United States should not act as though "we were an imperialist power, willy-nilly moving into capitals in that part of the world."

separate issues—interrogating Arab Americans at airports because people of Middle Eastern descent might be terrorists, and using secret evidence in court in prosecutions against alleged terrorists. But his onstage listeners did not seem to notice, nor did they point out that Bush's newly found civil libertarian stance ran counter to tendencies he had espoused in the past. Bush was renowned for being at odds with the American Civil Liberties Union. But now Bush was stealing a page right out of the ACLU playbook, arguing in effect that the use of secret evidence violated the constitutional right to due process of law. In fact, the ACLU had said the same thing in different words, asserting, "The incarceration and deportation of legal residents and others on the basis of secret evidence is a practice reserved for totalitarian countries, not the United States."

Bush's sudden about-face left the Democrats dumbfounded. But they were not about to attack him for adopting a civil libertarian position—even though he was campaigning with people who were later charged with supporting terrorism. Al Gore scurried to adopt the same position against secret evidence—but too late. Bush had been the first candidate to utter the code words—"racial profiling" and "secret evidence"—that unlocked Muslim-American support. "Within a few seconds I got thirty-one calls on my cell phone," said Usama Siblani, publisher of an Arab-American newspaper in Michigan. "People were excited."[60] The American Muslim Political Coordination Council (AMPCC), an umbrella organization of Muslim political groups, said Bush had shown "elevated concern" over the matter.*

George Salem was elated. "It is unprecedented in U.S. presidential debate history for a candidate for president of the United States to reference such support for Arab-American concerns, and to single out Arab Americans for attention," he said.[61]

The day after the debate, however, October 12, as the USS *Cole* was docked in Aden, Yemen, for refueling, a white fiberglass skiff with two men and five hundred pounds of a powerful plastic explosive

---

*Among the groups operating under the AMPCC are the American Muslim Alliance (AMA), American Muslim Council (AMC), Council on American-Islamic Relations, and Muslim Public Affairs Council (MPAC).

approached the navy destroyer and exploded, killing seventeen American sailors.[62] Counterterrorism czar Richard Clarke had no doubt that bin Laden was behind it and hoped to retaliate even though time was running out for the Clinton administration.[63]

In the presidential campaign, however, even the slaughter of seventeen more Americans did not make terrorism a major issue. Quietly, the Bush campaign was courting a number of Saudi-sponsored organizations and individuals such as Sami Al-Arian who were tied to the very same Islamic fundamentalist charities, such as the Holy Land Foundation and Palestinian Jihad, that counterterrorism officials were trying to investigate. But American voters would never learn that.

What they heard instead was a response by Bush that suggested he had compassion for those who had lost their lives: "Today, we lost sailors because of what looks like to be a terrorist attack." But as Bush continued, his response clearly showed he did not yet understand the new era of terrorism: "Terror is the enemy. Uncertainty is what the world is going to be about, and the next president must be able to address uncertainty. And that's why I want our nation to develop an antiballistic missile system that will have the capacity to bring certainty into this uncertain world." None of Al Qaeda's terrorist attacks had involved missiles, of course, and Bush's proposal of an antiballistic missile system suggests that he failed to understand that Al Qaeda's terrorism was fundamentally different from conventional warfare.

Meanwhile, in response to the three garbled sentences Bush had uttered about Arab Americans in the second debate, endorsements from Muslim groups rolled in for Bush. On Thursday, October 19, a Michigan umbrella group of more than twenty Arab-American groups came out for Bush. The *Detroit Free Press* reported, "What turned them to Bush, they said, was that he specifically mentioned Arab Americans in the second presidential debate and their concerns about airport profiling and the use of secret evidence."[64]

Four days later, the American Muslim Political Coordination Council called a press conference in Washington and announced its endorsement of George W. Bush. The head of the group, Agha Saeed, explained why: "Governor Bush took the initiative to meet with local and national representatives of the Muslim community. He also promised to address Muslim concerns on domestic and foreign policy issues."[65]

As an umbrella organization speaking for several major national Muslim groups, its endorsement meant thousands and thousands of votes to Bush on November 7—especially in Florida, where Al-Najjar's imprisonment was very much a live issue. The cliché was that every vote counted, and this time it would have fresh meaning in the closest and most controversial election in American history.

In the end, the outcome of the election would be decided by Florida's electoral college votes. And in Florida the result was so close, and so riddled with irregularities, that a recount was necessary. The battle over the recount soon worked its way to the U.S. Supreme Court. In an election with such a razor-thin margin, any one of dozens of factors can be held responsible. Ralph Nader's third-party candidacy had taken votes from Al Gore. Various efforts had been made to dissuade black voters from getting to the polls. The "butterfly" ballots of Palm Beach County were so confusing that they went uncounted. The "hanging chads" and "dimpled chads"—rectangular bits of paper that were not completely punched out of the punch-card ballots—led to counting irregularities.

But in the thousands of postmortems about the election, one factor was largely overlooked. According to an exit poll of Muslims in Florida conducted by the American Muslim Alliance, 91 percent voted for Bush, 8 percent for Ralph Nader, and only 1 percent for Al Gore. Likewise, the Tampa Bay Islamic Center estimated that fifty-five thousand Muslims in Florida voted and that 88 percent of them favored Bush.[66] All of which meant that the margin of victory for Bush among Florida Muslims was many, many times greater than his tiny statewide margin of victory of 537 votes.

With the Bush restoration in full swing, GOP partisans eagerly claimed whatever credit they might reasonably take for the Bush victory, and Grover Norquist was no exception. "George W. Bush was elected President of the United States of America because of the Muslim vote," he wrote in the right-wing *American Spectator.* "... That's right," he added, "the Muslim vote."[67]

Like every other group that contributed to Bush's victory, the

Islamists realized that the tiny margin of victory in Florida had increased their leverage. Agha Saeed, the AMPCC chairman, said, "It won't be long before political analysts realize that Muslim voters have played a historic role." And Sami Al-Arian, the engineering professor at the University of South Florida who was later to be arrested on charges relating to terrorism, asserted that the role of the Muslim vote in Florida was "crucial, even decisive."[68]

Even the party regulars agreed. As Tom Davis, the chairman of the National Republican Congressional Committee, put it, without the Muslim endorsements "Florida would have been reversed."[69] In other words, without the mobilization of the Saudi-funded Islamic groups, George W. Bush would not be president today.

CHAPTER THIRTEEN

Lost in Transition

EVEN BEFORE THE SUPREME Court decision awarded the presidency to the Republicans, the Bush team began behaving as if it had won. The election took place exactly ten years after the buildup of American troops in Saudi Arabia for the Gulf War, and to mark both that occasion and the impending Bush restoration, former president Bush and James Baker had proposed a hunting trip in Spain and England. The original guest list included the usual suspects from the Gulf War—the senior Bush; James Baker; Dick Cheney; General Norman Schwarzkopf, the commander of U.S. forces during the war; former national security adviser Brent Scowcroft; and, of course, Prince Bandar, whose enormous estate in Wychwood, England, had been an ancient royal hunting ground used by Norman and Plantagenet kings.[1]

The relationship between Baker and the elder Bush had been frayed as a result of the failed reelection campaign of 1992, but the two long-time friends had patched things up as the presidency of George W. Bush became increasingly probable. When he arrived in Austin, Texas, on Election Day, Baker went to Dick and Lynne Cheney's hotel suite to listen to the results.[2] However, by the next morning, Wednesday, November 8, Al Gore was contesting the Florida vote, so Baker was enlisted to lead the legal battle to win the presidency for Bush. As a result, both he and Cheney skipped the European hunting trip.

But the lavish gathering went on as planned. On Thursday, November 9, a private chartered plane from Evansville, Indiana, picked up former president Bush in Washington en route to Madrid, where the hunting trip was to begin. Already on board was a contingent from Indiana. One member was Bobby Knight, the highly successful but extraordinarily temperamental basketball coach who had just been fired from Indiana University.[3] Other hunters on the trip were powerful coal industry executives from the Midwest—Irl Engelhardt, the chairman and CEO of St. Louis's Peabody Energy, the world's largest coal company; and Steven Chancellor, Daniel Hermann, and Eugene Aimone, three top executives of Black Beauty Coal, a Peabody subsidiary headquartered in Evansville, Indiana.

During the campaign, Bush had proposed caps on the carbon dioxide emissions that scientists believe cause global warming, a regulatory measure that coal executives had not welcomed. But among them, the coal executives had contributed more than $700,000 to Bush and the Republicans.[4] They still had high hopes of participating in energy policy in a Bush administration and loosening the regulatory reins around the industry. Even though the recount battle was just getting under way in Florida, the Bush family was back in action, mixing private pleasure and public policy.

Once in Spain, Bush, Knight, and the executives were joined by Norman Schwarzkopf and proceeded to a private estate in Pinos Altos, about sixty kilometers from Madrid, to shoot red-legged partridges, the fastest game birds in the world. Bush impressed the hunting party as a fine wing shot and a gentleman—the seventy-six-year-old former president was not above offering to clean mud off the boots of his fellow hunters. Throughout the trip, Bush kept in touch with the election developments via e-mail. By Saturday, November 11, a machine recount had shrunk his son's lead in Florida to a minuscule 327 votes. "I kind of wish I was in the U.S. so I could help prevent the Democrats from working their mischief," he told another hunter in his party.[5]

On Tuesday, November 14, Bush and Schwarzkopf arrived in England, where Brent Scowcroft joined them and they continued their game hunting on Bandar's estate.[6] They kept a close eye on the zigs and zags of the recount battle. As a power play to demonstrate his confidence to the media, the Democratic Party, and the American populace, George W. Bush announced the members of his White House transition team even before the Florida vote-count battle was over.

Bandar eagerly anticipated seeing the Bush family back in Washington. Dick Cheney, Colin Powell, and Donald Rumsfeld were men Bandar already knew quite well. Others who would have access to a new President Bush—his father, James Baker, Brent Scowcroft—were also old friends.

Moreover, a Bush restoration would also strengthen Bandar's position in Saudi Arabia. During the twelve years of the Reagan-Bush era, Bandar had enjoyed unique powers—partly because of his close relationship to Bush, partly because he always had King Fahd's ear. But during the Clinton era, Bandar had lost clout. Never an insider in the Clinton White House, he had disliked what he called the "weak-dicked" foreign policy team of the Clinton administration.[7] Bandar had also lost ground in Riyadh because Crown Prince Abdullah, who had effectively replaced the ailing King Fahd, had never been particularly fond of Bandar. But now, on his estate in England, Bandar was once again wired into the real powers that be, and assuming that Bush won, he would be back in a position that no other prominent foreign official could come close to.

The anticipatory mood of the Bush-Bandar hunting trip contrasted sharply with what was going on in the White House, where, during the last days of the Clinton administration, the central figures in the battle against terrorism were frustrated beyond all measure. In the wake of the bombing of the USS *Cole* just a few weeks earlier, counterterrorism czar Richard Clarke—officially, head of the Counterterrorism Security Group of the National Security Council—felt acutely that the threat of Islamist terror was greater than ever. But since the Clinton administration was leaving office, it was unclear what he would be able to do about it.

A civil servant who had ascended to the highest levels of policy making, Clarke was a true Washington rarity. As characterized in *The Age of Sacred Terror,* he broke all the rules. He refused to attend regular National Security Council staff meetings, sent insulting e-mails to his colleagues, and regularly worked outside normal bureaucratic channels. Beholden to neither Republicans nor Democrats, the crew-cut, white-haired Clarke was one of two senior directors from the administration of the elder George Bush who were kept on by Bill Clinton, and abrasive as he was, he had continued to rise because of his genius for knowing when and how to push the levers of power.

Obsessed with the fear that bin Laden's next strike would take place on American soil, after the USS *Cole* bombing Clarke had prepared a proposal for a massive attack on Osama bin Laden and Al Qaeda in Afghanistan. But Clarke's plan faced one major obstacle. On Tuesday, December 12, the U.S. Supreme Court ruled by a vote of 5 to 4 that the recount of the disputed votes in Florida could not continue. In effect, it had awarded the presidency of the United States to George W. Bush.

Eight days later, on December 20, 2000, Clarke presented his plan to his boss, National Security Adviser Sandy Berger, and other principals on the National Security Council. But with only a month left in the Clinton administration, Berger felt it would be ill-advised to initiate military action just as the reins of power were being handed over to Bush.[8]

At the same time, Berger was obligated to make clear to the Bush team that bin Laden and Al Qaeda posed a national security threat that required urgent and aggressive action. As a result, in the early days of January 2001, Berger scheduled no fewer than ten briefings by his staff for his successor, Condoleezza Rice, and her deputy, Stephen J. Hadley.[9] Berger decided that it was not necessary for him to go to most of the briefings, but he made a point of attending one he felt was absolutely crucial. "I'm coming to this briefing to underscore how important I think this subject is," he told Rice.[10] At that meeting Clarke presented the incoming Bush team with an aggressive plan to attack Al Qaeda.

The meeting began at 1:30 p.m. on Wednesday, January 3, 2001, in Room 302 of the Old Executive Office Building, a room full of maps and charts that had become home base for Clarke and his chief of staff, Roger Cressey.[11] With Rice present, Clarke launched into a PowerPoint presentation on his offensive against Al Qaeda. Bush administration officials have denied being given a formal plan to take action against Al Qaeda. But the heading on slide 14 belies that denial. It read, "Response to al Qaeda: Roll back." Specifically, that meant attacking Al Qaeda's cells, freezing its assets, stopping the flow of money from Wahhabi charities, and breaking up Al Qaeda's financial network. It meant giving financial aid to countries fighting Al Qaeda such as Uzbekistan, Yemen, and the Philippines. It called for air strikes in Afghanistan and Special Forces operations. The Taliban had been in power in Afghanistan since 1996, and because they were providing a haven for and being supported by Osama bin Laden, Clarke proposed massive aid to the Northern Alliance, the last resistance forces against them.

Most significantly of all, Clarke called for covert operations "to eliminate the sanctuary" in Afghanistan where the Taliban was protecting bin Laden and his terrorist training camps.[12] The idea was to force terrorist recruits to fight and die for the Taliban in Afghanistan, rather than to allow them to initiate terrorist acts all over the world. The plan was budgeted at several hundred million dollars, and *Time* reported, according to one senior Bush official, it amounted to "everything we've done since 9/11."[13]

After the session, Berger underscored the challenge the next administration faced. "I believe that the Bush administration will spend more time on terrorism generally, and on Al Qaeda specifically, than any other subject," he told Rice.

It seems fair to say that until this point Condoleezza Rice had not taken Islamist terrorism seriously as a threat. Less than a year earlier, in a lengthy article in *Foreign Affairs,* Rice had voiced her contempt for the Clinton administration's foreign policies, and expressed her views on America's strategic foreign policy concerns.[14] Her brief references to terrorism in the article suggest she saw it as a threat only in terms of the state-sponsored terrorism of Iran, Iraq, Libya, and other countries that predated the transnational jihad of bin Laden and Al Qaeda. And in her speech before the Republican National Convention, Rice had not mentioned terrorism at all. Rather she had suggested that America's most difficult foreign policy challenges would come from China.[15]

After the briefing, Rice, who was about to become Clarke's boss, admitted to him that the dangers from Al Qaeda appeared to be greater than she had realized. Then she asked him, "What are you going to do about it?" According to Clarke, "She wanted an organized strategy review."[16] But she did not give Clarke a specific tasking.

During the changeover from an old administration to a new one, incoming officials frequently fall victim to "death by briefing" by each component of the government. Thus well-intentioned, carefully prepared plans from one administration may be sacrificed in turf wars or be lost in transition as a new administration takes office. Some members of the Bush team saw setting up a new missile defense system as their highest priority. For his part, Secretary of Defense Donald Rumsfeld wanted to overhaul the entire structure of the military. As a result, Bush, Cheney, and Rumsfeld all wanted to go after Iraq. Clarke's proposal sat there and sat there and sat there.

Nothing happened.

Meanwhile, the intricate private networks the Bushes had painstakingly assembled over four decades came alive again in the public sector with astonishing speed. Never before had the highest levels of an administration so nakedly represented the oil industry. Between them, the president, vice president, national security adviser, and secretary of commerce had held key positions in small independent oil companies (Arbusto, Bush Exploration, and Harken Energy), major publicly traded companies (Halliburton and Chevron), and one huge independent Texas oil company (Tom Brown). Secretary of the Army Thomas White was a former high-ranking Enron executive, and Robert Zoellick, the U.S. trade representative, was a member of Enron's advisory board. Others, including Karl Rove and Lewis "Scooter" Libby, Dick Cheney's chief of staff, owned large blocks of Enron stock when they joined the new Bush administration.[17]

But it was not just the oil industry that had access to the White House. Campaign contributors such as coal executives Irl Engelhardt and Steve Chancellor, both among the men who had gone hunting with George H. W. Bush in Spain, were named to Bush's Energy Transition Team.* Rewarding campaign contributors with direct access to White House policy makers was suddenly the rule, not the exception. According to the Center for Responsive Politics, Engelhardt and Chancellor were among 474 people named by the Bush cam-

---

*Less than two months after Bush took office, Engelhardt and Chancellor's huge contributions paid off many times over when Bush went back on his campaign promise to impose federal regulations on carbon dioxide released by power plants. His decision was a huge boon to the coal industry, but it drew sharp criticism from environmentalists. "He's turned his back on the weight of all the alarming scientific consensus that global warming is real, and that carbon dioxide is the main cause," said David Doniger, a spokesman for the Natural Resources Defense Council.

paign to serve as key policy advisers during the presidential transition who contributed a total of more than $5.6 million to federal candidates and party committees during the 2000 elections. Ninety-five percent of those campaign contributions went to Bush, other GOP candidates, or the Republican Party.*

All in all, if one looked at George W. Bush's new administration and the people he had brought in from his father's, the extraordinary confluence of power in the public and private sectors created an enormous potential for conflicts of interest and colored serious policy questions—especially with regard to energy policy and the Middle East. Tens of billions of dollars were at stake. The Bush administration could help decide which companies would be awarded lucrative defense contracts, how to resolve regulatory questions regarding the energy industry, whether sanctions should prohibit trade with oil-producing terrorist states such as Iran, Iraq, and Libya, and a host of other multibillion-dollar issues. Did the long history of incestuous relationships give friends, relatives, and political allies of the Bushes an inside track on winning defense contracts? Would they affect regulation of the energy industry, the Bush administration's position on trade sanctions against Iran and Iraq, or oversight of industry giants such as Enron? Given the Bush family's relationship with the House of Saud, not to mention its new alliance with Islamist groups in America, how closely would the new administration examine the rise of Islamist terrorism?

As the day approached when George W. Bush would be sworn in to power, the Saudis and the Bushes decided that the occasion called

*Among the most generous of the contributors were Dick Farmer, chairman of the uniform producer Cintas Corporation ($685,000 total, all of it to Republicans), who was named to the Veterans Advisory Team; Richard Egan of EMC Corporation ($567,100 total, $561,100 to Republicans), the world's number-one maker of mainframe computer memory hardware and software, who was named to the Commerce Advisory Team; John Chambers, CEO of tech giant Cisco Systems ($372,500 total, $304,000 to Republicans), who was named to the Education Advisory Team; Kenneth Lay, head of energy giant Enron ($318,050 total, $310,050 to Republicans), who was named to the Energy Advisory Team; Ken Eldred of Eldred Enterprises ($311,727 total, all of it to Republicans), who was named to the Commerce Advisory Team; and Charles Dolan of Cablevision Systems, Inc. ($270,000 total, $262,000 to Republicans), who was named to the FCC Advisory Team.

for a joint celebration. On Friday, January 19, the night before the inauguration, the Baker Botts law firm threw a party for the elder George Bush and Prince Bandar at the Ronald Reagan Building, the mammoth international trade center just a few blocks from the White House. Not long afterward, unprompted, one of Bandar's aides at the Saudi embassy told a visitor, "Happy days are here again."[18]

Now that the Bush team had retaken the White House, its friends in the private sector had more clout than ever. Just after the inauguration, in early February, Rumsfeld met with fellow Princeton wrestling teammate Frank Carlucci, also a former secretary of defense, who had led the way for the Carlyle Group's massive defense acquisitions. Carlucci said the meeting did not constitute a conflict because he was not lobbying his old friend.[19] "I've made it clear that I don't lobby the defense industry," Carlucci stated. But at the time, Carlyle still had several projects under consideration by the Pentagon that were potentially worth billions in contracts, and Carlucci, James Baker, Richard Darman, and other Bush allies might profit from them.* Most notable among these projects was United Defense's $11-billion contract for the Crusader tank, a gigantic Cold War-inspired weapon that was widely seen as obsolete, but which managed to stay in the budget.[20]†

Bush's allies were also well positioned to take advantage of the new administration's close ties to the Saudis. On February 5, just two weeks after the inauguration, Baker Botts announced that it had established a new office in Riyadh, presumably to better service its Saudi clients. "The kingdom has opened its doors to Western clients," explained managing partner Richard Johnson, "so we need to have a presence in the region."[21] Later that year, the firm acquired another

---

*According to a Carlyle spokesman, George H. W. Bush himself had no investments in Carlyle's defense companies. Instead, he was compensated at $80,000 to $100,000 per speaking engagement and could reinvest that money in various Carlyle funds.

†In April 2001, a government advisory panel recommended abandoning the Crusader tank, which is made by Carlyle subsidiary United Defense, but it stayed in the budget until Rumsfeld finally killed it at the end of 2002. Even with the program shut down, United Defense still did quite well with it. According to the *Washington Post*, the company took in more than $2 billion from the Crusader.

powerful friend in the region when Bush named the new ambassador to Saudi Arabia—Robert Jordan, the Baker Botts attorney who had represented Bush during the SEC's investigation into the Harken Energy insider trading allegations against him. In addition to representing such oil giants as ExxonMobil, ARCO, BP Amoco, and Halliburton, all of which did business with the Saudis, Baker Botts enjoyed the confidence of corporate clients whose businesses could be affected by the administration's policies. Highest on this list were the Carlyle Group and Dick Cheney's company, Halliburton, both of which had hundreds of millions of dollars in business with the Saudis.

Reporters have widely noted that Halliburton also stood to benefit from the friendly new administration. Almost immediately after the inauguration, Halliburton opened an office in Tehran, a move that, according to the *Wall Street Journal,* was "in possible violation of U.S. sanctions." Halliburton publicly called for lifting the sanctions against working in Iran, but insisted it was not violating U.S. laws because the company in question was a Halliburton subsidiary, not the domestic company itself.[22]

Rather than crack down on Halliburton, however, the Bush administration's Energy Task Force, which was headed by Cheney, presented a draft report in April 2001 saying the United States should reevaluate the sanctions against Iran, Iraq, and Libya that prohibited U.S. oil companies from "some of the most important existing and 'prospective' petroleum-producing countries in the world." Cheney asserted there was no conflict on his part because "Since I left Halliburton to become George Bush's vice president, I've severed all my ties with the company, gotten rid of all my financial interest."[23] Cheney neglected to mention that he was still due approximately $500,000 in deferred compensation from Halliburton and could potentially profit from his 433,333 shares of unexercised Halliburton stock options.[24]*

But more to the point, Cheney, as secretary of defense during the Gulf War, had begun a warm relationship with the Saudis. Even

---

*A Congressional Research Service report requested by Senate Democrats concluded that unexercised stock options in a private corporation, as well as deferred salary received from a private corporation, were "retained ties" or "linkages" to a former employer and should be reported as "financial interests."

though he had little experience in the private sector, after he left his cabinet post, Halliburton had selected Cheney as CEO because of such contacts, so that the oil giant might expand its largely domestic portfolio into foreign markets, including Saudi Arabia.* In his last year at Halliburton, Cheney had received $34 million from the company. Now Cheney was back on the other side of the revolving door, in a position to do business with his benefactors, and he had been uniquely sensitized to Saudi needs.

Meanwhile, the biggest foreign-policy initiative in the early days of the administration was a secretive one—how to get rid of Saddam Hussein. "It was all about finding a way to do it," said former secretary of the treasury Paul O'Neill, who as a cabinet secretary was a member of the National Security Council. "That was the tone of it. The president saying, 'Go find me a way to do this.' For me the notion of preemption, that the U.S. has a unilateral right to do whatever we decide to do, is really a huge leap." O'Neill added that such questions as "Why Saddam?" and "Why now?" were never discussed.[25]

According to O'Neill, as reported in *The Price of Loyalty* by Ron Suskind, plans for occupying Iraq were discussed just days after the inauguration in January 2001. By March, the Pentagon had drawn up a document entitled "Foreign Suitors for Iraqi Oilfield Contracts."

Ironically, three key figures in the administration—Dick Cheney, who had been a prominent Republican congressman, Secretary of State Colin Powell, who had been national security adviser, and Donald Rumsfeld, who had been Reagan's special presidential envoy to Iraq—had all played vital roles in giving Saddam Hussein a pass back in the Reagan-Bush era. Cheney and Rumsfeld had since become quite hawkish on Iraq—both were part of the Project for a New American Century—but Colin Powell remained convinced that Saddam was not a real threat. "Frankly, the sanctions [against Iraq] have worked," he said in February 2001. "Saddam has not deployed any significant capability with respect to weapons of mass destruction. He is unable to project conventional power against his neighbors."[26†]

---

*In July 2001, Halliburton announced that its profits had tripled and that the drilling outlook was bright in Saudi Arabia, among other places.

†On October 26, 2003, on *Meet the Press*, Powell was asked about this quote and said, "I did not think he had a significant capability but he did have a capability. And

* * *

As the first year of the Bush administration got under way, throughout the intelligence world analysts again and again heard in the "chatter" of monitored conversations that a major new Al Qaeda operation was in the works. At times, the intelligence was so cluttered with rumors, misinformation, and disinformation that, understandably, it was almost impossible to ferret out the vital clues. At other times, veteran FBI and CIA agents repeatedly discovered suspicious activity that they reported to their superiors. Not all, but substantial numbers of these reports found their way to the most senior counterterrorism official in the country, Richard Clarke.

In 2001, Clarke and Roger Cressey stayed on at the NSC with the new administration. They followed up their briefings with Condoleezza Rice with a memo on January 25, 2001, saying that more Islamist terrorist attacks had been set in motion since the bombing of the USS *Cole*. Worse, they reported that U.S. intelligence now believed that there were already Al Qaeda "sleeper cells" in America.[27]

Clarke and Cressey were not alone in their awareness of the growing threat. Six days later, on January 31, a bipartisan commission led by former senators Gary Hart and Warren Rudman warned Congress that a devastating terrorist attack on U.S. soil could be imminent. In the report, seven Democrats and seven Republicans unanimously approved fifty recommendations in hopes of addressing the commission's assessment that "the combination of unconventional weapons proliferation with the persistence of international terrorism will end the relative invulnerability of the U.S. homeland to catastrophic attack."[28]

Not long after the commission's report was released, on February 7, CIA director George Tenet testified in Congress that "Osama bin

---

... everybody agreed with that assessment. Foreign intelligence sources agreed with it. The previous administration, President Clinton and his administration, agreed with it. The United Nations agreed with that assessment year after year, resolution after resolution. And the information we presented earlier this year and the presentation that I made before the United Nations on the fifth of February of this year was the best judgments that were made by the intelligence community, all members of the intelligence community of the United States coming together, and it was a judgment that was shared by a number of other countries around the world."

Laden and his global network of lieutenants and associates remain the most immediate and serious threat" to American security.[29]

Nevertheless, even with CIA support, the recommendations of the Hart-Rudman Commission didn't get far. As Hart later lamented, "Frankly, the White House shut it down. The president said, 'Please wait, we're going to turn this over to the vice president. We believe FEMA [Federal Emergency Management Agency] is competent to coordinate this effort.' And so Congress moved on to other things, like tax cuts."

By early February, intelligence analysts had definitively nailed down Al Qaeda's involvement in bombing the USS *Cole*. As a candidate, in the wake of the attack, Bush had said, "I hope that we can gather enough intelligence to figure out who did the act and take the necessary action. There must be a consequence."[30] Richard Clarke had a specific response in mind. He now argued for striking Al Qaeda's training camps at Tarnak Qila and Garmabat Ghar in Afghanistan—easy targets that were important because thousands of terrorist recruits trained there to fight the Northern Alliance, the Afghan rebel coalition, or against American interests.

But the Bush administration did not go along with it. Condoleezza Rice and her deputy, Stephen J. Hadley, reportedly admired Clarke's fervor. But they believed Clarke's strategy of battling Al Qaeda would not work. "The premise was, you either had to get the Taliban to give up Al Qaeda, or you were going to have to go after both the Taliban and Al Qaeda together," Hadley told the *Washington Post*. "As long as Al Qaeda is in Afghanistan under the protection of the Taliban ... you're going to have to treat it as a system and either break them apart, or go after them together."[31]

In the Clinton administration, Clarke's colleagues had been on watch during the attacks against Americans in Riyadh, Kenya, Tanzania, and on the USS *Cole*, and terrorism came up at cabinet meetings nearly every week. But according to army lieutenant general Donald Kerrick, who managed the National Security Council staff and stayed at the NSC through the spring of the new administration's first year, Bush's advisers were not focused on it. "That's not being derogatory," Kerrick said. "It's just a fact. I didn't detect any activity but what Dick Clarke and the CSG were doing."[32] Without a clear-cut consensus behind them at the highest levels of the Bush administration, Clarke's proposals had to be subjected to a policy review that would take months. In the meantime, there was nothing to take their place. As a result, the tough rhetoric against terrorism espoused by Bush during the campaign was not backed up by action.

One development that typified the bureaucratic inertia was the Bush administration's failure to use the Predator aerial vehicle—an unmanned drone that, without risk to human life, was able to deliver thousands of photos of Al Qaeda's terrorist training camps. It had been deployed quite successfully during the Clinton administration, but now it was not even being used because of arguments between the Pentagon and the CIA over who should pay for it.[33]

Meanwhile, bin Laden's operatives were on the move. Some had already entered the United States. Over the next few months, others completed their training in Afghanistan and prepared to enter the United States. One already in the United States was a Saudi named Hani Hanjour, from the resort town of Taif. In January and February, Peggy Chevrette, a manager at the JetTech flight school in Phoenix, notified the Federal Aviation Administration three times that Hanjour lacked the necessary flying skills for the commercial pilot's license he had obtained in 1999. In response, an FAA inspector checked Hanjour's license and even sat next to him in a class. But the FAA said the inspector observed nothing that warranted further action.[34]

On February 26, 2001, Osama bin Laden attended the wedding of his son Mohammed, in the southern Afghan town of Kandahar, and read aloud a poem that appeared to refer to the bombing of the USS *Cole*. According to the Saudi paper *al-Hayat*, the poem read:

Your brothers in the East prepared their mounts and Kabul has
    prepared itself and the battle camels are ready to go.
A destroyer: even the brave fear its might. It inspires horror in the
    harbor and in the open sea. She goes into the waves flanked
    by arrogance, haughtiness, and fake might. To her doom she
    progresses slowly, clothed in a huge illusion.
Awaiting her is a dinghy, bobbing in the waves, disappearing and
    reappearing in view.

Many Bin Ladens had claimed they were completely estranged from Osama. But the wedding was reportedly also attended by a senior member of the Bin Laden family, and a number of siblings.[35] In addition, at roughly the same time, also in February, pro-West intelligence operatives alleged they saw two of Osama bin Laden's sisters taking cash to an airport in Abu Dhabi in the United Arab Emirates, where, the *New Yorker* reported, they were "suspected of handing it to a member of bin Laden's Al Qaeda organization."[36]

A few days after the wedding in Kandahar, thirteen Al Qaeda operatives recorded farewell videos before ending their training. In one of them, which was broadcast on the Arab TV news station Aljazeera in September 2002, Ahmed Alhaznawi pledged to send a "bloodied message" to Americans by attacking them in their "heartland."[37] In a similar video, Abdulaziz Alomari, another Al Qaeda operative, who was a graduate of an Islamic college in the Saudi province of El Qaseem, made an apparent reference to his last testament: "I am writing this with my full conscience and I am writing this in expectation of the end, which is near .... God praise everybody who trained and helped me, namely the leader Sheikh Osama bin Laden."[38] Other videos showed operatives studying maps and flight manuals in preparation for their mission.

In March, the Italian government gave the Bush administration information based on wiretaps of two Al Qaeda agents in Milan who talked about "a very, very secret plan" to forge documents for "the brothers who are going to the United States."[39]

On April 18, U.S. airlines got a memo from the FAA warning that they should demonstrate a "high degree of alertness" because Middle Eastern terrorists might try to hijack or blow up an American plane.[40] By this time, airlines had been receiving one or two such warnings per month—but the threats were so frequent and, often, so vague, they had little impact on security. Likewise, beginning in May, over a two-month period, the National Security Agency reported "at least thirty-three communications indicating a possible, imminent terrorist attack." But, according to congressional testimony, none of the reports provided specific information on where, when, or how an attack might occur.[41] There were so many warnings that officials grew numb to them.

Yet inexplicably, in the context of so many warnings, the Bush administration introduced policies that could only be counterproductive. Far from cracking down on the Taliban, in May, Colin Powell announced that the United States was actually giving $43 million to the Taliban because of its policies against growing opium. "Enslave your girls and women, harbor anti-U.S. terrorists, destroy every vestige of civilization in your homeland, and the Bush administration will embrace you," wrote columnist Robert Scheer in the *Los Angeles Times*. "All that matters is that you line up as an ally in the drug war, the only international cause that this nation still takes seriously .... Never mind that Osama bin Laden still operates the leading anti-American terror operation from his base in Afghanistan, from which, among other crimes, he launched two bloody attacks on American embassies in Africa in 1998."[42]

Then, in June, the American embassy in Saudi Arabia initiated new security measures that could only be described as absurd, announcing that its new Visa Express program would allow any Saudi to obtain a visa to the United States—*without actually appearing at the consulate in person*. The United States waives visas for twenty-eight countries, mostly in Western Europe. But Saudi Arabia was to be the only nation to enjoy the privileges of this new program, launched, in the most fertile breeding ground for terrorists in the world, for a simple reason: convenience. An official embassy announcement said, "Applicants will no longer have to take time off from work, no longer have to wait in long lines under the hot sun and in crowded waiting rooms."[43]

According to Jessica Vaughan, a former consular officer, Visa Express was "a bad idea" because the issuing officer "has no idea whether the person applying for the visa is actually the person [listed] in the documents and application."

Another official described the program as "an open-door policy for terrorists."[44]

And it was—quite literally. Before the program was in place, eleven Al Qaeda operatives had already made their way to the United States in preparation for September 11. But thanks to Visa Express, three Saudis—Abdulaziz Alomari, about twenty-eight years old, Khalid Almidhar, twenty-five, and Salem Alhazmi, twenty—began their journey to September 11 without the inconvenience of even having to wait in line.

* * *

Meanwhile, Bush had not forgotten that one of the constituencies that helped get him to the White House consisted of Islamic fundamentalists. Having depended so heavily on Muslim-American organizations during the Florida campaign, the Bush administration continued its "outreach" to Muslims. On June 22, 2001, Karl Rove addressed 160 members of the American Muslim Council on Bush's faith-based agenda in the Eisenhower Executive Office Building, which is adjacent to the White House and part of the White House complex.

The meeting stirred up controversy even before it took place. The scheduled speaker had actually been Cheney. But that morning, a front-page headline in the *Jerusalem Post* read, "Cheney to host pro-terrorist Muslim group." Citing logistical conflicts, Cheney canceled and Rove took his place.[45] Conservative pro-Israeli activists felt the Bush administration should be more careful about the Muslim activists that Grover Norquist was bringing into the White House. In this case, they had argued against the meeting because of concerns about the AMC's stance on Hamas, a sponsor of suicide bombings in Israel.[46] Nevertheless, the meeting went forth as scheduled, and Abdurahman Alamoudi, one of AMC's founders, attended even though less than a year earlier he had appeared at a White House demonstration where he said, "We are all supporters of Hamas."[47] In a written response, Alamoudi later said, "I regret that I made an emotional statement in the heat of the moment and I retract it."

The Secret Service requires White House visitors to submit their Social Security number and birth date for security reasons. But on this occasion, someone of even more dubious background than Alamoudi slipped by them—Sami Al-Arian, the professor at the University of South Florida who had campaigned for Bush. At the time, Al-Arian had been under investigation by the FBI for at least six years, and several news accounts had reported that federal agents suspected he had links to terrorism.

At roughly the same time Bush's staff was wooing Al-Arian, counterterrorism agents were digging up detailed information on terrorists that could be acted upon—but even then they were thwarted. In July

2001, a highly regarded forty-one-year-old FBI counterterrorism agent in Phoenix named Kenneth Williams was investigating suspected Islamic terrorists when he noticed that several of them were taking lessons to fly airplanes.[48] Williams became more suspicious after he heard that some of the men had been asking questions about airport security procedures. His supervisor, Bill Kurtz, thought Williams might be onto something and proposed monitoring civil aviation schools to see if bin Laden's operatives had infiltrated them. But, according to *Newsweek*, in Washington, Kurtz's proposal was completely ignored. Because George Bush had criticized the practice of racial profiling of Arab Americans in his presidential campaign, the FBI now pointedly avoided such measures. In addition, after John Ashcroft, the new attorney general, had taken office in January, the Justice Department had been directed to focus on child pornography, drugs, and violent crime—not counterterrorism.

Other bin Laden operatives were on the move. In early 2000 two of bin Laden's operatives, Khalid Almidhar and Nawaf Alhazmi, arrived in Los Angeles fresh from an Al Qaeda planning summit in Kuala Lumpur, Malaysia. In L.A., they were soon befriended by Omar al-Bayoumi, the Saudi who had received payments from Prince Bandar's wife, Princess Haifa bint Faisal.[49] In addition to throwing a party for them in San Diego to welcome them to the United States, al-Bayoumi guaranteed the lease on their apartment and, *Newsweek* reported, also paid $1,500 for the first two months' rent.* In July 2001, al-Bayoumi left the United States, but the monthly payments from Princess Haifa of about $3,500 allegedly began flowing instead to his associate, Osama Basnan. According to *Newsweek*, it was unclear whether the money given to the hijackers came from al-Bayoumi or Basnan. There is no evidence that Princess Haifa or Prince Bandar knew they may have been indirectly subsidizing Al Qaeda. Bandar has denied all allegations that he or his wife knowingly aided terrorists.

* * *

*Officials said it was possible that Almidhar and Alhazmi may have repaid the money at an undetermined date.

Another reason Prince Bandar looked forward to the return of the Bushes was that he expected the incoming president to help resolve the Israeli-Palestinian crisis. In the final days of the Clinton era, Bandar had quietly gone back and forth between Washington and Palestinian leader Yasir Arafat in a frantic attempt to resolve the Palestinian issue. Hardly a fan of Clinton's, even Bandar recognized that Clinton's new peace plan, which would have given the Palestinians 97 percent of the occupied territories, much of Jerusalem, and $30 billion in compensation, was the best deal ever offered to Arafat. Conditions in the Middle East were always volatile—the Palestinians, Israelis, Arabs, and the United States all had their own internal politics to contend with—it was possible that the opportunity for a settlement could quickly vanish.

But in January 2001, as Inauguration Day approached, the obstinate Arafat turned the deal down. The negotiations had failed. Exhausted, Bandar still hoped that the intractable conflict could finally be resolved. According to the *New Yorker,* before Bush was sworn in, Colin Powell assured Bandar that the new administration would enforce the same Middle East deal that Clinton had negotiated.[50] Within a few weeks, however, Bandar met with the new president and emerged quite upset: Bush had told him that he did not intend to take an aggressive role in mediating the conflict.[51] Historically, the House of Saud had refrained from intervening as forcefully as it might have on the side of the Palestinians. But Israel had killed 307 Palestinians and injured 11,300 during the previous year,[52] and now a great opportunity for peace was slipping away. In February, the hawkish Ariel Sharon was elected to replace Ehud Barak as prime minister of Israel. The violence in Israel continued to escalate. Now that satellite TV was broadcast throughout the Arab world, the news was relentless in Riyadh. Saudis who turned to Aljazeera saw Israeli soldiers attacking Palestinians hour after hour, day after day. On March 3, Palestinians were killed by Israelis in three separate incidents.[53] In April, a Palestinian cabinet minister accused Israel of using a car bomb in an attempt to assassinate a Fatah activist. That same month, Israelis shot dead a fourteen-year-old Palestinian in the West Bank village of Beit Ummar.[54]

Yet the Bush administration blamed all the violence on Arafat. In private conversations with the Saudis, people in the administration said that the president would not waste his slim political capital on what he saw as an unsolvable mess.[55] Their calculus made sense: Bush had been president for only a few months, needed to press his domestic agenda, and was barely legitimate in the eyes of many Americans.

But as a result, Bush's standing in the House of Saud suddenly plummeted. He appeared to be drawing too close to Ariel Sharon and was doing nothing to help the Middle East peace process. In May, Saudi crown prince Abdullah even turned down an invitation to the White House. "The U.S. enjoys a distinguished position as the leader of the new world," he said. "And like it or not, this requires it to meet crises before they get out of hand."[56] Never before had Abdullah been so blunt in criticizing the United States.

"We want them [the United States] to ... consider their own conscience," he told a *Financial Times* reporter. "Don't they see what is happening to the Palestinian children, women, the elderly, the humiliation, the hunger?"[57]

The Saudis were not alone in their assessment. Even old Saudi hands like Brent Scowcroft, who had served as national security adviser for Bush's father, criticized the administration for letting down its Arab friends during the conflict.[58]

The rupture was so precipitous that former president Bush himself felt obliged to intervene on his son's behalf. The elder George Bush still kept his hand in foreign policy, an area in which his son was untutored, and continued to receive regular briefings from the CIA. It was a privilege granted to all former presidents, but one that Bush, a former CIA director himself, used far more than anyone else—perhaps in part because he had a son in the White House who had so little experience in foreign affairs.[59] At the CIA, the briefings were jokingly called the "president's daddy's daily briefing."

In late June, Bush senior called Abdullah to tell him that his son's "heart is in the right place" and that his son was "going to do the right thing."[60] Effectively, he was assuring Abdullah that his son's policies in the Middle East would be similar to his own—i.e., that his son was not too pro-Israel. The tone of the conversation was said to be warm and familiar, and according to the *New York Times*, the president himself was in the room with the elder Bush at the time of the call.

For the time being, the relationship between the Bushes and the House of Saud appeared to be back on track.

As the terrorists continued their preparation through the summer, warning signs reached Richard Clarke. On July 5, he assembled officials from a dozen federal agencies—the Coast Guard, the FBI, the Secret Service, the Immigration and Naturalization Service, and others—in the White House Situation Room. "Something really spectacular is going to happen here, and it's going to happen soon," Clarke told them.[61] By here, he meant within the United States. According to the *Washington Post,* Clarke then ordered every counterterrorist office to put domestic rapid-response teams on shorter alert, to cancel vacations and defer nonvital travel; in short, to be in the highest possible state of readiness against an imminent attack.

By this time, the reality of the threat had reached the Oval Office. Not long after Clarke's exercise, according to *Time,* President Bush told CIA director George Tenet, "Give me a sense of what Al Qaeda can do inside the U.S."[62]

On August 4, President Bush traveled to his sixteen-hundred-acre ranch in Crawford, Texas. The new Western White House was not exactly a popular choice for the reporters who covered him. In summers past, Clinton had taken the White House press corps to such glamorous resorts as Martha's Vineyard, Massachusetts, or Jackson Hole, Wyoming. Covering Bush senior in August had meant passing time on the gorgeous rugged coast in Kennebunkport, Maine. By contrast, Crawford—population 705—was located smack in the middle of nowhere and offered few diversions. On the Vineyard or at Kennebunkport, there were clambakes and lobsters; in Crawford, haute cuisine meant a "Bush burger" at the Coffee Station, the only restaurant in town. In Crawford, the town's first sidewalk was still under construction. About sixty reporters camped out in a muggy gym seven miles from the ranch, constantly calling presidential aides to get tidbits of news.[63] And every day in the flat scrub plains of Crawford, it was one hundred degrees in the day, eighty at night, one hundred in the day, eighty at night.

To make matters worse, Bush had decided to spend more than just a couple of weeks in Crawford. He was going to repose there for the entire month of August to take nature walks and fish for bass. Bush defended his long vacation. "I just want to remind you all I love to go walking out there, seeing the cows," he said. "Occasionally, they talk to me, being the good listener that I am."

But the press didn't like it.

"By the time President Bush returns to Washington on Labor Day after the longest presidential vacation in 32 years, he will have spent all or part of 54 days since the inauguration at his parched but beloved ranch," the *Washington Post* observed. "That's almost a quarter of his presidency .... Throw in four days last month at his parents' seaside estate in Kennebunkport, Maine, and 38 full or partial days at the presidential retreat at Camp David, and Bush will have spent 42 percent of his presidency at vacation spots or en route."[64]

In response, the White House spin factory made clear that this was a "working" vacation, and in truth, Bush had a lot on his mind. There was a paralyzing energy crisis in California. There was the controversy over whether to allow stem cell research, which placed Bush between medical scientists and the evangelical right. And there was the Israeli-Palestinian conflict.

In addition, the concerns about bin Laden and Al Qaeda had not abated. Ordinarily, one of the key starting points of the day for any president is the President's Daily Briefing, or PDB, which represents the CIA's chance to funnel its priorities onto the president's agenda. The briefing is customarily delivered before the White House national security team—sometimes by the CIA director himself. During the vacation, one of the Agency's briefers had relocated to Crawford to help out with the PDB.

On August 6, the PDB was crafted to answer Bush's query about the threat of an Al Qaeda attack on American soil.[65] That hot Texas morning, he had already gone for a four-mile run and returned with dust on his sweats, then changed into what the press called his "Crawford casual" ensemble—jeans with a big belt buckle, a short-sleeved button-down shirt, and cowboy boots—for the meeting.[66]

The memo, which is classified and which the Bush administration had refused to release, was to become a matter of extraordinary controversy. Even its title was a matter of debate. Bush press secretary Ari Fleischer said it was called "Bin Laden Determined to Strike the

U.S." But other sources said Fleischer had left out a critical preposition, and it was really "Bin Laden Determined to Strike *in* the U.S."

Condoleezza Rice was not actually present as the briefing was given. But she discussed it with Bush immediately afterward, as was her practice. According to Rice, the memo was merely analytical and historical, discussing the practices Al Qaeda had used in the past. She said that just one or two sentences dealt with hijacking and they did not raise the possibility that a hijacked plane would ever be flown into a building. She and other administration officials repeatedly said that the memo contained only general information and had no specific threats upon which the president could act. White House spokesman Ari Fleischer later said, "I think it's fair to say that if I walked up to you in August of 2001 and said, 'We have information that Muslim extremists seek to hijack American airplanes,' you'd have said, 'So what? Everybody's known that for a long, long time.'"[67]

But other accounts characterized the briefing differently, as indicative of the serious threat of terrorism on American soil. NBC reported that biological and chemical weapons were discussed and that the president was informed Al Qaeda was "planning to strike us, probably here," meaning in the United States.[68] According to the *Washington Post*, the memo explicitly said that bin Laden's followers might hijack U.S. airliners.[69]

Without knowing the actual contents of the classified memo, it is difficult to know what options might have been appropriate for the president. But by that hot day in early August 2001, concerns about terrorism on American soil had clearly reached the highest official in the land. Clearly, also, Richard Clarke's detailed, multifaceted plan to strike back at Al Qaeda had been sitting on Bush's desk since he had taken the oath of office and remained unimplemented; Al Qaeda had suffered no major retaliation for the killing of nineteen Americans on the USS *Cole*.

After the security briefing, President Bush placed a white cowboy hat on his head and drove off in his truck to the canyons.[70] He spent the rest of the day fishing for bass in his pond.[71]

Over the next thirty days, President Bush had no further meetings about terrorism. Yet the threats were more serious than ever. The FBI had learned that Abu Zubaydah, a Saudi who had been chief of operations for Al Qaeda since 1996 and was in charge of training thousands of Muslim terrorists,[72] was in touch with a Middle Eastern student at a flight school in Arizona. That alarming piece of information, however, was never forwarded to the White House.[73] In addition, on August 21, the CIA notified the Immigration and Naturalization Service (INS) that two other Al Qaeda operatives, Khalid Almidhar and Nawaf Alhazmi, should be put on the terrorist watch list. Unlike the FBI, the INS responded quickly, and, according to *The Age of Sacred Terror*, came back with even more startling information: the two men had already entered the United States. The INS told both the CIA and the FBI, but this astonishing revelation—that two terrorists, one of whom may have participated in the bombing of the USS *Cole*, were already in the country—was not forwarded to the White House or to Richard Clarke's counterterrorism team.[74]

Even without such vital information, Clarke still saw bin Laden's threat as imminent. But when it came to putting his policies into action, he remained enormously frustrated. Under Clinton, he and his bull-in-a-china-shop approach had been given a relatively free hand by both Anthony Lake and Sandy Berger, Clinton's two national security advisers—even when it came to butting heads with powerful cabinet officials like Treasury Secretary Robert Rubin.[75] But the Bush White House gave Clarke far less leeway to wreak havoc in bureaucratic squabbles—something that was inevitable if anything was to be accomplished. Clarke was one of only three White House officials who carried a weapon for protection—a .357 Magnum SIG-Sauer semiautomatic with jacketed hollow-point bullets. The running joke was that he might well have to use it "for interagency combat."[76]

On September 4, Clarke was finally given the chance to present his strategy at a meeting of the administration's so-called Principals Committee, a group of high-level cabinet-ranking policy makers. Even though the Bush administration had been in power seven and a half months, it was only their second meeting about terrorism—out of ninety to a hundred meetings since Bush had taken office.[77]*

---

*A Clinton official said that after the 1998 African embassy bombings, they met every two or three weeks about terrorism and more frequently in times of heightened alerts.

This was the moment Clarke had been waiting for. He would finally get a hearing with the upper echelon of the Bush administration.
Those present included Condoleezza Rice, CIA director George
Tenet, Secretary of the Treasury Paul O'Neill, and General Richard
Myers, the vice chairman of the Joint Chiefs of Staff. Deputy Secretary of Defense Paul Wolfowitz substituted for his boss, Donald
Rumsfeld. President Bush was not attending, but the goal of the
meeting was to reach an agreement on a National Security Presidential Directive (NSPD). Clarke's strategy had three key elements—
arming the Northern Alliance, which was providing resistance
against the Taliban inside Afghanistan; mobilizing Uzbekistan,
which shared a border with Afghanistan and whose rulers hated bin
Laden; and putting the Predator into action against bin Laden.

If the group reached a consensus, Clarke's proposals would finally
be sent to the president and set in motion.

Clarke delivered his presentation, and one of the first people to
respond, George Tenet, was unqualifiedly supportive. "We really
need to aggressively go after these guys," he said.[78]

Going after Al Qaeda was not a tough call. With Sandy Berger
present, Clarke had made that case to Rice and her deputy back in
January, and now it was even stronger. But pushing the policy
through the bureaucracy was another story. Hundreds of millions
of dollars were needed for Clarke's program. Where would the
money come from? The principals decided that the Office of
Management and Budget and the CIA should try to figure that out
later.[79] But the question remained unanswered—a bad sign that suggested bureaucratic will was lacking. If attacking Al Qaeda was really such a high priority, one of the agencies could pay for it out of its
existing budget. Under Rumsfeld, however, the Pentagon certainly
did not see counterterrorism as an urgent matter, a fact that was
borne out five days later when he threatened to urge a veto if the
Senate went ahead with a plan to shift $600 million from missile
defense to counterterrorism.[80]*

*Other governmental departments, such as the Justice Department under John
Ashcroft, did not make counterterrorism a terribly high priority either. According to
the *New York Observer*, "As of Sept. 10, 2001, the Attorney General's final budget
request for the coming fiscal year asked to increase spending on 68 programs, 'none
of which directly involved counterterrorism He had rejected the F.B.I.'s request for

Then Clarke put forth the boldest part of his proposal. The Predator drone, the unmanned airborne device he championed, had been refitted with Hellfire missiles. Over the summer, tests showed that while flying two miles high, the Predator could find and kill men inside buildings four miles away. To a counterterrorism official, this was truly the "holy grail,"[81] and Clarke wanted to send it after Osama bin Laden.[82]

For a few minutes, there was a discussion about whether the Predator's weaponry was effective enough. Would it do the job?

Then Condoleezza Rice asked an even tougher question: Who would be in charge of the Predator?[83] As director of Central Intelligence, Tenet asserted that it would be wrong for *him* to deploy it. Others made it clear that the decision to actually fire the weapon should be left to the president. But if any of the armed forces was charged with carrying out the mission, General Myers argued, they might as well use a cruise missile, which, with a range of up to two thousand miles, was a different kind of weapon entirely. The Predator was essentially a weaponized surveillance device that had been designed for covert operations, and that should remain in the purview of the CIA.

In the end, the NSPD was forwarded to the White House. But there were many unanswered questions about funding and the Predator. Because no one could decide who would be in charge of the Predator, no strategy with regard to using it was sent to the president.[84] Once again, nothing happened.*

If the White House was not keenly focusing on bin Laden, one reason may have been that its alliance with Saudi Arabia was facing one of the deepest rifts in its history—a crisis that had begun to come to a head twelve days earlier. On August 23, a day when Israeli tanks had pen-

... funding to hire hundreds of new field agents, translators and intelligence analysts to improve the bureau's capacity to detect foreign terror threats. Moreover, among his proposed cuts was a reduction of $65 million in a Clinton program that made grants to state and local authorities for radios, decontamination garb and other counterterror preparedness measures."

*According to an NBC report, the NSPD was forwarded to the White House on September 9, but it had not been reviewed by the president at the time of the September 11 attacks.

etrated deeper than ever before into the West Bank, Crown Prince Abdullah had seen a TV news report in which an Israeli soldier held an elderly Palestinian woman to the ground by putting his boot on her head.[85] The image left Abdullah enraged, but when it was juxtaposed with what he saw on television the next day, according to one Saudi official, he "just went bananas."[86] From the comfort of his luxurious Riyadh palace, Abdullah listened to President Bush hold forth on the recent violence in the Middle East. "The Israelis will not negotiate under terrorist threat, simple as that," Bush said. "And if the Palestinians are interested in a dialogue, then I strongly urge Mr. Arafat to put one hundred percent effort into ... stopping the terrorist activity. And I believe he can do a better job of doing that."[87]

In the seven months or so that Bush had been president, high-level Saudis had not been terribly impressed by him. One used the word *goofy* to describe him.[88] Some thought of him as a lightweight who had not mastered foreign policy. Bandar thought Condoleezza Rice's lack of familiarity with the Middle East was partially to blame.[89]

What they especially didn't like was that Bush, pushed in part by neoconservatives in his administration who were close to Israel's Likud party, was blaming all the violence on the Palestinians. Two months earlier Bush senior had assured Abdullah that his son would toe the line. But now, those words appeared to be hollow promises. To the Saudis, it was as if the president of the United States had again become nothing more than a mouthpiece for Israeli prime minister Ariel Sharon.

Prince Bandar happened to be watching the same news conference at his $36-million Rocky Mountain retreat in Aspen, Colorado, when the phone rang.[90] It was Abdullah, directing him to confront the White House. He knew well that the United States still relied on the Saudis for vast amounts of oil, as it had for decades. And the United States still hoped for strategic support from the Saudis in other Middle East regional issues even though their shared interests were less clear than they had been a decade earlier. It was time to use that leverage to the fullest. Less than a year earlier, Bandar had gone hunting on his English estate with Bush senior, his close friend of two decades. Now he was going to draw a line in the sand with Bush's son—and push the Bush-Saudi relationship to the brink.

On August 27, with Bush still in Crawford, Bandar met with Condoleezza Rice in her White House office. "This is the hardest message I've had to deliver between our two countries since I started working in this country in 1983," Bandar said, using a twenty-five-page document from Abdullah as his script.[91] As related by a senior Saudi official, the message said, "We believe there has been a strategic decision by the United States that its national interest in the Middle East is 100 percent based on Israeli prime minister Ariel Sharon."[92]

According to an article in the *Washington Post* by Robert G. Kaiser and David B. Ottaway, Bandar noted that this was America's right, but that Saudi Arabia could not abide by that decision. The message was both full of moral indignation and deliberately provocative in tone. "I reject this extraordinary, un-American bias whereby the blood of an Israeli child is more expensive and holy than the blood of a Palestinian child," it said, "... that when you kill a Palestinian, it is defense; when a Palestinian kills an Israeli, it's a terrorist act."[93]

The message made clear that the Saudis had concluded that Bush was a lost cause. "Starting from today, you're from Uruguay, as they say. You Americans, go your way; I, Saudi Arabia, go my way. From now on, we will protect our national interests, regardless of where America's interests lie in the region."[94]

And Bandar left no room for compromise. Now was the time to "get busy rearranging our lives in the Middle East," he said.[95] He was instructed not to have any further discussions with the United States. Could it be that the two countries' sixty-year alliance was finally coming to an end?

Shocked by this ultimatum, Rice told Bandar that there had been no change in U.S. policy. She agreed to take the message to the president.[96]

For his part, Bush still had no intention of getting involved in the sticky Middle East peace process. Nevertheless, Bush was so stunned by the Saudi threat that he immediately did an about-face. Within thirty-six hours, Bandar returned to Riyadh with a groundbreaking personal message written by the president to mollify Abdullah. "I am troubled and feel deeply the suffering of ordinary Palestinians in their day to day life and I want such tragedies and sufferings to end," Bush wrote.[97] "I firmly believe that the Palestinian people have a right to self-determination and to live peacefully and securely in their own state in their own homeland."

Bush was not just getting involved. For the first time, he was publicly supporting a Palestinian state—and he had done it in writing. He also addressed the Saudi moral concerns, saying he believed the blood of all innocent people was the same—whether they be Israeli or Palestinian, Jewish, Christian, or Muslim.[98]*

Abdullah had played the game well. He had banged his fist and the United States had jumped. He was so thrilled with his victory, the *Post* reported, that he proudly showed off his correspondence—Bush's two-page letter and the long message he had given Bandar—as trophies to Arab leaders in Syria, Egypt, and Jordan.

Ever the diplomat, Bandar explained Bush's capitulation in a way that allowed the president to save face. The letter was so compelling, Bandar said, that he was certain it was not drafted in response to the Saudi ultimatum, but had been in the works for some time. "This must have been something ... that the administration was thinking about, that they just didn't share with everybody [but] were waiting for the right time," he said.

At Abdullah's invitation, Yasir Arafat came all the way from South Africa to Riyadh especially to read it. Then Abdullah sent Bandar back to Washington to help transform the words into deeds—and to convince the president to make public that he was calling for a Palestinian state.

On Friday, September 7, three days after Richard Clarke's attempt to lobby his proposal to fight Al Qaeda through the administration, Bandar met with Condoleezza Rice, Dick Cheney, Colin Powell, and President Bush in Washington and told them how happy he was to discover that he had misinterpreted the White House's policy toward the Middle East. The administration reiterated its desire to pursue new peace initiatives immediately.[99]

Many questions were unresolved about how to pursue such initiatives, but suddenly there was enough goodwill that discussions continued between the two countries over the weekend of September 8 and 9. At issue was whether Colin Powell or President Bush should make the speech announcing the new plans. Bush was even willing to meet with Arafat at the United Nations—a prospect that pleased the

Saudis immensely. And lest anyone doubt that Bush would follow through this time, he had invited Bandar to the White House the following Thursday to pursue these matters.

And so, on that Monday night, Prince Bandar bin Sultan bin Abdul Aziz was, in his own words, "the happiest man in the world." As he told the *Washington Post,* he decided to relax in the indoor swimming pool of his lavish McLean residence, smoking a cigar. He had been back and forth between Saudi Arabia and Washington with the Bush response and then the Saudi response. He had worked through the entire weekend, until three or four o'clock in the morning, and then he had worked all day Monday. He deserved a rest, so he called his office. He told them he was taking Tuesday off—Tuesday, September 11, 2001.[100]

CHAPTER FOURTEEN

9/11

JUST BEFORE 6 A.M. on September 11, President Bush awoke at the Colony Beach and Tennis Resort, an island enclave in the Gulf of Mexico, near Sarasota, Florida. He put on his running shorts and, accompanied by his Secret Service men, took a four-mile jog.[1]

Meanwhile, in Washington, the top brass of the Carlyle Group and scores of prospective investors began getting ready for an investors' conference at the Ritz Carlton Hotel in Washington. It was their custom to serve coffee and breakfast pastries at about 7:30 and to start the presentations half an hour later. Among those attending were James Baker, Frank Carlucci, and, representing the bin Laden family, Shafig bin Laden, one of Osama's many brothers.

At 7:59 a.m., American Airlines Flight 11 took off from Boston's Logan International Airport en route to Los Angeles. Five Al Qaeda operatives were seated aboard, one of whom, Abdulaziz Alomari, had gained entrée to the United States without even having to go to the consulate himself—thanks to the Visa Express program recently instituted in Saudi Arabia.

At about the same time, Khalid Almidhar and Nawaf Alhazmi, the two Saudis who indirectly received money from Prince Bandar's wife, Princess Haifa, stood in Washington's Dulles International Airport, getting ready to board American Airlines Flight 77 to Los Angeles scheduled to leave at 8:10. They were accompanied by three compatriots—Salem Alhazmi, who was possibly Nawaf's brother, Majed Moqed, a twenty-four-year-old operative about whom little is known, and Hani Hanjour, the Saudi who took flying lessons in Phoenix and who, the FBI had noted, was so curious about airplane security. Two of the Saudi operatives on the plane, Khalid Almidhar and Salem Alhazmi, also had entered the United States using the Visa Express program.

At about 8:13, the hijacking of American Airlines Flight 11 began.* It soon veered dramatically off course from its scheduled destination, L.A., and went toward New York instead. At 8:46, the plane crashed into the north tower of the World Trade Center.

At that moment, President Bush's motorcade was on its way to the Emma E. Booker elementary school in Sarasota. When he arrived just before 9:00, Karl Rove rushed up to the president, took him aside in a hallway, and told him about the plane crash. "What a horrible accident!" Bush replied. According to White House communications director Dan Bartlett, who was also present, Bush, a former pilot, asked if the cause had been bad weather.[2] Accounts differ as to whether Bush was informed about the attack before this or not, but it is clear he had been told about the first crash by nine o'clock.[3]

At about 9:03 Bush entered the second-grade classroom. The occasion was an opportunity to promote his education policies. Altogether, with his staff, members of the media, and the students, there were about 150 people in the room. Bush was introduced to the students and posed for pictures with them. Then the teacher led the

---

*One tantalizing detail whose meaning has never been fully explained concerns an unpublished memo from the FAA based on a phone call from a flight attendant on board Flight 11 who asserted, contrary to subsequent reports that only box cutters and plastic utensils had been used as weapons, that a hijacker had shot and killed a passenger on board. The memo said, "The American Airlines FAA Principal Security Inspector (PFI) was notified by Suzanne Clark of American Airlines Corporate Headquarters that an on board flight attendant contacted American Airlines Operation Center and informed [sic] that a passenger located in seat 10B shot and killed a passenger in 9B at 9:20 am. The passenger killed was Daniel Lewin, shot by Satam al-Suqama. One bullet was reported to have been fired."

However, according to Laura Brown, a spokeswoman for the FAA, "Events were unfolding minute by minute like they would in any crisis. People were reporting what they believed to be happening, but the preliminary information is frequently wrong. If you talk to the FBI about it, they have absolutely no information that there was a shot, and they have reviewed all the tapes."

Because the plane crashed into the World Trade Center, it is unlikely that a gun could have been found in the wreckage even if it had been on the plane. The memo can be found on the website of journalist Edward Jay Epstein at edwardjayepstein.com/nether_fictoid9popup.htm.

students in reading exercises. At this point there was no reason for Bush to think the crash was anything more than a tragic accident.

Just as Bush entered the classroom, however, United Airlines Flight 175, which had also been hijacked after its departure from Boston, crashed into the second World Trade Center tower.

One of the many ironies of the attack was that Marvin Bush, the president's brother, owned stock in and had served as a director of a company, Stratesec, that handled security for three clients that figured prominently in the attack—United Airlines; Dulles Airport, from which American Airlines Flight 77 was hijacked; and the World Trade Center itself. Conspiracy theorists have tried, with little success, to make something of the connection, even though Marvin Bush left the board of Stratesec prior to 9/11.*

At the Ritz Carlton Hotel in Washington, D.C., those attending the Carlyle Group's investment conference were glued to TV monitors showing the attack in progress. According to one source, after the second plane hit, Shafig bin Laden removed his name tag. He and James Baker, the source added, left shortly thereafter in separate cars.

Captain Deborah Loewer, the director of the White House Situation Room, who was traveling with Bush, also saw the second crash on television while she was at the elementary school in Sarasota. "It took me about thirty seconds to realize that this was terrorism," she said.[4]

She immediately told Andrew Card, the White House chief of staff, who whispered to Bush, still in the classroom full of second-graders, "Captain Loewer says it's terrorism."

Then the classroom was silent for about thirty seconds.[5] In the back of the room, press secretary Ari Fleischer held up a pad of paper

---

*Nonetheless, this connection between the House of Bush and the breakdown in airport security, potentially a political embarrassment, never gained prominence in the mainstream press. It is worth noting, however, that one of Marvin Bush's coinvestors was Mishal al-Sabah, a member of the Kuwaiti royal family, which was rescued and restored to power by Marvin's father during the Gulf War of 1991. The al-Sabah family is the same ruling Kuwaiti family that helped the elder George Bush make his fortune through Zapata Off-Shore forty years earlier. And, of course, it is the family of Nayirah, the fifteen-year-old girl whose false congressional testimony helped launch the Gulf War.

for Bush to see. "Don't Say Anything Yet" was written on it in big block letters.[6] Bush nodded his assent. Finally, he picked up the book to read a story called "The Pet Goat" with the children. In unison, the children read aloud, "The Pet Goat. A-girl-got-a-pet-goat. But-the-goat-did-some-things-that-made-the-girl's-dad-mad." As the reading continued, Bush said, "Really good readers, whew! ... These must be sixth-graders!"[7]

The reading continued for eight or nine minutes, and at 9:12, Bush left the room.[8]

By this time, the entire world was aware that a truly historic event was taking place. Thousands were dead or dying. Millions of people across the country, especially in New York and Washington, were in a state of panic.

At 9:30, Bush addressed the nation. "Today we had a national tragedy," he said. "Two airplanes have crashed into the World Trade Center in an apparent terrorist attack on our country."

Then he vowed "to hunt down and to find those folks who committed this act. Terrorism against our nation will not stand."

To the overwhelming majority of Americans the attacks had come completely out of the blue. Within the intelligence world, however, many knew who was behind them and Richard Clarke was one of those people. "This is Al Qaeda," he said as soon as a third hijacked jet crashed, this one into the Pentagon.[9]

CIA director George Tenet was eating breakfast with former senator David Boren at the St. Regis Hotel in Washington when he was told about the hijackings. He instantly came to the same assessment. "This has bin Laden's fingerprints all over it," he said.[10] At 10:06, a fourth hijacked plane, United Airlines Flight 93 from Newark, crashed about eighty miles southeast of Pittsburgh, its hijackers apparently having been overpowered by passengers.

It did not take long to confirm that bin Laden was the perpetrator. Almost immediately after the attacks, celebratory phone calls from bin Laden operatives were intercepted by the National Security Agency.

But over the next chaotic few hours, rather than move to strike just Al Qaeda, various high-ranking officials within the Bush administration saw the attack as an opportunity to pursue another agenda. At 2:40 p.m., Donald Rumsfeld ordered the military to begin working on retaliatory plans—not just to take out Osama bin Laden, but also to go after Iraq's Saddam Hussein.

According to notes taken by a Rumsfeld aide that day and later obtained by CBS News's David Martin, Rumsfeld said he wanted "best info fast, judge whether good enough to hit SH"—meaning Saddam Hussein—"at the same time, not only UBL," the initials used to identify Osama bin Laden. "Go massive," the notes quote Rumsfeld as saying, "sweep it all up, things related and not."[11]

In 1998, Rumsfeld had been a signatory to the Project for a New American Century's "Rebuilding America's Defenses" letter, which had called for the removal of Saddam Hussein. Perhaps this was the "new Pearl Harbor" that had to take place if PNAC's policies were to be implemented.

Meanwhile, the president spent the day flying around the country in Air Force One from Florida to Louisiana to Nebraska before returning to Washington. For much of the day, he was protected by U.S. Air Force servicemen in full combat gear. That night, before going to bed, President Bush dictated some observations into his diary. "The Pearl Harbor of the 21st century took place today."[12]

He added that because he was not a military tactician, he would have "to rely on the advice and counsel of Rumsfeld, [General Henry] Shelton [then chairman of the Joint Chiefs of Staff], [General Richard] Myers and Tenet."[13]

Several people were conspicuously absent from the list—Colin Powell, Condoleezza Rice, Dick Cheney, and others. But chief among them was Richard Clarke. The man who knew more about Osama bin Laden and Al Qaeda than anyone in the country and who had devoted his professional life to defeating them went unmentioned.

Prince Bandar did not go to the Saudi embassy in Washington on the day of the disaster,[14] but he was no doubt very busy. The relationship between the House of Bush and the House of Saud that he had so laboriously reassembled just before the attacks was now in tatters. It was as if in one horrifying moment all the extraordinary contradictions in that relationship—one that married the guardians of Israel with the guardians of Wahhabi Islam, that joined a secular, consumerist democracy with a puritanical theocratic monarchy—had suddenly been exposed. Thousands of innocent people had been killed in America and most of the killers were Saudi.

In good times, Bandar was known for his ingratiating charm and bonhomie, for his dazzling parties "where there was more chilled vodka in little shot glasses than I've ever seen," as one guest remembered.[15] There was also the Bandar who delighted in weaving a web of intrigue and participating in covert operations. Now came the Bandar who could be a commanding presence in a time of international crisis.

A virtuoso at spinning the media, he quickly conjured up a reality that entirely dissociated his country from bin Laden and the terrorists and reaffirmed Saudi Arabia's solidarity with the United States—as if the secret brinksmanship of two weeks earlier had never taken place. He swiftly launched an international media campaign with PR giant Burson-Marsteller.

He went on every network news show imaginable, repeating the message that the alliance was still strong. Saudi Arabia was America's friend in a hostile Arab world. Saudi Arabia had nothing to do with terrorism. "We in the kingdom, the government and the people of Saudi Arabia, refuse to have any person affiliated with terrorism to be connected to our country," he told a press conference.[16]

In every venue, he told the world that the widespread reports that Osama bin Laden was a Saudi were wrong because "his citizenship was terminated a long time ago because of his terrorist activities." And when he was asked about the financing of terrorism, Bandar told a reporter that charity was required by Islam and that the Saudi government had no evidence that Saudi money was going to Al Qaeda.[17]

Even as Bandar emphasized his friendship with the United States, he had another pressing item on his agenda. For hundreds of wealthy Saudis, it was not unusual to spend most of the summer in the United States. Some stayed over for the racehorse sales in Lexington, Kentucky, in September and then returned home in the fall. But now Arabs were being arrested all over the United States. Hundreds of

Saudis in the United States—members of the royal family and relatives of Osama bin Laden among them—feared reprisals if they stayed in the country. They needed to leave immediately. King Fahd himself had mandated that everything possible be done to protect them and return them to the kingdom. Fear was not the only motivation. "It's a perception issue for them back home," said a source who participated in the events that followed. "It looks really bad [to Wahhabi clerics] if the royal family is in the lap of luxury in the U.S. during a crisis." It was essential that the Saudis be granted special permission to return even while U.S. airspace was severely restricted.

At the time, in the aftermath of the terrorist attacks, key figures in the Bush administration who could facilitate such an operation were holed up in the Situation Room, a small underground suite with a plush eighteen-by-eighteen-foot conference room in the West Wing of the White House. Live links connected the room's occupants to the FBI, the State Department, and other relevant agencies. Dick Cheney, Condoleezza Rice, and other officials hunkered down and devoured intelligence, hoping to ascertain whether other terrorist attacks were imminent. The most powerful officials in the administration came and went, among them Colin Powell, George Tenet, and Donald Rumsfeld.

Within the cramped confines of that room, Richard Clarke chaired an ongoing crisis group making hundreds of decisions related to the attacks. Sometime shortly after 9/11—he doesn't remember exactly when—Clarke was approached in the Situation Room about quickly repatriating the Saudis.

"Somebody brought to us for approval the decision to let an airplane filled with Saudis, including members of the bin Laden family, leave the country," Clarke says. "My role was to say that it can't happen until the FBI approves it. And so the FBI was asked—we had a live connection to the FBI—and we asked the FBI to make sure that they were satisfied that everybody getting on that plane was someone that it was O.K. to leave. And they came back and said yes, it was fine with them. So we said, 'Fine, let it happen.'"[18]

Clarke, who left the government in March 2003 to run a consulting firm in Virginia, adds that he does not recall who initiated the request, but that it was probably either the FBI or the State Department. Both agencies deny playing any role whatsoever in the episode.* "It did not come out of this place," says one source at the State Department. "The likes of Prince Bandar does not need the State Department to get this done."

A White House official says that no such operation took place.

Richard Clarke's approval for evacuating the Saudis had been conditional upon the FBI's vetting them. "I asked [the FBI] to make sure that no one inappropriate was leaving," he says. "I asked them if they had any objection to Saudis leaving the country at a time when aircraft were banned from flying." Clarke adds that he assumed the FBI had vetted the bin Ladens prior to September 11. "I have no idea if they did a good job," he says. "I'm not in any position to second-guess the FBI."

But despite the evidence to the contrary, FBI officials assert that the Bureau had no part in the Saudi evacuation. The Bureau played no role in facilitating these flights, according to Special Agent John Iannarelli, the FBI's spokesman on counterterrorism activities.

Bandar, however, went on CNN and said that the FBI played a critical role in the evacuation.[19]

On Thursday, September 13, Bandar had planned to meet Bush at the White House to discuss the Middle East peace process. The meeting went forward as scheduled, but in the aftermath of the attacks, even the urgent demands of the peace process had to take a backseat to the historic catastrophe two days earlier. Until this meeting, Bandar had seen Bush as someone who did not measure up to his father, but on this occasion he seemed to be truly his own man.[20] The two men went out on the Truman Balcony where they lit up cigars and discussed how they might best deal with captured Al Qaeda operatives.

It is not known whether the two men talked about the evacuation at that time. In any case, the operation to begin flying out approximately 140 Saudis had already been initiated by Bandar. According to

*After a section of this book was published in *Vanity Fair*, Colin Powell, in a September 7, 2003, appearance on *Meet the Press*, was asked about the repatriation. "I don't know the details of what happened," he said. "But my understanding is that there was no sneaking out of the country; that the flights were well-known, and it was coordinated within the government. But I don't have the details about what the FBI's role in it might or might not have been."

Nail al-Jubeir, a spokesman for the Saudi embassy, the flights received approval from "the highest level of the U.S. government."[21] Al-Jubeir added that he did not know if there were private conversations in which Prince Bandar and the president discussed letting the bin Ladens and other Saudis begin to travel even while U.S. airspace was shut down. The White House declined to comment on the issue.

Thus, there are many unanswered questions about who authorized the operation. Did the president know? Did the elder George Bush or James Baker intervene? Or did Bandar go through his old friend Colin Powell in the State Department? Both the elder George Bush and James Baker declined requests for interviews for this book.

Nevertheless, a massive and elaborate operation to fly the Saudis out of the United States was already under way. At about 4:30 that afternoon, Dan Grossi and Manuel Perez, the two private detectives in Tampa, had already departed for Lexington, Kentucky, in a LearJet, accompanying three young Saudi men—even though private aircraft were still banned from U.S. skies. Sources familiar with the flight said that one of the men was a young Saudi royal. According to the *Tampa Tribune*, another was the son of a Saudi army commander.[22] The third Saudi passenger has not been identified.

According to Grossi, about one hour and forty-five minutes after takeoff they landed at Blue Grass Airport in Lexington, a frequent destination for Saudi horse-racing enthusiasts, the most famous of whom was Prince Ahmed bin Salman, a nephew of King Fahd. The father of the forty-two-year-old Prince Ahmed, Prince Salman bin Abdul Aziz, was the powerful governor of Riyadh and one of the Sudairi Seven and had worked closely with Osama bin Laden and his Afghan Arabs during the Afghanistan War in the eighties. Ahmed had gone to college at the University of California at Irvine and eventually become chairman of Saudi Arabia's Research and Marketing Group, a publishing company with offices in Saudi Arabia and England. But in Kentucky and the world of horse-racing, Ahmed was far better known as the owner of many of the top racehorses in the world. In 1994, he and a college friend launched the Thoroughbred Corporation, which bought and trained famous horses such as Sharp Cat, Lear Fan, Royal Anthem, and the greatest of all, the 2001 Horse of the Year, Point Given, which won two legs of racing's Triple Crown.[23]

Prince Ahmed had come to Lexington for the annual September yearling sales. The sale of young racehorses had been suspended on September 11 but resumed the very next day, during which Ahmed bought two horses. "America is home to me," he said. "I am a businessman. I have nothing to do with the other stuff. I feel as badly as any American and I am extremely astonished by [the terrorism]. We have had terrorism in Saudi Arabia and we know how painful it is."[24] Meanwhile, he made plans to leave the country as quickly as possible.

According to the *New York Times*, sometime after the attacks but before September 14, members of the bin Laden family were driven or flown under FBI supervision first to a secret assembly point in Texas and later to Washington.[25]*

On Friday, September 14, the nation's 200,000 private planes were cleared to fly. The paralyzed air transportation system slowly ramped up again with new security measures instituted all over the country to thwart hijackers. Initially, Bandar's operation had required, and obtained, White House approval. Now such permission was no longer necessary to fly. But the Bush administration had launched a global war against terror. Within days of the attacks, the FBI was circulating a list of more than one hundred suspects to airlines and more than eighteen thousand law-enforcement organizations. FBI director Robert Mueller said the investigation had generated more than thirty-six thousand leads. There were hundreds of search warrants and sub-poenas, and seizures of computers and documents. Agents conducted hundreds of interviews around the country.[26] All over the United States, Arabs were being detained. Attorney General John Ashcroft asserted that the government had to take "people into custody who have violated the law and who may pose a threat to America."[27]

The central question now became whether Saudi royals and their friends would get special treatment from the Bush White House when a massive international crackdown was under way. In the context of the global manhunt and war on terror, didn't it make sense to at least interview Osama bin Laden's relatives and other Saudis who, inadvertently or not, may have funded him? Nevertheless, as Bandar's massive operation to get the Saudis out of the United States continued,

*The FBI said the *Times* report was "erroneous."

the FBI repeatedly declined to interrogate or conduct extended interviews with the Saudis.

In addition to the Tampa-Lexington flight, at least seven other planes were made available for the operation. According to itineraries, passenger lists, and interviews with sources who had firsthand knowledge of the flights, members of the extended bin Laden family, the House of Saud, and their associates also assembled in Los Angeles, Las Vegas, Dallas, Houston, Cleveland, Orlando, Washington, D.C, Boston, Newark, and New York.

Arrangements for the flights were made with lightning speed. One flight, a Boeing 727 that left Los Angeles late on the night of September 14 or early in the morning of the fifteenth, required FAA approval, which came through in less than half an hour. "By bureaucratic standards, that's a nanosecond," said a source close to the flight.[18]

Payments for the charter flights were made in advance through wire transfer from the Saudi embassy. A source close to the evacuation said such procedures were an indication that the entire operation had high-level approval from the U.S. government. "That's a totally traceable transaction," he said. "So I inferred that what they were doing had U.S. government approval. Otherwise, they would have done it in cash."

According to the source, a young female member of the bin Laden family was the sole passenger on the first leg of the flight, from Los Angeles to Orlando. In the immediate aftermath of 9/11, boarding any airplane was cause for anxiety. But now that the name Osama bin Laden had become synonymous with mass murder, boarding a plane with his family members was another story entirely. To avoid unnecessary dramas, the flight's operators made certain that the cockpit crew was briefed about who the passengers were—the bin Ladens—and the highly sensitive nature of their mission.

However, they neglected to brief the flight attendants.

On the flight from Los Angeles, the bin Laden girl began talking to an attendant about the horrid events of 9/11. "I feel so bad about it," she said.

"Well, it's not your fault," replied the attendant, who had no idea who the passenger really was.

"Yeah," said the passenger. "But he was my brother."

"The flight attendant just lost it," the source said.[29]

When the 727 landed in Orlando, Khalil Binladin, whose estate in Winter Garden was nearby, boarded the plane.[30] After a delay of several hours, it continued to Washington.

Meanwhile, in Las Vegas, the Saudis had chartered a customized DC 8 that belonged to the president of Gabon and was equipped with two staterooms (bedrooms) and sixty-seven seats. According to a source who participated in the operation, the Saudis had hoped to leave Las Vegas on September 14, but were not able to get permission for two days. "This was a nightmare," said a source. "The manifest was submitted the day before. It was obvious that someone in Washington had said okay, but the FBI didn't want to say they could go, so it was really tense. In the end, nobody was interrogated." According to the passenger list, among the forty-six passengers were several high-level Saudi royals with diplomatic passports. On Sunday, September 16, the flight finally left for Geneva, Switzerland. The FBI did not even get the manifest until about two hours before departure. Even if it had wanted to interview the passengers—and the Bureau had shown little inclination to do so—there would not have been enough time.[31]

At the same time, an even more lavish Boeing 727 was being readied for Prince Ahmed bin Salman and about fourteen other passengers who were assembling in Lexington. If they felt they had to leave the country, at least it could be said that they were leaving in luxury. The plane, which was customized to hold just twenty-six passengers, had a master bedroom suite furnished with a large upholstered double bed, a couch, night stand, and credenza. Its master bathroom had a gold-plated sink, double illuminated mirrors, and a bidet. There were brass, gold, and crystal fixtures. The main lounge had a fifty-two-inch projection TV. The plane boasted a six-place conference room and dining room with a mahogany table that had controls for up and down movement.[32] The plane left Lexington at 4 p.m. on Sunday, September 16, and stopped in Gander, Newfoundland, en route to London.

And so they flew, one by one, mostly to Europe, where some of the passengers later returned home to Saudi Arabia. On September 17, a flight left Dallas for Newark at 10:30 p.m.[33] On September 18 and 19, two flights left Boston, including the 727 that had originated in Los Angeles. According to a person with firsthand knowledge of the flights, there is no question that they took place with the knowledge and approval of the State Department, the FBI, the FAA, and many other government agencies. "When we left Boston every governmental authority that could be there was there," says the source. "There were FBI agents at every departure point. In Boston alone, there was the FBI, the Department of Transportation, the FAA, Customs, the Immigration and Naturalization Service, the Massachusetts state police, the Massachusetts Port Authority, and probably the Bureau of Alcohol, Tobacco, and Firearms. There were more federal law-enforcement officials than passengers by far."[34]

In Boston, airport authorities were horrified that they were being told to let the bin Ladens go. On September 22, a flight went from New York to Paris, and on September 24, another flight from Las Vegas to Paris. According to passenger lists for many but not all of the flights, the vast majority of passengers were Saudis, but there were also passengers from Egypt, England, Ethiopia, Jordan, Lebanon, Morocco, Nigeria, Norway, the Philippines, Sudan, and Syria. "Not many Saudis like to do menial work," said a source, explaining the other nationalities.

Passengers ranged in age from seven years old to sixty-two.[35] The vast majority were adults. There were roughly two dozen bin Ladens.

"Here you have an attack with substantial links to Saudi Arabia," says John L. Martin, who as chief of internal security in the Criminal Division of the Justice Department supervised investigation and prosecution of national security offenses for eighteen years.[36] "You would want to talk to people in the Saudi royal family and the Saudi government, particularly since they have pledged cooperation. And you would want them to voluntarily submit to interviews that would not necessarily be hostile."

Martin further says that he was particularly surprised at the way the Saudis seemed to be making the rules. "It is an absolute rule of law enforcement that the agent or officers conducting the interviews control the interview, and that the persons of interest, suspects, or prospective defendants do not set the ground rules for the interview," he says.[37]

* * *

On September 20, while the Saudi evacuation was still quietly under way, President Bush formally declared a global war on terror in a dramatic speech before Congress. Fortress America, supposedly impregnable, was in a state of shock. The grisly totals were always changing, but at the time, the estimated number of the dead, missing, and injured people was more than thirteen thousand.[38] For security reasons, Vice President Cheney did not even attend the president's address in the capital.

America was united behind the president as never before. "Our war on terror ... will not end until every terrorist group of global reach has been found, stopped, and defeated," President Bush vowed.[39]

"We will starve terrorists of funding, turn them one against another, drive them from place to place until there is no refuge or no rest," he added. "And we will pursue nations that provide aid or safe haven to terrorism. Every nation in every region now has a decision to make: Either you're with us, or you are with the terrorists.

"From this day forward, any nation that continues to harbor or support terrorism will be regarded by the United States as a hostile regime."[40]

Four days later, on September 24, President Bush held a press conference with Colin Powell and treasury secretary Paul O'Neill at which he announced the freezing of assets of twenty-seven individuals or entities that may have been funneling money to terrorists. Although the list looked substantial, in fact many of the named targets had been identified by Richard Clarke long before.

Both Bush and Powell made a point of praising the Saudis. "As far as the Saudi Arabians go ... they've been nothing but cooperative," Bush said. "Our dialogue has been one of—as you would expect friends to be able to discuss issues. And my discussions with the foreign minister, as well as the ambassador, have been very positive."[41]

"That's exactly right, Mr. President," Powell added. "They have not turned down any requests that we have presented to them."

But in fact, the United States was not particularly demanding of Saudi Arabia. Even after the attacks, Visa Express, the program that allowed three of the 9/11 hijackers to enter the United States without even having to stop by the consulate, and which was described by a consular official as "an open-door policy for terrorists," was continued.[42] In the thirty days *after* 9/11, the U.S. consulate in Jeddah interviewed only 2 out of 104 applicants. No one was rejected.[43]

And when the United States did make demands of them, the Saudis were not particularly helpful. When U.S. troops attacked the Taliban in Afghanistan after 9/11, the Saudis refused to allow the United States to use Saudi territory to stage military operations. All over Europe authorities rounded up suspected terrorists and froze bank accounts—but Saudi officials did not follow suit. "Saudi Arabia is completely unsupportive as of today," Robert Baer, the former CIA officer and author of *Sleeping with the Devil,* said a month after 9/11. "The rank-and-file Saudi policeman is sympathetic to bin Laden. They're not telling us who these people were on the planes."[44]

Vincent Cannistraro, the former chief of counterterrorism operations for the CIA who worked in Saudi Arabia for that agency, added that even though tens of millions of dollars were flowing from Saudi Arabia to Al Qaeda, "We're getting zero cooperation now [from the Saudis]."[45]

William Hartung, a foreign policy and arms industry analyst at the World Policy Institute, attributed the Bush administration's softness on the Saudis to its vast shared economic interests. "If there weren't all these other arrangements—arms deals and oil deals and consultancies—I don't think the U.S. would stand for this lack of cooperation," Hartung said. "Because of those relationships, they have to tread lightly."[46]

Indeed, even as the fires at Ground Zero continued to burn, even as America measured its grief, new deals with the Saudis were in the works or already being signed.[47] Chief among them was a $25-billion gas-exploration project in Saudi Arabia involving eight huge oil companies,[48]* spearheaded by Crown Prince Abdullah and the minister for foreign affairs, Prince Saud al-Faisal, and with James Baker's firm, Baker Botts, playing a key advisory role.[49†]

*ExxonMobil, British Petroleum, Royal Dutch Shell, Philips Petroleum, Occidental Petroleum, Marathon Oil, Conoco, and France's TotalFinalElf.

†In October 2001, George Goolsby, the head of the energy law practice at Baker Botts, said the firm was "excited" about the openings for international energy firms in Saudi Arabia's gas sector, and that its Riyadh office was involved with "two to three clients, particularly in the second phase" of the project. He added that the

On September 14, Stephen Matthews, a partner at Baker Botts, lauded the Saudis for removing bureaucratic obstacles and for other developments "that have increased Saudi Arabia's attractiveness as an investment destination."

On Friday, September 21, Robert Jordan, the Baker Botts attorney who had been nominated earlier as ambassador to Saudi Arabia, finally testified in confirmation hearings before the Senate. Jordan, who had represented President Bush during the Harken insider trading fracas, appeared at the hearing accompanied by James Doty, a Baker Botts partner who had represented Bush when he bought into the Texas Rangers baseball team and who had been general counsel of the SEC during the Harken investigation, and by James A. Baker IV, a Baker Botts partner whose father was the former secretary of state.[50] Also accompanying him at the hearing was Steven Miles, another Baker Botts partner, who launched the firm's Riyadh office ten years earlier and who had played a key role in expanding its Middle East practice.[51]

Jordan testified that the day after the attacks of September 11, "Saudi Arabia released a statement in which it declared Saudi oil exports to the U.S. to be stable, adding that any export shortfalls on the international market will be filled by OPEC. These are welcome words, indeed." When it came to the Saudi role in 9/11, he said, "The tragedies of this magnitude show us who our real friends are. We call on the Saudis to fulfill their pledge of cooperation, and we seek with them to build an international coalition against terrorism. They have answered that call superbly."[52]

... opportunities are "still at a very conceptual stage." A few weeks later, in November 2001, Dick Cheney's old firm, Halliburton, also a Baker Botts client, won a $140-million deal to develop Saudi oil fields.

In January 2002, Neil Bush, the president's brother, would travel to the Middle East to help line up investors for his educational software company, Ignite! Learning (Michael Isikoff, "Neil Bush Raising Money for Educational Software Firm," *Newsweek*, February 4, 2002). In a speech at the Jeddah Economic Forum at the Hilton Hotel, he advised Saudis that it was time for them to fight the U.S. media by engaging in a massive PR campaign: "The U.S. media campaign against the interests of Arabs and Muslims and the American public opinion on the Israeli-Palestinian conflict could be influenced through a sustained lobbying and PR effort" (Khalil Hanware and K. S. Ramkumar, "Win American Hearts Through Sustained Lobbying: Neil Bush," *Middle East Newsfile*, January 22, 2002).

Jordan added that he was extremely interested in potential investments in the oil and gas sector in Saudi Arabia. "[I] have been really gratified, Senator, to note the gas concession that has been granted to three consortiums, two of which are led by Exxon-Mobil, into development of the gas fields in Saudi Arabia .... I certainly will have this high on my agenda."[53]

Jordan was not asked about nor did he comment on the fact that many high-level Saudis refused to accept that Saudis were involved in the attacks, and instead blamed 9/11 on unnamed "Zionists." Even a year later, Prince Nayef Ibn Abd-Al-Aziz, the powerful minister of the interior, made such charges. "Who committed the events of September 11 and who benefited from them?" he asked. "... I think [the Zionists] are behind these events .... It is impossible that nineteen youths, including fifteen Saudis, carried out the operation of September 11."[54]

Jordan's approach to Saudi Arabia was not out of sync with the policies that had linked the United States and the Saudis for several decades, policies that were deeply flawed because they were blind to the rise of Islamist terror, but that in many ways had been spectacularly fruitful for the United States, producing a stable, secure flow of oil that had lasted for decades. No two figures played a bigger role in those policies than George H. W. Bush and James Baker.

But at certain points in history, a policy outlives its utility. By the mid to late nineties, the Clinton administration had recognized that it was no longer advisable to craft Saudi-American policy solely with an eye toward the pursuit of oil as a strategic resource. Certainly by the time of the 1998 bombings of the American embassies in Kenya and Tanzania, security officials had begun the delicate task of pressuring the Saudis to crack down on terrorism.

Now, however, even in the wake of one of the worst catastrophes in American history, the Bush administration continued to ignore the Saudi role in terrorism. It had approved the Saudi evacuation and it continued to act as if the House of Saud and the Saudi merchant elite could in no way be complicit with the act of terror that had just taken place.

Just how wrong this decision was became apparent several months later, when the war in Afghanistan was in full swing. On Thursday,

March 28, 2002, acting on electronic intercepts of telephone calls, heavily armed Pakistani commando units, accompanied by American Special Forces and FBI SWAT teams, raided a two-story house in the suburbs of Faisalabad, in western Pakistan.[55] They had received tips that one of the people in the house was Abu Zubaydah, the thirty-year-old chief of operations for Al Qaeda who had been head of field operations for the USS *Cole* bombing and who was a close confidant of Osama bin Laden's.

Two days later, on March 30, news of Zubaydah's capture was spreading all over the world. At first, the administration refused to corroborate the reports; then it celebrated the capture of the highest-ranking Al Qaeda operative ever to be taken into custody. "This represents a very significant blow to Al Qaeda," said White House spokesman Ari Fleischer. He called Zubaydah "a key terrorist recruiter, an operational planner and a member of Osama bin Laden's inner circle."

Donald Rumsfeld told a news conference that Zubaydah was "being given exactly the excellent medical care one would want if they wanted to make sure he was around a good long time to visit with us."[56]

The international media speculated as to what Zubaydah might know, what he might say. On Sunday, March 31, three days after the raid, the interrogation began. For the particulars of this episode there is one definitive source, Gerald Posner's *Why America Slept*, and according to it, the CIA used two rather unusual methods for the interrogation.* First, they administered thiopental sodium, better known

---

*Posner's account is quite controversial, so it is worth noting that his reputation as an investigative reporter has been made largely from *debunking* conspiracies, as he did in *Case Closed*, his book on the assassination of President John F. Kennedy. As to his methodology in reporting this episode, he writes, "The information about those raids, the capture of top al Qaeda operative Abu Zubaydah, and his subsequent transfer, interrogation, and the results of those questioning sessions comes from two government sources, both in a position to know the details of Zubaydah's capture and interrogation, as well as his admissions. Both sources separately provided information. Their accounts often overlapped and confirmed each other in important aspects. Without any possibility of independently verifying much of the information, I have had to make a judgment about the sources themselves. In this instance, I believe them to be credible, knowledgeable, and truthful about what transpired. Additionally, an intelligence report on the dispersal and capture of Al Qaeda operatives has confirmed some of the interrogation techniques discussed in this

under its trademarked name, Sodium Pentothal, through an IV drip, to make Zubaydah more talkative. Since the prisoner had been shot three times during the capture, he was already hooked up to a drip to treat his wounds and it was possible to administer the drug without his knowledge. Second, as a variation on the good cop-bad cop routine, the CIA used two teams of debriefers. One consisted of undisguised Americans who were at least willing to treat Zubaydah's injuries while they interrogated him. The other team consisted of Arab Americans posing as Saudi security agents, who were known for their brutal interrogation techniques. The thinking was that Zubaydah would be so scared of being turned over to the Saudis, ever infamous for their public executions in Riyadh's Chop-Chop Square, that he would try to win over the American interrogators by talking to them.[57]

In fact, exactly the opposite happened. "When Zubaydah was confronted with men passing themselves off as Saudi security officers, his reaction was not fear, but instead relief," Posner writes. "The prisoner, who had been reluctant even to confirm his identity to his American captors, suddenly started talking animatedly. He was happy to see them, he said, because he feared the Americans would torture and then kill him. Zubaydah asked his interrogators to call a senior member of the ruling Saudi family. He then provided a private home number and cell phone number from memory. 'He will tell you what to do,' Zubaydah promised them."[58]

The name Zubaydah gave came as a complete surprise to the CIA. It was Prince Ahmed bin Salman bin Abdul Aziz, the owner of many legendary racehorses and one of the most westernized members of the royal family. On September 16, 2001, Prince Ahmed, of course, had boarded the flight in Lexington as part of the evacuation plan approved by the Bush White House.

Prince Ahmed was well known not just in Saudi Arabia, but also in publishing circles in London and horse-racing circles in Kentucky. He was such an unlikely name that the interrogators immediately assumed that Zubaydah was lying to buy time. According to Posner,

... chapter. And finally, a Defense Intelligence Agency employee has independently also acknowledged the accuracy of some of the interrogation methods" (*Why America Slept*, p. 181).

the interrogators then kept their prisoner on a "bare minimum" of pain medication and interrupted his sleep with bright lights for hour after hour before restarting the Sodium Pentothal drip.[59]

When they returned, Zubaydah spoke to his faux Saudi interrogators as if *they*, not he, were the ones in trouble. He said that several years earlier the royal family had made a deal with Al Qaeda in which the House of Saud would aid the Taliban so long as Al Qaeda kept terrorism out of Saudi Arabia. Zubaydah added that as part of this arrangement, he dealt with Prince Ahmed and two other members of the House of Saud as intermediaries, Prince Sultan bin Faisal bin Turki al-Saud, a nephew of King Fahd's, and Prince Fahd bin Turki bin Saud al-Kabir, a twenty-five-year-old distant relative of the king's. Again, he furnished phone numbers from memory.[60]

According to Posner, the interrogators responded by telling Zubaydah that 9/11 had changed everything. The House of Saud certainly would not stand behind him after that. It was then that Zubaydah dropped his real bombshell. "Zubaydah said that 9/11 changed nothing because Ahmed ... knew beforehand that an attack was scheduled for American soil that day," Posner writes. "They just didn't know what it would be, nor did they want to know more than that. The information had been passed to them, said Zubaydah, because bin Laden knew they could not stop it without knowing the specifics, but later they would be hard-pressed to turn on him if he could disclose their foreknowledge."[61]

Two weeks later, Zubaydah was moved to an undisclosed location. When he figured out that the interrogators were really Americans, not Saudis, Posner writes, he tried to strangle himself, and later recanted his entire tale.[62] To date no one has convincingly refuted Posner's account.

Meanwhile, the subject of Zubaydah's story, Prince Ahmed, had very different concerns on his mind—horse racing. The previous year Ahmed had experienced extraordinary success with his three-year-old colt, Point Given. Ahmed had been devastated when Point Given came in fifth in the Kentucky Derby.

In early April 2002, while Zubaydah was still being interrogated,

Prince Ahmed, knowing he didn't have a horse for the Kentucky Derby, was watching satellite TV in Riyadh when he saw War Emblem win the Illinois Derby by six lengths. "I was very impressed, so we got the door open, got the horse for a reasonable price and we go for it," the prince told a *New York Times* sports reporter. "We were thinking Derby."[63]

And why wasn't the CIA thinking Prince Ahmed, who was due to return to the United States for the Derby? According to Posner, senior CIA officials had ordered a thorough investigation to see whether there was any truth to the assertions Zubaydah had made during his interrogation. About a month afterward, they issued a report that corroborated some statements he had made but that was largely inconclusive. Then they quietly approached Saudi intelligence to ask whether Prince Ahmed could have been an Al Qaeda contact. The Saudis assured them that that could not possibly be the case. That left the administration with nowhere to go—unless it wanted to create an international incident.

And so, on May 7, 2002, Prince Ahmed's War Emblem entered the Kentucky Derby as a 20–1 shot. It was a gorgeous day at Churchill Downs racetrack in Louisville. Eight months after 9/11, however, America was still in mourning, and at 5:15 p.m., about fifty minutes before the race, a trumpet played taps, and the crowd of 145,000 attending the country's premier horse racing event fell silent. Firefighters from New York City's Ladder Company 3 on East Twenty-ninth Street were the guests of honor, standing at attention in front of the winners' circle. Twelve members of the company had lost their lives in the World Trade Center attack.[64]

Post time was 6:04. War Emblem had the number-five position in the wide-open, nineteen-horse field with no strong favorite. Before the gun, the trainer gave jockey Victor Espinoza his instructions: Sit still. The horse likes a quiet jockey. "I've never seen this horse before," Espinoza said. "Just don't move until the last minute, he told me probably a hundred times. Finally, I listened to him."[65]

War Emblem broke cleanly at the gate and took the lead in front of Proud Citizen. And that was it. He pulled away at midstretch, holding the lead wire to wire, winning by four lengths.

A few people jeered as Prince Ahmed made his way to the winners' circle, but that did not seem to bother him. "Everyone respects me here," he said. "Everybody actually makes me feel so good, sometimes I'm embarrassed. The American public treats me better than in Saudi Arabia."[66]

"It's a great achievement," he added. "This was important for me and it's an honor to be the first Arab to win the Kentucky Derby."

Columnist Jimmy Breslin, covering the Derby for *Newsday,* did not fail to notice Prince Ahmed's self-satisfaction. "Prince Ahmed bin Salman of Saudi Arabia held up the winner's cup and gloated with the thought of the million and more he made with the win, and did this in the presence of firefighters from Ladder 3," Breslin wrote. "... I wondered right away if Prince Ahmed had done anything to let us know he was sorry and could he do anything to assist after what bin Laden and other homegrown degenerates did to this city .... But the guy did nothing. What are you bothering me for, the prince said in Louisville, I am in horse racing, not politics."[67]

Two weeks later, War Emblem won the Preakness Stakes in Baltimore. Prince Ahmed's colt now had a shot at being the first Triple Crown winner since Seattle Slew in 1977. After the win, a reporter asked Ahmed how much he wanted to win the triple. "As badly as I want my son and daughter to get married," he replied. "Really bad. To win the Triple Crown would really knock me out."

But on June 8, Prince Ahmed did not even show up at the Belmont Stakes, the third part of the Triple Crown. "I'm disappointed the prince wasn't here," said trainer Bob Baffert.[68] Ahmed was said to be tending to family obligations in Riyadh. An associate said that he did not know the nature of the obligations. In any case, War Emblem stumbled as he came out of the starting gate and came in eighth.

About six weeks later, on July 22, Prince Ahmed was dead. News reports said the forty-three-year-old nephew of King Fahd had died in his sleep due to a heart attack.[69]

As Gerald Posner has reported, Ahmed was not the only person named by Zubaydah to suffer ill. The next day, July 23, Ahmed's cousin, Prince Sultan bin Faisal bin Turki al-Saud, was killed in a one-car crash while en route to Ahmed's funeral. A week later, on July 30, Prince Fahd bin Turki bin Saud al-Kabir, a third member of the royal family who had been named by Zubaydah, was found in the desert, having apparently died of thirst.[70]*

In and of themselves, the three mysterious deaths do not conclusively confirm Posner's assertion that Zubaydah was telling the truth about Osama bin Laden and his high-level links to the House of Saud.

Now, of course, the three men cannot be interviewed—not that the FBI didn't have its chance at one of them. On September 16, 2001, after the Bush administration had approved the Saudi evacuation, Prince Ahmed boarded the 727 in Lexington, Kentucky. He had been identified by FBI officials, but not seriously interrogated. It was an inauspicious start to the just-declared war on terror. "What happened on September 11 was a horrific crime," says John Martin, a former Justice Department official. "It was an act of war. And the answer is no, this is not any way to go about investigating it."

As for the Saudis, they were not offering any answers. On September 4, 2003, almost two years after 9/11, Saudi embassy spokesman Nail al-Jubeir appeared on CNN and was asked by newscaster Paula Zahn, "Can you tell us unequivocally tonight that no one on board [these planes] had anything to do with either the planning or the execution of the September 11 plot?"

"There are only two things that I'm sure about," al-Jubeir replied. "That there is the existence of God and then we will die at the end of the world. Everything else, we don't know."[71]

---

*Nor was that the end of it. During his interrogation, Zubaydah had also said that Osama bin Laden had struck a deal with Pakistani air force chief Air Marshal Mushaf Ali Mir, and had told him that there would be unspecified attacks on American soil on 9/11. Seven months after the Saudi deaths, on February 20, 2003, Mir and sixteen others were killed when their plane crashed in a northwest province of Pakistan. Sabotage was widely speculated to be behind the crash but could not be proved.

CHAPTER FIFTEEN

Print the Legend

IN AMERICA, MANY FORCES battle to shape the collective narrative. Nowhere is this conflict addressed more elegantly than in *The Man Who Shot Liberty Valance,* the epic Western movie directed in 1962 by the great John Ford. The story is told as a flashback, with the idealistic character played by Jimmy Stewart recounting to a newspaper reporter how he came to the small Western town of Shinbone many years earlier as a naive tenderfoot. Because he dared to challenge and duel a vicious bandit, Stewart has become mythologized as "the man who shot Liberty Valance." He has since gone on to become a U.S. senator and a national icon.

Jimmy Stewart's character, Ransom Stoddard, is unable to live with a lie, however, and he decides to tell the reporter the truth. The reporter, Maxwell Scott, listens intently as Stoddard demystifies himself with the startling revelation that he did not really shoot Liberty Valance. It was John Wayne, hiding in the shadows.

But as Stewart finishes, Scott dramatically rises to his feet and, with a flourish, starts tearing up his notes.

"You're not going to use the story, Mr. Scott?" Stewart asks.

"No, sir," Scott says. "This is the West, sir. And when the legend becomes fact, print the legend."[1]

When it comes to 9/11, for the most part, America has printed the legend. Because Al Qaeda's attacks seemingly came out of the blue, a simplistic narrative has emerged: America good, terrorists bad. Stand behind the president. It is a storyline that holds some unassailable truths. Heroic firemen, police officers, and others gave their lives so that their fellow citizens might live. But, as put forth by the Bush administration, the official narrative allows little room for complexity and none for doubt.

Yet the real story is full of startling paradoxes and subtle nuances and they have started to come into view. In the wake of the attacks, reports on the Saudi role in fostering terrorism have gradually made their way into the American press. Allegations that specific members of the royal family, or members of the Saudi merchant elite, had prior knowledge of 9/11 or knowingly financed Al Qaeda are grave charges indeed, and should not be made unless they can be backed up by strong evidence. Some of these questions may be answered in the $1-trillion civil suit brought by families of the victims of 9/11 against hundreds of individuals and entities, many of whom are prominent Saudis.

As to exactly how guilty the Saudis have been in aiding terror, Richard Clarke sees a spectrum of complicity. "Some of them were clearly sympathetic to Al Qaeda," he says. "Some of them thought that if they allowed a certain degree of cooperation with Al Qaeda, Al Qaeda would leave them alone. And some of them were merely reacting in a knee-jerk, instinctive way to what they believed was interference in their internal affairs."[2]

But there is also the sin of omission—the failure to crack down on terrorists—and on that score there is no ambiguity about the role played by America's great ally in the Middle East. The evidence is overwhelming that the House of Saud did little to stem the rise of Islamist terror that started in the mid-nineties, that it continued to finance terrorists, inadvertently or otherwise, and that it refused to cooperate with the United States again and again—even after the events of 9/11.

In his address to the nation just after the catastrophe, Bush promised, "We will make no distinction between the terrorists who committed these acts and those who harbor them."

How does the president reconcile this solemn vow with his alliance with a state that bears more responsibility for 9/11 than does any other nation? He does not. The most cogent explanation for the Bush administration's soft line toward the Saudis is best expressed by Richard Clarke. "There's a realization that we have to work with the government we've got in Saudi Arabia," Clarke says. "The alternatives could be far worse. The most likely replacement to the House of Saud is likely to be more hostile—in fact, extremely hostile to the U.S."[3]

Clarke is right, of course. Nevertheless, if the House of Saud were a genuine ally, the Bush administration could have pressured it about the Saudi role in terrorism, aggressively gone after Al Qaeda after the USS *Cole* bombing, and still maintained a productive alliance. But that didn't happen, and other explanations for Bush's pro-Saudi policies are less benign. "It's always been very clear that there are deep ties between the Bush family and the Saudis," says Charles Lewis, head of the Center for Public Integrity, a Washington, D.C., foundation that examines issues of ethics in government. "It creates a credibility problem. When it comes to the war on terror, a lot of people have to be wondering why we are concerned about some countries and not others. Why does Saudi Arabia get a pass?"[4]

Is it a factor that more than $1.4 billion has made its way from the House of Saud to individuals and entities tied to the House of Bush? "You would be less inclined to do anything forceful or dynamic if you are tied in with them financially," says Lewis, addressing the particular issue of Bush-Saudi ties within the Carlyle Group. "That's common sense."

Even if the president were somehow immune to the fact that in large measure he owed both his personal and political fortunes to the Saudis, it would be astonishing if he did not fall prey to a kind of groupthink as to who they really were. How could George W. Bush possibly perceive that policies hailed as great successes in the short run were actually so deeply flawed that in the long run they could lead to a catastrophe such as 9/11? To do so would require breaking a taboo. After all, the men he had grown up with—his father, James Baker— were *giants.* They were not only his elders, they were the most powerful men on earth. Surely, it was not possible for him to imagine that Prince Bandar and Princess Haifa, such longtime friends of the family, could have been connected to the disaster. After *Newsweek* reported that Princess Haifa's donations had ended up in the bank account of a Saudi who helped two of the 9/11 hijackers, the Bush family reaction was revealing. Not only did the White House fail to call for an investigation, but the Bushes rallied to her side. First Lady Laura Bush called

Princess Haifa to express her sympathies. Bush senior and his wife, Barbara, did so as well. "I felt horribly about the attacks on her," the elder Bush told the *New Yorker*.[5]

Nor did the news hurt Prince Bandar's relationship with the president himself. When Bandar arrived at the West Wing of the White House on December 3, 2002, just after the revelations, to meet with Condoleezza Rice, President Bush dropped by and insisted that Bandar join the family for dinner.[6]

In one respect, however, President Bush has not followed so resolutely in the footsteps of his father. In the immediate aftermath of 9/11, Bush temporarily resisted the urge to attack Saddam Hussein. But by early 2002, the White House had begun rattling sabers at Iraq. To the hard-line, militaristic, neocon faction in the administration, 9/11 presented an opening to execute their grandiose plan for overhauling the entire Middle East. The ascendancy of the neocons also meant that for the first time a militantly anti-Saudi bloc had a voice in the Bush administration—a stance that would have appalled Bush senior and James Baker. On July 10, 2002, an incendiary Pentagon briefing, by Rand Corporation analyst Laurent Murawiec, even characterized Saudi Arabia as "a kernel of evil, the prime mover, the most dangerous opponent" of the United States.

Murawiec, who was invited to give the briefing to the Defense Policy Board by Richard Perle, asserted that "The Saudis are active at every level of the terror chain, from planners to financiers, from cadre to foot-soldier, from ideologist to cheerleader .... Saudi Arabia supports our enemies and attacks our allies."[7]

Much of this was old news to Saudi critics. But then Murawiec went too far. One of the last slides of his presentation argued for a takeover of Saudi Arabia's most precious resources: "What the House of Saud holds dear can be targeted: Oil: the oil fields are defended by U.S. forces, and located in a mostly Shiite area."[8]

In the widely reported furore that followed, the White House frantically assured the Saudis that the briefing in no way represented administration policy and was not to be taken seriously.

While the rogue briefing created friction, the Bush-Saudi relationship was under greater strain for another reason. Bush's campaign against Iraq was in full swing. On August 26, 2002, Dick Cheney addressed the issue at the Veterans of Foreign Wars national convention. "Simply stated, there is no doubt that Saddam Hussein now has weapons of mass destruction," he said.[9] An American invasion, however, would create real problems for the Saudis. How could the House of Saud support "infidel" U.S. troops in a neighboring Arab country?

Yet two weeks later, on September 12, President Bush himself took the issue to the United Nations. "Right now, Iraq is expanding and improving facilities that were used for the production of biological weapons," he declared in a speech before the General Assembly.[10]

As 2002 drew to an end, the noose drew tighter around Iraq. "If he declares he has [no weapons of mass destruction], then we will know that Saddam Hussein is once again misleading the world," said presidential press secretary Ari Fleischer at a December 2 press briefing.[11]

That same day, the administration announced the appointment of Elliott Abrams as special assistant to the president and senior director for Near East and North African affairs, with responsibilities in the National Security Council that included overseeing Arab-Israeli relations. A controversial figure in the Reagan-Bush era who pleaded guilty in 1987 to withholding information from Congress during the Iran-contra hearings, Abrams was later pardoned by George H. W. Bush in 1992. His appointment was widely seen as a victory for the hard-line neocon camp that was opposed to pursuing the "road map" to peace in the Middle East—the same road map that President Bush had agreed to follow after his rapprochement with the Saudis mere days before 9/11.

In February 2003, as American troops massed in Qatar for an Iraqi invasion, Abrams cleaned house at the NSC. According to Yossef Bodansky, director of the Congressional Task Force on Terror and Unconventional Warfare, Abrams called over Ben Miller, a highly regarded analyst who had the Iraqi file at the NSC, and "led Miller to an open window and told him to jump."

"That's his [Abrams's] management style," Bodansky told UPI.[12] Miller, of course, did not jump. But he left shortly after, and two other officials, Flynt Leverett and Hillary Mann, left at about the same time. Miller's departure was especially significant in that he was sympathetic to CIA analysts who were less intent on war with Iraq. According to Tony Cordesman, Middle East specialist at the Center for Strategic and International Studies, Miller, Mann, and Leverett "were among the saner minds discussing the Arab-Israeli issue."

Even before Abrams installed hard-liners at the NSC, Secretary of Defense Donald Rumsfeld had set up a new agency called the Office of Special Plans to make sure intelligence that supported the imminent invasion of Iraq made its way to the highest levels of the administration. What was taking place was the creation of what the *New Yorker's* Seymour Hersh dubbed "the stovepipe"—an institutionalized means for funneling upward selectively chosen intelligence to serve ideological ends. According to Kenneth Pollack, a former National Security Council specialist on Iraq, who supported military action to oust Saddam, Bush officials dismantled "the existing filtering process that for fifty years had been preventing the policy makers from getting bad information. They created stovepipes to get the information they wanted directly to the top leadership. Their position is that the professional bureaucracy is deliberately and maliciously keeping information from them.[13]

"They always had information to back up their public claims, but it was often very bad information," Pollack continued. "They were forcing the intelligence community to defend its good information and good analysis so aggressively that the intelligence analysts didn't have the time or the energy to go after the bad information."

As all these events were taking place, the man who was best qualified to lead a real war on terror decided he had had enough. On February 21, 2003, Richard Clarke resigned from the Bush administration. Three weeks later, he was asked how he was adjusting to leaving government. "I already don't miss it," he said. Then he elaborated. "You know that great feeling you get when you stop banging your head against a wall?"[14]

Having excluded from the decision-making process the government officials who knew the most about Iraq—certain CIA analysts and State Department officials who had studied it for years—the United States went to war against Iraq on March 19, 2003, based on a wide variety of startlingly false assumptions. Allegations that Iraq's nuclear weapons program was alive and well turned out to be based on forged documents from Niger. Charges about Iraq's role in 9/11 or its links to Al Qaeda turned out to be wildly exaggerated or baseless. The premise for the preemptive strike—that Saddam's weapons of mass destruction posed an immediate threat to the United States—appears to have been completely false.

The policy makers in the Bush administration also grandly assumed and asserted that U.S. soldiers would be greeted by the Iraqi masses with flowers as conquering heroes; that after a short, low-intensity occupation of three months or so, democracy would flourish; that the deep-seated historical antagonisms among Shiites, Baathists, and Kurds would not create postwar conflict; that Iraqi oil production could be dramatically boosted from 3 million barrels a day to 6 million; that the invasion would create a domino effect in which one autocratic regime after another in Iraq, Syria, Libya, and Iran would fall, paving the way for a new democratic Middle East.

Even though fighting continued after the U.S. military victory, many Americans, temporarily at least, saw the war as a qualified success. When the war on terror began, President Bush had framed the hunt for bin Laden in the terms of the old American West: *Bin Laden, Wanted Dead or Alive.* Now, by constantly harping on Saddam's links to terrorism, the Bush administration had succeeded in switching villains to the extent that 70 percent of Americans ultimately believed Saddam Hussein was linked to 9/11.

At the same time that the White House put forth this misleading impression, it made sure that other pieces of the terrorism puzzle were suppressed. In July 2003, Congress released a nine-hundred-page report on 9/11. But the Bush administration refused to declassify important passages, including a twenty-eight-page section dealing with the Saudis, and as a result those pages were deleted. According to Senator Bob Graham, the reason was simple. "They are protecting a foreign government," he said. *Time* reported that blacked-out pages produced "the smell of a cover-up of complicity in the worst terrorist attack in U.S. history."[15]

Soon, however, the White House regained control of the narrative, thanks to another spectacle, the capture of Saddam on December 13, 2003, which appeared to have satisfied America's desire for revenge.

* * *

277

Yet as 2003 drew to a close, American soldiers continued to die—in bombings, shootings, and missile attacks on helicopters. Far from coming to fruition, the neocons' rosy scenario of a newly democratic Iraq had inarguably devolved into a bloody, ongoing, and costly adventure that widened the potential for historically disastrous American involvement in the region. After the capture of Saddam Hussein, violence in Iraq continued. Thousands of Islamist militants kept flooding through Iraq's porous borders. "Iranians have some fifteen thousand, perhaps twenty thousand armed, trained, and intelligence-equipped Hezbollah-style [militants] inside Iraq," says Youssef Ibrahim, a member of the Council on Foreign Relations and the man-aging director of the Dubai-based Strategic Energy Investment Group. "They are successfully infiltrating the Iraqi intelligence and the U.S. intelligence system, gathering information and preparing."[16]

Few in the United States liked to admit it, but by switching the venue of America's response to 9/11 to Iraq, the United States may have inadvertently played directly into Al Qaeda's and Osama bin Laden's hands. More than twenty years earlier, bin Laden had gone to Afghanistan to lure another superpower into a land war inside a Muslim country. America's Cold Warriors had cackled with glee when the Soviets took the bait, and the long and brutal war that ensued helped lead to the demise of the Soviet empire. In the mountains of Afghanistan, Osama bin Laden had learned that he and his band of impassioned warriors could defeat a superpower in a guerilla war. And for George H. W. Bush, it had been his finest hour.

Is it possible that the United States has stepped into the same trap, that this time around we are the Soviets? Is it possible that in terms of the geopolitical chessboard, putting 135,000 American troops in a land war in a Muslim country was not a smart move? According to Ibrahim, far from being in control of Iraq, the American troops may actually be closer to being hostages. "The Iranians think they've got American forces 'surrounded' inside Iraq—not the other way around," he says.[17]

In fact, more than two years after 9/11, Osama bin Laden has fared far better than the Bush administration likes to admit. Bin Laden's jihad against the United States includes two specific two goals: the complete removal of U.S. troops from Saudi Arabia and the overthrow of the House of Saud. In May 2003, after the Iraq War started, Osama's first wish came true, as the small number of U.S. soldiers left the Arabian peninsula, in part to ease pressure on the Saudi regime from militants. On December 17, the State Department warned American families to leave Saudi Arabia because it was no longer safe for them to live there. Then, two weeks later, Osama bin Laden issued an audiotape, broadcast on Aljazeera TV, referring to the recent capture of Saddam Hussein and calling on Muslims to "continue the jihad to check the conspiracies that are hatched against the Islamic nation."

As for bin Laden's second wish, for decades, observers have prematurely predicted the demise of the House of Saud. At this writing, the House of Saud may or may not be experiencing its last days, but at the very least, the kingdom has entered a historic new era. In the past, Al Qaeda's attacks in Saudi Arabia have been aimed at foreigners rather than the House of Saud itself. But beginning with a bombing in Riyadh on May 12, 2003, a low-intensity civil war had begun. "There is now an openly declared war by Al Qaeda within the kingdom," says Ibrahim, who was the Middle East correspondent for the *New York Times* for many years. "Stability and security have gone by the wayside. You have a regime that is manifestly unable to deliver on its promises, and even unable to defend the expatriates living there."

And with the advent of Aljazeera's Qatar-based satellite TV news, non-state-controlled, non-Saudi voices are fanning the flames. Caught between its exposure to the West and the puritanical strain of Islam that controls its most powerful political institutions, a division embodied by Crown Prince Abdullah, who still believes the country has to crack down on terrorists and accommodate the West, and Interior Minister Prince Nayef, who leans toward the militant clerics, the House of Saud is in a state of paralysis. Initiating timid reforms while fearful of plunging the country into strife, the kingdom has no clear path to follow. As 2004 began, Saudi Arabia was being torn apart from the inside. "Not to be too melodramatic about it, but it is High Noon," says Ibrahim.

And for the moment, if the House of Saud were to be toppled, there is no alternative political force except militant clerics who are sympathetic to Osama bin Laden—not exactly a pleasant prospect.

In American policy circles, wild scenarios abound for dealing with such a crisis, including the seizure of Saudi oil fields by the American military. Perhaps not coincidentally, a 1973 U.S. plan to do exactly that surfaced on January 1, 2004. It should be noted, however, that such a course of action is far easier to talk about than to execute. "You cannot take over oil fields," explains Ibrahim, noting continuing attacks on the fields in Iraq during the current American occupation. "They are too vast and too vulnerable, both under the ground and over the ground. All it takes is a match."

If the past is any guide, if a militant Islamic fundamentalist regime were to take over Saudi Arabia, the prognosis is not pretty. In 1979, in Iran, when fundamentalists overturned the pro-Western shah and ended up with control of the oil fields, the price of oil skyrocketed. The same outcome could occur again, and this time the whole picture would be complicated by the fact that the Saudis control one-fourth of the known oil reserves in the world. In addition, rapidly escalating oil consumption in China and the rest of Asia will only increase competition among America's rivals for those resources. Thus, the relationship between the House of Bush and the House of Saud appears to be coming to a difficult end—at a time when the steady supply of oil for America is more vulnerable than ever to the highly volatile forces of Islamic fundamentalism.

How the United States will deal with these twin threats—Islamist terror and the potential loss of its most important source of energy— is one of the great issues the country will confront in the immediate future. As for terrorism, it may be that even if President Bush had implemented Richard Clarke's proposals to take on Al Qaeda, such measures would not have stopped 9/11. We will never know. But switching the villain from Osama bin Laden to Saddam Hussein and Iraq appears to have been a dangerous and costly diversion at best.

And it is undeniable that a new American vision is needed. But it is unlikely to come from an administration that in December 2003 appointed James Baker to oversee the "restructuring" of Iraq's $100-billion-plus debt, which includes $25 billion owed to Iraq's biggest creditor, none other than the House of Saud. Moreover, it is difficult to believe that the answers can come from a man in the White House whose personal and political fortunes, from Harken Energy to the

Carlyle Group, are so deeply entwined with the House of Saud, whose extended political family has taken in more than $1.4 billion from the Saudis, whose relationship with them goes back more than two decades, and who apparently feels so indebted to the House of Saud that he has censored twenty-eight pages in Congress's 9/11 report—as if the billionaire Saudi royals are somehow more worthy of the government's concern than are the victims of 9/11.

Meanwhile, as the 2004 presidential election approaches, President Bush has assiduously cultivated an image as an indomitable commander-in-chief who remains unassailable on the issue of national security—an image that is belied by one incontrovertible fact: Never before has an American president been so closely tied to a foreign power that harbors and supports our country's mortal enemies.

APPENDIX A

CAST OF CHARACTERS

House of Bush

James A. Baker III—Former presidential chief of staff, secretary of state, and secretary of the treasury, James Baker is a senior counselor and partner at the Carlyle Group, which had many Saudi investors, including members of the bin Laden family and, according to his attorney, Abdulrahman bin Mahfouz as well. Baker is also a partner at Baker Botts, the powerful energy-industry law firm whose clients include members of the Saudi royal family, ExxonMobil, ARCO, Schlumberger, BP Amoco, Halliburton, and other major energy companies. The firm defended Saudi royals, including Prince Bandar's father, Prince Sultan, in a $1-trillion lawsuit brought by families of the 9/11 victims. Baker's business links to the Saudis date back to 1981, when Khalid bin Mahfouz helped develop a seventy-five-story office building for the Texas Commerce Bank, in which Baker owned more than $7 million in stock. In late 2003, George W. Bush assigned Baker the task of reconciling the massive debt compiled by Iraq, whose biggest creditor was Saudi Arabia.

George H. W. Bush—The forty-first president of the United States, Bush has been close friends with Prince Bandar for more than twenty years. Both were key figures in the Iran-contra scandal in the eighties and, along with James Baker, they waged the Gulf War together in 1991. An independent Texas oil-man before he entered politics, after his presidency Bush served as senior adviser to the Carlyle Group until October 2003, and spoke before potential investors in Carlyle, including prominent Saudis. After his son became president, he attempted to mollify Crown Prince Abdullah to heal a rift between the Saudis and the White House in the summer of 2001.

George W. Bush—The forty-third president of the United States, Bush also started out as an independent oilman in Texas. When he was director of Harken Energy, the company was bailed out by Saudis and other investors with links to BCCI, the corrupt, Saudi-dominated bank. During his presidency, approximately 140 Saudis, including Prince Ahmed and about two dozen members of the bin Laden family, were evacuated immediately after the events of 9/11 with White House approval—without having been seriously questioned.

Frank Carlucci—Former secretary of defense and managing director and chairman emeritus at the Carlyle Group, Carlucci helped build Carlyle into a defense-industry powerhouse by buying defense companies whose prices were depressed after the end of the Cold War. "I've made it clear that I don't lobby the defense industry," Carlucci said after a meeting with his old Princeton wrestling teammate Donald Rumsfeld, who had just become the newly appointed secretary of defense.

The Carlyle Group—The giant private equity firm that became a home to James Baker, George H. W. Bush, Frank Carlucci, Richard Darman, John Major, and other powerful figures from the Reagan-Bush era, Carlyle now owns companies with assets of more than $16 billion. An element in its ascendancy has been its lucrative relationships with the Saudis, including Saudi royals, the bin Ladens, and the bin Mahfouz family, both as investors and as clients for defense contractors owned by Carlyle.

Dick Cheney—Vice president of the United States under George W. Bush, Cheney had been a prominent Republican congressman and served as secretary of defense under Bush senior during the Gulf War. As CEO of Halliburton between 1995 and 2000, Cheney received $34 million in compensation during his last year at the company and became vice president without relinquishing more than 400,000 stock options in it.

Donald Rumsfeld—In 1983 and 1984, as a presidential envoy for the Reagan-Bush administration, Rumsfeld met Saddam Hussein and assured Iraqi leaders that even though the United States would publicly denounce Iraq for using chemical weapons, the issue should not interfere with developing a warm relationship between the two countries. In 2002, however, he turned against Saddam and led the war against Iraq the following year.

House of Saud

Crown Prince Abdullah bin Abdul Aziz—The de facto ruler of Saudi Arabia and heir to the throne now held by King Fahd, Prince Abdullah threatened the Bush administration with ending the special Saudi-U.S. relationship just before 9/11.

Prince Ahmed bin Salman—A nephew of King Fahd's who is best known as the owner of 2002 Kentucky Derby winner War Emblem and other great racehorses, Prince Ahmed was named by Al Qaeda boss Abu Zubaydah as the terror group's contact within the House of Saud. Zubaydah also said that Ahmed had foreknowledge that Al Qaeda would attack inside the United States on 9/11. Shortly after 9/11, Ahmed left the United States as part of the White House–approved evacuation of Saudis. He died of a heart attack at age forty-three not long after the Saudis were informed of Zubaydah's allegations. He was a son of Prince Salman bin Abdul Aziz, the governor of Riyadh, who is one of the relatively pro-West Sudairi Seven, but who had a close working relationship with Osama bin Laden back in the eighties.

Abdullah Taha Bakhsh—A major investor in Harken Energy, the struggling oil company of which George W. Bush was a director, Bakhsh was one of several people who had ties to BCCI and came to Harken's rescue when Bush's father was president. His representative on Harken's board, Talat Othman, later gained President George H. W. Bush's ear in the lead-up to Operation Desert Storm in 1990, and ten years later addressed the GOP convention at which George W. Bush was nominated. Bakhsh is a Saudi real estate magnate with ties to Khalid bin Mahfouz.

Prince Bandar bin Sultan—The longtime ambassador to the United States and close friend of George H. W. Bush and his family, Prince Bandar went on vacations and hunting trips with the elder Bush and also waged war with him and participated in covert operations. He oversaw the evacuation of approximately 140 Saudis, including members of the royal family, just after 9/11. He once remarked, "If the reputation ¼ builds that the Saudis take care of friends when they leave office, you'd be surprised how much better friends you have who are just coming into office." Bandar has reportedly been an investor in the Carlyle Group with the elder George Bush. He gave $1 million to the George H. W. Bush Presidential Library and a $1-million painting to President George W. Bush. He is a nephew of King Fahd.

King Fahd bin Abdul Aziz—nominal ruler of Saudi Arabia, incapacitated by a 1995 stroke. Half brother of Crown Prince Abdullah and uncle of Prince Bandar.

Princess Haifa bint Faisal—Prince Bandar's wife, Princess Haifa indirectly may have provided funds to two of the 9/11 hijackers. After *Newsweek's* revelations about her role in the funding, both Laura Bush and former president Bush called to console her.

Khalid bin Mahfouz—A billionaire Saudi banker, bin Mahfouz joined Salem bin Laden in creating the Houston-Jeddah connection through James Bath. A major shareholder in BCCI and longtime owner of the National Commercial Bank of Saudi Arabia, bin Mahfouz was for many years the most powerful banker in the kingdom. He helped develop a seventy-five-story sky-scraper in Houston for the Texas Commerce Bank, in which James Baker was a major shareholder. According to the family attorney, two of his sons invested $30 million in the Carlyle Group.

Salem bin Laden—Osama's half brother and longtime manager of the Saudi Binladin Group, Salem was a contemporary and friend of Khalid bin Mahfouz, the billionaire Saudi banker. The two men began establishing contacts in the United States through James R. Bath, a Texas Air National Guard buddy of George W. Bush. Salem died in a 1988 plane crash.

The Sudairi Seven—King Abdul Aziz, the founder of modern Saudi Arabia, had forty-three sons and the Sudairi Seven refers to the seven sons by his favored wife. They include King Fahd; Defense Minister Prince Sultan, who is Prince Bandar's father; Riyadh governor Prince Salman, who is the father of the late Prince Ahmed; Interior Minister Prince Nayef; business leader Prince Abdul Rahman; Prince Ahmad; and Prince Turki bin Abdul Aziz, who is not to be confused with Prince Turki bin Faisal, the longtime minister of intelligence. This powerful faction within the ruling family is considered pro-West, save for Prince Nayef, who maintains close relations with militant clergy and has blamed the events of 9/11 on Zionists.

Other Key Players

Sami Al-Arian—A professor at the University of South Florida who campaigned for George Bush and later visited him in the White House, Al-Arian was has been closely linked to the Palestinian Islamic Jihad. In 2003, he was arrested on dozens of charges, among them conspiracy to finance terrorist attacks that killed more than a hundred people, including two Americans.

James Bath—Beginning in the mid-seventies, the Houston-based Bath served as business representative for Salem bin Laden, Osama's older brother and the head of the Saudi Binladin Group, and billionaire banker Khalid bin Mahfouz. Bath also served in the Texas Air National Guard with George W. Bush and knew the elder George Bush, James Baker, and John Connally. A key figure in introducing the Saudis to the United States, he was also an investor in Arbusto, George W. Bush's first oil company.

Richard Clarke—The nation's first counterterrorism czar as head of the National Security Council's Coordinating Subgroup. Appointed initially to the NSC by George H. W. Bush, Clarke rose to power under Clinton. He devised an early and forceful strategy to confront Al Qaeda but his plans were largely ignored by the administration of George W. Bush.

Grover Norquist—A powerful conservative strategist, Norquist invented the Muslim Strategy to win the votes of millions of Muslim Americans through alliances between George W. Bush and Islamic extremists such as Sami Al-Arian and Abdurahman Alamoudi. "George W. Bush was elected President of the United States of America because of the Muslim vote," he wrote in the right-wing publication *American Spectator*. "... That's right," he added, "the Muslim vote."

Osama bin Laden—Scion to the multibillion-dollar bin Laden construction fortune and archterrorist of the early twenty-first century, Osama bin Laden rose to prominence in the 1980s as a leader of the "Afghan Arabs" fighting the Soviets in the Afghanistan War. Originally backed by the House of Saud, the Saudi merchant elite including the bin Mahfouz and bin Laden families, and the United States, he launched a jihad against the United States after American troops went to Saudi Arabia for the Gulf War of 1991. As the leader of Al Qaeda, he has been charged with orchestrating attacks on U.S. embassies in Nairobi and Tanzania, bombing the USS *Cole*, and perpetrating the 9/11 attacks among many other terrorist acts.

Abu Zubaydah—High-ranking Al Qaeda leader who was captured in March 2002 and who, while being interrogated, asserted that Prince Ahmed bin Salman, the wealthy racehorse owner and nephew of King Fahd, was an intermediary between Al Qaeda and the royal family. Zubaydah tried to strangle himself when he realized that he had been tricked by the agents who were interrogating him.

APPENDIX B
CHRONOLOGY

1924 George H. W. Bush is born on June 12.

1938 The first oil deposits are discovered in Saudi Arabia.

1945 President Franklin D. Roosevelt meets King Abdul Aziz of Saudi Arabia aboard the USS *Quincy* in the Suez Canal on Valentine's Day, initiating the modern U.S.-Saudi relationship based on oil for security. 1946 George W. Bush is born on July 6.

1957 Osama bin Laden is born on March 10.

1966 George H. W. Bush sells his shares in Zapata, his oil company, for $1 million and embarks on a career in politics.

1968 Billionaire Saudi construction mogul Mohammed bin Laden dies in a plane crash, leaving his son Osama a large inheritance.

1970 U.S. oil production peaks and begins a decades-long decline, while American oil consumption continues to grow, beginning a trend that leads to the nation becoming dependent on foreign oil.

1973 OPEC's oil embargo begins in the wake of the Arab-Israeli war. 1976 George W. Bush founds Arbusto, a small independent Texas oil company

1979 On November 4, fifty-two Americans are taken hostage when Iranian militants seize the American embassy in Tehran a few months after the shah is ousted and replaced with a fundamentalist regime.

On November 20, more than a thousand members of the Muslim Brotherhood invade Mecca and seize control of the Grand Mosque. Mahrous bin Laden is later accused of playing a role.

On December 26, the USSR invades Afghanistan. Zbigniew Brzezinski writes, "We now have the opportunity to give Russia its own Vietnam War." U.S. support for the Afghan Arabs had begun earlier that summer and would later grow to more than $700 million a year. Within days, Osama bin Laden decides to join the battle against the Soviet "infidels."

1980   On September 22, Iraq invades Iran, launching the Iran-Iraq War.

On November 4, Ronald Reagan is elected president. George H. W. Bush becomes vice president and James Baker becomes chief of staff to the president.

1981   Thanks to the lobbying of Prince Bandar and the support of Vice President George H. W. Bush, the U.S. Senate narrowly approves the $5.5-billion sale of AWACS aircraft to Saudi Arabia on October 28. It is the birth of a policy that eventually sends approximately $200 billion in U.S. weapons to Saudi Arabia.

Khalid bin Mahfouz develops the seventy-five-story Texas Commerce Bank building in Houston in partnership with the bank itself, which was founded by James Baker's family. At the time Baker owns approximately $7 million of the bank's stock.

1982   In January, George W. Bush sells 10 percent of Arbusto, his tiny, struggling oil company to New York investor Philip Uzielli, a longtime friend of James Baker, at a grossly inflated price.

On June 13, Crown Prince Fahd bin Abdul Aziz becomes king of Saudi Arabia.

1983   Prince Bandar is appointed ambassador to the United States by King Fahd in October.

On December 20, Donald Rumsfeld travels to Baghdad as a presidential special envoy to meet Saddam Hussein. Although Iraq is using chemical weapons almost daily, Rumsfeld does not raise the issue with Saddam. He returns in March 1984 to assure Iraq that U.S. protests against the use of chemical weapons should not interfere with a warm relationship between the two countries.

1984   With the approval of Vice President George H. W. Bush, Prince Bandar begins funding the right-wing contra rebels' attempts to topple the Sandinista government in Nicaragua on June 22 even though James Baker has warned that such an arrangement may constitute an impeachable offense.

1987   The Carlyle Group is founded by David Rubenstein and three other partners. It will become a private-sector home to some of the great icons of the Reagan-Bush era—George H. W. Bush, James Baker, Frank Carlucci, Richard Darman, and John Major.

1990   Having been bailed out by a number of people and institutions linked to BCCI, Harken Energy, the small oil company of which George W. Bush is a director, astonishes oil-industry analysts by winning a lucrative exploration contract in January to drill offshore of Bahrain.

On June 20, despite warnings from Harken's general counsel against insider trading, George W. Bush unloads 212,140 shares of Harken stock for $848,560 just before the company announces major losses.

On August 2, Iraq invades Kuwait. "This will not stand," says President George H. W. Bush. As the United States and Saudi Arabia prepare for war against Iraq, Osama bin Laden warns the House of Saud not to invite American troops into Saudi Arabia and offers his Afghan Arab warriors instead. He is rebuffed.

On September 18, the Carlyle Group buys BDM International and its subsidiary Vinnell, companies that service the Saudi Air Force and train the Saudi Arabian National Guard.

On November 5, Rabbi Meir Kahane of the right-wing Jewish Defense League is shot and killed by a militant Islamist. He is the first casualty of Al Qaeda on American soil.

1991 The Gulf War begins on January 16.

1992 Khalid bin Mahfouz is indicted in New York on July 2, for allegedly having fraudulently obtained $300 million from BCCI depositors. The matter is later settled without admission of guilt.

1993 On February 26, the World Trade Center is bombed by militants including El Sayed Nosair, the man who killed Meir Kahane.

On March 11, James A. Baker joins the Carlyle Group as one of its first seven partners.

1995 On November 13, a car bomb in Riyadh, widely attributed to followers of Osama bin Laden, kills seven people, including five Americans, and wounds several American advisers with Vinnell, the Carlyle-owned firm that trains the Saudi Arabian National Guard.

1996 On August 23, Osama bin Laden signs a declaration of jihad against the United States.

1997 The Carlyle Group buys United Defense, makers of the Crusader gun and the Bradley Fighting Vehicle

1998 On August 7, the seventh anniversary of the arrival of U.S. troops in Saudi Arabia for the Gulf War, Al Qaeda operatives bomb U.S. embassies in Dar es Salaam, Tanzania, and Nairobi, Kenya, killing about 260 and wounding 5,000. America responds less than two weeks later with cruise missile attacks on Afghanistan and Sudan.

2000 While campaigning for the presidency, George W. Bush and his wife, Laura, meet Sami Al-Arian and other Muslim leaders at a mosque in Tampa, Florida, on March 12. Al-Arian is later arrested on charges relating to the terrorist group Palestinian Islamic Jihad.

In September, the neoconservative Project for a New American Century releases an influential paper, "Rebuilding America's Defenses," a blueprint for U.S. global hegemony that urges, among other things, the overthrow of Saddam Hussein. Those affiliated with PNAC include Dick Cheney, Donald Rumsfeld,

and Paul Wolfowitz, all of whom will become key members of
George W. Bush's administration.

On October 11, at the second presidential debate of the 2000
election, Bush wins over Arab Americans by saying he is against
the use of secret evidence to prosecute alleged terrorists and that
he is against racial profiling of Arab Americans.

On election day, November 7, Bush's courtship of Arab Americans
pays off, particularly in Florida, where exit polls by the American
Muslim Alliance say that more than 90 percent voted for Bush.

On December 12, the U.S. Supreme Court stops the recount of
disputed votes in Florida, effectively awarding the presidency to
George W. Bush.

On December 20, counterterrorism czar Richard Clarke presents
National Security Adviser Sandy Berger with a plan to "roll back"
Al Qaeda. The plan is postponed pending the arrival of the new
administration, presented to the new national security adviser,
Condoleezza Rice, and then ignored.

2001   On January 25, Richard Clarke follows up his briefing with
Condoleezza Rice with a memo saying U.S. intelligence believes
that there are now Al Qaeda sleeper cells in the United States.

On July 5, Clarke assembles officials from a dozen federal agencies
in the White House Situation Room and tells them, "Something
really spectacular is going to happen here, and it's going to
happen soon."

On August 4, Bush sets out for Crawford, Texas, on the longest
presidential vacation in thirty-two years. He does not return to
the White House until September 3.

On August 6, Bush, still in Crawford, is given a briefing saying that
bin Laden and Al Qaeda are planning an attack on American soil.

On September 4, Richard Clarke finally meets with the Principals
Committee and presents his plan to attack Al Qaeda. No action is
taken.

On September 11, Al Qaeda hijacks four airplanes. Two hit the
World Trade Center towers, one hits the Pentagon, and one
crashes near Shanksville, Pennsylvania. Almost three thousand
people are killed.

At about 2 p.m., Secretary of Defense Donald Rumsfeld orders up
plans to take out Saddam Hussein, not just Osama bin Laden.
"Go massive," the notes quote Rumsfeld as saying, "sweep it all
up, things related and not."

Two days later, on September 13, Prince Bandar meets President
Bush for a private conversation on the Truman balcony in the
White House. At the same time, a massive operation to evacuate

140 Saudis, including about two dozen members of the bin Laden family, has begun. The first flight leaves Tampa, Florida, for Lexington, Kentucky, that day.

On September 16, as part of the White House-approved evacuation, Prince Ahmed bin Salman, a nephew of King Fahd's who is best known as the owner of famous racehorses, boards a flight in Lexington, Kentucky, to leave the United States. FBI officials meet and identify him, but he is not interrogated. Later, Al Qaeda boss Abu Zubaydah names Prince Ahmed as a liaison between Al Qaeda and the House of Saud and says that Prince Ahmed knew in advance that there would be attacks by Al Qaeda in the United States on September 11.

On September 19, Bush declares war: "Our war on terror ... will not end until every terrorist group of global reach has been found, stopped, and defeated." However, the Visa Express program, through which Saudis are allowed to get a visa without even appearing at a consulate, is allowed to continue.

On October 7, U.S. and British forces begin air strikes against the Taliban in Afghanistan.

2002   On March 31, Abu Zubaydah, a high-ranking Al Qaeda operative, is captured by Pakistani commandos, U.S. Special Forces, and FBI SWAT teams in the suburbs of Faisalabad, Pakistan.

On May 7, Prince Ahmed appears at the Kentucky Derby to see his horse War Emblem, a 20-1 shot, win.

On July 22, Prince Ahmed dies of an apparent heart attack in Riyadh at the age of forty-three. He is the first of three prominent Saudis named by Zubaydah as links between the royal family and Al Qaeda to die that week.

2003   On March 20, U.S forces begin bombing Baghdad.

On May 12, a suicide bomb set off by Al Qaeda kills at least 11 people in Riyadh and injures more than 120. The explosion takes place in a compound that houses mainly Arab families and is seen as a direct attack on the House of Saud rather than Westerners.

On July 25, the White House deletes twenty-eight pages in a nine-hundred-page congressional report on 9/11. According to Senator Bob Graham, the reason for the censorship was simple. "They are protecting a foreign government," he said. The government in question was clearly Saudi Arabia.

On December 13, U.S. forces capture Saddam Hussein.

On December 17, the State Department warns American families to leave Saudi Arabia. The decision has come after suicide bombings by Al Qaeda in May and November and is based on a review of the threat level to American interests in Saudi Arabia.

2004   On January 4, Aljazeera TV airs an audiotape purported to be from Osama bin Laden that refers to the recent capture of Saddam Hussein and calls on Muslims to "continue the jihad to check the conspiracies that are hatched against the Islamic nation." Bin Laden says the U.S. war against Iraq was the beginning of the "occupation" of Gulf states for their oil.

On January 14, the Senate Finance Committee asked the IRS for secret tax and financial records of Muslim charities and foundations, as part of a congressional probe into terrorist funding. Muslim-American leaders assailed the investigation as a "fishing expedition." "Are they now going to start a witch hunt of all the donors ... so that Muslims feel they're going to be targeted?" asked Ibrahim Hooper, a spokesman for the Council on American-Islamic Relations (CAIR). (Dan Eggen and John Mintz, "Muslim Groups' IRS Files Sought," *Washington Post,* January 14, 2004.) CAIR is a member of the American Muslim Political Coordination Council, which endorsed George W. Bush in 2000.

According to the *Wall Street Journal,* federal banking regulators began examining tens of millions of dollars in transactions in Saudi Arabian embassy accounts at a Washington bank that were not properly reported. The investigation began after reports showed that money from Princess Haifa's account ended up with two 9/11 hijackers. Initially, the irregularities were thought to involve only a few thousand dollars. But the U.S. Treasury Department charged the bank with failing to observe money-laundering regulations that require analysis of transactions for suspicious characteristics. (Glenn R. Simpson, "Probe of Saudi Embassy Widens," *Wall Street Journal,* January 14, 2004.)

In February, the 9/11 commission continued its investigation. A source close to the commission said that it was being "stonewalled" by the Bush administration in terms of getting crucial information about the tragedy.

APPENDIX A
THE NUMBER—$1,477,100,000

What follows is a compilation of financial transactions through which individuals and entities connected with the House of Saud transferred money to individuals and entities closely tied to the House of Bush. The House of Bush is defined here as George W. Bush, George H. W. Bush, James A. Baker III, Dick Cheney, and the major institutions that they are tied to, including the George H. W. Bush Presidential Library, the Carlyle Group, and Halliburton. The House of Saud includes members of the Saudi royal family, companies controlled by them, and members of the Saudi merchant elite such as the bin Laden and bin Mahfouz families, whose fortunes are closely tied to the royal family.

The list is by no means complete. It was not possible to obtain the particulars of many business dealings between the House of Bush and the House of Saud, and as a result, those figures are not included. For example, the client list of the Houston law firm of Baker Botts includes Saudi insurance companies, the Saudi American Bank, and members of the House of Saud itself, which Baker Botts is defending in the $1-trillion lawsuit filed by the families of the victims of 9/11. Because the payments made to Baker Botts are not publicly disclosed, they are not included. Likewise, Khalid bin Mahfouz was a partner in developing the Texas Commerce Bank skyscraper at a time when Baker was a major stockholder in the bank. Because the exact size of bin Mahfouz's investment could not be determined, it is not included.

It is worth adding that many other figures in the administration have close ties to Saudi Arabia through various other corporations that are not included in this list. Condoleezza Rice served on the board of directors of Chevron from 1991 to 2001. Among Chevron's business links to Saudi Arabia—which date back to the 1930s—are a 50 percent stake in Chevron Phillips Saudi Arabia to build a $650-million benzene and cyclohexane plant in Jubail, Saudi Arabia, and a joint venture with Nimir Petroleum, a Saudi company in which Khalid bin Mahfouz is a principal. These figures are not included. Finally, the Carlyle Group has owned a number of other major defense firms such as United Defense and Vought Aircraft that have had major contracts with Saudi Arabia, but their contracts are not included either. As a result, what follows is likely a conservative figure that may significantly understate the total sum involved.

The Carlyle Group: $1,268,600,000

Saudi Investors in Carlyle: $80 million

Former president George H. W. Bush, James Baker, and former prime minister John Major of Great Britain all visited Saudi Arabia on behalf of Carlyle, and according to founding partner David Rubenstein, the Saudis invested at least $80 million in the Carlyle Group.[1] With the exception of the bin Laden family, who extricated themselves from Carlyle not long after 9/11, Carlyle declined to disclose who the investors were. But other sources say that Prince Bandar, several other Saudi royals, and Abdulrahman and Sultan bin Mahfouz were prominent investors and that it was an explicit policy of the House of Saud to encourage Saudi investment in Carlyle.

Contracts between Carlyle-owned corporations Carlyle and Saudi Arabia— BDM (including its subsidiary Vinnell): $1,188,600,000

The Carlyle Group owned defense contractor BDM from September 1990 until early 1998.[2] One BDM subsidiary, Vinnell, has trained the Saudi National Guard since 1975 thanks to a controversial contract that allowed it to be the first U.S. private firm to train foreign forces.[3] While under Carlyle ownership, BDM's and Vinnell's contracts with Saudi Arabia included the following:

In 1994, BDM received a $46-million contract to "provide technical assistance and logistical support to the Royal Saudi Air Force."[4]
Between 1994 and 1998, Vinnell serviced a $819-million contract to provide training and support for the Saudi Arabian National Guard (SANG).[5]
In 1995, Vinnell signed a $163-million contract to modernize SANG.[6]
In 1995, BDM signed a $32.5-million contract to "augment Royal Saudi Air Force staff in developing, implementing, and maintaining logistics and engineering plans and programs."[7]
In 1996, BDM got a $44.4-million contract from the Saudis to build

housing at Khamis Mshayt military base.[8]

In 1997, BDM received $18.7 million to support the Royal Saudi Air Force.[9]

In 1997, just before BDM was sold to defense giant TRW, the company signed a $65-million contract to "provide for CY 1998 Direct Manning Personnel in support of maintenance of the F-15 aircraft." [10]

Halliburton: $180 million

Vice President Dick Cheney served as CEO of Halliburton from 1995 to 2000. At press time, he continued to hold 433,333 shares of Halliburton in a charitable trust." Among Halliburton's dealings with the Saudis, those whose details have been made public include:

In November 2000, Halliburton received $140 million to develop Saudi oil fields with Saudi Aramco.

In 2000, Halliburton subsidiary Kellogg, Brown, and Root was hired, along with two Japanese firms, to build a $40-million ethylene plant.[12]

Harken Energy: $25 million

After George W. Bush became a director of Harken Energy, several entities and individuals connected to BCCI, the scandal-ridden bank, suddenly came to Harken's rescue. When that financing fell through, Abdullah Taha Bakhsh.[13]

Charitable Donations: $3.5 million

It is worth pointing out that in terms of charitable donations, the House of Saud has been truly bipartisan and has contributed to every presidential library over the last thirty years. Many members of the House of Saud have directed their largesse to charities important to powerful Americans, including a $23-million donation to the University of Arkansas soon after Bill Clinton became president. The donations below represent those from the House of Saud to charities of personal importance to the Bush family:

1989: King Fahd gave $1 million to Barbara Bush's campaign against illiteracy.[14]

1997: Prince Bandar gave $1 million to the George Bush Presidential Library and Museum in College Station, Texas.[15]

2002: Prince Alwaleed bin Talal gave $500,000 to Andover to fund a George Herbert Walker Bush scholarship.[16]

2003: Prince Bandar gave a $1-million oil painting of an American Buffalo hunt to President Bush for use in his presidential library after he leaves the White House.[17]

ACKNOWLEDGMENTS

This book would not have been possible without the help of many people who assisted me every step of the way. At Scribner, I was fortunate to have an extraordinary editor, Colin Harrison, who was attentive to every aspect of the book from the breadth of its narrative scope to its finest details. His editorial judgment is superb and it has been a privilege to work with him. I am also grateful to Susan Moldow and Nan Graham, who were wonderfully supportive throughout the writing of this book and who oversaw a terrific team of people who treated the book with the highest level of professionalism. They include John Fulbrook, Erich Hobbing, Sarah Knight, Roz Lippel, Cynthia Mann, John McGhee, and Allison Murray. My thanks also go to Elisa Rivlin, for her comprehensive legal review, and to Pat Eisemann, who devoted her-self to the book's publicity.

My agent, Elizabeth Sheinkman of the Elaine Markson Agency, was one of the first people to recognize the possibilities of this book. She was always there with wise advice.

Daniel Benaim, my research assistant, and Cynthia Carris, my photo editor, both performed with grace and professionalism under deadline pressure. I am especially grateful to Daniel for his help in compiling the amount of money transferred from the House of Saud to the House of Bush. My thanks also go to James Hamilton for the author's photo.

This book was backed by a grant from the Florence and John Schumann Foundation. I am grateful to Bill Moyers, the president of the foundation, and Lynn Welhorsky, its vice president, for their generous support and encouragement. The grant was administered by the Nation Institute. My thanks there go to Victor Navasky, Katrina Vanden Heuvel, and Taya Grobow.

In the past, I have written about George H. W. Bush and George W. Bush for the *New Yorker, Esquire,* and *Vanity Fair* magazines. The *New Yorker* article, "In the Loop," was an investigative piece on George H. W.

Bush's role in Iran-contra and Iraqgate that I co-wrote with investigative reporter Murray Waas in 1992. Murray did an excellent job of reporting for the piece and I thank him for his permission to adapt parts of it for this book.

In addition, part of the book appeared in *Vanity Fair* in October 2003. I am indebted to Graydon Carter and Michael Hogan there for publishing the piece.

In the course of my earlier work on the Bushes and additional reporting for this book I interviewed, by phone or in person, three directors of the Central Intelligence Agency: Stansfield Turner, the late William Colby, and James Woolsey; and Saudi Arabia's minister of intelligence, Prince Turki bin Faisal. I would also like to thank Michael Anton at the White House for his time and for showing me exactly how the Bush administration deals with the press. In addition, there are many people in and out of government who spoke to me on condition of anonymity, including several members of the National Security Council staff in the administration of George W. Bush and high-level officials at the FBI. I am particularly indebted to them.

Others I'd like to acknowledge are Nail Al-Jubeir at the Saudi embassy, Don Albosta, Frank Anderson, David Armstrong, Gerry Auerbach, Robert Baer, James Bath, Dan Benjamin, Terry Bennett, Tom Blanton at the National Security Archive, Jack Blum, Richard Clarke, Casey Cooper, Dan D'Aniello, Alan Gerson, Dan Grossi, Armond Habiby, Dee Howard, Youssef Ibrahim, John Iannarelli, Thomas Kinton, Don Leavitt, Terry Lenzner, Charles Lewis, John Loftus, John L. Martin, Adil Najam, Nawaf Obaid, Bob Parry, Manuel Perez, Gerald Posner, Richard Rechter, Oliver "Buck" Revell, David Rubenstein, Cherif Sedky, Joe Trento, Dale Watson, Will Wechsler, Jonathan Winer, and James Zogby. Chris Ullman at the Carlyle Group was always gracious and responsive, belying the reputation for secrecy that the firm has acquired.

Helpful as such sources have been, this book relies extensively on declassified government documents, congressional investigations, and news accounts from thousands of newspapers and journals from all over the world. It would have been impossible to research this book without the Internet and I am especially grateful to people and institutions who have built the Internet research tools that enabled me to search through such vast amounts of material so quickly.

Specifically, my thanks go to Gary Sick and Columbia University's Gulf/2000, an Internet group that afforded me e-mail and telephone access to hundreds of scholars, diplomats, and policy makers who specialize in the Middle East. Gulf/2000's vast Internet archives of clippings were of great value and the thousands of e-mails they sent out enabled me to be privy to a dialog with hundreds of specialists in the field.

The Center for Cooperative Research (www.cooperativeresearch.org/)

is another valuable Internet tool. Because I made a practice of citing original sources, it does not appear in my notes nearly as often as it might. However, its timelines about 9/11 and related issues often helped me find exactly what I was looking for. I highly recommend it to anyone doing research on 9/11 and I encourage its support.

The National Security Archives (www.gwu.edu/~nsarchiv) has also performed a valuable public service through years of filing Freedom of Information Act requests to declassify secret documents, many of which it has posted on the Internet. These documents were useful to me again and again and are often cited in my notes. I also recommend the website of the Federation of American Scientists (www.fas.org), which makes many government documents readily accessible, including the 1992 Senate investigation into the BCCI scandal. Understanding that Byzantine affair was vital to putting together a template for the events in this book.

E-mail groups I joined that I found useful include Truthout (www.truthout.org) and the Weekly Spin (www.prwatch.org).

I should add that the notes offer a far more complete list of people and published sources that have contributed to the book. Wherever possible I have tried to include web addresses for those interested in further information.

Many friends and colleagues helped either by contributing in one way or another to the book itself or through much-needed moral support. They include John Anderson, Sidney Blumenthal, Peter Carey, Joe Conason, Martin Kilian, Don Leavitt, Robin and Susan Madden, Pazit Ravina, John "Print the Legend" Strahinich, and Lynne Faljian Taylor. My friends Len Belzer and Emily Squires generously provided their friendship and a house in the country for weekend R and R. And finally, my gratitude goes to my family—my mother, Barbara; my father, Roger; Chris, Shanti, and Thomas; and Jimmy, Marie-Claude, Adam, and Matthew.

NOTES

Chapter 1: The Great Escape

1. Warren King, *Seattle Times*, May 2, 2000.
2. Hank Kurz Jr., "Organ Network Gets Clearance for Charter Flights," Associated Press, September 13, 2001.
3. The heart Cortez was waiting for was brought in by helicopter and arrived just in time for surgery. However, throughout the United States, the entire organ transplant system was disrupted by the grounding of planes. In Salt Lake City, Utah, twenty-three-year-old Kenny Robison's heart transplant was canceled when the heart he had been waiting for could not be transported in time. A girl awaiting a liver transplant at a Stanford University hospital had her operation put on hold because the liver could not be flown in. Normally, transplanted organs go to those who need them most, but while America was grounded, geographical proximity became a far more important criterion.
4. John Bradley, "Are the Saudis Sunk?" *American Prospect*, September 2003.
5. Robert Kaiser, "Enormous Wealth Spilled into American Coffers," *Washington Post*, February 11, 2002.
6. Robert G. Kaiser and David B. Ottaway, "Saudi Leader's Anger Revealed Shaky Ties," *Washington Post*, February 10, 2002, p. 1.
7. Evan Thomas and Christopher Dickey, with Eleanor Clift, Roy Gutman, Debra Rosenberg, and Tamara Lipper, "The Saudi Game," *Newsweek*, November 19, 2001, p. 32.
8. Jack O'Dwyer, *Jack O'Dwyer's Newsletter*, October 17, 2001.
9. *ABC News Special Report: America Under Attack*, ABC News, September 12, 2001.
10. Interview with Prince Bandar, *Larry King Live*, October 1, 2001, www.cnn.com/transcripts/0110/01/lkl.00.html.
11. Jane Mayer, "The House of Bin Laden," *New Yorker*, November 12, 2001, www.newyorker.com/fact/content/?O11112fa_FACT3.
12. "Dreamland: A Hint of Florida Comes to Cairo," *Middle East Economic Digest*, April 2, 1999, p. 7.
13. Daniel Golden, James Bandler, and Marcus Walker, "Bin Laden Family Could Profit," *Wall Street Journal*, September 27, 2001.
14. Patrick Tyler, "Fearing Harm, Bin Laden Kin Fled from *U.S.*," *New York*

Times, September 30, 2001, p. A1.

15. "Authorities Search US Apartments of bin Laden's Relatives," Agence France-Presse, September 19, 2001.
16. Jacob Silberberg, "Tufts U. Wooed Binladin Family Members," *Tufts Daily* via University Wire, October 22, 2001.
17. Alison Leigh Cowan, Kurt Eichenwald, and Michael Moss, "Bin Laden Family, with Deep Western Ties, Strives to Re-establish a Name," *New York Times*, October 28, 2001, sec. 1B, p. 9.
18. "Authorities Search US Apartments of bin Laden's Relatives," Agence France-Presse.
19. Mayer, "House of Bin Laden."
20. Todd Venezia and Chris Wilson, "Osama Niece Fled NY," *New York Post*, October 6, 2001.
21. "Osama Kin on Shopping Spree," *New York Post*, October 28, 2001, p. 10.
22. Associated Press, September 23, 2001.
23. Holly Stepp, "Bin Laden's Half Brothers Are University of Miami Alumni," *Miami Herald*, September 20, 2001, p. 23A.
24. Tyler, "Fearing Harm, Bin Laden Kin Fled From U.S.," p. A1.
25. "America Prepares; Allies Respond," *Boston Globe*, October 1, 2001, p. A8.
26. Kathy Steele with Brenna Kelly and Elizabeth Lee Brown, "Phantom Flight from Florida," *Tampa Tribune*, October 5, 2001.
27. Elsa Walsh, "The Prince: How the Saudi Ambassador Became Washington's Indispensable Operator," *New Yorker*, March 24, 2003.
28. "Prince Bandar, Saudi Arabia Ambassador, Holds News Conference," FDCH Political Transcripts, Federal Document Clearing House, September 12, 2001.
29. Walsh, "The Prince," p. 48.
30. A search of all American newspapers two years later using Nexis-Lexis showed that no other paper had reported on the Tampa flight.
31. Interview with Dan Grossi.
32. Interview with Manuel Perez.
33. Interview with Dan Grossi.
34. Ibid.
35. Steele with Kelly and Brown, "Phantom Flight from Florida."
36. Inteview with John Iannarelli.
37. Kevin Cullen and Andrea Estes, "Bin Laden Kin, Family Weighed Staying in the US," *Boston Globe*, September 21, 2001.
38. Interview with Dale Watson, former FBI agent.
39. John Harris, "Bush Gets More International Support," *Washington Post*, September 17, 2001.
40. Kingdom of Saudi Arabia, *Information on Current Issues*, 2003, p. 2; also Saudi embassy website, saudiembassy.net/reportlink/update_final.pdf.
41. "Our Resolve Must Not Pass," Text of President Bush's Speech to Congress," *Columbus Dispatch*, September 20, 2001, p. A4.
42. Marcella Bombardieri and Neil Swidey, "America Prepares the Personal and Political; in Cambridge, a Binladin Breaks Family Silence," *Boston Globe*, October 7, 2001.
43. Interview with Tom Kinton.
44. Ibid.
45. Ibid.
46. Virginia Buckingham, "My Side of the Story," *Boston Globe Magazine*, September 8, 2002, p. 10.

47. Ibid.
48. "Osama: The Black Sheep," *Hotline*, September 19, 2001.
49. Charles M. Madigan, "Bush Boosts Police Powers," *Chicago Tribune*, September 19, 2001, p. 1.
50. Jonathan Wells, Jack Meyers, and Maggie Mulvihill, "Saudi Elite Tied to Money Groups Linked to bin Laden," *Boston Herald*, October 14, 2001.
51. Mayer, "The House of Bin Laden."
52. Walsh, "The Prince," p. 48.

Chapter 2: The Houston-Jeddah Connection

1. Interview with James Bath.
2. Ibid.
3. Unattributed, biography of Osama bin Laden, PBS *Frontline* Online.
4. Michael Field, *The Merchants*, p. 105.
5. Ibid.
6. Lowell Bergman and Martin Smith, "Saudi Time Bomb," PBS *Frontline*, November 15, 2001.
7. Interview with Adil Najam.
8. Field, *The Merchants*, p. 106.
9. Interview with Jamie Etheridge, analyst for Strategic Forecasting.
10. Jane Mayer, "The Contractors," *New Yorker*, May 5, 2003, p. 35.
11. Interview with James Bath.
12. Interview with Gerry Auerbach.
13. Suzanne Hoholik and Travis E. Poling, *San Antonio Express-News*, August 22, 1998, pt. A, p. 1.
14. Pavlo Solodko, "The Bin Ladin Business" [in Ukrainian], *Lviv Halytski Kontrakty*, no. 45, pp. 8, 24.
15. Dee Howard, telephone interview.
16. Mike Ward, "Bin Laden Relatives Have Ties to Texas," *Austin American-Statesman*, November 9, 2001, p. A1.
17. Interview with Terry Bennett.
18. Torch Lewis, *Business & Commercial Aviation*, December 2001, p. 112.
19. Dennis McLellan, "Obituary: Mohammed al-Fassi," *Los Angeles Times*, December 31, 2002, pt. 2, p. 10.
20. Dan Balz, "The Saudi Connection," *Washington Post*, April 19, 1981, p. C1.
21. Interview with a Houston associate of bin Mahfouz.
22. Robert Baer, *Sleeping with the Devil*, p. 41; and interview with bin Laden pilots.
23. Scott Farwell, "Saudi Arabia Asks Iran for Son of bin Laden," *Dallas Morning News*, September 8, 2003.
24. Interview with Heinrich Rupp.
25. Sandra Mackey, *The Saudis*, p. 45.
26. International Council of Shopping Centers, "The Impact of Shopping Malls," www.icsc.org.
27. Daniel Yergin, *The Prize*, p. 84; and Herbert S. Parmet, *George Bush*, p. 69.
28. Yergin, *The Prize*, p. 84.
29. Parmet, *George Bush*, p. 69.
30. Edward Vulliamy, "The Dark Heart of the American Dream," *Observer* (London), June 16, 2002, p. 22.
31. Yergin, *The Prize*, p. 300.
32. Ibid., pp. 287-91.

33. Ibid., p. 591.
34. "The Arming of Saudi Arabia," transcript of PBS *Frontline* #1112, February 16, 1993.
35. California Energy Commission, "Historical Yearly Average California Gasoline Prices per Gallon," www.energy.ca.gov/gasoline/statistics/gasoline_cpi_adjusted.html.
36. Steve Emerson, *The American House of Saud*, p. 53.
37. Balz, "The Saudi Connection," p. C1.
38. Mimi Swartz, "Oscar Wyatt," *Texas Monthly*, September 2001.
39. City of Houston, Office of the Mayor, Mayoral Speeches, www.ci.houston.tx.us/city/govt/mayor/speeches/020701.htm.
40. Balz, "The Saudi Connection," p. C1.
41. Anthony Cordesman, *Saudi Arabia*, p. 7.
42. Mackey, *The Saudis*, p. 293.
43. Robert Baer, "The Fall of the House of Saud," *Atlantic Monthly*, May 2002, p. 55.
44. *Washington Post*, February 11, 2002, p. A17; and Prince Bandar bin Sultan bin Abdul Aziz al-Saud, U.S.–Saudi Arabian Business Council, Third Plenary Meeting, Washington, D.C., October 2, 1996.
45. Interview with Nawaf Obaid.
46. Interview with Prince Turki.
47. Gay Jervey and Stuart Taylor Jr., "From Statesman to Front Man: How Clark Clifford's Career Crashed," *American Lawyer*, November 1992, p. 49.
48. Jonathan Beaty and S. C. Gwynne, *The Outlaw Bank*, p. 149; and James Ring Adams and Douglas Frantz, *A Full Service Bank*, p. 36.
49. Adams and Frantz, *A Full Service Bank*, p. 32.
50 Beaty and Gwynne, *The Outlaw Bank*, p. 149.
51. Adams and Frantz, *A Full Service Bank*, p. 27.
52. Ibid., p. 34; and *The BCCI Affair: A Report to the Committee on Foreign Relations, United States Senate*, by Senator John Kerry and Senator Hank Brown, December 1992, 102nd Cong., 2nd sess., Senate Print 102-140. NB: This December 1992 document is the penultimate draft of the Senate Foreign Relations Committee report on the BCCI affair. After it was released by the committee, Senator Hank Brown, reportedly acting at the behest of Henry Kissinger, pressed for the deletion of a few passages, particularly in chapter 20, "BCCI and Kissinger Associates." As a result, the final hard-copy version of the report, as published by the Government Printing Office, differs slightly from the committee's soft-copy version at www.fas.org/irp/congress/1992_rpt/bcci/04crime.htm.
53. Beaty and Gwynne, *The Outlaw Bank*, p. 150.
54. Ghaith Pharaon's profile on his website at www.pharaon.com.
55. "Hunting bin Laden," PBS *Frontline;* www.pbs.org/wgbh/pages/frontline/shows/binladen/who/family.html.
56. Alexander Stuart, "Citizen Connally: The Businessman You Never Knew," *Fortune*, July 31, 1978, p. 86.
57. James Ring Adams and Kenneth Timmerman, *American Spectator*, May 1997.
58. *The BCCI Affair*, Senate Print 102-140.
59. Ibid.
60. Ibid.
61. Jonathan Beaty with reporting by S. C. Gwynne, "A Mysterious Mover of Money and Planes," *Time*, October 28, 1991, p. 80.
62. Interview with James Bath.

63. Ibid.
64. Jerry Urban, "Feds Investigate Entrepreneur Allegedly Tied to Saudis," *Houston Chronicle,* June 4, 1992, p. A21.
65. Beaty with Gwynne, "A Mysterious Mover of Money and Planes," p. 80.
66. Interview with James Bath.
67. Ibid.
68. Daniel Golden, James Bandler, and Marcus Walker, "Special Report: Aftermath of Terror—Bin Laden Family Could Profit from a Jump in Defense Spending Due to Ties to U.S. Bank," *Wall Street Journal,* September 27, 2001.
69. Urban, "Feds Investigate Entrepreneur."
70. Beaty with Gwynne, "A Mysterious Mover of Money and Planes," p. 80.
71. Associated Press, August 18, 1977.
72. Brad Kuh, "BCCI Tentacles Reached Far, Even into Central Florida," *Orlando Sentinel Tribune,* August 11, 1991, p. A1.
73. .Paul Galloway, "Bankrupt Hunt Brothers Bid Adieu to Art Collections Worth Millions," *Chicago Tribune,* May 10, 1990, p. C1.
74. .Roy Rowan, "A Hunt Crony Tells All," *Fortune,* June 30, 1980, p. 54.

Chapter 3: The Ascendency of George H. W. Bush

1. Ron Rosenbaum, *New York Observer,* April 23, 2001, p. 1.
2. Ed Vulliamy, "Dark Heart of the American Dream," *Observer* (London), June 16, 2002, p. 22; Herbert S. Parmet, *George Bush,* p. 25; and Elizabeth Mitchell, *W: Revenge of the Bush Dynasty.*
3. George Bush, *Looking Forward,* p. 56.
4. Parmet, *George Bush,* p. 78.
5. Daniel Yergin, *The Prize,* p. 753.
6. Parmet, *George Bush,* p. 81.
7. "Bush's Energy Policy Is No Policy at All," *Atlanta Journal and Constitution,* February 26, 1991, p. 12.
8. Parmet, *George Bush,* p. 83.
9. Ibid., pp. 30–31.
10. Barry Bearak, "His Great Gift, to Blend In; Team Player Bush: A Yearning to Serve," *Los Angeles Times,* November 22, 1987, p. 1; and Bill Minutaglio, *First Son,* p. 218.
11. Richard Ben Cramer, *What It Takes,* pp. 86–88.
12. George Lardner Jr. and Lois Romano, "George Bush: A Texas Childhood," *Washington Post,* July 26, 1999, p. A1.
13. Parmet, *George Bush,* p. 85.
14. Ibid., p. 135.
15. Walter Pincus and Bob Woodward, "George Bush: Man and Politician, Part 2," *Washington Post,* August 8, 1988, p. A1.
16. John Loftus and Mark Aarons, *The Secret War Against the Jews,* p. 369.
17. Minutaglio, *First Son,* pp. 166–67.
18. Bush, *Looking Forward,* p. 153.
19. Historic Houston website, www.neosoft.com/~sgriffin/houstonhistory/whoswho/history11hof.htm.
20. Parmet, *George Bush,* p. 140.
21. Jill Abramson and Thomas Petzinger, *Wall Street Journal,* June 11, 1992; and "Periscope," *Newsweek,* September 29, 1980, p. 19.
22. Parmet, *George Bush,* p. 189.

23. Bob Woodward, "To Bones Men, Bush Is a Solid 'Moderate,'" *Washington Post,* August 7, 1988, p. A18.
24. Parmet, *George Bush,* p. 209.
25. Vulliamy, "The Dark Heart of the American Dream."
26. Maureen Dowd and Thomas Friedman, "The Fabulous Bush & Baker Boys," *New York Times,* May 6, 1990, sec. 6, p. 34.
27. James A. Baker III, *The Politics of Diplomacy,* p. 18.
28. Dowd and Friedman, "The Fabulous Bush & Baker Boys."
29. Ibid.
30. Ibid.
31. Jacob V. Lamar, "The Cool Texan: Master of the Game," *Time,* October 3, 1988, p. 21.
32. Kenneth J. Lipartito and Joseph A. Pratt, *Baker & Botts in the Development of Modern Houston,* p. 17.
33. Burt Solomon, "The President's Peer," *National Journal,* January 7, 1989, p. 6.
34. Dowd and Friedman, "The Fabulous Bush & Baker Boys."
35. Bearak, "His Great Gift," p. 1.
36. Dowd and Friedman, "The Fabulous Bush & Baker Boys."
37. Harry F. Rosenthal, Associated Press, March 4, 1980.
38. Sidney Blumenthal, "I, Baker: George Bush's Final Gambit," *New Republic,* November 2, 1992, p. 17.
39. Ibid.; and Dowd and Friedman, "The Fabulous Bush & Baker Boys."
40. Blumenthal, "I, Baker," p. 17.
41. Ibid.
42. Parmet, *George Bush,* p. 235
43. Blumenthal, "I, Baker," p. 17.
44. Ibid.
45. "Hour by Hour: The Deal That Got Away," *U.S. News & World Report,* July 28, 1980, p. 22.
46. Clarence Page, "Here's Who'll Help Bush," *Chicago Tribune,* July 20, 1988, p. 20.
47. Solomon, "The President's Peer"; and "Molly Ivins Discusses New Collection of Columns," CBS News Transcripts, *This Morning,* October 3, 1991.
48. Bill Peterson, "For Bush, a Potential for the Spotlight," *Washington Post,* January 20, 1981, p. 16.
49. Jonathan Kwitny, "The Mexican Connection: A Look at an Old George Bush Business Venture," *Barron's,* September 19, 1988.
50. Alexandre de Marenches and David Andelman, *The Fourth World War,* pp. 253-54.
51. Parmet, *George Bush,* pp. 204, 289.
52. Interview with Susan Clough.
53. Gary Sick, *October Surprise,* p. 24.
54. "Unauthorized Transfers of Nonpublic Information During the 1980 Presidential Election," report prepared by the Subcommittee on Human Resources of the Committee on the Post Office and Civil Service, May 17, 1984, pt. 1, p. 10.
55. Ibid., p. 34.
56. Craig Unger, "October Surprise," *Esquire,* October 1991.
57. "Unauthorized Transfers," Committee on the Post Office and Civil Service, May 17, 1984, pt. 1, p. 35.
58. Ibid., p. 3.
59. Howard Kurtz, "Reagan '80 Campaign Sought Data on US Probe of Billy Carter," *Washington Post,* May 24, 1984, p. 16.

60. One of the key figures in Casey's operation had been Bush's national policy director, Stefan Halper. Halper, the son-in-law of CIA deputy director Ray Cline, set up a complex in Arlington, Virginia, that used former CIA operatives to monitor the Carter administration. All of the men working under Halper later denied participating in covert operations for the Reagan-Bush campaign. And Halper said that the existence of an intelligence network spying on the Carter administration was "absolutely false." Nevertheless, sensitive documents from the Carter-Mondale campaign repeatedly came into their possession. Halper told congressional investigators that he did not know how that could have happened.

In September 1980, however, Halper sent three memos to Ed Meese, the campaign's chief of staff, who later became attorney general. The memos indicated that Halper had sources inside the Carter administration or the Carter-Mondale campaign. Each memo was accompanied by materials from the Democrats.

Halper was not the only one close to Bush who had moles inside the Carter organization. In the latter days of the campaign, Bush's brother, Prescott Bush Jr., wrote three letters to James Baker about Herb Cohen, a consultant to the Justice Department and the FBI. The letters asserted that Cohen had reliable sources on Carter's National Security Council and was ready to expose the administration's handling of the hostage situation. Cohen later objected to the way he was characterized in these letters.

The pilfered papers consisted of a black loose-leaf notebook that had been in the office of Zbigniew Brzezinski, Carter's national security adviser. The Albosta Report concluded, "The presumption, therefore, is that these materials were improperly taken for use by the opposition campaign." This apparent theft must have created a special problem for James Baker. As a lawyer in Houston, Baker had a reputation as a model of probity. It was said that he gave up litigation early in his career because of the unsavory practices it entailed.

At the same time, part of Baker's job was to supervise people who prepared the debate briefing books for Reagan. The Albosta Report found that at least thirteen members of the Reagan-Bush team either received the Carter debate material or saw it at one time or another. One was Baker himself, who, in an affidavit, admitted that he had in his possession "materials apparently intended or designed to be used in the preparations of briefings for President Carter." Baker said he passed the material on to other staffers.

And how did Baker get them? "My best recollection is that I received the material ... from William Casey," he explained.

And where did Casey get them? Baker said he did not know. For his part, the perpetually disheveled Casey, who mumbled so much during his congressional testimony that many could barely understand him, said he did not recall giving any such materials to Baker. The Albosta Report concluded that both Baker and Casey could not be telling the full truth. But that left the essential questions unanswered.

As the investigation neared its unsatisfactory conclusion, Congressman Albosta considered upping the ante by calling for a special prosecutor ? la Watergate. But a young Republican congressman from Wyoming dropped by Albosta's office—the same man whom Albosta suspected of giving the papers to Casey. It was Dick Cheney.

"Cheney came over to my office and pleaded with me not to investigate anymore," said Albosta. "I was at the end where I was going to drop it anyway. The reason he gave was the nice-guy reason—him being a nice guy and he didn't want to get involved.

"There were suspicions in my mind about him. The papers were supposedly in Cheney's hands, in Bill Casey's hands, and Casey handed them to Baker. But he was one of the people I had to work with and I didn't want to make waves anymore. If I had done any more, I think he would have been teed off with me."

And so, the Albosta investigation sputtered to a halt with his committee unable to get the Justice Department to appoint a special prosecutor to investigate. Many of Bush's men appeared to have played key roles in a sophisticated intelligence operation directed against the Carter campaign, but Bush himself emerged entirely unscathed.

As it turned out, the Republicans were already so teed off at Albosta's investigation that they had resolved to make sure he was defeated that fall. "I was the number-one house member they [the Republicans] targeted in the elections," recalls Albosta. "They labeled me the number one to get rid of." As the November election approached, President Reagan himself went to Albosta's district in rural Michigan to campaign against him, as did Vice President George Bush, Secretary of Commerce Malcolm Baldrige, Agriculture Secretary John Block, and other high-level cabinet members.

"They put in more than a million dollars in soft money against me. They bought up every minute of television time for advertising," Albosta added. He lost to Republican Bill Schuette in the November election and later retired to a farm in rural Michigan.

Sick, *October Surprise,* p. 24; "Unauthorized Transfers," Committee on the Post Office and Civil Service, pt. 1, pp. 36, 39, 55, 100, 102, 124, 1086, 1105; United Press International, July 24, 1983; Laurence I. Barrett, *Gambling with History,* p. 383; and Donald Albosta, telephone interview.

61. Nina Hyde, "Having Designs on the First Lady," *Washington Post,* January 18, 1981, p. A9.

62. Barry Schweid, "US, Iran Close to Hostage Accord," Associated Press, January 18, 1981.

63. United Press International, January 19, 1981.

64. Richard Harwood and T. R. Reid, "U.S. Announces Resolution of Dispute Blocking Return of Hostages from Iran," *Washington Post,* January 20, 1981, p. A1.

65. E. J. Dionne, "Albany Plea on Arab Bank Bid," *New York Times,* May 13, 1981, p. D3.

66. Dan Balz, "The Saudi Connection: The Next Best Thing to Mecca Is Houston; Houston as the Mecca for the Saudis," *Washington Post,* April 19, 1981, p. C1.

67. Cherif Sedky, interview by e-mail, September 7, 2002.

68. *American Banker,* December 24, 1985.

69. James Conaway, "The Texas Connection: James Baker and George Bush Represent a New Kind of Lone Star Politician in the White House—the Texas Preppie," *Washington Post Magazine,* December 13, 1981, p. 18; and Alexander Stuart, "Texan Gerald Hines Is Tall in the Skyline," *Fortune,* January 28, 1980, p. 101.

70. Thomas Friedman, "Baker Selling His Stocks to Avoid Any Conflict in State Dept. Role," *New York Times,* February 15, 1989, p. A1.

71. Interview with Gerry Auerbach.

Chapter 4: Three-Dimensional Chess

1. "Looking for Answers: Egypt," PBS *Frontline,*

www.pbs.org/wgbh/pages/frontline/shows/terrorism/egypt/.

2. U.S. Department of State, *Patterns of Global Terrorism, 2001*, May 2002, library.nps.navy.mil/home/tgp/hamas.htm.
3. Don Rothberg, Associated Press, July 18, 1980.
4. Murray Waas and Craig Unger, "In the Loop," *New Yorker*, November 2, 1992, p. 64ff.
5. Walter Pincus, "Secret Presidential Pledges Over Years Erected US Shield for Saudis," *Washington Post*, February 9, 1992, p. A20.
6. The entire cost of the package has sometimes been reported as $8.5 billion.
7. Bob Woodward, *The Commanders*, p. 200.
8. Elsa Walsh, "The Prince: How the Saudi Ambassador Became Washington's Indispensable Operator," *New Yorker*, March 23, 2003, p. 48.
9. Rory O'Connor, writer and producer, "The Arming of Saudi Arabia," PBS *Frontline* #1112, February 16, 1993.
10. Ibid.
11. One of the chief beneficiaries of the AWACS deal was the Bechtel Corporation, of which Reagan's secretary of state, George Shultz, and secretary of defense, Caspar Weinberger, had served as president and general counsel, respectively.
12. O'Connor, "The Arming of Saudi Arabia."
13. Ibid.
14. Ibid.
15. "Al Salaam Slow Down," *Middle East Defense News*, April 19, 1993.
16. O'Connor, "The Arming of Saudi Arabia."
17. Ibid.
18. Robert Baer, "The Fall of the House of Saud," *Atlantic Monthly*, May 2003, p. 60.
19. Wayne King with reporting by Jeff Gerth and Wayne King, "Private Pipeline to the Contras: A Vast Network," *New York Times*, October 22, 1986, p. A1.
20. Walsh, "The Prince," p. 48.
21. Waas and Unger, "In the Loop."
22. Ibid.
23. Ibid.
24. Ibid.
25. Theodore Draper, *A Very Thin Line*, p. 77.
26. Jane Mayer, "The House of bin Laden," *New Yorker*, November 12, 2001, www.newyorker.com/fact/content/?011112fa_FACT3.
27. Patrick Tyler, "Officers Say US Aided Iraq in War Despite Use of Gas," *New York Times*, August 18, 2002, p. 1.
28. Waas and Unger, "In the Loop"; Robert Parry, "Saddam's Green Light," *Consortium News*, www.consortiumnews.com/archive/xfile5.html; and Dilip Hiro, *The Longest War*.
29. Richard Sale, "Saddam Key in Early CIA Plot," UPI, April 10, 2003.
30. Adel Darwish, *Unholy Babylon*, pp. 201-8.
31. F. Gregory Gause III, "Iraq and the Gulf War: Decision-Making in Baghdad," University of Vermont,www.ciaonet.org/casestudy/gafO1/#note22.
32. Said Aburish, *The Rise, Corruption and Coming Fall of the House of Saud*, p. 52.
33. Elaine Sciolino, "Threats and Responses: The Iranians; Iraq Chemical Arms Condemned, but West Once Looked the Other Way," *New York Times*, February 13, 2002, p. A18.
34. Tyler, "Officers Say US Aided Iraq in War Despite Use of Gas," p. 1.

35. Alan Friedman, *Spider's Web*, p. 25.
36. Before the new administration took office—in fact, the day after the November 1980 election—Iraq began reaching out to Bush, with Iraqi deputy foreign minister Ismat Kittani, a good friend of Bush's from his days at the United Nations, flying especially to the United States to congratulate the vice president-elect and send him flowers.
37. Friedman, *Spider's Web*, p. 4.
38. "Iraq Use of Chemical Weapons," unclassified memo from Jonathan Howe to the secretary of state, November 1, 1983, National Security Archives, www.gwu.edu/ ~ nsarchiv/NSAEBB/NSAEBB82/iraq24.pdf.
39. "Iraqi Use of Chemical Weapons," from Jonathan T. Howe and Richard Murphy to Lawrence Eagleburger, November 21, 1983, National Security Archives, www.gwu.edu/ ~ nsarchiv/NSAEBB/NSAEBB82/iraq25.pdf.
40. "U.S. Documents Show Embrace of Saddam Hussein in Early 1980s Despite Chemical Weapons," National Security Archives, www.gwu.edu/ ~ nsarchiv/NSAEBB/NSAEBB82/press.htm.
41. Joyce Battle, ed., *Shaking Hands with Saddam Hussein: The US. Tilts toward Iraq, 1980-1984* (National Security Archives Electronic Briefing Book no. 82, February 25, 2003),www.gwu.edu/ ~ nsarchiv/NSAEBB/NSAEBB82/index.htm.
42. Dana Priest, "Rumsfeld Visited Baghdad in 1984 to Reassure Iraqis, Documents Show," *Washington Post,* December 19, 2003. Documents were originally obtained by the National Security Archives.
43. "Measures to Improve U.S. Posture and Readiness to Respond to Developments in the Iran-Iraq War," National Security Decision Directive (NSDD) 139 of April 5, 1984, National Security Archives, www.gwu.edu/ ~ nsarchiv/NSAEBB/NSAEBB82/iraq53.pdf.
44. Dean Foust and John Carey, "A U.S. Gift to Iraq: Deadly Viruses," *Business Week,* September 20, 2002, www.businessweek.com/bwdaily/dnflash/sep2002/nf20020920_3025.htm.
45. Ibid. After the Gulf War, a Senate investigation determined that the United States allowed the export of a wide range of disease-producing and poisonous biological material to Iraq during the eighties, thanks to licensing by the Department of Commerce of "dual-use" exports that could be used for chemical and biological warfare. According to the investigation, among the approved sales to Iraq was the often fatal anthrax bacterium; the botulinum toxin, which causes vomiting, constipation, thirst, general weakness, headache, fever, dizziness, double vision, dilation of the pupils, and paralysis of the muscles involving swallowing; and *Histoplasma capsulatum,* which can lead to pneumonia and enlargement of the liver and spleen and is often fatal; see Donald W. Riegle Jr. and Alphonse M. D'Amato, "A Report of the Committee of Banking, Housing and Urban Affairs with Respect to Export Administration, US Chemical and Biological Warfare-Related Dual Use Exports to Iraq and Their Possible Impact on the Health Consequences of the Persian Gulf War with Respect to May 25, 1994," www.gulflink.osd.mil/medsearch/FocusAreas/riegle_report/report/report_s01.htm#Chapter%201.%20Iragi%20Chemical%20and%20Biological%20Warfare%20Capability.
46. Richard Ben Cramer, *What it Takes*, p. 15.
47. Waas and Unger, "In the Loop."
48. Ibid.
49. Ibid.

50. Ibid.

51. Herbert S. Parmet, *George Bush,* p. 292.

52. Joe Conason, "The George W. Bush Success Story," *Harper's,* February 2000.

53. Waas and Unger, "In the Loop."

54. Bob Woodward, *Veil,* p. 397.

55. Waas and Unger, "In the Loop."

56. On May 20, 1985, Fuller wrote a Special National Intelligence Estimate (SNIE), a closely held memo that was circulated to the president. The memo became the basis for renewed arms sales to Iran and the ensuing Iran-contra scandal.

57. Waas and Unger, "In the Loop."

58. Ibid.

59. Ibid.

60. Ibid.

61. Ibid.

62. Ibid.

63. Ibid.

64. Ibid.

65. Ibid.

66. Ibid.

67. Woodward, *The Commanders,* p. 203.

68. Waas and Unger, "In the Loop."

69. Maureen Dowd and Thomas Friedman, "The Fabulous Bush & Baker Boys," *New York Times,* May 6, 1990, sec. 6, p. 34; and Sidney Blumenthal, "I, Baker," *New Republic,* November 2, 1992, p. 17.

70. "World Oil Market and Oil Price Chronologies: 1970-2002," Energy Information Administration, Department of Energy, www.eia.doe.gov/cabs/chron.html.

71. *The BCCI Affair: A Report to the Committee on Foreign Relations, United States Senate,* by Senator John Kerry and Senator Hank Brown, December 1992, 102nd Cong., 2nd Sess. Senate Print 102-140. NB: This December 1992 document is the penultimate draft of the Senate Foreign Relations Committee report on the BCCI Affair. After it was released by the committee, Senator Hank Brown, reportedly acting at the behest of Henry Kissinger, pressed for the deletion of a few passages, particularly in chapter 20, "BCCI and Kissinger Associates." As a result, the final hard-copy version of the report, as published by the Government Printing Office, differs slightly from the committee's soft-copy version at www.fas.org/irp/congress/1992_rpt/bcci/11intel.htm.

72. Jonathan Beaty and S. C. Gwynne, *The Outlaw Bank,* p. 316.

73. Jonathan Beaty and S. C. Gwynne, "Not Just a Bank; You Can Get Anything You Want Through BCCI," *Time,* September 2, 1991, p. 56.

74. Peter Truell and Larry Gurwin, *False Profits,* pp.133-34.

75. Douglas Farah, "Al Qaeda's Road Paved with Gold," *Washington Post,* February 17, 2002, p. A1.

76. Joost Hiltermann, "America Didn't Seem to Mind Poison Gas," *International Herald Tribune,* January 17, 2003; and Lee Stokes, "Iran Asks for UN Probe of Chemical Warfare," UPI, April 23, 1988.

77. Jeffrey Goldberg, "Wartime Friendships," *New Yorker,* April 14, 2003, p. 30.

78. Stuart Auerbach, "1.5 Billion in U.S. Sales to Iraq: Technology Products Approved up to Day before Invasion," *Washington Post,* March 11, 1991, p. A1.

79. Peter W. Galbraith, "The Wild Card in Post-Saddam Iraq," *Boston Globe Magazine,* December 15, 2002.

80. *The BCCI Affair,* Senate Print 102-140.
81. Waas and Unger, "In the Loop."
82. Ibid.

Chapter 5: The Double Marriage

1. Alan Friedman, *Spider's Web,* p. 84.
2. Stephen Schwartz, *The Two Faces of Islam,* p. 74.
3. Ibid., p. 75.
4. Madawi Al-Rasheed, *A History of Saudi Arabia,* p. 19.
5. Schwartz, *The Two Faces of Islam,* p. 105.
6. David E. Long, "Whither Saudi Arabia?" *Jewish Daily Forward,* September 5, 2003, www.forward.com/issues/2003/03.09.05/arts1.long.html.
7. Schwartz, *The Two Faces of Islam,* p. 69.
8. Ibid., p. 118.
9. Ibid., p. 73.
10. Daniel Benjamin and Steve Simon, *The Age of Sacred Terror,* p. 54.
11. Schwartz, *The Two Faces of Islam,* p. 106.
12. "Saudi Arabia: Religious Police Role in School Fire Criticized," *Human Rights News,* March 15, 2002, hrw.org/press/2002/03/saudischool.htm.
13. Said Arburish, *The Rise, Corruption and Coming Fall of the House of Saud,* p. 14.
14. Ibid., p. 24.
15. Ibid., p. 27; and "Saudi Executioner Tells All," BBC radio broadcast, June 6, 2003.
16. Arburish, *The Rise, Corruption and Coming Fall of the House of Saud,* p. 68.
17. Ibid., p. 55.
18. Robert Baer, "The Fall of the House of Saud," *Atlantic Monthly,* May 2003, p. 56.
19. Tina Marie O'Neill, "Sands Shift Under House of Saud," *Sunday Business Post,* August 11, 2002.
20. Seymour Hersh, "King's Ransom," *New Yorker,* October 22, 2001, p. 35.
21. Ibid.
22. "Jihad, About Islam and Muslims," www.unn.ac.uk/societies/islamic/jargon/jihad1.htm.
23. Ibid.
24. F. Gregory Gause, "Be Careful What You Wish For," www.house.gov/ international_relations/107/gaus0522.pdf .
25. Evan Thomas and Christopher Dickey, with Eleanor Clift, Roy Gutman, Debra Rosenberg, and Tamara Lipper, "War on Terror: The Saudi Game," *Newsweek,* November 19, 2001, p. 32.
26. Interview with Prince Bandar, "Looking for Answers," PBS *Frontline,* www.pbs.org/wgbh/pages/frontline/shows/terrorism/interviews/bandar.html.
27. Elaine Sciolino, "Ally's Future," *New York Times,* November 4, 2001, sec. 1B, p. 4.
28. Bandar bin Sultan, *New York Times,* July 10, 1994, p. 20.
29. Al-Rasheed, *A History of Saudi Arabia,* p. 124.
30. "U.S. Oil Consumption and Imports, 1973-2000," Office of Transportation Technologies, www.ott.doe.gov/facts/archives/fotw191.shtml.
31. Schwartz, *The Two Faces of Islam,* p.115.
32. Anonymous, *Through Our Enemies' Eyes,* p. 81.
33. Michael Field, *The Merchants,* p. 105.
34. Anonymous, *Through Our Enemies' Eyes,* p. 82.

35. Ibid.
36. Jason Burke, "The Making of the World's Most Wanted Man," *Observer* (London), October 28, 2001.
37. Interview with Dee Howard.
38. Peter Bergen, *Holy War, Inc.,* p. 45.
39. Anonymous, *Through Our Enemies' Eyes,* p. 84.
40. Ibid., p. 83; and Edward Girardet, "A Brush with Laden on the Jihad Front Line," *Christian Science Monitor,* August 31, 1998, p. 19.
41. Malise Ruthven, *A Fury for God,* pp. 197-98.
42. Ibid.
43. Anonymous, *Through Our Enemies' Eyes,* p. 84.
44. Lawrence Wright, "The Man Behind Bin Laden," *New Yorker,* September 16, 2002, www.lawrencewright.com.
45. Robert Siegel, "Sayyid Qutb's America," *All Things Considered,* National Public Radio, May 6, 2003, www.npr.org/display_pages/features/feature_1253796.html
46. Anonymous, *Through Our Enemies' Eyes,* p. 85; and Gregory Palast, "FBI and US Spy Agents Say Bush Spiked Bin Laden Probes," *Guardian* (London), November 7, 2001.
47. Paul Berman, "Al Qaeda's Philosopher," *New York Times Magazine,* March 23, 2003, p. 27.
48. Wright, "The Man Behind Bin Laden."
49. Ismail Royer, e-mail correspondence.
50. Anonymous, *Through Our Enemies' Eyes,* p. 85.
51. Ibid., p. 85.
52. "Hunting bin Laden," PBS *Frontline,* www.pbs.org/wgbh/pages/frontline/shows/binladen/who/family.html.
53. Neil MacKay, "Family Ties: The Bin Ladens," *Sunday Herald* (Scotland), October 7, 2001, www.sundayherald.com/19047.
54. "Hunting bin Laden," PBS *Frontline.*
55. Robert Baer, *Sleeping with the Devil,* p. 166.
56. Kim Willenson, with Nicholas Proffitt and Lloyd Norman, "Persian Gulf: This Gun for Hire," *Newsweek,* February 24, 1975, p. 30; and William Hartung, "Bombings Bring U.S. 'Executive Mercenaries' into the Light," *Orlando Sentinel,* May 19, 2003.
57. MacKay, "Family Ties," p. 14.
58. Anonymous, *Through Our Enemies' Eyes,* p. 87.

Chapter 6: Another Frankenstein

1. Zbigniew Brzezinski, "For the Record: American Tragedy," *New African,* November 1, 2001, p. 6. Originally published by *Le Nouvel Observateur* in January 1998.
2. Bob Woodward, *Veil,* pp. 136-37.
3. Gordon Negus, "Afghan Resistance," November 5, 1982, National Security Archives, www.gwu.edu/ ~ nsarchiv/NSAEBB/NSAEBB57/us3.pdf.
4. George Crile, *Charlie Wilson's War,* p. 238.
5. Interview with Prince Turki.
6. Crile, *Charlie Wilson's War,* pp. 239-40.
7. Steve Galster, "Afghanistan: The Making of US Policy, 1973-1990," October 9, 2001, National Security Archives, www.gwu.edu/ ~ nsarchiv/NSAEBB/NSAEBB57/essay.html.

8. Edward Girardet, "Arab Extremists Exploit Afghan Jihad," *Christian Science Monitor,* February 23, 1989, p. 1.
9. Interview with Armond Habiby.
10. Ahmed Rashid, *Taliban,* p. 131.
11. Roland Jacquard, *In the Name of Osama bin Laden,* p. 21.
12. "Usama bin Laden: Islamic Extremist Financier," CIA memo, National Security Archives, www.gwu.edu/ ~ nsarchiv/NSAEBB/NSAEBB55/ciaubl.pdf.
13. Yossef Bodansky, *Bin Laden,* p. 10.
14. Jacquard, *In the Name of Osama bin Laden,* p. 11.
15. "Hunting bin Laden," PBS *Frontline,* www.pbs.org/wgbh/pages/frontline/shows/binladen/who/family.html.
16. Anonymous, *Through Our Enemies' Eyes,* p. 80.
17. Michael Field, *The Merchants,* p. 106.
18. Anonymous, *Through Our Enemies' Eyes,* p. 80.
19. Interview with John Loftus.
20. Federation of American Scientists, 216.239.39.100/search?q=cache:sXX_KfWXrGUJ:www.library. cornell.edu/colldev/mideast/gaida.htm+MAK+and+Afghanistan&h1=en&ie =UTF-8.
21. Daniel Benjamin and Steven Simon, *The Age of Sacred Terror,* p. 103.
22. Interview with Prince Bandar, "Looking for Answers," PBS *Frontline,* www.pbs.org/wgbh/pages/frontline/shows/terrorism/interviews/bandar.html.
23. Ibid.
24. Rashid, *Taliban,* p. 132.
25. Jane Mayer, "The House of Bin Laden," *New Yorker,* November 12, 2001, www.newyorker.com/fact/content/?011112fa_FACT3.
26. Mary Anne Weaver, "Blowback," *Atlantic Monthly,* May 1996, www. theatlantic.com/issues/96may/blowback.htm.
27. Interview with Prince Turki.
28. Robert Marquand, with Jane Lampman, Scott Peterson, Ilene R. Prusher, and Warren Richey, as well as Sarah Gauch and Dan Murphy, "The Tenets of Terror, Part II," *Christian Science Monitor,* October 18, 2001.
29. Anonymous, *Through Our Enemies' Eyes,* p. 90.
30. "The Soviet Invasion of Afghanistan: Five Years After," a CIA Intelligence assessment produced jointly by the Office of Near Eastern and South Asian Analysis and the Office of Soviet Analysis, released as sanitized, 1999 CIA Historical review program, National Security Archives, www.gwu.edu/ ~ nsarchiv/NSAEBB/NSAEBB57/us5.pdf.
31. Joseph Persico, *Casey,* p. 225.
32. Steve Coll, "Anatomy of a Victory: CIA's Covert Afghan War," *Washington Post,* July 19, 1992.
33. Federation of American Scientists, Military Analysis Network, "FIM-92A Stinger Weapons System: RMP & Basic," www.fas.org/man/dod-101/sys/land/stinger.htm.
34. Persico, *Casey,* p. 312.
35. Marin Strmecki, "Among the Afghans," *Washington Quarterly,* vol. 11, no. 3 (summer 1988), p. 227.
36. Weaver, "Blowback."
37. Ibid.
38. Ibid.

39. Charlotte Edwardes, "My Brother Osama" *Sunday Telegraph* (London), December 16, 2001.
40. Anonymous, *Through Our Enemies' Eyes,* p. 91.
41. Ibid.
42. William Claiborne, "Bush at the Khyber Pass," *Washington Post,* May 18, 1984, p. A23.
43. Anonymous, *Through Our Enemies' Eyes,* p. 99.
44. "The Costs of Soviet Involvementin Afghanistan," Directorate of Intelligence, prepared by the Office of Soviet Analysis, February 1987, National Security Archives, www.gwu.edu/nsarchiv/NSAEBB/NSAEBB57/us8.pdf.
45 "Bush Asserts 'Iron Curtain' Remains, but It's Rusting," Gerald Boyd, *New York Times,* October 19, 1988, p. B6.
46. Galster "Afghanistan: The Making of US Policy."
47. Lawrence Lifschut "Bush, Drugs, and Pakistan: Inside the Kingdom of Heroin," *Nation,* November 14, 1988.p. 477; and B. Raman, "Heroin, Taliban and Pakistan," Financial Times Asia Africa Intelligence Wire, August 10, 2001.
48. Interview with Frank Anderson.
49. Interview with former Senate investigator.
50. Galster "Afghanistan: The Making of US Policy."
51. Persico, *Casey,* p. 313.
52. Patrick Tyler, "Possible Diversion of Stinger Missile to Terrorists Causes Concern," *Washington Post,* April 8, 1986, p. A12.
53. Michael Springman, interview on BBC as reported in the in the *Sydney Morning Herald,* November 7, 2001, www.smh.com.au/0111/07world100.html.
54. Interview with Frank Anderson.
55. "Bush OKs Military Aid for Rebels," Associated Press, February 12, 1989.
56. "Zbigniew Brzezinski: How Jimmy Carter and I Started the Mujahideen," interview with Zbigniew Brzezinski, *Nouvel Observateur,* Jan15–21, 1988.
57. *Meet the Press,* NBC News Transcripts, October 14, 2001.
58. Weaver, "Blowback"; and Rashid, *Taliban,* p. 132.
60. Tony Barthleme, "King of Torts," *Post and Courier* (Charleston, S.C.), June 22, 2003.
61. Barthleme, "Seized Bosnian Documents Links Saudis to Terror Funding, Lawyers Say," p. 17.
62. Kaplan et al., "Playing Offense," p. 18.
63. Golden Chain List Analysis, investi.virtualave.net/Golden%20Chain%20Analyses.htm.
64. Barthleme, "Seized Bosnian Documents Links Saudis to Terror Funding, Lawyers Say," p. 17.
65. Glen Simpson, "List of Early a Qaeda Donors Points to Saudi Elite, Charities," Wall Street Journal, March 18, 2003.
66. Glen Simpson, Wall Street Journal, online corrections and amplifications, updated March 18, 2003, 10:48 p.m., online.wsj.com/article/0,,SB104794563734573400,00.html#CX.
67. Interview with Robert Baer.
68. Interview with Cherif Sedky, attorney for Khalid bin Mahfouz.

Chapter 7: Friends in High Places

1. Molly Ivins and Lou Dubose, *Shrub,* p. *xxi.*
2. Michael Lind, *Made in Texas,* pp. 7-9.

3. Bill Minutaglio, *First Son*, p. 121.
4. George Lardner Jr., "Texas Speaker Reportedly Helped Bush Get into Guard," *Washington Post*, September 21, 1999, p. A4. In 1999, a spokesman for Bush, who was then governor of Texas, said, "Governor Bush did not need and did not ask anybody for help."
5. Chris Williams, "Did Bush Serve? Claims He Was in Alabama Guard, but There's No Record," Associated Press, June 25, 2000.
6. Francis S. Greenlief, Major General, Chief, National Guard Bureau, September 29, 1972, www.talion.com/suspension.html.
7. "Not rated for the period 1 May 1972 through 30 April 1973. Report for this period not available for administrative reasons," www.talion.com/admin.html.
8. George Lardner, Jr. and Lois Romano, "George Walker Bush," *Washington Post*, July 30, 1999, p. Al.
9. Ivins and Dubose, *Shrub*, pp. 22, 23.
10. Lardner and Romano, "George Walker Bush," p. Al.
11. Ibid.
12. Eric Pooley, *Time*, June 14, 1999, www10.cnn.com/ALLPOLITICS/time/1999/06/14/bush.groove.html.
13. "World Oil Market and Oil Price Chronologies: 1970-2002," Energy Information Administration, Department of Energy, www.eia.doe.gov/emeu/cabs/chron.html.
14. "The Bush-Saudi Axis," *Time*, September 15, 2003, www.time.com/time/covers/1101030915/#.
15. Minutaglio, *First Son*, p. 208.
16. Lardner and Romano, "George Walker Bush," p. Al.
17. Thomas Petzinger Jr., Peter Truell, and Jill Abramson, "Family Ties: How Oil Firm Linked to a Son of Bush Won Bahrain Drilling Pact," *Wall Street Journal*, December 6, 1991, p. Al.
18. Lardner and Romano, "George Walker Bush," p. Al.
19. Petzinger, Truell, and Abramson, "Family Ties," p. Al.
20. Pooley, *Time*.
21. Ibid.
22. Petzinger, Truell, and Abramson, "Family Ties," p. Al.
23. Paul Krugman, "Succeeding in Business," *New York Times*, July 7, 2002.
24. Richard Behar, "The Wackiest Rig in Texas," *Time*, October 28, 1991, p. 78.
25. Interview with Cherif Sedky, attorney for Khalid bin Mahfouz.
26. E-mail correspondence with Cherif Sedky.
27. Interviews with James Bath and Cherif Sedky.
28. Interview with Cherif Sedky.
29. Ibid.
30. Interview with source who boarded bin Mahfouz's planes.
31. Bin Mahfouz's attorney, Cherif Sedky, says that even though bin Mahfouz had invested nearly $1 billion in BCCI, he was little more than a passive figure in its operations. "You have to take everything in scale and context," says Sedky. "A billion is a lot of money, but it is not out of scale when I say 'passive.'" In an e-mail, Sedky added, "To the best of [Khalid bin Mahfouz's] present and unrefreshed recollection, he attended no more than three meetings of the board." "Outlaw Bank," *Financial Times*, July 13, 1992; and Douglas Farah, "Al Qaeda's Road Paved with Gold," *Washington Post*, February 17, 2002, p. A1.
32. Petzinger, Truell, and Abramson, "Family Ties," p. A1.
33. Ibid.

34. Larry Gurwin and Adam Zagorin, "All That Glitters," *Time,* November 6, 1995, p. 52.
35. Petzinger, Truell, and Abramson, "Family Ties," p. A1.
36. E-mail correspondence with Cherif Sedky.
37. Ibid.; and Petzinger, Truell, and Abramson, "Family Ties," p. A1.
38. E-mail to author from Cherif Sedky.
39. Interview with Nawaf Obaid.
40. *The BCCI Affair: A Report to the Committee on Foreign Relations, United States Senate,* by Senator John Kerry and Senator Hank Brown, December 1992, 102nd Cong., 2nd Sess., Senate Print 102-140.
41. Interview with Harken source.
42. Micah Morrison, "Who Is David Edwards?" *Wall Street Journal,* March 1, 1995, p. 14.
43. Toni Mack, "Fuel for Fantasy," *Forbes,* September 3, 1990, p. 37.
44. Michael Kranish and Beth Healy, "Board Was Told of Risks Before Bush Stock Sale," *Boston Globe,* October 30, 2002, www.boston.com/dailyglobe2/303/nation/Board_was_told_of_risks_before_Bush_stock_sale+.shtml.
45. Glenn Simpson, "Harvard Was Unlikely Savior of Bush Energy Firm Harken," *Wall Street Journal,* October 9, 2002, online.wsj.com/article_email/0,,SB1034111592892893796,00.html.
46. Kranish and Healy, "Board Was Told of Risks Before Bush Stock Sale."
47. Ibid.
48. White House spokesman Dan Bartlett pointed out that the memo was addressed to the Harken board and did not mention Bush by name. "This is a general memo that goes through the perfunctory guidelines of a rights offering," Bartlett said. "It was not specific to the transaction that the president was contemplating"; ibid.
49. Kelly Wallace, "Senators: Release Records on Bush Stock Sale," CNN Washington Bureau, July 16, 2002, www.cnn.com/2002/ALLPOLITICS/07/14/bush.stock.sale/.
50. Kranish and Healy, "Board Was Told of Risks Before Bush Stock Sale."
51. Mike Allen and George Lardner Jr., "Harken Papers Offer Details on Bush Knowledge," *Washington Post,* July 14, 2002, p. A1.
52. Bennett Roth, "Clerical Mix-up Blamed in Bush Stock Sale Filing," *Houston Chronicle,* July 4, 2002, p. A1.
53. Allen and Lardner, "Harken Papers Offer Details on Bush Knowledge," p. A1.
54. Petzinger, Truell, and Abramson, "Family Ties," p. A1.
55. *The BCCI Affair,* Senate Print 102-140.
56. Ibid.
57. Ibid.
58. Laurence Marks and Barry Hugill, "The BCCI Scandal," *Observer,* July 21, 1991, p. 19.
59. Interview with Cherif Sedky.
60. Interview with Jason Stanford.
61. Associated Press Worldstream, November 3, 1994.
62. Petzinger, Truell, and Abramson, "Family Ties," p. A1.

Chapter 8: War Drums

1. James A. Baker III, *The Politics of Diplomacy,* pp. 262-63.
2. Ibid., p. 264.

3. "Richard Perle: The Making of a Neo-Conservative," transcript, interview with Ben Wattenberg, Public Broadcasting System's *Think Tank,* www.pbs.org/thinktank/transcript1017.html.
4. Baker, *The Politics of Diplomacy,* p. 268.
5. Bob Woodward, *The Commanders,* p. 200.
6. Ibid.
7. Ibid., p. 213.
8. Stephen Engelberg, "U.S.-Saudi Deals in 90's Shifting Away from Cash Toward Credit," *New York Times,* August 23, 1993, p. A1.
9. Evan Thomas, with John Barry, Thomas M. Defrank, and Douglas Waller, "The Reluctant Warrior," *Newsweek,* May 13, 1001, p. 18.
10. Woodward, *The Commanders,* p. 200.
11. David B. Ottaway, "Been There, Done That; Prince Bandar, One of the Great Cold Warriors, Faces the Yawn of an Era," *Washington Post,* July 21, 1996, p. F1.
12. Woodward, *The Commanders,* p. 202.
13. Murray Waas and Craig Unger, "In the Loop," *New Yorker,* November 2, 1992, p. 64ff.
14. Douglas Frantz, "Bush Denial on Iraq Arms Aid Challenged," *Los Angeles Times,* September 24, 1992, p. A24.
15. Carlyle Murphy, "Iraq Accuses Kuwait of Plot to Steal Oil, Depress Prices; Charge Seen as Part of Gulf Power Move by Saddam Hussein," *Washington Post,* July 18, 1990.
16. Caryle Murphy, "Iraq Takes Hard Line as Talks Open; Baghdad Press Insists That Kuwait Accede to Demands," *Washington Post,* July 31, 1990, p. A14.
17. Woodward, *The Commanders,* p. 232.
18. Murphy, "Iraq Takes Hard Line as Talks Open," p. A14.
19. "CIA Support to the US Military During the Persian Gulf War," Persian Gulf Illnesses Task Force, Director of Central Intelligence, June 16, 1997, National Security Archives, www.gwu.edu/%7Ensarchiv/NSAEBB/NSAEBB63/doc6.pdf.
20. Molly Moore, "Bush Stresses Saddam's Isolation After the Arab League Vote," *Washington Post,* August 12, 1990, p. A21.
21. R. Jeffrey Smith, "Iraqis Fortify Defense in Kuwait; Ground Battle Would Result in Significant U.S. Casualties, Officials Warn," *Washington Post,* August 21, 1990, p. Al.
22. Woodward, *The Commanders,* p. 226.
23. Herbert S. Parmet, *George Bush,* p. 458.
24. Baker, *The Politics of Diplomacy,* pp. 304-5.
25. Kevin Philips, "Bush's Worst Political Nightmare," *Los Angeles Times,* January 13, 1991, p. M4; and Anthony Kimery, "A Well of a Deal," *Common Cause,* Spring 1991.
26. Woodward, *The Commanders,* p. 214.
27. George Bush and Brent Scowcroft, *A World Transformed,* p. 320.
28. Ibid., p. 321.
29. Woodward, *The Commanders,* p. 243.
30. Baker, *The Politics of Diplomacy,* p. 289.
31. Evans and Novak, November 8, 1990.
32. John Elvin, "Inside the Beltway," *Washington Times,* December 14, 1990, p. A6.
33. John R. MacArthur, *Second Front,* p. 43.
34. Ibid., p. 44.

35. David Hoffman, "Gulf Crisis Tests Baker as Diplomat," *Washington Post,* November 2, 1990, p. Al.
36. John Stauber and Sheldon Rampton, *Toxic Sludge Is Good for You* (Common Courage Press, 1995), web version from PRWatch.org.
37. Ibid.
38. *O'Dwyer's FARA Report, vol.* 5, no. 1 (January 1991), pp. 8, 10.
39. MacArthur, *Second Front,* p. 150.
40. Ibid., pp. 57-58.
41. Ibid., p. 58.
42. Ibid., p. 60.
43. Ibid., p. 65.
44. Ibid., p. 66.
45. Ibid., p. 70.
46. Ibid., pp. 68-69.
47. Ibid., p. 73.
48. Ibid., p. 74.
49. John MacArthur, "Remember Nayirah, Witness for Kuwait?" *Seattle Post-Intelligencer,* January 12, 1992, p. Dl.
50. MacArthur, *Second Front,* p. 173.
51. Ned Zeman, "Periscope," *Newsweek,* December 3, 1990, p. 6.
52. MacArthur, *Second Front,* p. 174.
53. Zeman, "Periscope," p. 6.
54. Jean Heller, "Photos Don't Show Buildup," *St. Petersburg Times,* January 6, 1991, p. Al.
55. MacArthur, *Second Front,* p. 174.
56. Ibid., pp. 177-78.
57. Bush and Scowcroft, *A World Transformed,* p. 489.
58. "The War Behind Closed Doors," PBS *Frontline,* www.pbs.org/wgbh/pages/frontline/shows/iraq/etc/wolf.html.

Chapter 9: The Breaking Point

1. Douglas Jehl, "Holy War Lured Saudis as Rulers Looked Away," *New York Times,* December 27, 2001, p. Al.
2. Yossef Bodansky, *Bin Laden,* p. 29.
3. Jehl, "Holy War Lured Saudis as Rulers Looked Away," p. Al.
4. Ibid.
5. Bodansky, *Bin Laden,* p. 29.
6. Anonymous, *Through Our Enemies' Eyes,* p. 114.
7. Bodansky, *Bin Laden,* p. 29; and Arnaud de Borchgrave, "Osama's Saudi Moles," *Washington Times,* August 1, 2003, p. A19.
8. Bodansky, *Bin Laden,* p. 30.
9. Robert Mackay, "U.S. Sending Aircraft, Troops to Saudi Arabia," UPI, August 7, 1990.
10. Elsa Walsh, "The Prince: How the Saudi Ambassador Became Washington's Indispensable Operator," *New Yorker,* March 24, 2003, p. 48.
11. Arab supporters of the U.S. military action in the Gulf War included Syria, Egypt, Bahrain, Saudi Arabia, the United Arab Emirates, Oman, and Qatar.
12. Tehran TV, November 18, 1990, Gulf/2000 archives.
13. *New York Times,* November 20, 1990, p. 12.
14. Judith Caesar, "Rumblings Under the Throne," *Nation,* December 17, 1990, p. 762.

15. Anonymous, *Through Our Enemies' Eyes,* p. 115.
16. Ibid., p. 114.
17. Bodansky, *Bin Laden,* p. 250.
18. Ibid., p. 30.
19. Michael Specter and Laurie Goodstein, "Thousands of U.S. Jews Mourn Militant Kahane," *Washington Post,* November 7, 1990, p. 18.
20. Sam Donaldson, ABC *Nightline,* November 5, 1990.
21. Evan Thomas et al., "The Road to September 11," *Newsweek,* October 1, 2001, p. 38.
22. John Miller, Michael Stone, and Chris Mitchell, *The Cell,* p. 49.
23. Michael Daly, "Terror Clues in '90 Killing," *Daily News* (New York), May 29, 2002, p. 5; and Simon Reeve, "Blind Sheikh Behind New Terror Wave," *Scotland on Sunday,* November 23, 1997, p. 17.
24. Arieh O'Sullivan, "Osama bin Laden's Links to the Palestinians Widening," *Jerusalem Post,* September 13, 2001, p. 6; and John Miller, interviewed by Terry Gross, *Fresh Air,* National Public Radio, August 21, 2002.
25. Thomas et al., "The Road to September 11," p. 38.
26. Peter Bergen, *Holy War, Inc.,* p. 67.
27. Miller, *Fresh Air;* and John Miller, "The *Esquire* Timeline," *Esquire,* October 2003, p. 80.
28. James C. McKinley, "Suspect in Kahane Slaying Kept List of Prominent Jews," *New York Times,* December 1, 1990, p. 29.
29. Daly, "Terror Clues in '90 Killing," p. 5.
30. Daniel Benjamin and Steven Simon, *The Age of Sacred Terror,* p. 235.
31. Bodansky, *Bin Laden,* p. 30.
32. Anonymous, *Through Our Enemies' Eyes,* p. 118.
33. Benjamin and Simon, *The Age of Sacred Terror,* p. 109.
34. Ibid., p. 111.
35. Bodansky, *Bin Laden,* p. 70.
36. Robert Fisk, "Anti-Soviet Warrior Puts His Army on the Road to Peace," *Independent* (London), December 6, 1993, p. 10.
37. "Osama bin Laden, a Chronology of His Life," PBS *Frontline,* www.pbs.org/wgbh/pages/frontline/shows/binladen/etc/cron.html.
38. There was another terrorist attack on American soil as a result of U.S. policy toward the Muslims, though it was never tied to bin Laden or Al Qaeda. On January 25, 1993, just five days after Bill Clinton was sworn in as president, a man with an AK-47 got out of his car near CIA headquarters in McLean, Virginia, and fired ten times at vehicles lined up to get into the agency. The gunman, a Pakistani named Mir Aimal Kansi, killed two agency employees and wounded three others. Kansi was executed in 2002 for the murders.
39. Miller, Stone, and Mitchell, *The Cell,* pp. 91-92.
40-. Ibid., p. 123.
41. Ibid., p. 94.
42. Miller, *Fresh Air.*
43. Miller, Stone, and Mitchell, *The Cell,* p. 123.
44. Colum Lynch and Vernon Loeb, "Bin Laden's Network: Terror Conspiracy or Loose Alliance?" *Washington Post,* August 1, 1999, p. A1.
45. "Osama bin Laden," PBS *Frontline.*
46. February 19, 1994, Associated Press.
47. Charles Richards, "Times Have Changed for Terrorists Today," *Ottawa Citizen,* August 16, 1994, p. A2.

48. "Unemployment Will Cause Unrest in Gulf," Reuters, February 5, 1995.
49. "Gulf Citizen, No Qualifications, Seeks Well-Paid Job," *Economist*, April 12, 1997, p. 41.
50. Lisa Beyer et al., "After 9/11: The Saudis: Friend or Foe," *Time*, September 15, 2003, p. 38; and interview with Richard Clarke.
51. Howard Schneider, "Rote Schooling in Saudi Arabia Leaves Students Ill-Suited to Work," *Washington Post*, June 12, 1999, p. A13.
52. Walsh, "The Prince," p. 48.
53. Ibid.
54. Patricia Dane Rogers, "A Princely View: A Bird's-Eye Tour of the Saudi Ambassador's Residence," *Washington Post*, September 8, 1994, p. T12.
55. David Whitford, "Entrepreneur of the Year," *Inc.*, December 1993, p. 102.
56. Robert G. Kaiser and David Ottaway, "Oil for Security Fueled Close Ties; But Major Differences Led to Tensions," *Washington Post*, February 11, 2002, p. A1.

Chapter 10: Masters of the Universe

1. Interview with David Rubenstein.
2. Robert H. Williams, "Postscript," *Washington Post*, June 27, 1977, p. A3.
3. Michael Lewis, "The Access Capitalists—Influence-Peddling: The Next Generation; The Carlyle Group," *New Republic*, October 18, 1993, cover story.
4. Williams, "Postscript," p. A3.
5. Greg Schneider, "Connections and Then Some; David Rubenstein Has Made Millions Pairing the Powerful with the Rich," *Washington Post*, March 16, 2003, p. F1.
6. Lewis, "The Access Capitalists."
7. Ibid.
8. Interview with David Rubenstein.
9. Carlyle website, www.thecarlylegroup.com/eng/industry/12-industry495.html.
10. Melanie Warner, "What Do George Bush, Arthur Levitt, Jim Baker, Dick Darman, and John Major All Have in Common?" *Fortune*, March 18, 2002, p. 104.
11. Tim Shorrock, "Crony Capitalism Goes Global," *Nation*, April 1, 2002.
12. Interview with David Rubenstein.
13. Christopher Connell, "Malek Juggles Jobs to Plan Economic Summit," Associated Press, April 21, 1990.
14. Beth Ewen, "Malek Brings Cargo of Controversy to NWA," *Minneapolis—St. Paul City Business*, October 9, 1989, p. 1.
15. David Rubenstein, speech to the Los Angeles County Employees Retirement Association, www.pacifica.org/programs/dn/030703.html.
16. David Ignatius, "Bush's Fancy Financial Footwork," *Washington Post*, August 6, 2002, p. 15.
17. "Profile on Frank Carlucci: From the Knives of the Congo to Darkest Pentagon," *Times* (London), November 8, 1987.
18. Lewis, "The Access Capitalists."
19. Ibid.
20. Ibid.
21. Interview with David Rubenstein.
22. Erica Copulsky, "Gadzooks! —The Super LBO Players Increasingly Are Those That Are Expanding Their Reach into New Product Lines or Geographic

Regions," *Investment Dealers Digest*, August 17, 1998.

23. Lewis, "The Access Capitalists."
24. Ibid.; and Alison Leight Cowan, "Carlyle Getting Part of Ford Aerospace," *New York Times*, September 19, 1990, p. D5.
25. Katie Fairbank, "Carlyle Builds Defense Portfolio," *Dallas Morning News*, June 18, 2000; and PR Newswire Association, October 27, 1994.
26. Leslie Wayne, "Elder Bush in Big G.O.P. Cast Toiling for Top Equity Firm," *New York Times*, March 5, 2001, p. A1.
27. Interview with David Rubenstein.
28. *Hotline*, August 20, 1993; and Louis Dubose, "O Brother, Where Art Thou?" *Austin Chronicle*, March 16, 2001.
29. Alan Friedman, "Big Names at Little Known Investment House," *Financial Times*, September 30, 1993, p. 27.
30. Baker Botts website, www.bakerbotts.com.
31. Michael Carroll, "Doing the Washington–Wall Street Shuffle," *Institutional Investor*, September 1996, pp. 48–66.
32. Interview with David Rubenstein.
33. Said K. Aburish, *The Rise, Corruption and Coming Fall of the House of Saud*, p. 82.
34. Kenneth Gilpin, "Little-Known Carlyle Scores Big," *New York Times*, March 26, 1991, p. D1.
35. Nigel Dempster, "Desert Storm Costs Saudi Prince ?76M," *Daily Mail*, August 6, 1998, p. 33.
36. Interview with Texas oil executive.
37. Interview with Chris Ullman, vice president, Carlyle Group; and Cherif Sedky, attorney for the bin Mahfouz family, via e-mail.
38. globalarchive.ft.com/globalarchive/article.html?id=0003140010338&query= Carlyle+Group+and+Saudi.
39. Interviews with Chris Ullman and David Rubenstein.
40. Interview with oil analyst.
41. Robert G. Kaiser, "Enormous Wealth Spilled into American Coffers," *Washington Post*, February 11, 2002, p. A17.
42. Interview by e-mail with Cherif Sedky.
43. Ibid.
44. Laura Litvan and Jay Mallin, "Race Is On for Kuwait Projects," *Washington Times*, March 5, 1991, p. A1.
45. PR Newswire, June 29, 1993.
46. "BDM Seeks to Buy 25pc of ISE," Moneyclips Ltd., April 10, 1995.
47. PR Newswire, October 27, 1994.
48. PR Newswire, May 3, 1995.
49. Charles J. Hanley, "Saudi Guard Gets Quiet Help," Associated Press, March 22, 1997.
50. PR Newswire, July 20, 1995.
51. Martin Walker and David Pallister, "Saudi Bomb Targets U.S. Military Role," *Guardian*, November 14, 1995, p. 13.
52. Richard Oppel, "Aerospace Deals Could Aid Area," *Dallas Morning News*, February 17, 1994, p. ID.
53. "Corporate Profile for United Defense," *Business Wire*, February 27, 1998.
54. Shorrock, "Crony Capitalism Goes Global."
55. Warner, "What Do George Bush, Arthur Levitt, Jim Baker, Dick Darman, and John Major All Have in Common?" p. 104.

Chapter 11: A House Divided

1. Christopher Dickey and Gregory Vistica, "Attack on the House of Saud," *Newsweek,* November 27, 1995, p. 44.
2. Yossef Bodansky, *Bin Laden,* p. 138.
3. Anonymous, *Through Our Enemies' Eyes,* p. 199.
4. Anthony H. Cordesman, *Saudi Arabia: Guarding the Desert Kingdom,* p. 42.
5. Bruce W. Nelan et al., "Gulf Shock Waves," *Time,* July 8, 1996, p. 20.
6. Bodansky, *Bin Laden,* p. 138.
7. CBS *This Morning,* November 13, 1995.
8. Interview with Chris Ullman, vice president, Carlyle Group.
9. Sidney Blumenthal, *The Clinton Wars,* p. 656.
10. Tim Weiner and David Johnston, "Roadblocks Cited in Efforts to Trace Bin Laden's Money," *New York Times,* p. A1.
11. George Gordon, "Clinton Sends In FBI," *Daily Mail,* November 14, 1995, p. 15
12. Daniel Benjamin and Steven Simon, *The Age of Sacred Terror,* p. 242.
13. Interview with Steven Simon.
14. Bodansky, *Bin Laden,* p. 245.
15. Kathy Gannon, Associated Press Worldstream, May 31, 1996.
16. Sig Christenson, "Bin Ladens Building U.S. Troops' Housing," *San Antonio Express-News,* September 14, 1998, p. 7A.
17. "Osama bin Laden, a Chronology of His Life," PBS *Frontline,* www.pbs.org/wgbh/pages/frontline/shows/binladen/etc/cron.html.
18. Interview with Will Wechsler.
19. Benjamin and Simon, *The Age of Sacred Terror,* pp. 242-45.
20. Ibid., p. 246.
21. Weiner and Johnston, "Roadblocks Cited in Efforts to Trace Bin Laden's Money," p. A1.
22. David B. Ottaway, "Been There, Done That: Prince Bandar, One of the Great Cold Warriors, Faces the Yawn of a New Era," *Washington Post,* July 21, 1996, p. F1.
23. Benjamin and Simon, *The Age of Sacred Terror,* p. 242.
24. Ibid., p. 301.
25. A decentralized, risk-averse bureaucracy, the FBI has a culture that does not appreciate taking orders from policy makers. In addition, FBI agents are trained to react after a crime has been committed, not to investigate situations that might foster terrorism. The FBI's horrendous failure to see the assassination of Meir Kahane as part of a larger terrorism problem typified the problems with its approach. Astonishingly, it had not even bothered to translate Arabic documents that pointed out future targets such as the World Trade Center. In addition, under Freeh the FBI had endured fiascos in handling crises at Ruby Ridge, at Waco, and in the investigation of Timothy McVeigh in the Oklahoma City bombing.
26. Benjamin and Simon, *The Age of Sacred Terror,* p. 301.
27. Ibid., p. 302.
28. Robert Siegel interview with Elsa Walsh, *All Things Considered,* National Public Radio, May 7, 2001.
29. Benjamin and Simon, *The Age of Sacred Terror,* p. 302.
30. Ottaway, "Been There, Done That," p. F1.
31. William F. Wechsler and Lee S. Wolosky, *Terrorist Financing,* report of an

Independent Task Force sponsored by the Council on Foreign Relations, p. 13; and Bodansky, *Bin Laden*, p. 304.

32. *Litigation for the Victims of 9/11*, U.S. District Court for the District of Columbia, 1:02CV01616(JR) Second Amended Complaint, p. 564, www.motleyrice.com/911_victims/911_victims_relevant_documents.html.
33. Ibid., p. 563.
34. Jack Kelley, "Saudi Money Aiding bin Laden," *USA Today*, October 29, 1999.
35. Interview with Cherif Sedky.
36. U.S. Department of Treasury press release, October 12, 2001, part of court papers in the *Litigation for the Victims of 9/11*, p. 583.
37. "Bin Laden's Sister-in-Law Speaks," UPI, October 24, 2001.
38. Craig Unger, "Saving the Saudis," *Vanity Fair*, October 2003.
39. Documents were given to the author by David Armstrong, an investigator for the Public Education Center, the Washington, D.C., foundation that obtained the documents.
40. *Litigation for the Victims of 9/11*, p. 612.
41. Unger, "Saving the Saudis"; and interview with Casey Cooper.
42. Michael Isikoff et al., "The Saudi Money Trail," *Newsweek*, December 2, 2002, p. 28.
43. Mark Matthew, "Saudis Admit Money Trail Leads to Envoy," *Baltimore Sun*, November 25, 2002.
44. Interview with Nawaf Obaid.
45. Interview with Nail al-Jubeir.
46. *Washington Post*, November 15, 2003, final ed.
47. Interview with Will Wechsler.
48. Interview with Richard Clarke.
49. Ibid.
50. "Turki Appeals for Egypt's Help," *Intelligence Newsletter*, November 23, 1995.
51. Bodansky, *Bin Laden*, p. 173.
52. Interview with Robert Baer.
53. Bodansky, *Bin Laden*, p. 139.
54. Ibid., p. 304.
55. Middle East Media Research Institute, www.memri.org/bin/articles.cgi?Page=countries&Area=saudiarabia&ID=SR1 703#_ednref2.
56. David Jackson et al., "Saudi's Cash Funds Terrorism, U.S. Says: Ex-Chicagoan's Assets Are Frozen," *Chicago Tribune*, October 28, 2001, p. 1.
57. Interview with Will Wechsler.
58. George Gedda, "Clinton Vows Justice for Terrorists," Associated Press, August 7, 1998.
59. Bodansky, *Bin Laden*, p. 258.
60. "Riyadh Accused of Detaining Shiite Clerics as Sunnite Dissident Calls for Jihad Against U.S. Troops," *Mideast Mirror*, vol. 10, no. 172, September 4, 1996.
61. "Hunting bin Laden," PBS *Frontline*, www.pbs.org/wgbh/pages/frontline/shows/binladen/etc/cron.html.
62. *Litigation for the Victims of 9/11*, Third Amended Complaint, p. 213, www.motleyrice.com/911_victims/FinalThirdAmendedComplaint.pdf.
63. Shaykh Usamah Bin-Muhammad Bin-Ladin; Ayman al-Zawahiri, amir of the Jihad Group in Egypt; Abu-Yasir Rifa'i Ahmad Taha, Egyptian Islamic Group; Shaykh Mir Hamzah, secretary of the Jamiat-ul-Ulema-e-Pakistan; Fazlur

Rahman, amir of the Jihad Movement in Bangladesh, "Jihad Against Jews and Crusaders," World Islamic Front Statement, February 23, 1998, www.fas.org/irp/world/para/docs/980223-fatwa.htm.

64. Anonymous, *Through Our Enemies' Eyes*, p. 197.

65. Benjamin and Simon, *The Age of Sacred Terror*, p. 355.

66. Ibid., p. 353.

67. Daniel Benjamin and Steven Simon, "A Failure of Intelligence," *New York Review of Books*, December 20, 2001. Jamal Ahmed al-Fadl's testimony:

> Q. Did you ever travel to the section of Khartoum called Hilat Koko with any member of al Qaeda?
> A. Yes, I did... .
> Q. Tell us about the time you went to Hilat Koko with Abu Hajer al Iraqi, what you discussed.
> A. I learn that in this building they try to make chemical weapons with regular weapons ...
> Q. Returning to your conversation with Abu Hajer al Iraqi, did he discuss with you who it was that was trying to make the chemical weapons in the area there of Hilat Koko?
> *A. He tell me the al Qaeda group try to help Islamic National Front to do these weapons, to make these weapons* [italics added in *New York Review*].
> Q. Okay. So I'm asking you, do you know that chemical weapons are used to kill people?
> A. Yes, that's what I hear from them.
> Q. You know that, for example, they use gas to kill people, right?
> A. Yes.
> Q. And whoever is in the area where that gas goes runs the risk of being killed?
> A. Yes.

68. Peter Worthington, "An Honourable Man Would Resign," *Toronto Sun*, December 22, 1998, p. 16.

69. Benjamin and Simon, *The Age of Sacred Terror*, p. 361.

70. Ibid., p. 359.

71. Interview with Frank Anderson; and Vernon Loeb, "A Dirty Business; Because of a Cupful of Soil, the U.S. Flattened This Sudanese Factory," *Washington Post*, July 25, 1999, p. F1.

72. Benjamin and Simon, *The Age of Sacred Terror*, p. 363.

73. Loeb, "A Dirty Business," p. F1.

74. Benjamin and Simon, *The Age of Sacred Terror*, p. 363.

75. James Zogby, "The Attack on Sudan," *Mideast Mirror*, August 16, 1999; and James V. Grimaldi, "An Arab American Charitable Connection That Might Be Too Close for Comfort," *Washington Post*, December 17, 2001, p. E6.

76. Barbara Bush, *Reflections*, p. 234.

77. E-mail from Cherif Sedky.

78. E-mail from Jean Becker.

79. Interviews and e-mails with David Rubenstein and Chris Ullman.

Chapter 12: The Arabian Candidate

1. Stuart Stevens, *The Big Enchilada*, p. 146.

2. Bush had gotten religion in 1985 when the Reverend Billy Graham visited the Bushes at their summer home in Kennebunkport, Maine. "He planted a seed in my heart and I began to change," he said. "... I realized that alcohol was beginning to crowd out my energies and could crowd, eventually, my affections for other people. To put it in spiritual terms, I accepted Christ"; and Lois Romano and George Lardner Jr., "1986: A Life-Changing Year; Epiphany Fueled Candidate's Climb," *Washington Post,* July 25, 1999, p. A1.
3. Joan Didion, "Mr. Bush & the Divine," *New York Review of Books,* November 6, 2003.
4. Ibid.
5. Ibid.
6. Interview with source who worked with Bush in the Reagan-Bush administration.
7. Didion, "Mr. Bush & the Divine"; and Skipp Porteous, "Bush's Secret Religious Pandering," adapted from *Penthouse,* November 2000.
8. Didion, "Mr. Bush & the Divine."
9. Letter to President William J. Clinton, January 26, 1998, signed by Elliott Abrams, Richard L. Armitage, William J. Bennett, Jeffrey Bergner, John Bolton, Paula Dobriansky, Francis Fukuyama, Robert Kagan, Zalmay Khalilzad, William Kristol, Richard Perle, Peter W. Rodman, Donald Rumsfeld, William Schneider Jr., Vin Weber, Paul Wolfowitz, R. James Woolsey, and Robert B. Zoellick, www.newamericancentury.org/iraqclinton-letter.htm.
10. "Rebuilding America's Defenses, Strategy, Forces and Resources for a New Century," Project for a New American Century, www.newamericancentury.org/RebuildingAmericasDefenses.pdf.
11. Ann McFeatters, "Bush Drafting Call for Saddam's Ouster," *Pittsburgh Post-Gazette,* November 24, 1999.
12. Sidney Blumenthal, *The Clinton Wars,* p. 721.
13. Ibid.; and Dana Milbank, *Smashmouth,* p. 197.
14. Mark Sherman and Ken Herman, "McCain Blasts Bush Ad Blitz 'That Knows No Depths,' " *Atlanta Journal and Constitution,* March 5, 2003.
15. *Journeys with George,* HBO documentary directed by Alexandra Pelosi.
16. Jacob Epstein, "The Complete Bushisms," *Slate,* slate.msn.com/id/76886/.
17. Stevens, *The Big Enchilada,* p. 121.
18. *Journeys with George.*
19. Ibid.
20. Ibid.
21. *Intelligence Newsletter,* March 2, 2000.
22. Craig Unger, "Saving the Saudis," *Vanity Fair,* October 2003.
23. *Time,* September 15, 2003; www.andover.edu/news/bush_scholars.htm; *Chicago Tribune,* July 4, 2003; and Associated Press, July 18, 2003, final ed.
24. Alexander Rose, "How Did the Muslims Vote in 2000?" *Middle East Quarterly,* vol. 8, no. 3 (Summer 2001), www.meforum.org/article/13/; the U.S. Census does not put together data on Muslims, and estimates of the population of Muslims in the United States range from 6 million to 12 million; and Cornell University study on American Muslims, April 2002, www.aljazeerah.info/Special%20Reports/Different%20special%20reports/Snapshot%20of%20Moslims%20in%20America.htm.
25. Rose, "How Did the Muslims Vote in 2000?"
26. Eric Boehlert, "'Betrayed' by Bush," *Salon,* April 3, 2002.

27. Stephen Schwartz, *The Two Faces of Islam*, p. 233.
28. Testimony of Stephen Schwartz, Director, Islam and Democracy Program, Foundation for the Defense of Democracies, before the Senate Judiciary Committee Subcommittee on Terrorism, Technology and Homeland Security, June 26, 2003.
29. Ibid.
30. David E. Kaplan, "The Saudi Connection," *U.S. News and World Report*, December 15, 2003, www.usnews.com/usnews/issue/031215/usnews/15terror.htm.
31. Testimony of Stephen Schwartz.
32. Frank Gaffney Jr., "A Troubling Influence," FrontPageMagazine.com, December 2003, www.frontpagemag.com/Articles/ReadArticle.asp?ID=11209.
33. Mona Charen, "Saudi Tendrils," Creators Syndicate, February 18, 2003, www.townhall.com/columnists/monacharen/mc20030218.shtml.
34. Ibid.
35. Rose, "How Did the Muslims Vote in 2000?"
36. Jeff Jacoby, "The Islamist Connections," *Boston Globe*, February 27, 2003, p. A15; and Glenn Simpson, "Muslim School Used by Military Has Troubling Ties," *Wall Street Journal*, December 3, 2003.
37. Gaffney, "A Troubling Influence."
38. Bob McKeown, *Dateline NBC*, October 28, 2001.
39. Mike Allen and Richard Leiby, "Alleged Terrorist Met With Bush Adviser, Al-Arian Part of Muslim Outreach," *Washington Post*, February 22, 2003, p. A10.
40. Ibid.
41. Juan Gonzales, "Call Stirs Fears of Jihad Air Terror," *Daily News* (New York), July 19, 1996, p. 30.
42. Michael Fechter, "Ties to Terrorists," *Tampa Tribune*, May 28, 1995, p. 1.
43. Steven Emerson, *American Jihad*, p. 122.
44. Peter Katel and Mark Hosenball, "Foreign Thugs, U.S. Soil: Did Islamic Jihad Have a Covert Base in Florida?" *Newsweek*, May 6, 1996, p. 35.
45. Kenneth Timmerman, "Arrested Prof Was Guest at Bush White House," *WorldNetDaily, Insight Magazine*, February 21, 2003, www.worldnetdaily.com/news/article.asp?ARTICLE_ID=31172. See also Emerson, *American Jihad*, p. 225.
46. Timmerman, "Arrested Prof Was Guest at Bush White House"; and Frank Gaffney, "What's Wrong with This Picture?" *Washington Times*, February 27, 2003.
47. *United States of America v. Sami Al-Arian et al.*, U.S. District Court, Middle District of Florida, Tampa Division, www.usdoj.gov/usao/flm/pr/022003indict.pdf.
48. David Frum, "The Strange Case of Sami Al-Arian," *National Review*, www.nationalreview.com/frum/diary022103.asp.
49. Ibid.
50. Nora Boustany, "One Man, Making a Difference," *Washington Post*, August 2, 2000.
51. Rose, "How Did the Muslims Vote in 2000?"
52. Ibid.
53. Gaffney, "A Troubling Influence."
54. Rose, "How Did the Muslims Vote in 2000?"
55. Sami Al-Arian, "A Worthy Struggle," *Tampa Tribune*, August 18, 2002, p. 1.
56. "Rebuilding America's Defenses," Project for a New American Century.

57. Ibid.
58. Jake Tapper, *Salon,* March 11, 2003; David Sanger, "A Special Report; Rivals Differ on U.S. Role in the World," *New York Times,* October 29, 2000, p. A1; and Glenn Kessler, "U.S. Decision on Iraq Has Puzzling Past; Opponents of War Wonder When, How Policy Was Set," *Washington Post,* January 12, 2003.
59. Timothy Edgar, ACLU legislative counsel, "Secret Evidence Measure Resoundingly Defeated," archive.aclu.org/news/2001/n110801c.html.
60. Rose, "How Did the Muslims Vote in 2000?"
61. Ibid.
62. Ian Brodie, "US Crew Waved as Suicide Bomb Boat Drew Near," *Times* (London), October 23, 2000.
63. Judith Miller, Jeff Gerth, and Don Van Natta Jr., written by Ms. Miller, "Many Say U.S. Planned for Terror but Failed to Take Action," *New York Times,* December 31, 2001, www.nytimes.com/2001/12/30/national/30TERR.html?pagewanted=1&ei=5 070&en=5038154b0e30023d&ex=1070859600.
64. *Detroit Free Press,* October 20, 2000.
65. "American Muslim PAC Endorses George W. Bush for President," www.iiie.net/Articles/MPACBushEndors.html.
66. Rose, "How Did the Muslims Vote in 2000?"
67. Grover Norquist, "The Natural Conservatives: Muslims Deliver for the GOP," *American Spectator,* June 2001.
68. Rose, "How Did the Muslims Vote in 2000?"
69. Ibid.

Chapter 13: Lost in Transition

1. Maureen Dowd, "A Golden Couple Chasing Away a Black Cloud," *New York Times,* November 27, 2002.
2. Jeffrey Toobin, *Too Close to Call,* p. 41.
3. Chris Dufresne, *Los Angeles Times,* November 16, 2000, p. S2.
4. Center for Responsive Politics, www.opensecrets.org/pressreleases/BushTransitionTeams.htm.
5. Interview with Richard Rechter, a participant in the hunting trip.
6. Elsa Walsh, "The Prince: How the Saudi Ambassador Became Washington's Indispensable Operator," *New Yorker,* March 24, 2003.
7. Ibid., p. 48.
8. Michael Elliott, "They Had a Plan," *Time,* August 12, 2002.
9. Ibid.
10. Ibid.
11. Barton Gellman, "A Strategy's Cautious Evolution," *Washington Post,* January 20, 2002, p. A1.
12. Elliott, "They Had a Plan."
13. Ibid.
14. Condoleezza Rice, "Promoting the National Interest," *Foreign Affairs,* January/February 2000.
15. "Remarks by Condoleezza Rice, Gov. George W. Bush's International Affairs Adviser, to the Republican National Convention on Tuesday," Associated Press, August 1, 2000.
16. Gellman, "A Strategy's Cautious Evolution."
17. Andrew Leonard, "Will Bush Be Tarnished by Enron's Collapse?" *Salon,*

November 30, 2001, dir.salon.com/tech/col/leon/2001/11/30/enron_collapse/index.html?pn=1.

18. Walsh, "The Prince," p. 48.

19. Leslie Wayne, "Elder Bush in Big G.O.P. Cast Toiling for Top Equity Firm," *New York Times,* March 5, 2001.

20. Walter Pincus, "Crusader a Boon to Carlyle Group Even if Pentagon Scraps Project," *Washington Post,* May 14, 2002, p. A3.

21. "Baker Botts Opens in Riyadh with Two Arent Fox Partners," *Lawyer,* February 5, 2001, p. 13.

22. Peter Behr and Alan Sipress, "Energy Panel Seeks Review of Sanctions," *Washington Post,* April 19, 2001, p. A13.

23. *Hotline,* February 1, 2001.

24. "Democrats Mount Effort to Strip Cheney of Corporate Salary and Stock Options," U.S. Newswire, October 14, 2003.

25. Lesley Stahl, "Bush Sought Way to Invade Iraq," CBS News.com, January 11, 2004, www.cbsnews.com/stories/2004/01/09/60minutes/printable592330.shtml.

26. "Slick Deals: Bush Advisers Cashed In on Saudi Gravy Train," *Boston Herald,* December 11, 2001.

27. Interview on NBC's *Meet the Press,* October 26, 2003.

28. Gellman, "A Strategy's Cautious Evolution."

29. Jake Tapper, "We Predicted It," *Salon,* September 12, 2001, dir.salon.com/ politics/feature/2001/09/12/bush/index.html.

30. Robert Burns, "CIA Chief Calls bin Laden Biggest Threat to U.S. Security," Associated Press, February 7, 2001.

31. Gellman, "A Strategy's Cautious Evolution."

32. Ibid.

33. Ibid.

34. Elliott, "They Had a Plan."

35. John Solomon, "Fighting Terror/Early Signs; FAA Was Warned of Pilot," Associated Press, May 11, 2002.

36. "'To Her Doom': Bin Laden Reads Poem About USS *Cole's* Fate at Son's Wedding," Reuters, March 1, 2001, abcnews.go.com/sections/world/DailyNews/afghanistan010301_binladen.html.

37. Jane Mayer, "The House of Bin Laden," *New Yorker,* November 12, 2001, www.newyorker.com/fact/content/?011112fa_FACT3.

38. Julian Borger, "Arab TV Network Broadcasts First Taped Testimony by a Hijacker," *Guardian,* April 16, 2002, www.guardian.co.uk/international/story/0,3604,685102,00.html.

39. Peter Finn, "Hamburg's Cauldron of Terror," *Washington Post,* September 11, 2002.

40. Carl Cameron, "Clues Alerted White House to Potential Attacks," Fox News, May 17, 2002, www.foxnews.com/story/0,2933,53065,00.html.

41. Jonathan D. Salant, Associated Press, May 18, 2002, www.newsday.com/news/local/newyork/ny-airlines0519,0,1731679.story.

42. "Joint Inquiry Staff Statement, Part 1," Eleanor Hill, Staff Director, Joint Inquiry Staff, Senate Select Committee on Intelligence, September 18, 2002, www.cooperativeresearch.org/timeline/2002/senatecommittee091802.html.

43. Robert Scheer, "Bush's Faustian Deal with the Taliban," *Los Angeles Times,* May 22, 2001.

44. Edward T. Pound, "The Easy Path to the United States for Three of the 9/11

Hijackers," *U.S. News and World Report,* December 12, 2001, www.usnews.com/usnews/news/terror/articles/visa011212.htm.

45. Joel Mowbray, "Open Door for Saudi Terrorists: The Visa Express Scandal," *National Review Online,* June 14, 2002, www.nationalreview.com/comment/comment-mowbray 061402.asp.

46. Mike Allen and Richard Leiby, "Alleged Terrorist Met with Bush Adviser," *Washington Post,* February 22, 2003.

47. Mary Jacoby, "Friends in High Places," *St. Petersburg Times,* March 11, 2003.

48. Michael Hirsh and Michael Isikoff, "What Went Wrong?" *Newsweek,* May 27, 2002.

49. Michael Isikoff, "9–11 Hijackers: A Saudi Money Trail?" *Newsweek,* November 22, 2002.

50. Walsh, "The Prince."

51. Ibid.

52. Steven Mufson, "Israel Cited for 'Excessive Force'; State Dept. Report on Human Rights Also Faults Palestinians," *Washington Post,* February 27, 2001, p. A20.

53. "World," Reuters; "In Brief," *Washington Post,* March 4, 2001, p. A25.

54. Wafa Amr, "Palestinian: Israel Set Car Bomb," Reuters; *Washington Post,* April 13, 2001, p. A20.

55. Walsh, "The Prince."

56. "Saudi Arabia: Political Outlook," MEED, Janet Matthews Information Services, Quest Economics Database, September 3, 2001.

57. Walsh, "The Prince."

58. Jane Perlez, "Bush Senior, on His Son's Behalf, Reassures Saudi Leader," *New York Times,* July 15, 2001.

59. Ibid.

60. Ibid.

61. Barton Gellman, "Before Sept. 11, Unshared Clues and Unshaped Policy," *Washington Post,* May 17, 2002, p. A1.

62. Michael Elliott, "How the U.S. Missed the Clues," *Time,* May 27, 2002.

63. Mike Allen, "A White House on the Range, Bush Retreats to Ranch for 'Working Vacation,'" *Washington Post,* August 7, 2001.

64. Terry Moran, *ABC World News Tonight,* August 3, 2001.

65. Elliott, "How the U.S. Missed the Clues."

66. Scott Lindlaw, "President Bush Vacationing in Texas," Associated Press, August 6, 2001.

67. Dan Rather, *CBS News,* May 16, 2002.

68. "White House Defends Response to Pre-9/11 Intelligence Reports," *Bulletin's Frontrunner,* May 17, 2002.

69. Bob Woodward and Dan Eggen, "Sources: Aug. 6 Memo Focused on al-Qaida," *Washington Post,* May 18, 2002, p. A3.

70. Lindlaw, "President Bush Vacationing in Texas."

71. Frank Rich, "Thanks for the Heads-Up," *New York Times,* May 25, 2002, p. A17.

72. Gerald Posner, *Why America Slept,* p. 183.

73. Benjamin and Simon, *The Age of Sacred Terror,* p. 347.

74. Ibid.

75. Barton Gellman, "Anti-Terror Pioneer Turns In the Badge," *Washington Post,* March 13, 2003.

76. Ibid.

77. Ted Bridis, "Bush's Top Security Advisers Met Just Twice on Terrorism Before Sept. 11 Attacks," Associated Press, June 29, 2002.
78. Benjamin and Simon, *The Age of Sacred Terror,* p. 345.
79. Ibid.
80. Elliott, "They Had a Plan"; and Joe Conason, "Ashcroft's Failures Deserve a Hearing," *New York Observer,* www.nyobserver.com/pages/story.asp? ID=5970.
81. Gellman, "A Strategy's Cautious Evolution."
82. Gellman, "Anti-Terror Pioneer Turns In the Badge."
83. Benjamin and Simon, *The Age of Sacred Terror,* p. 345.
84. Ibid.
85. Robert G. Kaiser and David B. Ottaway, "Saudi Leader's Anger Revealed Shaky Ties," *Washington Post,* February 10, 2002; and Walsh, "The Prince," p. 48.
86. Kaiser and Ottaway, "Saudi Leader's Anger Revealed Shaky Ties."
87. Ibid.
88. Ibid.
89. Walsh, "The Prince," p. 48.
90. Charlie Brennan, "The Brightest Star in Starwood," *Rocky Mountain News,* December 28, 2002.
91. Walsh, "The Prince," p. 48.
92. Kaiser and Ottaway, "Saudi Leader's Anger Revealed Shaky Ties."
93. Ibid.
94. Ibid.
95. Ibid.
96. Walsh, "The Prince," p. 48.
97. Ibid.
98. Kaiser and Ottaway, "Saudi Leader's Anger Revealed Shaky Ties."
99. Ibid.
100. Ibid.

Chapter 14: 9/11

1. "George and Laura," *Early Show,* November 1, 2002, www.cbsnews.com/ stories/2002/10/29/earlyshow/leisure/books/main527361.shtml.
2. Sharon Churcher, "The Day the President Went Missing," *Daily Mail,* September 8, 2002.
3. "Springfield Native Told President of Terrorist Attacks," Associated Press, November 26, 2001, www.directsourceradio.com/links/11262001120N.html.
4. Ibid.
5. Jennifer Barrs, "From a Whisper to a Tear," *Tampa Tribune,* September 1, 2002, www.unansweredquestions.org/timeline/2002/tampatribune090102.html.
6. Ari Fleischer, "Voices of 9-11: 'God Bless You, Mr. President,'" *National Journal,* August 31, 2002.
7. Nancy Gibbs, "Special Report: The Day of the Attack," *Time,* September 12, 2001, www.time.com/time/nation/article/0,8599,174655–3,00.html.
8. David E. Sanger and Don Van Natta Jr., "In Four Days, a National Crisis Changes Bush's Presidency," *New York Times,* September 16, 2001.
9. Judith Miller, Jeff Gerth, and Don Van Natta Jr., "Planning for Terror but Failing to Act," *New York Times,* December 30, 2001.
10. Charles Gibson, "Terror Hits the Towers," *ABC News,* September 14, 2001,

abcnews.go.com/onair/DailyNews/sept11momentsi.html.

11. David Martin, "Notes from an Aide to Defense Secretary Rumsfeld Say Iraq Was Considered an Attack Target as Far Back as 9/11 Despite No Evidence of Involvement," *CBS News,* September 4, 2002.

12. Bob Woodward, *Bush at War,* p. 37.

13. Ibid.

14. Interview with Nail al-Jubeir.

15. Maureen Dowd, "A Golden Couple Chasing Away a Black Cloud," *New York Times,* November 27, 2002.

16. "America Under Attack," *ABC News* Special Report, September 12, 2001.

17. Judith Miller with Kurt Eichenwald, "A Nation Challenged: The Investigation; U.S. Set to Widen Financial Assault," *New York Times,* October 1, 2001.

18. Interview with Richard Clarke.

19. Carol Costello, David Ensor, and Rula Amin, "Bin Laden Family Believes Osama Is Alive," CNN *Daybreak,* March 19, 2002.

20. Elsa Walsh, "The Prince: How the Saudi Ambassador Became Washington's Indispensable Operator," *New Yorker,* March 24, 2003. p. 48.

21. Interview with Nail al-Jubeir.

22. Kathy Steele, Brenna Kelly, and Elizabeth Lee Brown, "Phantom Flight from Florida," *Tampa Tribune,* October 5, 2001.

23. Cindy Pierson Dulay, Horse-races.net, www.horse-races.net/library/aa072202.htm.

24. Bill Christine, "Bomb Scare Interrupts Card," *Los Angeles Times,* September 13, 2001, pt. 4, p. 3.

25. Patrick E. Tyler, "Fearing Harm, Bin Laden Kin Fled From U.S.," *New York Times,* September 30, 2001, p. Al.

26. Jules Crittenden, "Attack on America: Feds Make First Arrest in Manhunt; U.S. Air Force Lost Frantic Race Against Time During Hijackings," *Boston Herald,* September 15, 2001.

27. Charles M. Madigan, "Bush Boosts Police Powers," *Chicago Tribune,* September 19, 2001, p. 1.

28. Interview with source with firsthand knowledge of the flight.

29. Ibid.

30. Kevin Cullen and Andrea Estes, "Bin Laden Kin, Family Weighed Staying in U.S.," *Boston Globe,* September 21, 2001.

31. Interview with source with firsthand knowledge of the flight.

32. Specification sheet for BOEING 727-100 EXEC.

33. Confirmation of flight/vendor agreement.

34. Interview with source with firsthand knowledge of the flights.

35. Passenger lists prepared by Saudi embassy.

36. Interview with John L. Martin.

37. Ibid.

38. Byron York, "The bin Ladens' Great Escape," *National Review,* September 11, 2002.

39. "President Bush Addresses a Joint Session of Congress and the Nation Regarding Last Week's Terrorist Attacks," *CBS News* Special Report, September 20, 2001

40. "'Our Resolve Must Not Pass'; Text of President Bush's Speech to Congress," *Columbus Dispatch,* September 20, 2001, p. A4.

41. "President Bush Addresses a Joint Session of Congress and the Nation Regarding Last Week's Terrorist Attacks," *CBS News* Special Report,

September 20, 2001.

42. "President Freezes Terrorists' Assets," White House Press Releases, Office of the Press Secretary, September 24, 2001.

43. Joel Mowbray, "Open Door for Saudi Terrorists: The Visa Express Scandal," *National Review Online,* June 14, 2002, www.nationalreview.com/comment/comment-mowbray061402.asp.

44. Ibid.

45. David Willman and Greg Miller, "Saudi Aid to War on Terror Is Criticized," *Los Angeles Times,* October 13, 2001.

46. Ibid.

47. Jonathan Wells, Jack Meyers, and Maggie Mulvihill, "U.S. Ties to Saudi Elite May Be Hurting War on Terrorism; U.S. Businesses Weave Tangled Web with Saudis," *Boston Herald,* December 10, 2001.

48. Lisa Beyer, "Inside the Kingdom; Saudi Arabia," *Time,* September 15, 2003, p. 38.

49. Stephen Matthews, "Investing in Saudi Arabia," *Middle Eastern Economic Digest,* September 14, 2001.

50. "Analysis: Globalisation of Law Firms," *Petroleum Economist,* October 23, 2001.

51. Testimony of Robert Jordan, Ambassadorial Nominations, Chaired by Sen. Russell Feingold (D-WI), Federal News Service, September 21, 2001.

52. *Lawyer,* February 5, 2001.

53. Testimony of Robert Jordan.

54. Ibid.

55. Gerald Posner, *Why America Slept,* p. 181.

56. Bob Drogin, "U.S. Studies Loot Seized with Captured Al Qaeda Leader," *Los Angeles Times,* April 3, 2002.

57. Posner, *Why America Slept,* pp. 187-88.

58. Ibid., p. 188.

59. Ibid., p. 189.

60. Ibid., p. 190.

61. Ibid.

62. Ibid., p. 191.

63. William C. Rhoden, "Winning Formula? This Year It Was Money," *New York Times,* May 5, 2002.

64. Jimmy Breslin, "No Apology After Big Win," *Newsday,* May 7, 2002.

65. King Kaufman, "Still Life with Horse," *Salon,* May 5, 2002.

66. Rhoden, "Winning Formula? This Year It Was Money."

67. Breslin, "No Apology After Big Win."

68. Beth Harris, "War Emblem's Owner Skips Belmont Stakes," Associated Press, June 6, 2002.

69. "War Emblem Owner Dies," *Sports Network,* July 22, 2002.

70. Simon Wardell, "Three Royal Princes Die Within a Week," *World Markets Analysis,* July 30, 2002.

71. Paula Zahn, "Saudis Evacuated from United States After 9/11?" CNN, September 4, 2003, transcript # 090409CN.V94.

Chapter 15: Print the Legend

1. *The Man Who Shot Liberty Valance,* screenplay by James Warner Bellah and Willis Goldbeck, story by Dorothy M. Johnson, directed by John Ford.

2. Interview with Richard Clarke.

3. Ibid.

4. Interview with Charles Lewis.

5. Elsa Walsh, "The Prince: How the Saudi Ambassador Became Washington's Indispensable Operator," *New Yorker,* March 24, 2003.

6. Romesh Ratnesar, "A Twist of the Arm; Pushing Saudi Arabia to Up Its Antiterrorism Efforts, the U.S. Is Telling Riyadh It's Next on al-Qaeda's List," *Time,* December 9, 2002, p. 45.

7. Jack Shafer, "The PowerPoint That Rocked the Pentagon," *Slate,* August 7, 2002.

8. Ibid.

9. Dick Cheney, speech to Veterans of Foreign Wars convention, August 26, 2002, www.whitehouse.gov/news/releases/2002/08/20020826.html.

10. President George W. Bush, Speech to UN General Assembly, September 12, 2002, www.whitehouse.gov/news/releases/2002/09/20020912-1.html.

11. Ari Fleischer, press briefing, December 2, 2002, www.whitehouse.gov/news/releases/2002/12/20021202-6.html.

12. Richard Sale, "Staff Change Means Mideast Policy Shift," United Press International, February 26, 2003.

13. Ibid.

14. Seymour Hersh, "The Stovepipe," *New Yorker,* October 27, 2003, www. newyorker.com/fact/content/?031027fa_fact.

15. Lisa Beyer et al., "Inside the Kingdom," *Time,* September 15, 2003, p. 38.

16. Interview with Youssef Ibrahim.

17. Ibid.

Appendix C

1. Interview with David Rubenstein.

2. *New Republic,* October 18, 1993; and *Washington Post,* November 22, 1997.

3. *Washington Times,* May 14, 2003.

4. PR Newswire, October 27, 1994.

5. Associated Press, November 14, 1995.

6. www.icij.org/dtaweb/icij_bow.asp?Section=Database&Action=Operation&-OID=230.

7. *Defense Daily,* June 23, 1995.

8. *Boston Herald,* December 10; and Pentagon press release, April 1, 1996, Contract Number 175-96.

9. *Defense Daily,* February 4, 1997.

10. Pentagon press release, December 24, 1997.

11. CNN.com, October 25, 2003; FDCH Political Transcripts, September 25, 2003; and *New York Times,* October 1, 2003.

12. *Boston Herald,* December 10, 2001.

13. *Platt's Oilgram News,* January 29, 2003; and *Wall Street Journal,* December 6, 1991.

14. *Time,* September 15, 2003.

15. Ibid.

16. www.andover.edu/news/bush_scholars.htm.

17. Associated Press, July 18, 2003, Friday Final Edition.

SELECTED BIBLIOGRAPHY

Said K. Aburish, *The Rise, Corruption and Coming Fall of the House of Saud.* New York: St. Martin's Press, 1995.

James Ring Adams and Douglas Frantz, *A Full Service Bank: How BCCI Stole Billions Around the World.* New York: Pocket Books, 1992.

Madawi Al-Rasheed, *A History of Saudi Arabia.* New York: Cambridge University Press, 2002.

Anonymous, *Through Our Enemies' Eyes: Osama bin Laden, Radical Islam, and the Future of America.* Washington, D.C.: Brassey's, 2002.

Robert Baer, *See No Evil: The True Story of a Ground Soldier in the CIA's War on Terrorism.* New York: Three Rivers Press, 2002.

————, *Sleeping with the Devil.* New York: Crown, 2003.

James A. Baker III with Thomas DeFrank, *The Politics of Diplomacy: Revolution, War, and Peace.* New York: Putnam, 1995.

Benjamin R. Barber, *Jihad vs. McWorld: How Globalism and Tribalism Are Reshaping the World.* New York: Ballantine Books, 1996.

Laurence I. Barrett, *Gambling with History: Reagan in the White House.* New York: Penguin Books, 1983.

Jonathan Beaty and S. C. Gwynne, *The Outlaw Bank: A Wild Ride into the Secret Heart of BCCI.* New York: Random House, 1993.

Daniel Benjamin and Steven Simon, *The Age of Sacred Terror.* New York: Random House, 2002.

Peter L. Bergen, *Holy War, Inc.: Inside the Secret World of Osama bin Laden.* New York: Free Press, 2001.

Khalid bin Sultan et al., *Desert Warrior: A Personal View of the Gulf War by the Joint Forces Commander.* New York: HarperCollins, 1995.

Tom Blanton, ed., *White House E-mail: The Top-Secret Messages the Reagan/Bush White House Tried to Destroy.* New York: New Press, 1995.

Sidney Blumenthal, *The Clinton Wars.* New York: Farrar Straus & Giroux, 2003.

————, *Pledging Allegiance: The Last Campaign of the Cold War.* New York: Harper-Collins, 1990.

Yossef Bodansky, *Bin Laden: The Man Who Declared War on America.* Rocklin, Calif.: Forum, 1999.

Anthony Cave Brown, *Oil, God, and Gold: The Story of Aramco and the Saudi Kings.* Boston: Houghton Mifflin, 1999.

Frank Bruni, *Ambling into History: The Unlikely Odyssey of George W Bush*. New York: HarperCollins, 2002.

Zbigniew Brzezinksi, *The Grand Chessboard: American Primacy and Its Geostrategic Imperatives*. New York: Basic Books, 1997.

Barbara Bush, *Reflections: Life After the White House*. New York: Scribner, 2003.

George Bush with Victor Gold, *Looking Forward: The George Bush Story*. Garden City, N.Y.: Doubleday, 1987.

George Bush and Brent Scowcroft, *A World Transformed*. New York: Vintage Books, 1998.

Richard Butler, *The Greatest Threat: Iraq, Weapons of Mass Destruction, and the Crisis of Global Security*. New York: Public Affairs, 2000.

Jimmy Carter, *Keeping Faith: Memoirs of a President*. New York: Bantam Books, 1982.

Andrew Cockburn and Patrick Cockburn, *Out of the Ashes: The Resurrection of Saddam Hussein*. New York: HarperCollins, 1999.

Leslie Cockburn, *Out of Control: The Story of the Reagan Administration's Secret War in Nicaragua, the Illegal Arms Pipeline, and the Contra Drug Connection*. New York: Atlantic Monthly Press, 1987.

Joe Conason, *Big Lies: The Right-Wing Propaganda Machine and How It Distorts the Truth*. New York: St. Martin's Press, 2003.

John K. Cooley, *Unholy Wars: Afghanistan, America and International Terrorism*. Sterling, Va.: Pluto Press, 1999.

Anthony H. Cordesman, *Saudi Arabia: Guarding the Desert Kingdom*. Boulder, Colo.: Westview Press, 1997.

Richard Ben Cramer, *What It Takes: The Way to the White House*. New York: Random House, 1992.

George Crile, *Charlie Wilson's War: The Extraordinary Story of the Largest Covert Operation in History*. New York: Atlantic Monthly Press, 2003.

Adel Darwish, *Unholy Babylon: The Secret History of Saddam s War*. London: Gollancz, 1991.

Alexandre de Marenches and David Andelman, *The Fourth World War: Diplomacy and Espionage in the Age of Terrorism*. New York: William Morrow, 1992.

Theodore Draper, *A Very Thin Line—The Iran-Contra Affairs*. New York: Hill and Wang, 1991.

Michael Duffy and Dan Goodgame, *Marching in Place: The Status Quo Presidency of George Bush*. New York: Simon & Schuster, 1992.

Steven Emerson, *The American House of Saud: The Secret Petrodollar Connection*. New York: Franklin Watts, 1985.

————, *American Jihad: The Terrorists Living Among Us*. New York: Free Press, 2002.

Michael Field, *The Merchants: The Big Business Families of Saudi Arabia and the Gulf States*. Woodstock, N.Y.: Overlook Press, 1985.

Alan Friedman, *Spider's Web: The Secret History of How the White House Illegally Armed Iraq*. New York: Bantam, 1993.

Thomas Friedman, *From Beirut to Jerusalem*. New York: Anchor Books, 1989.

David Frum, *The Right Man: The Surprise Presidency of George W Bush*. New York: Random House, 2003.

Jack Germond and Jules Witcover, *Whose Broad Stripes and Bright Stars? The Trivial Pursuit of the Presidency, 1988*. New York: Warner Books, 1989.

Dore Gold, *Hatred's Kingdom: How Saudi Arabia Supports the New Global Terrorism*. Washington, D.C.: Regnery, 2003.

Stephen Graubard, *Mr. Bush's War: Adventures in the Politics of Illusion.* New York: Hill and Wang, 1992.

Dilip Hiro, *The Longest War: The Iran-Iraq Military Conflict.* New York: Routledge, 1991.

David Holden and Richard Johns, *The House of Saud: The Rise and Rule of the Most Powerful Dynasty in the Arab World.* New York: Holt, Rinehart, and Winston, 1982.

Samuel Huntington, *The Clash of Civilizations and the Remaking of World Order.* New York: Touchstone, 1997.

Molly Ivins, *Molly Ivins Can't Say That, Can She?* New York: Random House, 1991.

Molly Ivins and Lou Dubose, *Shrub.* New York: Vintage Books, 2000.

Roland Jacquard, *In the Name of Osama bin Laden: Global Terrorism and the bin Laden Brotherhood.* Durham, N.C.: Duke University Press, 2002.

Michael Kelly, *Martyr's Day: Chronicle of a Small War.* New York: Random House, 1993.

Peter Kornbluh and Malcolm Byrne, *The Iran-Contra Scandal: The Declassified History.* New York: New Press, 1993.

Peter Lance, *1000 Years for Revenge: International Terrorism and the FBI—the Untold Story.* New York: Regan Books, 2003.

Bernard Lewis, *What Went Wrong?: The Clash Between Islam and Modernity in the Middle East.* New York: Oxford University Press, 2002.

Kenneth J. Lipartito and Joseph A. Pratt, *Baker & Botts in the Development of Modern Houston.* Austin: University of Texas Press, 1991.

Michael Lind, *Made in Texas: George W Bush and the Southern Takeover of American Politics.* New York: Basic Books, 2003.

John Loftus and Mark Aarons, *The Secret War Against the Jews: How Western Espionage Betrayed the Jewish People.* New York: St. Martin's Press, 1994.

David E. Long, *The United States and Saudi Arabia: Ambivalent Allies.* Boulder, Colo.: Westview Press, 1985.

Sandra Mackey, *The Saudis: Inside the Desert Kingdom.* Boston: Houghton Mifflin, 1987.

John R. MacArthur, *Second Front: Censorship and Propaganda in the Gulf War.* New York: Hill and Wang, 1992.

Peter Marsden, *The Taliban: War and Religion in Afghanistan.* New York: Zed Books, 2002.

Robert C. McFarlane with Zofia Smardz, *Special Trust.* New York: Cadell & Davies, 1994.

Howard Means, *Colin Powell: Soldier/Statesman.* New York: Donald I. Fine, 1992.

Dana Milbank, *Smashmouth: Two Years in the Gutter with Al Gore and George W. Bush.* New York: Basic Books, 2001.

John Miller and Michael Stone, with Chris Mitchell, *The Cell: Inside the 9/11 Plot, and Why the FBI and CIA Failed to Stop It.* New York: Hyperion, 2002.

Bill Minutaglio, *First Son: George W Bush and the Bush Family Dynasty.* New York: Crown, 1999.

Elizabeth Mitchell, *W: Revenge of the Bush Dynasty.* New York: Hyperion, 2000.

Michael Moore, *Dude, Where's My Country?* New York: Warner Books, 2003.

Nawaf Obaid, *The Oil Kingdom at 100: Petroleum Policymaking in Saudi Arabia.* Washington, D.C.: Washington Institute for Near East Policy, 2001.

Herbert S. Parmet, *George Bush: The Life of a Lone Star Yankee.* New Brunswick, N.J.: Transaction, 2001.

Joseph Persico, *Casey: The Lives and Secrets of William J. Casey—from the OSS to the CIA.* New York: Viking, 1990.

Kenneth M. Pollack, *The Threatening Storm: The Case for Invading Iraq.* New York: Random House, 2002.

Gerald Posner, *Why America Slept: The Failure to Prevent 9/11.* New York: Random House, 2003.

Sheldon Rampton and John Stauber, *Weapons of Mass Deception: The Uses of Propaganda in Bush's War on Iraq.* New York: Tarcher/Penguin, 2003.

Ahmed Rashid, *Taliban: Militant Islam, Oil, and Fundamentalism in Central Asia.* New Haven: Yale University Press, 2000.

Dr. Nasser Ibrahim Rashid and Dr. Esber Ibrahim Shaheen, *Saudi Arabia: All You Need to Know.* Joplin, Mo.: International Institute of Technology, 1995.

Jeffrey Robinson, *Yamani: The Inside Story.* London: Simon & Schuster, 1988.

Malise Ruthven, *A Fury for God: The Islamist Attack on America.* New York: Granta, 2002.

Pierre Salinger, *America Held Hostage: The Secret Negotiations.* New York: Doubleday, 1981.

Stephen Schwartz, *The Two Faces of Islam: The House of Sa'ud from Tradition to Terror.* New York: Doubleday, 2002.

Gary Sick, *October Surprise: America's Hostages in Iran and the Election of Ronald Reagan.* New York: Random House, 1991.

Micah L. Sifry and Christopher Cerf, eds., *The Gulf War Reader.* New York: Times Books, 1991.

Stuart Stevens, *The Big Enchilada: Campaign Adventures with the Cockeyed Optimists from Texas Who Won the Biggest Prize in Politics.* New York: Free Press, 2001.

Howard Teicher and Gayle Radley Teicher, *Twin Pillars to Desert Storm: America's Flawed Vision in the Middle East from Nixon to Bush.* New York: William Morrow, 1993.

Edward Tivnan, *The Lobby: Jewish Political Power and American Foreign Policy.* New York: Simon & Schuster, 1987.

Jeffrey Toobin, *Too Close to Call: The Thirty-six-Day Battle to Decide the 2000 Election.* New York: Random House, 2001.

Peter Truell and Larry Gurwin, *False Profits: The Inside Story of BCCI, the World's Most Corrupt Financial Empire.* Boston: Houghton Mifflin, 1992.

Alexei Vassiliev, *The History of Saudi Arabia.* New York: New York University Press, 2000.

Lawrence E. Walsh, *Iran-Contra, the Final Report.* New York: Times Books, 1994. Bob Woodward, *Bush at War.* New York: Simon & Schuster, 2002.

————, *The Commanders.* New York: Simon and Schuster, 1991.

————, *Veil: The Secret Wars of the CIA, 1981-1987.* New York: Simon & Schuster, 1987.

Robin Wright, *Sacred Rage: The Wrath of Militant Islam.* New York: Touchstone, 1985.

Daniel Yergin, *The Prize: The Epic Quest for Oil, Money, and Power.* New York: Simon & Schuster, 1991.

INDEX